300 best Stir-Fry recipes

Nancie McDermott

Robert
ROSE

300 Best Stir-Fry Recipes
Text copyright© 2007 Nancie McDermott
Photographs copyright© 2007 Robert Rose Inc.
Cover and text design copyright© 2007 Robert Rose Inc.

For complete cataloguing information, see page 345.

Disclaimer
The recipes in this book have been carefully tested by our kitchen and our tasters. To the best of our knowledge, they are safe and nutritious for ordinary use and users. For those people with food or other allergies, or who have special food requirements or health issues, please read the suggested contents of each recipe carefully and determine whether or not they may create a problem for you. All recipes are used at the risk of the consumer. Consumers should consult their convection oven manufacturer's manual for recommended procedures and cooking times.

We cannot be responsible for any hazards, loss or damage that may occur as a result of any recipe use.

For those with special needs, allergies, requirements or health problems, in the event of any doubt, please contact your medical advisor prior to the use of any recipe.

Design & Production: PageWave Graphics Inc.
Editor: Carol Sherman
Recipe Editor: Jennifer MacKenzie
Proofreader: Sarah Silva
Photography: Colin Erricson
Food Styling: Kate Bush and Kathryn Robertson
Prop Styling: Charlene Erricson

Cover image: Pork Slices with Bursting Peas (page 88)

We acknowledge the financial support of the Government of Canada through the Book Publishing Industry Development Program (BPIDP) for our publishing activities.

Published by Robert Rose Inc.
120 Eglinton Avenue East, Suite 800
Toronto, Ontario, Canada M4P 1E2
Tel: (416) 322-6552   Fax: (416) 322-6936

Printed in Canada
2 3 4 5 6 7 8 9 CP 15 14 13 12 11 10 09 08

Contents

Acknowledgments

MY HEARTFELT THANKS go to the many people whose excellent work and creative energy flavor every page of this book. I am grateful to Bob Dees, publisher of Robert Rose Inc., for entrusting me with his concept of a volume on stir-fry cooking, and for his generosity of spirit and ongoing infusions of humor and encouragement throughout the process of writing this book. I am profoundly thankful to my editor Carol Sherman, wordsmith extraordinaire, for her intelligent, insightful and creative attention to every letter on every page. She edited my efforts with the greatest patience and wit, diplomatically crafting even the roughest chunks of text into words that worked. Jennifer MacKenzie tested recipes expertly, while seeking out answers to questions and solutions to problems that arose along the way. Judith Finlayson stepped in to transform my clunky recipe titles into delightful, astute names that greatly brighten the book. I am thrilled with the way Daniella Zanchetta of PageWave Graphics transformed my words into such a handsome, inviting and useful design. I am grateful to the entire design team at PageWave, including Kevin Cockburn, Joseph Gisini and Andrew Smith. The photography team of Colin Erricson, Kate Bush, Kathryn Robertson, Charlene Erricson and Matt Johannsson cooked up a gorgeous batch of photographs with which to inspire my readers to get in the kitchen and start cooking. My literary agent, Lisa Ekus-Saffer, keeps my life as a writer and cooking teacher interesting and worthwhile, guiding me toward projects that offer rich rewards on every level, along with an abundance of laughter and fun. I am indebted to her staff at Lisa Ekus Public Relations, especially Jane Falla, Sarah Baurle and Dalyn Miller, for their tireless and creative efforts on my behalf. Food, family and friends go together and without my sisters, Susanne Settle and Linda McDermott, and my friends Debbie Gooch, Dean Nichols, Karen Johnson and Jill O'Connor, I might forget to slow down, step back and laugh out loud. At the end of every day, I get to sit down at the table with Will, Camellia and Isabelle, my wonderful family. They make my life a feast because they love me, listen to me, comfort me and nourish my spirit, no matter what I put on the table.

Introduction

THIS BOOK IS a recipe box, designed to introduce you to an ancient way of cooking, one that translates beautifully into the language and demands of the 21st-century kitchen. Simple in concept, essentially healthy and intrinsically quick, stir-frying makes sense for Western cooks, whether they are experts or novice cooks. With stir-frying in your kitchen repertoire, you have almost endless options for making delicious, healthful home-cooked meals, even on a busy day.

Wonderful as it is, stir-fry cooking is presented here not to replace the cooking methods you use now, but rather to offer you another technique to use in cooking wonderful, satisfying and delightful food in your kitchen. If you don't cook, it's an excellent place to get started. If you do cook, stir-fry cooking fits right in to what you already do, while expanding your options to create wonderful food.

I consider stir-fry cooking to be an essential part of my repertoire as a cook and I use it often to bring freshly cooked, beautiful and delicious food to our dinner table. I still stew, sauté, fry, steam and grill. I still make curries and soup and slow-cooker feasts, and I love having breakfast for dinner, meaning pancakes with maple syrup and sausage, or eggs and bacon and grits on a dark, wintry night. But stir-fry cooking is a cornerstone of my kitchen routine — a simple, endlessly varied kitchen technique that helps me cook weeknight dinners for my family and celebration meals for our extended family and friends.

The main course dishes in this book presume that you will enjoy them Asian-style, as a flavorful and substantial accompaniment to rice. Quantities of meat and vegetables in a given dish in most cases serve four people who are eating them along with a generous portion of rice or noodles or couscous or another satisfying accompaniment.

Unlike a European-style stew or a bowl of chili con carne, which can be a meal in a bowl along with an optional serving of bread, stir-fried dishes exist in tandem with rice or another grain or noodle. They are seasoned to this end, with generous amounts of salt, herbs, and other intense ingredients, so that the flavors of the stir-fry balance and brighten the "comfort food" portion of the meal, which traditionally consists of unseasoned rice.

One reason for this is that rice is what Asia has been eating for thousands of years, even before the wok appeared on the culinary scene as a tool for cooking. In Thailand, the very word for stir-fries and other substantial dishes, such as curries, steamed fish and soups, is "with-rice." It is a phrase, used as a noun, to encompass all that will be provided as a meal. It acknowledges that the traditional role of such dishes is to season, accompany and make more delightful the rice, which on any given evening was all that was available along with chiles, fish from the stream and greens from the garden.

I hope you enjoy learning how to stir-fry or that you find a few new recipes to add to your repertoire if you already know how. I hope that your cooking brings you pride and pleasure. I hope that it makes your table a place where you can set aside your cares and enjoy being here, now, eating good food, whether you are alone, with family, or with friends.

— Nancie McDermott

History of Stir-Fry Cooking

STIR-FRY COOKING IS an approach to preparing food that originated in China more than 2,000 years ago. This distinctive way of preparing and cooking food evolved in the ancient Chinese kitchen to address the particular challenges facing cooks at that time and place. Stir-frying made the best possible use of precious resources including fuel, ingredients and tools.

In the ancient world, cooking fuel was the on-going focus of a major investment of time and money. Asian kitchens depended on a steady supply of firewood or charcoal, along with twigs and straw. A hand-held fan served to boost the level of heat, and a covered jar by the small stove was the destination for excess red-hot coals when the cook wished to decrease the heat.

Getting ingredients to the kitchen called for a continuous effort, including frequent forays to the vegetable garden, the chicken coop and perhaps the waters of a nearby lake or stream. Water came from a well or from rain barrels. This gathered bounty was supplemented by frequent visits to the nearest fresh market. Cooking oil, meat and eggs were luxury items, and the cook's job was to serve up as much flavor and nutrition as possible in these circumstances, while enhancing the plain, unseasoned rice that anchored the meal.

The traditional stir-frying setup of wok and stove met these challenges well. With its generous bowl-like shape and high sides flaring out from the small round base, woks could cook quantities of food rapidly in a small amount of oil. Stir-frying allowed cooks to flavor a platterful of food, stretching costly ingredients to serve a group.

Stir-Frying and the Modern Kitchen

AS COOKS IN today's typical Western kitchens, we pay little attention to the costs of fuel for our stoves and oil for cooking our food. We twirl the dial on a gas or electric stove, an affordable and convenient source of kitchen heat. We shop in supermarkets and farmers' markets, stock our refrigerators and pantries, and often serve generous portions of an astounding array of foods.

Despite the huge contrast between kitchens past and present, stir-fry cooking suits today's cooks for a new set of reasons. Few of us gather firewood or fish for our supper, but modern life keeps many of us on busy, demanding schedules. Cooking oil is no longer a precious ingredient in terms of price or effort to obtain it, but we try to use it in moderation because of health concerns. Meat and protein are affordable and available, but vegetables and grains belong on the table in abundance as well.

Stir-frying is a cooking technique that meets all these challenges. It is intrinsically quick, with its components chopped into small pieces that cook quickly in a very hot pan. Vegetables step up while protein steps back. Meat and seafood play a major role in stir-fry cooking, but more often as an accent rather than a starring role. Kitchens have changed profoundly since stir-frying emerged as a cooking technique, but it fits perfectly into the 21st-century kitchen.

Prep Work for Stir-Fry Cooking

THE KEY TO stir-fry success is to prepare your ingredients well and then arrange them by the stove before you begin to cook. This differs from the standard order of things in Western cooking, where the use of an oven for extended, gradual and largely unattended cooking procedures, and a tradition of long-simmered stews and braises defines the cooking process.

In stir-fry cooking, none of the ingredients spends much time over the heat, so each must hit the hot pan ready to cook quickly, in a matter of minutes. Some things go in whole, such as baby spinach leaves, snow peas and peeled shrimp. Others are chopped, sliced, shredded or ground, creating surface area to receive seasonings as well as speed the cooking. These include carrots, shiitake mushrooms, broccoli, and all kinds of meat.

In addition to chopping, I suggest you do as I do and prepare all your seasonings, having them measured out and ready by the stove, before you heat up the pan. The serving plate on which you plan to present the finished dish should be there, along with utensils for cooking such as long-handled spatulas and spoons. Seasoning mixtures are often stirred up as a first step in these recipes and then added all at once toward the end of cooking.

If you are a veteran of stir-fry cooking, you may not need to measure everything out in advance. Observe the cooks stir-frying dishes in an Asian night market or in a Chinese restaurant in the West. Watch them ladle in a bit of oil, add a dash of fish sauce, toss in a handful of dried chile peppers, cooking away without measuring cups, spoons or kitchen scales. That is a fine way to stir-fry, but for me, preparing and measuring out everything in advance still makes sense, even though I have been doing it for more than 20 years. Having done my prep and set out my ingredients, I can enjoy the sizzling, live-action stir-fry process greatly, moving through the tasks quickly and turning my finished dish out onto the serving plate in a flash.

Though advance preparation can cut down on work at suppertime, I suggest you chop fresh leafy herbs, garlic, ginger and onions as close as possible to cooking time, since their bright flavor quickly changes or fades. Marinating is often a step in stir-fry cooking, but unlike marinades in the Western kitchen, the process tends to be brief (10 to 20 minutes) and to involve small amounts of seasonings, all of which are added to the pan along with the marinated meat or seafood.

To streamline the process on busy days, look for prepared ingredients in the supermarket. Chopped broccoli florets, trimmed green beans and shredded carrots are available in the fresh produce section. Frozen vegetables are an excellent staple for stir-fry cooking, with tiny peas, lima beans, corn and edamame beans being particular favorites in these recipes. Stock your pantry with cans of baby corn, straw mushrooms, water chestnuts, bamboo shoots and chicken or vegetable broth, so that you can "shop" in your own kitchen on a busy day and find yourself with lots of options without a trip to the store.

None of the recipes in this book demands a major investment of time, given that the subject is stir-fry cooking; but as you become accustomed to stir-fry cooking, or familiar with this book if you are already a stir-fry fan, you will find it easy to choose the dishes that suit you and your kitchen routine.

Equipment Glossary

STIR-FRYING IS FAR from a strange, new technique in Western kitchens. More than 30 years have gone by since Chinese cooking in general and stir-fry cooking in particular debuted on the culinary scene. Stir-fry cooking is well-known and viewed as a speedy, accessible, potentially healthful and delicious way to prepare food.

With just a few pieces of easy-to-find equipment, you can make stir-frying a part of your everyday kitchen routine. This section offers you an overview of pans and other tools worth considering.

The first piece of equipment essential for stir-fry cooking is a sturdy pan large enough to contain the ingredients throughout the tossing, scooping and seasoning which are part of the process. The two main options to which I refer in recipes throughout this book are a wok and a large deep skillet.

Woks

Developed more than 2,000 years ago in China expressly for stir-fry cooking, woks are widely available to modern cooks. They come in a remarkable variety of styles and materials, the differences addressing a range of kitchen circumstances and the preferences of many different cooks.

The two basic wok designs are Cantonese-style and Northern Chinese-style. Both styles are bowl-like, but the Northern-style wok has a deeper, rounder bowl. Handles differ more dramatically. The classic Cantonese-style wok has two loop-shaped handles placed opposite each other on the rim of the pan, while the classic Northern-style design has a long, sturdy handle on one side with a loop-shaped handle attached to the opposite rim. These two traditional styles of woks come in both carbon-steel and cast-iron versions. Carbon-steel woks are widely available in the West in a variety of styles, while cast-iron woks are available from shops and vendors specializing in Chinese cookware.

The best 20th-century innovation to this ancient cooking pan is the invention of the flat-bottomed wok. Made to adapt to the standard Western stove with its flat burners powered by electricity or gas, the flat bottom wok works very well, offering the traditional wok's large capacity for tossing food along with direct exposure to the heat source. Though smaller capacity woks are part of the modern wok marketplace in the West, a standard 14-inch (35 cm) wok is the best choice, since it is big enough for traditional stir-fry cooking.

Large deep skillets

Known in many a home kitchen as frying pans, skillets are pans with wide flat bottoms and shallow sides, sporting one large handle and the ability to withstand high heat. A large deep skillet can be used for stir-fry cooking with excellent results. Ideally it should be around 12 inches (30 cm) in diameter and around 2 inches (5 cm) deep.

Standard skillets with rounded sides work well, as do sauté pans, which are deep skillets with straight sides. (If you must work with a large shallow skillet, try to stir-fry with two utensils such as spatulas or slotted spoons, rather than one. By holding one in each hand, you can scoop and move the food about fairly quickly without sending the components of your dish sailing across the kitchen. A small skillet won't work, no matter how deep it is, since the food wouldn't have space to cook.)

The marketplace for both woks and large deep skillets is huge. You can explore your options in cooking specialty shops, the housewares section of department stores, restaurant supply houses and Asian markets. You'll find many sources online as well, a number of which specialize in Asian cookware and equipment.

Both woks and skillets come in nonstick finishes, as well as numerous standard cookware finishes. Nonstick pans are beloved for the easy cleanup they allow, but they often call for a lower heat level than that traditionally used in stir-fry cooking and special utensils to protect the surface.

Other Tools for Stir-Fry Cooking

Spatula or a long-handled spoon. Use in stirring, scooping and tossing the food as you cook it. A standard spatula made of metal or heatproof plastic will work. You can also look for a traditional wok spatula (Cantonese name is *wok chan*), which is a bit like a shallow shovel. Its scooping edge is gently curved, to mirror the wok's interior shape as well as to allow a little depth for scooping up more food than a flat "pancake turner" spatula could manage.

Long-handled cooking spoons are another option. A set of two is ideal, one slotted and one not, so that you can toss quickly with the slotted spoon and scoop out sauce and ingredients deftly with the regular spoon when swift action is needed. A long-handled Chinese-style ladle can be useful as an additional tool, with its broad shallow bowl for scooping up the food during or after cooking. This tool can be used upside-down, with its edge used to push food about the pan and its bowl used to toss everything up for stir-frying.

Knives. Good knife skills help you prepare food for cooking with confidence and ease. Seek out cooking classes or help from a friendly chef or experienced cook so that you can learn to use a knife safely and effectively. Use a Chinese-style cleaver or chef's knife for chopping and thinly slicing meat. A chef's knife makes a good substitute for a Chinese-style cleaver. A larger knife (8-inch/20 cm or 10-inch/25 cm) is ideal, as a heavier knife with a sizable blade aids you in chopping and slicing.

Cutting boards. A heavyweight cutting board is ideal for its sturdiness, and a dampened kitchen towel underneath to help keep it in place. Wet a clean kitchen towel well and wring out as much water as possible. Then spread it out on the counter and place the cutting board on top. This creates traction to keep it steady on your counter as you chop and slice.

Electric rice cooker. This is another piece of equipment that I often use in stir-frying cooking. Rice is the traditional accompaniment to stir-fried dishes and this appliance cooks it quickly and perfectly, once you've measured out water and rice and pressed the start button. You can also cook rice in a saucepan on the stove or enjoy your stir-fried dishes with noodles, pasta, couscous, tortillas and various kinds of whole grains instead. But if you enjoy eating rice, consider this as an investment in your stir-fry cooking.

Cleaning brushes. You will need a plastic scrubbing pad, a long-handled dish-washing brush with plastic bristles or a sponge with a gentle abrasive surface on one side — any of these in combination with hot water, and a little mild dish liquid on occasion as needed, are all you need for ongoing cleaning (see also Cleanup, page 10). If you should have a cleaning crisis that these tools will not solve, you will need to scrub down your pan with steel wool or another heavy-duty scouring pad (see Seasoning a Metal Wok or Skillet, page 11) and then re-season the cleaned pan, just as you did in originally seasoning the wok. The traditional bamboo brush that often comes with wok sets, made of long, very sturdy strips of bamboo bound together at the top, is more than you need for cleaning a home-kitchen wok. Designed for powerhouse cleaning of restaurant woks that are in use daily for many hours at extremely high heat, they are likely to scrub away some of the patina on your wok, the natural sheen which develops as a benefit of stir-fry cooking and careful cleanup over time. I do not recommend them.

Electric woks and skillets. While not my first choice, a good electric wok can work very well for stir-fry cooking. Look for a well-made, solid wok with the highest heating capacity you can find. Though their level of heat seldom matches what you can reach on top of the stove, they are sturdy and steady since they have a built-in base. Well-made ones provide respectable heat levels over the pan's surface, not just at the very bottom. Electric woks almost always come with a lid, which can be used during the latter phase of stir-fry cooking, to increase the level of heat and steam. Electric frying pans lack the wok's stir-fry-friendly shape, but they too can serve as a decent stir-fry pan. Use two utensils to scoop as you toss, and use the lid to boost the heat level. Both these pans offer the benefit of allowing you to turn any location into a stir-fry kitchen, as long as it has electrical outlets where you can plug in.

Lids. While essential for the technique of steaming food, lids are not often required for stir-fry cooking, but when they are the proper lid for a given wok is a bit smaller in diameter, so that it will fit down into the wok and rest on the sides, just a little below the rim. Wok lids are oversized, with a rounded or "plateau" shape, made from aluminum or another lightweight metal. They can be purchased separately from Asian cookware vendors (see Sources, page 346). If you have a lid for your wok or large deep skillet, you can use it when cooking vegetables. Covering the wok or skillet after greens and other vegetables have had their initial toss in oil causes them to cook a bit more quickly, since the lid increases the levels of heat and steam. Plan ahead as to where you will place the lid after you remove it to finish the stir-fry dish, as you will be holding a very big, very hot metal utensil that will most likely be dripping with condensed steam.

Cleanup

Whether you use a wok or a skillet, cleanup is simple if you make use of water and time. If food sticks or burns onto your stir-fry pan with a nonstick surface, simply add a good amount of water, to a point above the level in need of cleanup. You can leave the pan to soak for several hours or if you need to clean it right away, place it over medium heat and bring the water to a steaming level of heat. After the pan has either soaked extensively or heated to the steaming point, gently scrape with your spatula or spoon at the areas you want to clean until you can push off the burnt or stuck portion. Then drain well and clean the pan further if needed with a gently abrasive pad, one with a plastic surface to loosen without scraping away the cooking surface of the pan. Place the wet, newly cleaned pan back over medium-high heat to dry quickly or dry it well with a kitchen towel. (See also Cleaning brushes, page 9.)

Seasoning a Metal Wok or Skillet

A carbon-steel wok or cast-iron wok or skillet develops a natural patina, which discourages food from sticking. (A pan with a "sandwich" of different kinds of metal, such as a stainless-steel cooking surface over copper, aluminum or other metals, does not require seasoning, nor does an anodized aluminum pan.) To season a new carbon-steel or cast-iron pan, three steps are required.

1. Vigorously scrub the pan with a steel-wool scrubbing pad and dish washing liquid, since traditional pans are usually coated with oil to keep them from rusting during their indeterminate time in the marketplace prior to ending up in your kitchen. Scrub the pan clean inside and out, and rinse very well.

2. Oil the cleaned pan well over medium heat to begin developing its patina. This natural surface helps the pan to resist rust and discourages food from sticking as you cook. Place the scrubbed and rinsed pan over medium heat until it dries out completely and becomes hot all over. Add about 3 tbsp (45 mL) of vegetable oil and then slowly tilt and turn to spread it over the pan's surface. Crumple two paper towels into a makeshift sponge and use them to spread the oil over the entire interior surface of the wok, making sure that every inch is nicely coated. Now rub the oil into the pan's surface, using fresh paper towels as needed to do the job.

3. Wipe away any excess oil using a clean paper towel and leaving the pan with the beginnings of a handsome sheen. Now repeat the oiling process two more times, adding oil, coating the pan, rubbing it in, and then blotting away the excess. Then let the pan cool completely. Now it is ready for its first cooking session or for storing until time to cook. The pan will darken naturally as it seasons, and the darkening will probably be uneven in the beginning.

To maintain a seasoned pan, always dry it well after gentle cleaning, using hot water and a gentle scrubbing pad designed for nonstick cookware, and then drying it over medium heat. Avoid scrubbing it with abrasive cleansers and tools; use mild dish liquid if needed. (See Cleanup, page 10 for notes on everyday cleaning of your seasoned pan.) Should it occasionally require a serious and vigorous cleanup, simply do what needs to be done to remove burnt or stuck food, and then repeat the process of seasoning it to create a new patina.

Ingredient Glossary

Asian basil
With its purple stems and delicate, pointed leaves, Asian basil contributes its bright anise flavor and aroma to many dishes. Known in Thai as *bai horapah* and in Vietnamese as *rau que*, it is widely available in Asian markets and increasingly found in supermarkets. Any culinary variety of basil makes a very good substitute.

Asian fish sauce
The quintessential seasoning in kitchens throughout Southeast Asia, fish sauce is a salty essence of small saltwater fish such as anchovies. Known in Thai as *nahm plah* and in Vietnamese as *nuoc mam*, fish sauce is a thin, transparent liquid the color of whiskey or tea, and can be found in small bottles in many supermarkets or in large bottles in Asian markets. I have found brands imported from Thailand to be of consistently excellent quality. I avoid the very dark versions, which tend to be extremely salty. Fish sauce keeps indefinitely at room temperature.

Asian sesame oil
Made from white sesame seeds, which are toasted to a handsome brown to enhance their flavor, this extraordinarily delicious tea-colored oil is used more for seasoning than for cooking, since it tends to smoke and burn over high heat. (In Northern China and Korea it is used as a cooking oil.) Also called "toasted sesame oil," it is often added at the very end of cooking time, or sprinkled over a dish just after it is removed from the heat, or when it is in its serving dish. Store in the refrigerator for up to 6 months.

Balacang or blachan
(See Shrimp paste)

Bamboo shoots
Supermarkets carry small sliced bamboo shoots and Asian markets carry an array of canned bamboo shoots with varied shapes and sizes. Shredded, sliced or whole, they are ready to eat and can be cut to bite size and added to the pan just long enough to heat up and take on the seasonings of a given dish. Rinse and drain them before using. Refrigerate remaining bamboo shoots in a jar with water to cover them for up to 5 days, changing the water daily to keep them fresh.

Basil
(See Asian basil and Holy basil)

Basmati rice
(See Rice)

Bean paste
Made from fermented soybeans, this family of condiments originated in China and is widely used in sauce, marinades and dishes that are braised or roasted. Bean paste is a thick, salty, chocolate-brown purée, sold in small cans or tall jars. Some forms of bean paste contain sugar and are called "sweet bean paste." One form of sweet bean paste, hoisin sauce, is particularly popular with duck. Hot or Szechwan bean paste is spiked with chiles for a hot-and-spicy note. (Do not confuse the sweetened forms of this savory bean paste with red bean paste, which is made from red beans rather than from salted soybeans, and is used in Asian desserts.) Transfer canned bean paste to a jar and refrigerate for up to 6 months.

Bean sauce
Made from fermented soybeans, bean sauce is profoundly salty and delivers a tasty, pungent note to sauces, marinades and stir-fried dishes. It is particularly

popular paired with greens and vegetables in Southeast Asian cooking. You'll find both coarsely ground and whole-bean sauces in glass jars in textures ranging from watery and very thin to medium, with the salty beans whole or coarsely ground. Keep refrigerated for up to 6 months.

Bean thread noodles

Made from hard round mung beans (sometimes called "green beans" since their outer hull is a mossy shade of green), bean thread noodles are available only in dried form. They are wire-like in texture and translucent white in color, and wound up into varying sizes of skeins. Also known as glass noodles, cellophane noodles, silver noodles, *harusame*, *sai-fun* and long rice, they keep indefinitely and are an excellent pantry staple for soups, stews and noodle dishes. Soak the noodles in warm water until they are flexible enough to cut before using them in cooking. (See also Noodles.)

Black beans, fermented, or Black beans, salted

(See Salted black beans)

Bok choy

Known in Mandarin as *bai-cao*, but widely known by its Cantonese name, this delicious vegetable sports lush emerald-green leaves crowning its thick, rounded, celery-like white stalks. Bok choy keeps well and can be found in sizes from diminutive 6-inch (15 cm) long bunches to substantial ones weighing well over 1 pound (500 g). It makes a simple stir-fry on its own, and adds wonderful color, texture and flavor to stir-fried dishes containing meat and vegetables as well as soup and noodle dishes.

Celery cabbage

(See Napa cabbage)

Char sui pork

(See Chinese barbecued pork)

Chenkiang rice vinegar

Deep in flavor and color, this Chinese vinegar made from sticky rice has a surprisingly mild flavor. It provides richness and color to marinades, braised dishes and seasoning sauces. Sometimes called Chinese black vinegar, it is widely available in Asian markets. It keeps indefinitely at room temperature. You can use red wine vinegar in its place, though it lacks the color and contributes a tangier flavor, or balsamic vinegar, which provides both color and its own distinctive flavor note.

Chile garlic sauce

Look for this condiment with the words *tuong ot toi*, its Vietnamese-language name. It has pale small seeds in a rich red purée, which contains garlic as well as a little vinegar. It shines both as a condiment mixed with other ingredients to make marinades and seasoning mixtures, and as a hot pepper sauce, either straight from the bottle or mixed with other fresh ingredients to make a dipping sauce. You could substitute other hot pepper sauces with very good results.

Chile peppers

Whether they are harvested or purchased fresh or dried, ground to a paste, to flakes or to a fine powder, chile peppers in their numerous forms keep the culinary fires alight in the kitchens of Asia. As a general rule, the smaller the chile, the hotter its flavor will be in a given dish.

Fresh chiles

Tiny fresh Thai chiles, also called bird peppers, are diminutive, pointy and extremely hot. Known as *prik kii noo* in Thai, they are the central ingredient in green curry paste. Finger-length fresh chiles called *prik chii fah* are a bit milder and are used to garnish and season foods. Fresh green serrano and jalapeño chiles make good substitutes for Thai chiles in most recipes.

Dried red chiles

Small dried red chiles are used extensively in Southeast Asian cooking, as well as in the cuisines of the Eastern regions of China, notably Hunan and Szechwan provinces. You will find large cellophane packages of dried red chiles imported from China or Thailand in Asian markets. You could also use the *chiles de arbol* and *chiles japones*, which are widely available in the West.

Dried hot pepper flakes

Also known as dried red chile pepper flakes. Chopped and then ground to a coarse, seedy texture, dried hot pepper flakes light up sauces as well as stir-fried dishes and are widely available.

Chinese barbecued pork

Known as *char siu pork* in Cantonese and adored throughout Asia, these thick strips of sweet, rich oven-roasted pork begin with a red, sweet and pungent marinade usually containing honey, hoisin sauce and dark soy sauce, as well as food coloring to provide its signature red hue. Slow roasted to develop its flavors and color along with charring here and there on the strips of pork, it is delectable sliced and eaten along with rice and cucumbers. It is also sliced and tossed with rice, noodles and vegetables, or chopped and added to an array of Asian dishes. See page 332 for a recipe or purchase 1 to 2 lbs (500 g to 1 kg) when you visit a Chinese barbecue shop. You can freeze it for up to 4 months.

Chinese broccoli

(See Gai lan)

Chinese parsley

(See Cilantro)

Chinese sausage

Sweet and rich, this hard, reddish-brown pork sausage is beloved throughout Asia. It is used much like ham, as a salty accent to savory dishes. Known as *lap cheong* in Cantonese, it is air-dried to a very firm state, and is widely available in Asian markets, vacuum-sealed into shelf-stable packages of about 10 short links. It is often steamed before use, or thinly sliced, stir-fried and served over rice as a quick lunch. You can substitute an equal amount of ham in many recipes, reducing the cooking time a bit since ham is more tender than Chinese sausage.

Cilantro

Also known as Chinese parsley and coriander leaves (it is the plant which comes from coriander seeds), this intensely flavored and scented herb brightens the flavor and appearance of Asian dishes. Its delicate leaves can be used whole as a garnish, coarsely chopped as a finishing touch or added to a stir-fried dish during cooking. Widely available in Western supermarkets, it should be placed stems down in a jar or glass of water, very loosely covered with a plastic bag and placed in the refrigerator for 3 to 4 days. Or leave it out on the counter with its stems in water and use it within a day or two. Plan to chop it just before you use it in cooking, so that its signature flavor and aroma make their best impression.

Coconut milk

This thick white liquid is made from the grated meat of dried brown coconuts that are soaked in warm water and then squeezed over a fine sieve to extract a rich creamy essence used in sauces, soups, curries and stir-fried dishes. Look for unsweetened coconut milk in cans imported from Thailand, available in supermarkets as well as in Asian markets. Frozen coconut milk is often available in Asian markets and works wonderfully in recipes, and dried coconut powder, which is reconstituted with water, makes an acceptable substitute as well. (Avoid sweetened coconut milk products; any with sugar as an ingredient would work only in sweets and drinks, not in savory dishes.)

Coriander leaves
(See Cilantro)

Curry paste
A vibrant seasoning paste based on hot chile peppers, fresh or dried, garlic, shallots and an array of herbs and spices, this condiment makes a powerhouse addition to stir-fried dishes. Thai curry pastes contain lemongrass, galanga, toasted cumin and coriander seeds, while Indian-style curry pastes contain fresh ginger and an array of aromatic and intense ground dried spices with a milder burst of chile heat. There are various kinds of curry pastes that you can use interchangeably and still get a tasty dish. To make Thai-style curry paste at home, see page 338.

Dark soy sauce
(See Soy sauce)

Dark sweet soy sauce
(See Soy sauce)

Dried Chinese mushrooms
(See Shiitake mushrooms, dried)

Dried red chiles or
Dried red chile pepper flakes
(See Chile peppers)

Edamame beans
Newly welcomed onto the culinary scene in the West, edamame beans have long been a treat in Japan, where they are enjoyed hot or cold in their pods as a nibble with sushi. Look for them, shelled and cooked, in the produce section along with tofu and wonton wrappers. You will also find them frozen, either in their pods or shelled. Use them in stir-fried dishes directly from the freezer; no need to thaw them as they cook nicely along with the other stir-fried ingredients. Their beautiful intense green color is a plus but their nutty flavor adds greatly as well.

Five-spice powder
An aromatic and intense seasoning powder with sweet notes, particularly delicious when paired with pork or chicken. Used in marinades, braises, Chinese-style barbecue sauces and stir-fried dishes, five-spice powder is a mixture of ground star anise, cloves, cinnamon, Szechwan peppercorns and fennel seeds. Sealed airtight and stored away from heat and light, it will keep for up to 8 months.

Fresh hot green chiles
(See Chile peppers)

Fresh soybeans
(See Edamame beans)

Gai lan
Also known as Chinese broccoli, this deep green vegetable has thick stalks and smooth wide green leaves, sometimes sporting small clusters of white flowers depending on the season in which it is harvested. Its stalks are usually peeled before cooking. The chopped leaves and stalks are blanched just until vibrant green and tender-crisp and then drizzled with oyster sauce for a quick, delicious vegetable side dish. For stir-fry cooking, it should be peeled, sliced and blanched, or peeled and sliced very thinly so that the stalks cook quickly. Known in Thailand as *pahk ka-nah*, its barely bitter flavor has sweet notes, making it a very popular vegetable throughout Asia.

Gingerroot
Plump, knobby and covered with a smooth, almost-shiny beige skin, fresh gingerroot is an extraordinary source of vibrant flavor used ubiquitously in Asian cuisines. Widely available year-round in supermarkets as well as in Asian grocery stores, fresh gingerroot is a rhizome or underground stem, which grows in clusters of moist, golden-fleshed lobes. Gingerroot is most often chopped for

use in stir-frying, though it is sometimes thinly sliced crosswise to make delicate coins. These are added to hot oil to season it prior to cooking and then removed before the dish is served. To chop it for most stir-fried dishes, peel a section, slice it crosswise into very thin coins, stack them up and then slice the stacks into long, slender shreds. These can be used in shredded form or cut crosswise one more time to make finely chopped fresh gingerroot. Combined with garlic and sometimes onions or shallots as well, fresh gingerroot is a central flavor essence for many stir-fried dishes. If you can purchase it fresh on a regular basis, do so. If you need to store it for use over time, buy about 8 oz (250 g), peel it carefully and place it in a glass jar with a tight-fitting lid. Add dry sherry to cover it and store in the refrigerator for up to 4 months. Use a little more than the recipe calls for and slice and chop it just before cooking.

Holy basil

Rarely available in the West, holy basil is the classic variety of fresh basil used in Thai stir-fried dishes. Known as *bai gra-prao* in Thai, it has rounded leaves with a matte finish and serrated edges, rather than shiny pointed leaves with smooth edges. Fragile once picked, it should be used within a day of purchase. Look for seeds and plants (see Sources, page 346) if you would like to grow holy basil for your kitchen. Any culinary variety of basil makes an acceptable substitute.

Hoisin sauce

Made from salted, fermented soybeans, which are ground to a thick, dark brown paste, hoisin sauce is seasoned with sugar and garlic. It adds handsome color as well as flavor and is widely used both in cooking and as an ingredient in dipping sauces. It is particularly delicious with duck. (See also Bean sauce).

Hot pepper flakes
(See Chile peppers)

Jasmine rice
(See Rice)

Kaffir lime; kefir lime
(See Makrut lime leaves)

Lemongrass

This tropical herb is used extensively in the cooking of Thailand and Vietnam, as well as in the cuisines of their Southeast Asian neighbors. It grows in patches of grassy stalks, enjoying the sunshine while it sends out countless stalks with a flavorful purple-tinged base that harbors a delicate citrus-flavored center. It is central to Thai-style curry pastes and as an ingredient in *tome yum* and other classic Thai soups.

Makrut lime leaves

Look for these aromatic and flavorful leaves in Asian markets, often packaged in small plastic bags with a dozen or so leaves to each bag. They grow in pairs attached stem-to-stem and have brilliant deep green leaves with a delicate sheen. Also known as kaffir or kefir lime leaves, they are added to dishes whole or torn into large pieces, since they infuse their flavor but are seldom eaten. Occasionally they are sliced thread thin and included in a dish to be eaten. They grow on small citrus trees with major thorns; the trees are sometimes available through Asian markets and nurseries. If you can't find them on a regular basis, buy several dozen when you do, transfer them to a jar or wide-mouthed bottle and store in the freezer. Use them straight from the freezer without thawing. Dried ones have no flavor or aroma; if you can't find them fresh or frozen, simply omit them.

Mushroom soy sauce
(See Soy sauce)

Nahm prik pao
(See Roasted chile paste)

Napa cabbage
Also known as celery cabbage, this plump, ivory-to-pale green cabbage with curly-leafed tops folding into a dense, pointed tip is delicious stir-fried simply with garlic and salt or combined with other ingredients in soups, noodle dishes and stir-fries. Widely available in supermarkets, it is usually available in large heads, often weighing more than 2 lbs (1 kg). Cut huge ones lengthwise in halves or quarters and refrigerate the unused portion in a plastic bag for up to 1 week.

Noodles
Noodles are cherished around the world as a main dish, as a component in soups and as an accompaniment to other dishes. Three types of noodles are widely used for stir-fry cooking: Rice noodles, wheat flour noodles made with or without egg, and bean thread noodles made from mung bean flour. Bean thread noodles are available only in dried form, while rice and wheat flour noodles are available both fresh and dried. In the West, fresh rice noodles are best the day they are made and therefore are rarely found outside metropolitan areas with large Asian communities. Dried rice noodles are widely available in various widths, from thread-thin to fettucine-fat. Once they are softened in hot water, they can be stir-fried easily. Fresh egg noodles can be refrigerated for several days, so they are widely available in Asian markets as well as in some supermarkets. Like dried egg noodles, they come in various widths and can be stir-fried once they have been cooked in boiling water to a tender-but-still-firm state.

Oyster sauce
This luscious, fluid condiment, standard in kitchens throughout Asia, is made from an extract of dried oysters. Beloved both as a cooking ingredient and a component in seasoning sauces, it is available in glass bottles in supermarkets as well as in Asian markets. Known as *sauce na-mahn hoy* in Thai, oyster sauce provides a delectable finishing touch to a steaming platter of blanched Asian greens, particularly Chinese broccoli (*gai lan*).

Rice
Unlike bread in Western cuisines, rice is central to the meal in the majority of Asian cuisines. Whether it is short- to medium-grain rice cooked so that it is moist enough to be eaten with chopsticks, or long-grain rice cooked to a fluffy state and eaten with spoons from a plate or a banana leaf, rice cooks first and then while it simmers away the cooking of its accompaniments begins. Stir-fried dishes exist as a means of seasoning and enhancing the unadorned rice that anchors the meal. Basmati rice, grown in the foothills of the Himalayas and treasured throughout India, Pakistan, Iran and Bangladesh, has extremely long, slender grains and creates a gentle nutty flavor in the kitchen as it cooks. Jasmine rice, an aromatic long-grain rice grown in Thailand and other Southeast Asian countries, emits an inviting nutty aroma as well. Brown rice is simply a less-processed form of rice in which the nutritious bran layer is left intact. It takes a bit longer to cook than polished white rice and has a pleasing substantial quality that goes wonderfully with stir-fried dishes. A majority of the dishes in this book are created as hearty accompaniments to rice and are seasoned accordingly. If you prefer, enjoy them with your favorite kind of noodles, cooked until tender but firm, and then tossed with a little Asian sesame oil and sliced green onions. Or serve couscous, barley, other grains or bread; as long as you have something satisfying with which to round out your meal.

Rice noodles
(See Noodles)

Roasted chile paste
A Thai-style seasoning paste with fantastic flavor, this is used in Thailand's classic shrimp and lemongrass soup, *tome yum*, as well as in sauces, marinades and stir-fried dishes. It is particularly popular stir-fried with clams in the shell or with shrimp. Made from dried red chiles, shallots and garlic, which are traditionally roasted over coals and then pounded to a fragrant and rustic purée, it is often seasoned with tamarind liquid and dried shrimp. You can buy it jars in Asian markets; one widely available brand bears the English-language description, "chilies in soya bean oil." You can also make a supply using the recipe on page 336.

Salted black beans
This pungent Cantonese-style ingredient is made from small black soybeans that are salted and fermented, a process that preserves them while simultaneously creating extraordinary flavor. (Don't confuse this pungent condiment with the plump dried black beans enjoyed as a main dish with rice in Mexican and Caribbean cooking.) Salted black beans are beloved in stir-fry cooking, particularly in combination with garlic and gingerroot as a seasoning for fish and seafood dishes. You will find them sealed inside plastic bags or in a round cardboard container. Salted black beans resemble raisins without the wrinkles and should be supple rather than dry. Usually chopped before use, they are often mashed into a coarse paste with garlic, ginger and other seasonings. Transferred to an airtight jar, salted black beans keep at room temperature for up to 1 year.

Sesame oil
(See Asian sesame oil)

Shallots
Cooks throughout Asia treasure shallots, as do cooks in France. In Thailand they are used along with garlic as the initial seasoning for most stir-fried dishes and are a major component of curry pastes, and of *nahm prik*, the pungent chile sauce enjoyed with fresh vegetables and rice. Though an equal amount of chopped onion can be used in their place, shallots deliver a subtle but distinctive flavor that makes it worthwhile to keep them on hand. Look for smaller ones with multiple cloves if you have a choice and consider it a plus if the batch you are using is reddish purple inside, a particularly tasty type. Store them at room temperature as you do onions, allowing them to stay dry and "breathe." Many Southeast Asian cooks keep a seasoning basket handy, so that shallots, garlic cloves, a hunk of fresh ginger and a handful of dried red chiles are never far from the cutting board and the stove.

Shiitake mushrooms, fresh
Ranging in color from a light caramel color to a rich coffee brown, shiitake mushrooms are a handsome and delicious addition to stir-fry cooking. Remove and discard their tough, fibrous stems (or add them to stocks) and then slice their round, flat caps into strips, or quarter them before cooking. Small caps can be left whole. Slicing or chopping them reveals the lovely contrast between their darker brown exterior and cream-colored interior and stir-frying gives them a luscious, velvety texture. Though they are expensive, they make a most worthwhile splurge for stir-fry cooking. You can substitute an equal amount of thinly sliced fresh button mushrooms for shiitakes in most recipes. Store them in a paper bag or perforated container so that they can "breathe" in the refrigerator for up to 3 days.

Shiitake mushrooms, dried

Dried shiitakes, also called dried Chinese mushrooms or dried black mushrooms, make an outstanding pantry staple, since they deliver an intense earthy flavor and keep well indefinitely in a glass jar or another airtight container. (In traditional Chinese cuisine they are valued over fresh shiitakes, due to the concentration of flavor they develop as they dry.) They range in color from medium brown to black and those with crackled surface are often the most prized. Soaked for 20 to 30 minutes in warm water, they swell to a plush tender state and make a delicious addition to soups, stir-fries and noodle dishes. Cut away and discard their tough stems (or use them in stocks), and then use their disk-shaped caps whole if they are small, or quartered or sliced into thin or thick strips if they are large.

Shaoxing rice wine

Fermented from sticky rice and other grains, this flavorful tea-colored spirit is widely used in stir-fry cooking, as well as in marinades and braised dishes. Several basic brands are widely available in Asian markets. Check Asian liquor stores for rarer and more expensive brands. Dry sherry makes an excellent substitute in stir-fry cooking, and sake or white wine are acceptable.

Shrimp paste

Made from tiny shrimp, which are cooked, salted, dried and then ground to a fine paste, this condiment is widely used in traditional cuisines throughout Asia. Textures vary from an almost fluid sauce enjoyed in East Asia, to Southeast Asia's moist cake or slab, solid enough to be sliced or grated. It is often wrapped in a piece of banana leaf or foil and roasted or dry fried to round out its flavor and aroma before it is added to sauces, dips or stir-fried dishes.

Soy sauce

This salty and pungent condiment is central to Chinese, Japanese and Korean cooking, and is valued as an important secondary ingredient in Southeast Asian kitchens. Made from salted, fermented soybeans, it provides a shelf-stable source of protein as well as an intense, deep flavor to soups, sauces, marinades, braises and stir-fried dishes. The familiar soy sauce widely available in the West is sometimes called "light" or "white" soy sauce in Asian cooking, to distinguish it from "heavy" or "black" soy sauce, a thicker version that is valued more for its richness, smoothness and the gorgeous deep brown color it gives to an array of savory dishes. Both versions are quite dark in color but they are generally not interchangeable in cooking. For this book and most English-language recipes, the simple term "soy sauce" is used to refer to the more common thin, salty form, and "dark soy sauce" is used to refer to the thicker, heavier, milder-flavored form that is treasured for its color. Dark soy sauce is available in three forms: regular dark soy sauce, the most commonly used kind; dark sweet soy sauce, which has molasses added to give it a mellow sweet note; and mushroom soy sauce, which has an essence of dried shiitake mushrooms added to it for a rich flavor note. The standard condiment of Indonesian cooking, *ketcap manis*, is a form of dark sweet soy sauce.

Szechwan peppercorns

Though reminiscent of peppercorns in the sharp, pungent heat it contributes to food, this intensely flavorful and aromatic brick red-colored spice is in fact a diminutive type of berry, harvested and dried in the midst of emerging from its tiny flower-like casing. Sometimes called "flower pepper" for this reason, it creates a delicious flavor sensation described paradoxically as both numbing and tingling, and is central to the cooking of Szechwan province. A key ingredient in five-spice powder, it is usually dry-roasted in a hot pan, tiny twigs and all, and then lightly crushed or finely ground before being added to marinades, sauces and many different dishes. Look for it in cellophane or plastic bags, and transfer it to a jar, where it will keep indefinitely.

Tamarind and tamarind liquid

The crescent-shaped fruit of the tamarind tree, an enormous and beautiful tropical hardwood tree, has a delicate and brittle, nut-brown peel enclosing a soft, luscious pulp. Its tangy and smoky flavor is simultaneously sour and sweet. Enjoyed in South and Southeast Asia in soups, stews, marinades, sauces, sweets and drinks, it is often available in Asian markets in blocks of partly processed fruit that has been peeled and seeded. This pulp is soaked in warm water and then pressed and scraped through a sieve, extracting a thick, rich purée. You can buy processed tamarind liquid, or substitute Indian-style tamarind chutney with good results. (See page xx for instructions on preparing tamarind liquid.)

Tofu

Tofu is a valued mainstay of Asian cuisines from Northern China to the Indonesian archipelago. Also known as bean curd and *dao-hu*, tofu is made from dried soybeans that are soaked, ground to a paste, combined with vinegar, lemon juice or another tangy ingredient to form delicate curds and then pressed into blocks. Tofu is appreciated throughout Asia as an appealing ingredient, which provides an economical and convenient source of protein, rather than simply as a vegetarian alternative to meat. The texture of this nutritious ingredient ranges from that of the most delicate custard to a sturdy firmness that stands up well to stir-fry cooking. Tofu absorbs pungent seasonings well, and is enjoyed fried, braised, in soups and even as a sweet. Market vendors often serve warm, soft tofu in small bowls with ginger syrup on wintry mornings. Supermarkets nowadays routinely stock tofu, either in shelf-stable packaging or in refrigerated tubs holding a block of tofu covered in water. Once opened, you can keep tofu for up to 3 days, provided you drain it and add fresh water to cover it each day. Firm or extra-firm tofu is ideal for stir-frying, since it can maintain its shape rather than crumbling into bits. (See page xx for instructions on how to press soft tofu to make firm tofu.)

Terasi or trassi
(See Shrimp paste)

Thai-style curry paste
(See Curry paste)

Turmeric

First cousin to gingerroot, turmeric is a rhizome or underground stem, its leaves and flowers poking out above the ground and its hair-like roots growing downward. Unlike knobby gingerroot, its shape is smooth and slender, with a dull, coppery outer skin marked with dark concentric rings. Cut into a chunk and you will find an amazing blaze of moist carrot-colored flesh endowed with a faint earthy aroma and flavor. Treasured for the intense and magnificent color it bestows on foods as diverse as curry powder and ballpark mustard, it is popular in its dried, powdered form as well as fresh. Ground turmeric is available in supermarkets and Asian markets.

Wild lime leaves
(See Makrut lime leaves)

Chicken

Thai Chicken with Broccoli and Oyster Sauce

Serves 4

Oyster sauce provides an earthy depth to many Asian dishes. In this Thai-style dish, it is paired with broccoli, a natural partner for its pleasantly salty flavor.

2 tbsp	oyster sauce	25 mL
2 tbsp	fish sauce	25 mL
1 tsp	granulated sugar	5 mL
1/2 tsp	freshly ground pepper	2 mL
1/3 cup	chicken stock or water	75 mL
8 oz	skinless boneless chicken breasts or thighs, cut into 1 1/2-inch (4 cm) pieces	250 g
2 tbsp	vegetable oil	25 mL
1 tbsp	chopped garlic	15 mL
1 cup	small broccoli florets	250 mL

1. In a small bowl, combine oyster sauce, fish sauce, sugar, pepper and chicken stock and stir well.

2. Heat a wok or a large deep skillet over high heat. Add oil and swirl to coat pan. Add garlic and toss well, until fragrant, about 15 seconds.

3. Add chicken and spread into a single layer. Cook, undisturbed, until edges turn white, about 1 minute. Toss well and cook for 30 seconds more.

4. Add broccoli florets and toss well. Cook, tossing once, until bright green, for 1 minute.

5. Add oyster sauce mixture and toss well. Cook, undisturbed, until chicken is cooked through and broccoli is tender-crisp, 2 to 3 minutes more. Transfer to a serving plate. Serve hot or warm.

Thai-Style Sweet-and-Sour Chicken

3 tbsp	fish sauce	45 mL
2 tbsp	granulated sugar	25 mL
1 tbsp	white or cider vinegar	15 mL
½ tsp	salt or to taste	2 mL
2 tbsp	vegetable oil	25 mL
1 tbsp	chopped garlic	15 mL
8 oz	skinless boneless chicken breasts or thighs, cut into 1-inch (2.5 cm) chunks	250 g
1 cup	small cauliflower florets	250 mL
½ cup	coarsely chopped onion	125 mL
2 tbsp	water	25 mL
½ cup	cubed cucumber (½-inch/1 cm cubes) (see Tip, right)	125 mL
½ cup	halved cherry tomatoes	125 mL

1. In a bowl, combine fish sauce, sugar, vinegar and salt and stir well. Set aside.
2. Heat a wok or a large deep skillet over high heat. Add oil and swirl to coat pan. Add garlic and toss well, until fragrant, about 15 seconds.
3. Add chicken and spread into a single layer. Cook, until edges turn white, about 1 minute. Toss well.
4. Add cauliflower florets and onion and toss well. Add water and cook, tossing once or twice, until cauliflower is tender, about 2 minutes.
5. Add fish sauce mixture and toss well. Cook, undisturbed, until chicken is cooked through, about 1 minute more. Add cucumber chunks and cherry tomatoes. Give one more good toss to mix everything well. Transfer to a serving plate. Serve hot or warm.

Serves 4

Thailand's take on sweet-and-sour dishes is bright in color, texture and flavors. Cauliflower, cucumbers and tomatoes make an inviting addition to a quick chicken stir-fry in a simple and tangy sauce.

TIP

If you can't find a long, tender English hothouse cucumber, or small, chunky pickling or Kirby cucumbers, you can work with a big dark green field cucumber. For ½ cup (125 mL), peel half of the cucumber, halve it lengthwise, scoop out seeds and then chop up into ½-inch (1 cm) cubes.

Gingery Chicken with Black Bean Sauce

Serves 4 to 6

This recipe gives you a feast of pungent black bean sauce along with chunks of chicken, onion and green peppers. Plan to serve this dish at once, to enjoy it at its peak of flavor. Serve this with lots of rice or noodles and pair it with a crisp green salad or cooked carrots.

TIP

The salted, fermented black beans used in Chinese cooking (also known as Chinese-style black beans or fermented black beans) provide a deliciously pungent flavor to stir-fried and steamed dishes. After you open a new package, transfer the soft, dark beans to a jar and store them airtight at room temperature for up to 6 months.

3 tbsp	chicken stock or water	45 mL
2 tbsp	dry sherry	25 mL
2 tbsp	water	25 mL
1 tbsp	soy sauce	15 mL
1 tbsp	cornstarch	15 mL
1 tsp	granulated sugar	5 mL
2 tbsp	chopped salted black beans (see Tip, left)	25 mL
2 tbsp	chopped fresh gingerroot	25 mL
2 tsp	chopped garlic	10 mL
2 tbsp	vegetable oil, divided	25 mL
½ cup	coarsely chopped green bell pepper (1½-inch/4 cm pieces)	125 mL
½ cup	coarsely chopped onion (1½-inch/4 cm pieces)	125 mL
12 oz	skinless boneless chicken breasts or thighs, cut into 1½-inch (4 cm) pieces	375 g
2 tsp	Asian sesame oil	10 mL

1. In a bowl, combine chicken stock, sherry, water, soy sauce, cornstarch and sugar and stir well into a smooth sauce. Set aside.
2. In a small bowl, combine black beans, ginger and garlic and using a spoon, stir and mash gently, just enough to mix together a bit, but not into a smooth paste. Set aside. Place a bowl next to stove to hold green peppers and onions after their initial cooking.
3. Heat a wok or a large deep skillet over high heat. Add 1 tbsp (15 mL) of the vegetable oil and swirl to coat pan.

4. Add peppers and onion and cook, tossing often, until peppers are softened and onion is fragrant, 1 minute. Transfer to reserved bowl, leaving behind as much oil as possible.

5. Add remaining vegetable oil, and as soon as it is hot, add black bean mixture. Toss well, until fragrant, about 15 seconds.

6. Add chicken and spread into a single layer. Cook, undisturbed, until edges turn white, about 1 minute.

7. Return green peppers and onion to pan, along with any accumulated juices. Cook, tossing occasionally, until chicken is cooked through and green peppers are tender-crisp, 1 to 2 minutes more.

8. Stir soy sauce mixture and add to pan, pouring in around sides. When it heats up and begins to bubble, toss well and cook, tossing once or twice, until it thickens into a glistening sauce on chicken and vegetables. Add sesame oil and toss once more. Transfer to a serving bowl. Serve hot.

Moo Goo Gai Pan

This satisfying and handsome dish is a great favorite in Chinese restaurants in the West. Its combination of chicken slices tumbled with gorgeous fresh snow peas, crunchy water chestnuts, and mushrooms is easy to love, and simple enough to cook at home. The name *moo goo gai pan* indicates a dish made with slices of chicken and lots of mushrooms. Have everything ready so that you can serve this dish hot, right out of the pan, at its fresh and beautiful best.

TIP

If you want to simplify and speed up this dish, cut chicken into big, bite-size chunks, adjusting cooking time to be certain these larger pieces are done. You could also buy sliced fresh mushrooms, allowing extra cooking time for them as well, since they tend to be thick. If you need more cooking time toward the end, add water 1 to 2 tbsp (15 or 25 mL) at a time around the side of the pan to avoid burning and drying out the food.

3 tbsp	chicken stock or water	45 mL
1 tbsp	soy sauce	15 mL
1 tbsp	dry sherry or Shaoxing rice wine	15 mL
1 tbsp	cornstarch	15 mL
1 tsp	salt or to taste	5 mL
½ tsp	granulated sugar	2 mL
¼ tsp	freshly ground pepper	1 mL
2 tbsp	vegetable oil	25 mL
1 tbsp	chopped garlic	15 mL
2 tsp	chopped fresh gingerroot	10 mL
8 oz	skinless boneless chicken breast, thinly sliced	250 g
1 cup	thinly sliced fresh mushrooms	250 mL
1 cup	trimmed snow peas (see Tips, page 36)	250 mL
½ cup	sliced drained canned water chestnuts	125 mL
2 tsp	Asian sesame oil	10 mL

1. In a small bowl, combine chicken stock, soy sauce, sherry, cornstarch, salt, sugar and pepper and stir well into a smooth sauce. Set aside. Place a bowl next to the stove to hold chicken temporarily after its initial cooking in the pan.

2. Heat a wok or large deep skillet over high heat. Add vegetable oil and swirl to coat pan. Add garlic and ginger and toss well, until fragrant, about 15 seconds.

3. Add chicken and spread into a single layer. Cook, until most of the edges turn white, about 1 minute. Toss well and cook until most pieces have changed color outside but are still not done, less than 1 minute. Transfer to reserved bowl, leaving behind as much oil as possible.

4. Add mushrooms to pan and spread out as much as possible. Cook for 1 minute and then toss well.

5. Return chicken and any juices to pan, toss well, and cook, tossing occasionally, for 1 minute more. Add snow peas and water chestnuts. Cook, tossing occasionally, for 1 minute more.

6. Stir soy sauce mixture and add to pan, pouring in around sides. When it heats up and begins to bubble, toss well and cook, tossing once or twice, until it thickens into a glistening sauce on chicken and vegetables. Add sesame oil and toss once more. Transfer to a serving plate. Serve hot.

Vietnamese-Style Lemongrass Chicken

2 tbsp	fish sauce	25 mL
1 tbsp	soy sauce	15 mL
2 tsp	granulated sugar	10 mL
1 tsp	cornstarch	5 mL
12 oz	skinless boneless chicken breasts or thighs, cut into 1-inch (2.5 cm) chunks	375 g
2	stalks fresh lemongrass	2
1/4 cup	chopped onion	50 mL
1/2 cup	chicken stock or water	125 mL
2 tbsp	vegetable oil	25 mL
1 tbsp	chopped garlic	15 mL
1/2 tsp	salt or to taste	2 mL
1/2 tsp	hot pepper flakes	2 mL
1/3 cup	chopped green onions	75 mL

Serves 4

For my version of this classic Vietnamese dish, grind up chopped fresh lemongrass in a blender or mini-food processor, speedily softening its fibrous texture and releasing its ethereal flavor into a delicious spicy sauce.

1. In a bowl, combine fish sauce, soy sauce, sugar and cornstarch and stir well into a smooth sauce. Add chicken, stirring to combine evenly. Set aside for about 15 minutes.

2. Meanwhile, trim lemongrass stalks, cutting away top half, leaving about a 6-inch (15 cm) base. Cut away dry root ends, leaving a smooth base just under the bulb. Remove any dry outer leaves. Cut stalks in half lengthwise and then crosswise into 1-inch (2.5 cm) pieces.

3. In a blender or mini-food processor, combine lemongrass, onion and chicken stock. Process well, stopping to scrape sides as necessary, to a fairly smooth paste.

4. Heat a wok or a large deep skillet over high heat. Add oil and swirl to coat pan. Add garlic and toss well, until fragrant, about 15 seconds.

5. Add chicken mixture and spread into a single layer. Cook, until edges turn white, about 1 minute.

6. Add lemongrass paste and toss well. Add salt and hot pepper flakes and cook, tossing occasionally, until chicken is cooked through, 2 to 3 minutes. Sprinkle with green onions and toss well. Transfer to a serving plate. Serve hot or warm.

Kung Pao Chicken

Serves 4

This wildly popular dish may have a long ingredient list, but it's mostly a matter of measuring out the two seasoning mixtures. Once that's done, there's a bit of chopping and then you're ready to cook. Many classic recipes include Szechwan peppercorns, but if you don't have them, it's still a delicious dish. The chicken needs to marinate for 1 hour, so plan on that and use the time to assemble the remaining ingredients for this spectacular dish.

Marinade

1 tbsp	soy sauce	15 mL
1 tbsp	dry sherry or Shaoxing rice wine	15 mL
1 tbsp	cornstarch	15 mL
1 tsp	vegetable oil	5 mL
12 oz	skinless boneless chicken breasts, cut into 1-inch (2.5 cm) chunks	375 g

Sauce

1 tbsp	soy sauce	15 mL
1 tbsp	dry sherry or Shaoxing rice wine	15 mL
1 tbsp	red wine vinegar or dark Chinese-style vinegar (see Tips, right)	15 mL
1 tbsp	granulated sugar	15 mL
1 tsp	cornstarch	5 mL
1 tsp	salt or to taste	5 mL
2 tbsp	vegetable oil	25 mL
5 to 10	small dried hot red chiles (see Tips, right)	5 to 10
1 tsp	finely ground Szechwan peppercorns, optional	5 mL
1 tbsp	chopped garlic	15 mL
1 tbsp	chopped fresh gingerroot	15 mL
¼ cup	chopped green onions	50 mL
¾ cup	roasted salted peanuts	175 mL
1 tsp	Asian sesame oil	5 mL

1. *Marinade:* In a bowl, combine soy sauce, sherry, cornstarch and oil and stir well into a smooth sauce. Add chicken, stirring to coat evenly. Set aside at room temperature for 30 minutes or cover and refrigerate for up to 1 day.

2. *Sauce:* In a small bowl, combine soy sauce, sherry, vinegar, sugar, cornstarch and salt and stir well into a smooth sauce. Set aside.

3. Heat a wok or a large deep skillet over high heat. Add vegetable oil and swirl to coat pan. Add chiles and Szechwan peppercorns, if using, and toss well.

4. Add chicken mixture and spread into a single layer. Cook, undisturbed, until edges turn white, about 1 minute. Toss well. Add garlic, ginger and green onions. Cook, tossing occasionally, until chicken has changed color, 1 to 2 minutes.

5. Stir sauce and add to pan. Cook, tossing often, until sauce thickens and coats everything evenly and chicken is cooked through, about 1 minute more. Add peanuts and sesame oil and toss once more. Transfer to a serving plate. Serve hot or warm.

TIPS

Chinese kitchens rely on several kinds of vinegar, including many varieties of dark vinegar. Chenkiang rice vinegar is one variety found in many Asian stores in the West. Though the color is intense, the flavor is strong and sweet rather than tangy and sharp. Red wine vinegar makes a decent substitute if you don't have Chinese-style vinegar.

Adjust the amount of hot red chiles to your heat preference. For a mild dish, add 5 small dried hot red chiles; 10 chiles will produce a lot of fiery heat.

Zesty Chicken with Crisp Asparagus

Serves 4

Enjoy this Southeast Asian-style stir-fry whenever fresh asparagus are in the marketplace. Served with rice or over noodles or polenta, it is a swift and delicious one-dish meal.

TIP

Chubby asparagus stalks are my favorite, but thin ones will work nicely in this recipe. Watch your cooking time and test for doneness as you go, since skinny spears will cook faster than bigger stalks. You could peel the larger stalks below their tips if you like, using a vegetable peeler.

2 tbsp	fish sauce	25 mL
1 tbsp	soy sauce	15 mL
½ tsp	salt or to taste	2 mL
½ tsp	freshly ground pepper	2 mL
½ tsp	granulated sugar	2 mL
8 oz	skinless boneless chicken breasts or thighs, thinly sliced	250 g
8 oz	fresh asparagus (see Tip, left)	250 g
2 tbsp	vegetable oil	25 mL
1 tbsp	chopped garlic	15 mL
2 tbsp	chicken stock or water	25 mL
2 tbsp	thinly sliced green onions	25 mL

1. In a bowl, combine fish sauce, soy sauce, salt, pepper and sugar and stir well. Add chicken, stirring to coat evenly. Set aside for about 15 minutes.

2. Meanwhile, trim asparagus by snapping off ends. Cut each asparagus spear on the diagonal into 2-inch (5 cm) lengths, leaving tips a little longer. You should have about 2 cups (500 mL) chopped asparagus.

3. Heat a wok or large deep skillet over high heat. Add oil and swirl to coat pan. Add garlic and toss well, until fragrant, about 15 seconds.

4. Add chicken mixture and spread into a single layer. Cook, undisturbed, until edges turn white, about 1 minute. Toss well. Cook, tossing once, for 1 minute more.

5. Add asparagus, stock and green onions. Cook, tossing occasionally, until asparagus is bright green and tender-crisp and chicken is cooked through, about 2 minutes more. Transfer to a serving plate. Serve hot or warm.

Chicken with Sweet and Hot Peppers

1 tbsp	cornstarch	15 mL
1 tbsp	water	15 mL
2 tsp	dry sherry or Shaoxing rice wine	10 mL
12 oz	boneless skinless chicken breasts, cut into 1-inch (2.5 cm) chunks	375 g
3 tbsp	chicken stock or water	45 mL
1 tbsp	soy sauce	15 mL
1 tsp	salt or to taste	5 mL
½ tsp	granulated sugar	2 mL
2 tbsp	vegetable oil	25 mL
1 tbsp	chopped garlic	15 mL
1 tbsp	finely chopped jalapeño peppers (see Tips, right)	15 mL
2 tsp	chopped fresh gingerroot	10 mL
1¼ cups	thin strips red, green and yellow bell pepper (see Tips, right)	300 mL

1. In a bowl, combine cornstarch, water and sherry and stir well. Add chicken and mix gently to coat evenly with marinade. Set aside for 20 minutes.

2. In a small bowl, combine chicken stock, soy sauce, salt and sugar and stir well.

3. Heat a wok or a large deep skillet over high heat. Add oil and swirl to coat pan. Add garlic, jalapeño peppers and ginger and toss well, until garlic and ginger are fragrant, about 15 seconds.

4. Add chicken mixture, quickly spreading into a single layer and cook, undisturbed, until edges turn white, 1 minute. Toss well and cook for 1 minute more. Add bell peppers and toss well. Reduce heat to medium.

5. Add chicken stock mixture and cook, until chicken is no longer pink inside and peppers are tender-crisp, 1 to 2 minutes more. Transfer to a serving platter. Serve hot or warm.

Serves 4

Bursting with vitamin C and ablaze with color, sweet bell peppers make an ideal ingredient in stir-fry dishes. You could use red, yellow and orange bell peppers, or just green ones from your summer garden. Jalapeños make a hot but not blazing spicy note here. If you want more heat, use fresh green or red serrano chile peppers, and if you want a fiery dish, use tiny Thai chiles instead.

TIPS

To chop jalapeño peppers, cut off stems and halve each pepper lengthwise, discarding seedy portions and most of the seeds. Chop lengthwise into thin strips and then crosswise to make small bits.

To make pepper strips, halve each pepper lengthwise and discard stem section and seeds. Cut off the rounded top and bottom portions and reserve for salad or other dishes. Cut enough of the remaining portion of each pepper into slender strips about 1½ inches (4 cm) long.

Gingery Chicken with Crisp Vegetables

Serves 4

Cool, crisp and ready to amplify the flavors of fresh ginger and soy sauce, bean sprouts are worth seeking out in the produce section. Buy them when you find them at their freshest: bright white, firm and stick-straight, and use them within a day or two.

1 tbsp	dry sherry or Shaoxing rice wine	15 mL
1 tbsp	soy sauce	15 mL
1 tbsp	water	15 mL
1½ tsp	cornstarch	7 mL
1 tsp	salt or to taste	5 mL
2 tbsp	vegetable oil	25 mL
2 tbsp	chopped fresh gingerroot	25 mL
2 tsp	chopped garlic	10 mL
½ cup	shredded carrot	125 mL
3 cups	bean sprouts	750 mL
8 oz	skinless boneless chicken breasts or thighs, thinly sliced	250 g
⅓ cup	chopped green onions	75 mL

1. In a small bowl, combine sherry, soy sauce, water, cornstarch and salt and stir well into a smooth sauce. Set aside.

2. Heat a wok or a large deep skillet over high heat. Add oil and swirl to coat pan. Add ginger, garlic and carrot and toss well, until ginger and garlic are fragrant, about 30 seconds.

4. Push carrots to the side and add chicken. Spread into a single layer and cook, undisturbed, until edges turn white, about 1 minute. Toss well. Cook, tossing occasionally, until chicken is cooked through, 2 to 3 minutes more. Add bean sprouts and toss once.

5. Add sherry mixture, pouring in around sides of pan. Cook, tossing once, until mixture comes to a gentle boil. As soon as sauce thickens, scatter in green onions. Toss once more. Transfer to a serving plate. Serve hot.

Chicken and Cherry Tomato Toss

3 tbsp	chicken stock	45 mL
1 tbsp	soy sauce	15 mL
1 tsp	dark soy sauce, optional (see Tips, right)	5 mL
1 tbsp	granulated sugar	15 mL
1 tsp	salt or to taste	5 mL
2 tbsp	vegetable oil	25 mL
1 tbsp	coarsely chopped garlic	15 mL
1 tbsp	finely chopped fresh gingerroot	15 mL
12 oz	skinless boneless chicken breasts, cut into 1½-inch (4 cm) pieces	375 g
⅓ cup	thinly sliced green onions, divided	75 mL
¾ cup	halved cherry tomatoes	175 mL

1. In a small bowl, combine chicken stock, soy sauce, dark soy sauce, if using, sugar and salt and stir well. Set aside.

2. In a wok or a large deep skillet, heat oil over medium-high heat. Add garlic and ginger and toss well, until fragrant, about 30 seconds.

3. Add chicken and spread into a single layer. Cook, undisturbed, until edges turn white, about 1 minute. Toss well. Cook, tossing occasionally, until no longer pink, about 1 minute more.

4. Add chicken stock mixture, pouring in around sides of pan. Cook, tossing occasionally, until chicken is cooked through and coated in a thin, smooth sauce, 1 to 2 minutes more.

5. Reserve a generous pinch of green onions for garnish, and add remaining green onions and cherry tomatoes to pan. Cook, tossing once, for 1 minute more.

6. Transfer to a serving plate. Sprinkle reserved green onions over chicken. Serve hot or warm.

> **Variation:** Use skinless boneless chicken thighs, cut into 1½-inch (4 cm) pieces, increasing the cooking time by a few minutes so that this slower-cooking meat has time to cook through.

Serves 4

This recipe is simply beautiful, and beautifully simple to cook. I keep fresh ginger, green onions and peeled garlic on hand and a chicken breast in the freezer. Serve with rice, couscous or noodles.

TIPS

Dark soy sauce adds handsome color and depth of flavor to stir-fry dishes, but is not essential to the recipe. Omit it if you don't have it on hand. It's a good background stir-fry seasoning, and keeps long and well, so consider buying a bottle if you stir-fry often.

You'll have a pleasing amount of dark, delicious sauce, perfect for spooning over rice along with the spicy chicken. The sauce will be thin, Thai-style, since no cornstarch is used to thicken it.

Peppery Shredded Chicken

Serves 4

I love this combination of bright green pepper with savory strips of chicken. If you like heat, chop up a spoonful of serrano or jalapeño peppers and add it with the green bell peppers. I like this dish with rice and a bowl of corn mixed with lima beans or peas.

TIP

You'll need most of 1 large green bell pepper for this recipe. Cut it in half lengthwise, and break off or cut out the stem sections from each half. Shake out any remaining seeds, and then cut off the rounded, bumpy portions at top and bottom, leaving two nice rectangles of green bell pepper. Slice these lengthwise to make up the amount needed for this recipe. Use any remainder in salads or roast in the oven or on a countertop grilling machine and enjoy on sandwiches or as a vegetable side dish with other roasted vegetables.

1 tbsp	soy sauce	15 mL
1 tbsp	dry sherry or Shaoxing rice wine	15 mL
1 tsp	cornstarch	5 mL
1 tsp	salt or to taste	5 mL
½ tsp	granulated sugar	2 mL
2 tbsp	vegetable oil	25 mL
2 tsp	chopped garlic	10 mL
1 tsp	chopped fresh gingerroot	5 mL
1½ cups	thinly sliced large green bell pepper (see Tip, left)	375 mL
8 oz	skinless boneless chicken breasts, thinly sliced	250 g
2 tsp	Asian sesame oil	10 mL

1. In a small bowl, combine soy sauce, sherry, cornstarch, salt and sugar and stir well into a smooth sauce. Set aside. Place a bowl next to the stove to hold the green peppers after their first cooking.

2. Heat a wok or a large deep skillet over high heat. Add vegetable oil and swirl to coat pan. Add garlic and ginger and toss well, until fragrant, about 15 seconds.

3. Add green peppers and spread into a single layer. Cook, tossing twice, until peppers begin to soften, about 30 seconds. Transfer to reserved bowl, leaving behind as much oil as possible.

4. Add chicken and spread into a single layer. Cook, undisturbed, until edges turn white, about 1 minute. Toss well. Cook, tossing once, until no longer pink, about 1 minute more.

5. Return green peppers to pan along with any accumulated juices. Toss to mix everything well and cook, tossing often, until chicken is cooked through, about 2 minutes more.

6. Add soy sauce mixture, pouring in around sides of pan. As soon as it begins to bubble, toss well to evenly coat chicken and vegetables. Add sesame oil and toss once. Transfer to a serving plate. Serve hot or warm.

Not-too-Corny Chicken with Red Peppers

1 tbsp	soy sauce	15 mL
1 tbsp	dry sherry or Shaoxing rice wine	15 mL
1 tsp	salt or to taste	5 mL
½ tsp	granulated sugar	2 mL
12 oz	skinless boneless chicken breasts or thighs, cut into 1-inch (2.5 cm) chunks	375 g
2 tbsp	vegetable oil	25 mL
1 tbsp	chopped garlic	15 mL
1 tbsp	chopped fresh gingerroot	15 mL
¾ cup	corn kernels, fresh, frozen or canned (see Tips, right)	175 mL
¼ cup	cubed red bell peppers (about ½-inch/1 cm pieces)	50 mL
2 tbsp	chicken stock or water	25 mL
3 tbsp	chopped green onions	45 mL
1 tsp	Asian sesame oil	5 mL

1. In a bowl, combine soy sauce, sherry, salt and sugar and stir well. Add chicken and mix to season evenly. Set aside for about 15 minutes.

2. Heat a wok or a large deep skillet over high heat. Add vegetable oil and swirl to coat pan. Add garlic and ginger and toss well, until fragrant, about 15 seconds.

3. Add chicken mixture and spread into a single layer. Cook, undisturbed, until edges turn white, about 1 minute. Toss well. Cook, tossing twice, until no longer pink, about 1 minute more.

4. Add corn and red peppers and toss well. Add chicken stock, pouring in around sides of pan. Cook, tossing often, until chicken is cooked through and vegetables are tender, about 2 minutes more. Add green onions and sesame oil and toss once more. Transfer to a serving plate. Serve hot or warm.

Serves 4

Make this with corn from the farmer's market during the summer, and then keep frozen or canned corn on hand so that you can enjoy it the rest of the year. You could substitute green bell peppers for the red ones or use a colorful mix of sweet peppers.

TIPS

If using frozen corn, add an extra tablespoon (15 mL) of water and allow an extra minute or two of cooking time, tasting a kernel to be sure it is hot and cooked through before completing the dish.

Frozen corn is best added straight from the freezer; but thawing it is fine as well. For canned corn, drain, rinse well with cold water, and drain again. Adjust cooking time depending on which you use: Frozen corn will take longer than fresh, canned or thawed. To determine doneness, simply sample a kernel or two when you think it is ready.

Dazzling Chicken with Snow Peas and Tomatoes

Serves 4

Snow peas and chunks of tomato team up with chicken in this delicious and brilliantly colored dish. Plum tomatoes work nicely here, but you could substitute any variety, including cherry tomatoes halved lengthwise.

TIPS

To keep ingredients from sticking and burning, be sure to reduce heat to medium after the chicken gets a good start. If you need more time and find the mixture sticking to the pan, add more water, 1 tbsp (15 mL) at a time, toward the end of cooking.

To trim snow peas, cut off and discard tip and cut stem end partway, pulling it down along the straight side of each snow pea to remove any strings.

1 tbsp	soy sauce	15 mL
1 tbsp	dry sherry or Shaoxing rice wine	15 mL
1 tbsp	water	15 mL
1 tsp	salt or to taste	5 mL
½ tsp	granulated sugar	2 mL
2 tsp	cornstarch	10 mL
2 tbsp	vegetable oil	25 mL
1 tbsp	chopped garlic	15 mL
1 tbsp	chopped fresh gingerroot	15 mL
8 oz	skinless boneless chicken breasts or thighs, cut into 1-inch (2.5 cm) chunks	250 g
1¼ cups	trimmed snow peas (see Tips, left)	300 mL
2	plum (Roma) tomatoes, chopped into large chunks and drained (1 cup/250 mL) (see Tip, page 45)	2

1. In a small bowl, combine soy sauce, sherry, water, salt, sugar and cornstarch and stir well into a smooth sauce. Set aside.

2. Heat a wok or a large deep skillet over high heat. Add oil and swirl to coat pan. Add garlic and ginger and toss well, until fragrant, about 15 seconds.

3. Add chicken and spread into a single layer. Cook, undisturbed, until edges turn white, about 1 minute. Cook, tossing occasionally, until no longer pink, about 1 minute more.

4. Push chicken to the side and add snow peas to center of pan, spreading out so they have as much contact with hot pan as possible. Cook for 1 minute. Reduce heat to medium (see Tips, left).

5. Add tomatoes and toss well. Stir soy sauce mixture and pour in around sides of pan. Cook, tossing occasionally, until snow peas are tender and chicken is cooked through, and both are coated with sauce, 1 to 2 minutes more. Transfer to a serving plate. Serve hot or warm.

Crunchy Quilted Chicken

1 tbsp	dry sherry or Shaoxing rice wine	15 mL
2 tsp	soy sauce	10 mL
2 tsp	cornstarch	10 mL
1 tsp	salt or to taste	5 mL
¼ tsp	granulated sugar	1 mL
2 tbsp	vegetable oil	25 mL
2 tsp	chopped garlic	10 mL
2 tsp	chopped fresh gingerroot	10 mL
¾ cup	shredded carrots	175 mL
8 oz	skinless boneless chicken breasts, thinly sliced	250 g
1 cup	thinly sliced fresh mushrooms	250 mL
3 cups	fresh spinach leaves	750 mL
2 tsp	Asian sesame oil	10 mL

Serves 4

This dish has color and flavor with a pleasing carrot crunch. You can chop chicken into big bite-size pieces and allow a little more time to cook them through.

1. In a small bowl, combine sherry, soy sauce, cornstarch, salt and sugar and stir well into a smooth sauce. Set aside.

2. Heat a wok or a large deep skillet over high heat. Add oil and swirl to coat pan. Add garlic, ginger and carrots and toss well, until garlic and ginger are fragrant, about 15 seconds.

3. Toss and push garlic-carrot mixture to sides of pan. Add chicken and spread into a single layer. Cook, undisturbed, until edges turn white, about 1 minute.

4. Toss well and add mushrooms. Cook, tossing occasionally, until chicken is cooked through, 1 to 2 minutes. Add sherry mixture, pouring in around sides of pan. Add spinach. Cook, tossing, until spinach is wilted, for 1 minute more.

5. Add sesame oil and toss once more. Transfer to a serving plate. Serve hot or warm.

Technicolor Chicken Stir-Fry

Serves 4

Though this dish has three different vegetables in addition to the chicken, it is easy to prepare and cooks quickly. Only the baby carrots need chopping. The dish looks wonderful with lots of color and texture, and looks are not deceiving in this case, because it tastes good, too.

TIPS

Instead of baby carrots, quarter the top portion of a medium carrot lengthwise, and then cut crosswise into thin pieces.

To freshen the flavor of canned baby corn, drain it well, cover with cold water and drain again. Transfer any leftover baby corn to a jar with fresh water to cover it, or chop it into plump little rounds and add them to soups and salads just before serving.

1 tbsp	cornstarch	15 mL
1 tbsp	water	15 mL
2 tsp	dry sherry or Shaoxing rice wine	10 mL
1 tsp	salt or to taste	5 mL
12 oz	skinless boneless chicken breasts, cut into 1-inch (2.5 cm) chunks	375 g
¼ cup	chicken stock	50 mL
2 tbsp	soy sauce	25 mL
1 tsp	dark soy sauce, optional (see Tip, page 33)	5 mL
½ tsp	granulated sugar	2 mL
2 tbsp	vegetable oil	25 mL
2 tsp	chopped garlic	10 mL
2 tsp	finely chopped fresh gingerroot	10 mL
½ cup	thinly sliced baby carrots (see Tips, left)	125 mL
1½ cups	baby corn (see Tips, left)	375 mL
½ cup	frozen tiny peas (see Tip, page 47)	125 mL

1. In a bowl, combine cornstarch, water, sherry and salt and stir well into a smooth sauce. Add chicken and mix gently to coat evenly with marinade. Set aside for 20 minutes.

2. In a small bowl, combine chicken stock, soy sauce, dark soy sauce, if using, and sugar and stir well. Set aside.

3. Heat a wok or a large deep skillet over high heat. Add oil and swirl to coat pan. Add garlic and ginger and toss well, until fragrant, about 15 seconds.

4. Add chicken mixture and spread into a single layer. Cook, undisturbed, until edges turn white, about 1 minute. Add carrots and cook, tossing, for 1 minute more.

5. Add chicken stock mixture and corn and toss well. Cook, tossing once or twice, until chicken is cooked through and carrots are tender-crisp, 1 to 2 minutes more. Add peas and cook, tossing once, until heated through, about 1 minute more. Transfer to a serving plate. Serve hot or warm.

Soy-Spiked Chicken with Shiitakes

2 tsp	soy sauce	10 mL
2 tsp	water	10 mL
1 tsp	salt or to taste	5 mL
½ tsp	granulated sugar	2 mL
1 cup	fresh shiitake mushrooms (4 oz/125 g)	250 mL
2 tbsp	vegetable oil	25 mL
2 tsp	chopped garlic	10 mL
2 tsp	chopped fresh gingerroot	10 mL
8 oz	skinless boneless chicken breasts or thighs, cut into 1-inch (2.5 cm) chunks	250 g
1 cup	shredded carrots	250 mL
3 tbsp	chopped green onions	45 mL
2 tsp	Asian sesame oil	10 mL

Serves 4

Fresh shiitakes are a beautiful and flavorful treat. I love the plush texture they provide to a stir-fried dish like this one.

1. In a small bowl, combine soy sauce, water, salt and sugar and stir well. Set aside.

2. Cut away and discard stems of shiitake mushrooms. Cut large caps into quarters, halve medium ones, and leave small ones whole. Set aside.

3. Heat a wok or a large deep skillet over high heat. Add oil and swirl to coat pan. Add garlic and ginger and toss well, until fragrant, about 15 seconds.

4. Add chicken and spread into a single layer. Cook, undisturbed, until edges turn white, about 1 minute. Add carrots and toss well. Cook, tossing twice, until chicken is no longer pink, about 1 minute.

5. Add mushrooms and toss to mix everything well. Cook, tossing often, until chicken is cooked through and mushrooms are tender and a rich, shiny brown, 1 to 2 minutes more.

6. Add soy sauce mixture, pouring in around sides of pan and toss to mix everything well. Add green onions and sesame oil and toss once more. Transfer to a serving plate. Serve hot or warm.

Orange-Spiked Chicken with Cilantro

Serves 4

Orange juice and a bit of orange zest give this dish a burst of sunny flavor. I like it with couscous or rice, along with a bowl of steamed broccoli or tiny peas.

TIP

If you don't have freshly squeezed orange juice, store-bought can be substituted and the zest omitted.

1 tbsp	soy sauce	15 mL
2 tsp	white vinegar	10 mL
2 tsp	cornstarch	10 mL
1 tsp	salt or to taste	5 mL
12 oz	skinless boneless chicken breasts, thinly sliced	375 g
1 tsp	grated orange zest	5 mL
3 tbsp	freshly squeezed orange juice (see Tip, left)	45 mL
1 tbsp	granulated sugar	15 mL
2 tbsp	vegetable oil	25 mL
2 tbsp	chopped fresh gingerroot	25 mL
½ cup	shredded carrot	125 mL
3 tbsp	chopped fresh cilantro	45 mL

1. In a bowl, combine soy sauce, vinegar, cornstarch and salt and stir well into a smooth sauce. Add chicken and stir well to coat evenly with marinade. Set aside.
2. In a small bowl, combine orange zest and juice and sugar and stir well. Set aside.
3. Heat a wok or a large deep skillet over high heat. Add oil and swirl to coat pan. Add ginger and carrot and toss well. Cook, tossing occasionally, until ginger is fragrant and carrots are beginning to soften, about 30 seconds.
4. Push carrots to sides of pan. Add chicken mixture and spread into a single layer. Cook, undisturbed, until edges turn white, about 1 minute. Cook, tossing occasionally, until chicken is cooked through, about 2 minutes more.
5. Add orange juice mixture, pouring in around sides of pan. When it begins to bubble, toss well to season chicken evenly. Add cilantro and toss well. Transfer to a serving plate. Serve hot or warm.

Vietnamese Chicken with Caramel-Ginger Sauce

2 tbsp	soy sauce	25 mL
2 tbsp	water	25 mL
1 tbsp	dark brown or light brown sugar	15 mL
½ tsp	salt or to taste	2 mL
2 tbsp	vegetable oil	25 mL
2 tbsp	chopped fresh gingerroot	25 mL
1 tbsp	chopped garlic	15 mL
12 oz	skinless boneless chicken thighs, cut into 1½-inch (4 cm) chunks	375 g
2 tbsp	chopped green onions	25 mL

1. In a small bowl, combine soy sauce, water, sugar and salt and stir well. Set aside.

2. Heat a wok or a large deep skillet over high heat. Add oil and swirl to coat pan. Add ginger and garlic and toss well, until fragrant, about 15 seconds.

3. Add chicken and spread into a single layer. Cook, until edges turn white, about 1 minute. Cook, tossing, until no longer pink, for 1 minute more.

4. Add soy sauce mixture, pouring in around sides of pan and toss again. Cook, tossing often, until chicken is cooked through and coated with sauce, about 2 minutes more. Add green onions and toss well. Transfer to a serving plate. Serve hot or warm.

Serves 4

This is my version of a delicious Vietnamese dish that traditionally braises gently in a clay pot. Here, I've stir-fried it quickly and used chicken thighs, but chicken breast would also work nicely. It's perfect for a busy night and can be made with chicken, pork or fish. You'll want lots of rice or French bread to help you savor the delectable sauce.

Thai-Style Chicken with Cilantro

Serves 4

This Thai-style dish makes a hearty main course, perfectly matched with a spinach salad, cucumber rounds and a spicy salsa or the deliciously fiery Thai chile sauce, Sriracha. This dish needs at least an hour of marinating time so plan ahead.

2 tbsp	chopped garlic	25 mL
2 tsp	soy sauce	10 mL
2 tsp	oyster sauce	10 mL
2 tsp	granulated sugar	10 mL
1 tsp	freshly ground pepper	5 mL
½ tsp	salt or to taste	2 mL
12 oz	skinless boneless chicken breasts or thighs, thinly sliced	375 g
3 tbsp	vegetable oil	45 mL
2 tbsp	chopped fresh cilantro	25 mL

1. In a bowl, combine garlic, soy sauce, oyster sauce, sugar, pepper and salt and stir well. Add chicken and turn to coat each piece evenly with marinade. Cover and refrigerate for at least 1 hour or for up to 8 hours.

2. Heat a wok or a large deep skillet over high heat. Add oil and swirl to coat pan. Add chicken mixture and spread into a single layer. Cook, undisturbed, until edges turn white, about 1 minute. Toss well. Cook, tossing often, until chicken is no longer pink, about 1 minute more.

3. Reduce heat to medium-high. Cook, tossing occasionally, until chicken is cooked through and is nicely browned, 1 to 2 minutes more. Add cilantro and toss well. Transfer to a serving plate. Serve hot or warm.

Gingery Chicken with Mushrooms and Red Pepper

1 tbsp	fish sauce	15 mL
1 tbsp	soy sauce	15 mL
1 tbsp	water	15 mL
1 tsp	granulated sugar	5 mL
2 tbsp	vegetable oil	25 mL
1 tbsp	chopped garlic	15 mL
8 oz	skinless boneless chicken breasts, thinly sliced	250 g
¾ cup	thinly sliced mushrooms	175 mL
⅓ cup	long thin strips fresh gingerroot (see Tip, right)	75 mL
⅓ cup	long thin strips red bell peppers	75 mL
¼ cup	chopped green onions	50 mL

1. In a small bowl, combine fish sauce, soy sauce, water and sugar and stir well. Set aside.

2. Heat a wok or a large deep skillet over high heat. Add oil and swirl to coat pan. Add garlic and toss well, until fragrant, about 15 seconds.

3. Add chicken and spread into a single layer. Cook, undisturbed, until edges turn white, about 1 minute. Add mushrooms and toss well. Cook, tossing occasionally, for 1 minute more.

4. Push chicken and mushrooms to the side. Add ginger to center of pan, spreading it out, and cook until ginger is fragrant and chicken is cooked through, 1 to 2 minutes more. Toss well.

5. Add fish sauce mixture, pouring in around sides of pan. Add red peppers to center of pan and toss well to season everything evenly. Add green onions and toss once more. Transfer to a serving plate. Serve hot or warm.

Serves 4

This dish calls for lots of fresh ginger, cut into long, thin shreds to provide maximum flavor to the dish. Pair it with steamed broccoli, a little salad of tomatoes and cucumbers, cut into large chunks, and lots of rice.

TIP

To prepare shredded ginger, start with firm, plump and shiny roots. Cut them into 2-inch (5 cm) long pieces and remove peel with a paring knife. Cut each section crosswise, against the grain, into very thin slices. Stack slices into even little piles, and then slice thinly with the grain into long, slender strips. Do this very close to cooking time, so that you will get maximum flavor from the ginger shreds.

Asian-Style Scrambled Eggs with Chicken

Serves 4

Throughout Asia, eggs are enjoyed throughout the day in delicious hearty dishes like this one, made to be savored with rice. I think it's also wonderful with toast, as long as you don't wait for breakfast time to enjoy it.

2 tbsp	fish sauce	25 mL
1 tbsp	water	15 mL
½ tsp	salt or to taste	2 mL
½ tsp	granulated sugar	2 mL
1 cup	sugar snap peas or snow peas	250 mL
2 tbsp	vegetable oil	25 mL
1 tbsp	chopped garlic	15 mL
8 oz	skinless boneless chicken breasts, thinly sliced	250 g
⅓ cup	coarsely chopped onion	75 mL
⅓ cup	chopped green onions	75 mL
4	eggs, well beaten	4
½ cup	halved cherry tomatoes	125 mL
3 tbsp	chopped fresh cilantro	45 mL

1. In a small bowl, combine fish sauce, water, salt and sugar and stir well. Set aside. Trim sugar snap peas, cutting off stem end and pulling it along straight edge to remove any strings. Set peas aside.

2. Heat a wok or a large deep skillet over high heat. Add vegetable oil and swirl to coat pan. Add garlic and toss well, until fragrant, about 15 seconds.

3. Add chicken and spread into a single layer. Cook, undisturbed, until edges have turned white, about 1 minute. Toss again and cook, tossing occasionally, for 1 minute more. Add fish sauce mixture and cook, tossing occasionally, for 30 seconds to season everything well.

4. Add sugar snap peas, onion and green onions and toss well. Cook, tossing often, until chicken is cooked through, about 2 minutes.

5. Add eggs, pouring in around sides of pan. Cook, undisturbed, until they begin to set, about 30 seconds. Toss gently. Cook, tossing occasionally, for 1 minute more.

6. Add cherry tomatoes and toss again, gently breaking up large chunks of egg and letting tomatoes heat up just a little on the pan. Add cilantro and toss well gently. Transfer to a serving plate. Serve hot or warm.

Luscious Chicken Curry in-a-Hurry

2 tbsp	vegetable oil	25 mL
½ cup	chopped onion (1-inch/2.5 cm chunks)	125 mL
½ cup	chopped green bell peppers (1-inch/2.5 cm chunks)	125 mL
1 tbsp	chopped garlic	15 mL
1 tsp	chopped fresh gingerroot	5 mL
½ tsp	salt or to taste	2 mL
½ tsp	granulated sugar	2 mL
2 tbsp	curry powder	25 mL
12 oz	skinless boneless chicken breasts, thinly sliced	375 g
2 tbsp	water	25 mL
2	plum (Roma) tomatoes, chopped into large chunks and drained (1 cup/250 mL) (see Tip, right)	2
3 tbsp	chopped fresh cilantro	45 mL
	Plain yogurt	

1. Heat a wok or a large deep skillet over high heat. Add oil and swirl to coat pan. Add onion and toss well. Cook, tossing twice, until fragrant and beginning to soften, about 1 minute.

2. Add green peppers, garlic, ginger, salt and sugar and toss well. Cook, tossing once, 30 seconds more.

3. Add curry powder and toss well. Add chicken and spread into a single layer. Cook, tossing twice, and adding water once most of the chicken has turned white, about 2 minutes.

4. Add tomatoes and cook, tossing occasionally, until chicken is cooked through and tomatoes are hot but still firm, about 1 minute more. Add cilantro and toss well. Transfer to a serving plate. Serve hot or warm with a dollop of yogurt over top.

Variation: You can substitute ½ cup (125 mL) halved cherry tomatoes instead of plum tomatoes here.

Serves 4

Serve this recipe with rice or another grain for a complete meal. Add hot curry powder if you want a fiery little feast.

TIP

To chop plum tomatoes, trim off stem end, and cut each tomato lengthwise into quarters. Cut each piece crosswise into 3 or 4 big chunks and transfer to a small bowl, leaving the juice and any easily released seeds behind on cutting board. Chopping the tomatoes in this way removes some of the juices and seeds and helps keep the sauce from diluting. Also, these chopped tomatoes should be big, so they are in the sauce more as a vegetable than as a seasoning.

Coconut Chicken Curry with Zucchini

Serves 4

Hearty and spicy hot, this recipe provides a robust curry sauce perfect for enjoying with rice or noodles. Once you have its standard Asian ingredients on hand, it's a quick meal on a busy night.

¼ cup	unsweetened coconut milk	50 mL
2 tbsp	fish sauce	25 mL
2 tbsp	water	25 mL
1 tbsp	brown sugar	15 mL
1	medium zucchini (or 2 small)	1
2 tbsp	vegetable oil	25 mL
2 tbsp	Thai-style red curry paste	25 mL
8 oz	skinless boneless chicken breasts or thighs, thinly sliced	250 g
2 tbsp	chopped green onions	15 mL

1. In a small bowl, combine coconut milk, fish sauce, water and brown sugar and stir well. Set aside.

2. Trim zucchini and cut lengthwise in half and then crosswise into half-circles about ¼ inch (0.5 cm) thick. Set aside.

3. Heat a wok or a large deep skillet over medium-high heat. Add oil and swirl to coat pan. Add red curry paste and cook, mashing and stirring to soften in the hot oil, about 30 seconds. Reduce heat if the mixture spatters and pops.

4. Add chicken and toss well. Spread into a single layer and cook, tossing often, until chicken is no longer pink and evenly coated with curry paste, 1 to 2 minutes.

5. Add coconut milk mixture and toss gently to mix well. Add zucchini and bring to a gentle boil. Cook, tossing gently once or twice, until chicken is cooked through and zucchini is tender and bright green, 1 to 2 minutes more. Add green onions and toss well. Transfer to a serving plate. Serve hot or warm.

Thai-Style Piquant Chicken Curry

¼ cup	unsweetened coconut milk	50 mL
2 tbsp	fish sauce	25 mL
2 tbsp	water	25 mL
1 tbsp	brown sugar	15 mL
2 tbsp	vegetable oil	25 mL
2 tbsp	Thai-style green curry paste	25 mL
12 oz	skinless boneless chicken breasts or thighs, thinly sliced	375 g
⅓ cup	frozen tiny peas (see Tip, right)	75 mL
¼ cup	fresh basil leaves	50 mL
	Basil sprigs, optional	

Serves 4

This spicy hot Thai-style dish is perfect with lots of rice or noodles to accompany its vibrant flavors. If you have Makrut lime leaves, fresh or frozen, cut them into quarters and add them to the pan along with coconut milk.

TIP

Frozen tiny peas are also referred to as "petite" and "baby." You can also use regular-size frozen peas, if you allow a little extra cooking time to heat them through.

1. In a small bowl, combine coconut milk, fish sauce, water and brown sugar and stir well. Set aside.

2. Heat a wok or a large deep skillet over medium-high heat. Add oil and swirl to coat pan. Add green curry paste and cook, mashing and stirring it to soften in the hot oil, about 30 seconds. Reduce heat if the mixture spatters and pops.

3. Add chicken and toss well. Spread into a single layer and cook, tossing often, until chicken turns white all over and is evenly coated with curry paste, 1 to 2 minutes.

4. Add coconut milk mixture and toss gently to mix well. When sauce comes to a gentle boil, add peas and cook, tossing gently once or twice, until chicken is cooked through and peas are hot, 1 to 2 minutes more.

5. Add fresh basil leaves, holding back a pretty sprig or two for garnish. Tear very large leaves in half as you add them. Toss gently once. Transfer to a serving plate and garnish with basil sprigs, if using. Serve hot or warm.

Peppery Basil Chicken

Serves 4

At my house, this Thai-inspired pairing of fragrant basil with chicken shows up often on our dinner table. We enjoy it with rice and steamed spinach or a simple salad. It's also good over couscous or noodles.

TIPS

For a hotter dish, add more hot pepper flakes. If you prefer less heat, add only ½ tsp (2 mL).

You'll have a pleasing amount of dark, delicious sauce — perfect for spooning over rice along with the spicy chicken. The sauce will be thin, Thai-style, since no cornstarch is used to thicken it.

3 tbsp	chicken stock	45 mL
1 tbsp	soy sauce	15 mL
1 tbsp	granulated sugar	15 mL
1 tsp	salt or to taste	5 mL
2 tbsp	vegetable oil	25 mL
½ cup	coarsely chopped onion	125 mL
1 tbsp	coarsely chopped garlic	15 mL
8 oz	skinless boneless chicken breasts, cut into 1½-inch (4 cm) pieces	250 g
1 tsp	hot pepper flakes or hot pepper sauce (see Tips, left)	5 mL
¼ tsp	freshly ground pepper	1 mL
1 cup	fresh basil or mint leaves	250 mL

1. In a small bowl, combine chicken stock, soy sauce, sugar and salt and stir well. Set aside.

2. Heat a wok or a large deep skillet over medium-high heat. Add oil and swirl to coat pan. Add onion and garlic and cook, tossing once or twice, until fragrant, about 30 seconds.

3. Add chicken and spread into a single layer. Cook, tossing once or twice to brown on all sides, 1 minute. Add chicken stock mixture and cook, tossing occasionally, until chicken is cooked through and seasonings form a thin, smooth sauce, 2 to 3 minutes more.

4. Add hot pepper flakes, pepper and basil and toss well. Transfer to a serving plate. Serve hot or warm.

> **Variation:** Use skinless boneless chicken thighs, increasing the cooking time by a few minutes so that this slower-cooking meat has time to cook through.

Spicy Minted Garlic Chicken with Green Beans

2 tbsp	fish sauce	25 mL
1 tbsp	water	15 mL
2 tsp	white vinegar	10 mL
2 tsp	granulated sugar	10 mL
1 tbsp	chopped garlic	15 mL
1 tbsp	chopped fresh gingerroot	15 mL
2 tbsp	chopped shallots or onion	25 mL
1	fresh green serrano chile or 3 Thai chiles	1
2 tbsp	vegetable oil	25 mL
12 oz	skinless boneless chicken breasts, cut into 1-inch (2.5 cm) pieces	375 g
½ cup	chopped fresh green beans (1-inch/2.5 cm pieces)	125 mL
⅓ cup	chopped red bell peppers (½-inch/1 cm pieces)	75 mL
⅓ cup	fresh mint leaves	75 mL

Serves 4

This one is hot stuff, with fresh chile peppers and ginger ground to a fiery seasoning paste. Use a mini-food processor or a blender to make the simple seasoning paste, or grind them using a mortar and pestle if you have one in your kitchen.

1. In a small bowl, combine fish sauce, water, vinegar and sugar and stir well. Set aside.

2. In a mini-food processor or a blender, combine garlic, ginger, shallots and chile. Process to a fairly smooth paste, pulsing and stopping to scrape down sides to mix everything well. Add 1 to 2 tbsp (15 to 25 mL) water if needed to help move the blade.

3. Heat a wok or a large deep skillet over medium-high heat. Add oil and swirl to coat pan. Carefully add garlic-chile paste (it will sizzle up wildly). Reduce heat to maintain a lively sizzle but avoid burning and popping. Cook, stirring and pressing, until fragrant and well combined with the oil, 1 to 2 minutes.

4. Add chicken and spread into a single layer. Cook, undisturbed, until edges turn white, about 1 minute. Toss well. Add green beans and toss again. Cook, tossing occasionally, until chicken is cooked through and beans are bright green, 2 to 3 minutes.

5. Add red peppers and toss well. Add fish sauce mixture, pouring in around sides of pan and cook, tossing, for 1 minute more. Add mint leaves and toss well. Transfer to a serving plate. Serve hot or warm.

Classic Chicken with Salted Cashews

Serves 4

Celery adds its cool crunch and cashews provide their luscious texture to this classic Chinese stir-fry combination.

2 tbsp	dry sherry or Shaoxing rice wine	25 mL
2 tbsp	water	25 mL
1 tbsp	soy sauce	15 mL
2 tsp	cornstarch	10 mL
½ tsp	granulated sugar	2 mL
½ tsp	salt or to taste	2 mL
12 oz	skinless boneless chicken breasts or thighs, cut into 1-inch (2.5 cm) pieces	375 g
2 tbsp	vegetable oil	25 mL
2 tsp	finely chopped garlic	10 mL
2 tsp	finely chopped fresh gingerroot	10 mL
¾ cup	sliced celery (about ½-inch/1 cm chunks)	175 mL
1 cup	dry-roasted salted cashews	250 mL
3 tbsp	chopped green onions	45 mL

1. In a bowl, combine sherry, water, soy sauce, cornstarch, sugar and salt and stir well. Add chicken and mix to coat well. Set aside for 15 minutes.

2. Heat a wok or a large deep skillet over medium-high heat. Add oil and swirl to coat pan. Add garlic and ginger and toss well, until fragrant, about 30 seconds.

3. Add chicken mixture and spread into a single layer. Cook, undisturbed, until edges turn white, about 1 minute. Toss well. Add celery and cook, tossing occasionally, until chicken is cooked through and celery is bright green, 1 to 2 minutes more.

4. Stir soy sauce mixture well and add to pan, pouring in around sides. When it begins to sizzle, add cashews and green onions and toss well. Cook, tossing once, for 30 seconds more. Transfer to a serving plate. Serve hot or warm.

Fiery Thai-Style Chicken with Cashews and Chiles

2 tbsp	fish sauce	25 mL
2 tbsp	water	25 mL
2 tsp	soy sauce	10 mL
½ tsp	granulated sugar	2 mL
3 tbsp	vegetable oil	45 mL
8	small dried red chiles (see Tip, right)	8
8 oz	skinless boneless chicken breasts, cut into 1-inch (2.5 cm) pieces	250 g
1 cup	very coarsely chopped onion	250 mL
½ cup	dry-roasted salted cashews	125 mL
⅓ cup	chopped green onions	75 mL

1. In a small bowl, combine fish sauce, water, soy sauce and sugar and stir well. Set aside. Place a bowl next to the stove to hold the chiles once they have been cooked in the hot oil.

2. Heat a wok or a large deep skillet over medium heat. Add oil and swirl to coat pan. Add chiles and toss well, letting them color but not burn, about 30 seconds. Transfer chiles to the reserved bowl and set aside, leaving behind as much oil as possible.

3. Increase heat to high. Add chicken and spread into a single layer. Cook, undisturbed, until edges turn white, 1 minute. Toss well and cook for 1 minute more. Add onion and cook, tossing occasionally, until onion is fragrant and beginning to wilt, 1 to 2 minutes.

4. Add fish sauce mixture, pouring in around sides of pan and toss well. Return chiles to pan. Add cashews and green onions. Cook, tossing occasionally, until chicken is cooked through and everything is evenly coated, 1 to 2 minutes more. Transfer to a serving plate. Serve hot or warm.

Chicken with Candied Walnuts

Serves 4

For this dish, plan ahead and cook up a big batch of Candied Walnuts (see recipe, page 341). Make extra, since they are a treat to have on hand as a snack and perfect in this recipe. If you don't have them, you can use toasted walnut halves instead.

TIP

To toast walnut halves, place on a baking sheet in a 350°F (180°C) oven and toast for 15 minutes to heighten their flavor.

2 tbsp	dry sherry or Shaoxing rice wine	25 mL
2 tbsp	water	25 mL
1 tbsp	soy sauce	15 mL
2 tsp	cornstarch	10 mL
½ tsp	granulated sugar	2 mL
½ tsp	salt or to taste	2 mL
12 oz	skinless boneless chicken breasts or thighs, cut into 1-inch (2.5 cm) pieces	375 g
2 tbsp	vegetable oil	25 mL
2 tsp	finely chopped garlic	10 mL
1 tsp	finely chopped fresh gingerroot	5 mL
1 cup	Candied Walnuts (see recipe, page 341) or toasted walnut halves (see Tip, left)	250 mL
2 tbsp	chopped green onions	25 mL

1. In a bowl, combine sherry, water, soy sauce, cornstarch, sugar and salt and stir well. Add chicken and mix to coat well. Set aside for 15 minutes.

2. Heat a wok or a large deep skillet over medium-high heat. Add oil and swirl to coat pan. Add garlic and ginger and toss well, until fragrant, about 30 seconds.

3. Add chicken mixture and spread into a single layer. Cook, undisturbed, until edges turn white, about 1 minute. Toss well. Cook, tossing occasionally, until chicken is cooked through, about 2 minutes more.

4. Toss well and add walnuts and green onions. Cook, tossing once or twice, for 1 minute more. Transfer to a serving plate. Serve hot or warm.

Gently Seasoned Chicken with Peas

2 tbsp	vegetable oil	25 mL
1 tbsp	chopped garlic	15 mL
8 oz	ground chicken or turkey	250 g
2 tbsp	soy sauce	25 mL
1 tsp	granulated sugar	5 mL
½ tsp	salt or to taste	2 mL
¼ cup	chicken stock or water	50 mL
½ cup	fresh or frozen peas	125 mL

1. Heat a wok or a large deep skillet over medium-high heat. Add oil and swirl to coat pan. Add garlic and toss well, until fragrant, about 30 seconds.

2. Add ground chicken, breaking up meat into small pieces with a spatula and spread in an even layer. Cook, undisturbed, for 1 minute. Toss well.

3. Add soy sauce, sugar and salt and cook until chicken has changed color, 1 to 2 minutes. Add chicken stock and peas and cook, tossing occasionally, until chicken is cooked through and peas are hot, 1 to 2 minutes more. Transfer to a serving plate. Serve hot or warm.

Variation: Since this flavorful dish has very little sauce, you can scoop some into a pita bread, adding shredded lettuce and some cherry tomatoes or cucumbers to make it a meal.

Serves 4

This dish is perfect for a busy night. It goes nicely with rice, couscous or noodles, accompanied by grilled zucchini or steamed spinach. You could also serve warm in lettuce cups for a hearty appetizer or a picnic entrée.

TIP
Resist the urge to toss and stir this dish too often. Ground meat needs time to cook directly on the hot surface of the pan, so use your spatula to turn it and chop it as it cooks.

Ground Chicken with Tofu in a Sherry Sauce

Serves 4

This dish provides pleasing flavor and texture, and since ground chicken is used, it can be made quickly. If you can't find firm tofu, you can buy soft tofu and press it to make it firm enough for stir-fry cooking (see page 198).

2 tbsp	soy sauce	25 mL
1 tbsp	dry sherry or Shaoxing rice wine	15 mL
1 tbsp	water	15 mL
2 tsp	cornstarch	10 mL
1 tsp	granulated sugar	5 mL
1 tsp	salt or to taste	5 mL
2 tbsp	vegetable oil	25 mL
2 tsp	chopped garlic	10 mL
1 tsp	chopped fresh gingerroot	5 mL
8 oz	ground chicken	250 g
6 oz	firm tofu, cut into $\frac{1}{4}$-inch (0.5 cm) cubes (about 1 cup/250 mL)	175 g
$\frac{1}{3}$ cup	chopped green onions	75 mL
2 tsp	Asian sesame oil	10 mL

1. In a small bowl, combine soy sauce, sherry, water, cornstarch, sugar and salt and stir well. Set aside.

2. Heat a wok or a large deep skillet over high heat. Add vegetable oil and swirl to coat pan. Add garlic and ginger and toss once, until fragrant, about 15 seconds.

3. Add ground chicken, breaking up meat into small pieces with a spatula and spread in an even layer. Cook, undisturbed, about 30 seconds. Toss well. Reduce heat to medium and toss well. Cook, tossing occasionally, and chopping big chunks down into smaller ones, until chicken has changed color almost completely, but is not yet done, 1 to 2 minutes.

4. Add tofu and cook, tossing occasionally, for 1 minute more. Stir sauce well and add to pan, pouring in around sides. Cook, tossing well, until sauce thickens and coats everything nicely, about 1 minute.

5. Add green onions and sesame oil and toss once more to combine. Transfer to a serving plate. Serve hot or warm.

Beef

Beef with Broccoli in Oyster Sauce

Serves 4

This classic Chinese dish is enjoyed throughout Asia, both in fine restaurants and in simple cafés. The standard vegetable used is a sturdy member of the cabbage family known as *gai lan* in Cantonese dialect and *jie lan* in Mandarin. I love this version using broccoli, which is easy to find, simple to trim, and cooks faster than *gai lan*.

TIP

If you have time and want very thin meat slices, place meat in the freezer for 30 to 40 minutes so that it is partially frozen. Then slice it across the grain into thin strips.

2 tbsp	oyster sauce	25 mL
1 tbsp	soy sauce	15 mL
1 tsp	granulated sugar	5 mL
½ tsp	freshly ground pepper	2 mL
⅓ cup	chicken stock or water	75 mL
2 tbsp	vegetable oil	25 mL
1 tbsp	coarsely chopped garlic	15 mL
8 oz	lean boneless beef, thinly sliced (see Tip, left)	250 g
12 oz	broccoli florets, halved lengthwise if large	375 g

1. In a small bowl, combine oyster sauce, soy sauce, sugar, pepper and chicken stock and stir well. Set aside.

2. Heat a wok or a large deep skillet over high heat. Add oil and swirl to coat pan. Add garlic and toss well, until fragrant, about 15 seconds.

3. Add beef and cook, tossing occasionally, until no longer pink, 1 to 2 minutes. Add broccoli florets and cook, tossing once, until tender-crisp, for 1 minute.

4. Add oyster sauce mixture, pouring in around sides of pan. Cook, tossing occasionally, until broccoli is tender and beef is cooked through, 3 to 4 minutes. Transfer to a serving plate. Serve hot or warm.

Chinese Pepper Steak

1 tbsp	dry sherry or Shaoxing rice wine	15 mL
1 tbsp	water	15 mL
2 tsp	cornstarch	10 mL
8 oz	lean boneless beef, thinly sliced	250 g
2 tbsp	soy sauce	25 mL
1 tbsp	chicken stock or water	15 mL
1 tsp	dark soy sauce or molasses, optional	5 mL
1 tsp	salt or to taste	5 mL
½ tsp	granulated sugar	2 mL
½ tsp	freshly ground pepper	2 mL
3 tbsp	vegetable oil, divided	45 mL
2 tsp	chopped garlic	10 mL
2 tsp	chopped fresh gingerroot	10 mL
2 cups	thinly sliced green bell peppers (see Tip, right)	500 mL

1. In a bowl, combine sherry, water and cornstarch and stir well into a smooth sauce. Add beef and stir to coat well. Set aside for 10 minutes.

2. In a small bowl, combine soy sauce, chicken stock, dark soy sauce, if using, salt, sugar and pepper and stir well. Place a bowl next to the stove to hold green peppers after their initial cooking.

3. Heat a wok or a large deep skillet over high heat. Add 1 tbsp (15 mL) of the oil and swirl to coat pan. Add garlic and ginger and toss well, until fragrant, about 15 seconds.

4. Add green peppers and toss well. Spread peppers and cook, tossing occasionally, for 1 minute. Transfer to the reserved bowl, leaving behind as much oil as possible. Set aside.

5. Add remaining oil to wok and swirl to coat pan. Add beef mixture and spread into a single layer. Cook, undisturbed, until edges change color, about 1 minute. Toss well and cook, tossing occasionally, until no longer pink, about 1 minute more.

6. Return green peppers to pan and toss well. Add soy sauce mixture, pouring in around sides of pan. Toss well and cook, until beef is cooked through and peppers are tender-crisp, about 1 minute more. Transfer to a serving plate. Serve hot or warm.

Serves 4

This dish of thinly sliced beef stir-fried with green pepper is a popular combination in American Chinese restaurants, dating back to the days when Egg Fu Yung and Sweet-and-Sour Pork were exotic fare on the dining scene. Its popularity is justified since the two ingredients contrast nicely in color and texture, and the bright flavor of green peppers lights up the dish. With bell peppers available year-round in many places, it's a warm-weather note in wintertime. When summer comes, you can make it with red, yellow and orange peppers and boost the color quotient.

TIP

To make bell pepper strips, halve each pepper lengthwise and discard the stem section and seeds. Cut off the rounded top and bottom portions and reserve for salad or other dishes. Cut the remaining portion of each pepper lengthwise into slender strips.

Onion-Flavored Beef

Serves 4

This robust dish works well accompanied by an array of grilled vegetables or a bowl of steamed broccoli and cauliflower. Green onions add flavor and color here, beautifully seasoning the meat and sauce.

TIP

To prepare green onions, trim away root ends and any wilted outer layers and tops. Then halve each one crosswise to separate the white base from the green tops. Cut white portions in half lengthwise, and then cut white and green portions crosswise into 2-inch (5 cm) lengths.

1 tbsp	soy sauce	15 mL
1 tbsp	water	15 mL
2 tsp	cornstarch	10 mL
12 oz	lean boneless beef, thinly sliced	375 g
1 tbsp	oyster sauce	15 mL
1 tbsp	dry sherry or Shaoxing rice wine	15 mL
1 tsp	granulated sugar	5 mL
½ tsp	freshly ground pepper	2 mL
2 tbsp	vegetable oil	25 mL
1 tbsp	chopped fresh gingerroot	15 mL
½ cup	chopped green onions (2-inch/5 cm lengths) (see Tip, left)	125 mL

1. In a bowl, combine soy sauce, water and cornstarch and stir well into a smooth sauce. Add beef and stir to coat well. Set aside for 10 minutes.

2. In a small bowl, combine oyster sauce, sherry, sugar and pepper and stir well. Set aside.

3. Heat a wok or a large deep skillet over high heat. Add oil and swirl to coat pan. Add ginger and toss well, until fragrant, about 15 seconds.

4. Add beef mixture and spread into a single layer. Cook, undisturbed, until edges change color, about 30 seconds. Toss well. Cook, tossing occasionally, until no longer pink, 1 minute more. Add green onions and toss well. Cook, tossing occasionally, until tender and fragrant, 1 minute more.

5. Add oyster sauce mixture, pouring in around sides of pan. Cook, tossing occasionally, until beef is evenly seasoned and cooked through, about 30 seconds more. Transfer to a serving plate. Serve hot or warm.

Soy-Spiked Beef with Bok Choy

1	head bok choy (about 1 1/4 lbs/625 g)	1
2 tbsp	soy sauce	25 mL
2 tbsp	water	25 mL
1 tbsp	dry sherry or Shaoxing rice wine	15 mL
1 tsp	salt or to taste	5 mL
1/2 tsp	granulated sugar	2 mL
3 tbsp	vegetable oil, divided	45 mL
1 tbsp	chopped garlic	15 mL
8 oz	lean boneless beef, thinly sliced	250 g

Serves 4

Beef and bok choy bring out each other's robust flavor beautifully. This makes a hearty main dish or a quick one-dish meal over rice or noodles.

1. Halve bok choy lengthwise and place each half cut side down on a cutting board. Cut crosswise into 2-inch (5 cm) pieces. Transfer to a large bowl and toss with your hands to separate into individual pieces. You will need about 6 cups (1.5 L).

2. In a small bowl, combine soy sauce, water, sherry, salt and sugar and stir well. Set aside. Place a bowl next to the stove to hold beef after its initial cooking.

3. Heat a wok or a large deep skillet over high heat. Add 2 tbsp (25 mL) of the oil and swirl to coat pan. Add garlic and toss well, until fragrant, about 15 seconds.

4. Add beef and spread into a single layer. Cook, undisturbed, until edges change color, about 30 seconds. Toss well and cook, tossing occasionally, until no longer pink, about 1 minute more. Transfer to reserved bowl and set aside.

5. Add remaining oil and swirl to heat and coat pan. Add bok choy and toss well. Cook, undisturbed, for 1 minute. Toss well. Cook, tossing occasionally, until bright green and beginning to wilt, about 1 minute more.

6. Return beef to pan and toss well. Add soy sauce mixture, pouring in around sides of pan. Cook, tossing occasionally, until beef is cooked through and bok choy is tender-crisp, about 2 minutes more. Transfer to a serving plate. Serve hot or warm.

Sesame-Scented Beef with Gai Lan

Serves 4

Gai lan is the Cantonese name for Chinese broccoli, a beautifully green vegetable with crunchy stems, sturdy leaves and a pungent flavor perfect for stir-frying with meat.

TIP

Chinese broccoli, also known as *jie lan* in Mandarin and *gai lan* in Cantonese, is increasingly available in grocery stores as well as in Asian markets.

2 tbsp	soy sauce	25 mL
1 tbsp	water	15 mL
1 tbsp	cornstarch	15 mL
12 oz	lean boneless beef, thinly sliced	375 g
1/4 cup	chicken stock or water	50 mL
2 tbsp	dry sherry or Shaoxing rice wine	25 mL
1/2 tsp	granulated sugar	2 mL
1/2 tsp	salt or to taste	2 mL
1 lb	Chinese broccoli (see Tip, left)	500 g
2 tbsp	vegetable oil, divided	25 mL
1 tbsp	chopped green onions	15 mL
2 tsp	chopped gingerroot	10 mL
1 tsp	chopped garlic	5 mL
2 tsp	Asian sesame oil	10 mL

1. In a bowl, combine soy sauce, water and cornstarch and stir well into a smooth sauce. Add beef and stir to coat well. Set aside for 15 minutes.

2. In a small bowl, combine chicken stock, sherry, sugar and salt and stir well. Set aside.

3. Trim away ends from Chinese broccoli. Peel outer layer from bottom 3 inches (7.5 cm) of the stem, and cut through stems to separate them from the leaves. Chop stems in half lengthwise, and then crosswise into 2-inch (5 cm) lengths. Stack leaves and cut them in half lengthwise. Stack again and cut them crosswise into 2-inch (5 cm) lengths. Place leaves and stems separately on a plate and set next to the stove, along with a bowl to hold broccoli after its initial cooking.

4. Heat a wok or a large deep skillet over high heat. Add 1 tbsp (15 mL) of the vegetable oil and swirl to coat pan. Add green onions, gingerroot and garlic and toss well, until fragrant, about 15 seconds.

5. Add Chinese broccoli stems and toss well. Cook, tossing occasionally, until bright green, about 30 seconds. Add leaves and toss again. Cook, tossing once, until leaves turn bright green and are beginning to wilt, about 1 minute. Transfer to reserved bowl, leaving behind as much oil as possible. Set aside.

6. Add remaining oil to pan and swirl to coat pan. Add beef mixture and spread into a single layer. Cook, undisturbed, until edges have changed color, about 30 seconds. Toss well. Cook, tossing occasionally, until no longer pink, about 1 minute more.

7. Add soy sauce mixture, pouring in around sides of pan. Toss to coat beef evenly. Add Chinese broccoli and toss well. Cook, tossing occasionally, until broccoli is hot and tender-crisp, beef is cooked through and sauce has thickened a bit, about 1 minute more. Add sesame oil and toss well. Transfer to a serving plate. Serve hot or warm.

Tomato Beef

This Cantonese favorite can be made with plum tomatoes, as well as with plump ripe tomatoes. It makes a beautiful and satisfying dish, served with rice or noodles on a busy day, or with other dishes as part of a special-occasion menu.

TIP

To chop plum tomatoes, trim off stem end, and cut each tomato lengthwise into quarters. Cut each piece crosswise into 3 or 4 big chunks and transfer to a small bowl, leaving the juice and any easily released seeds behind on cutting board. Chopping the tomatoes in this way removes some of the juices and seeds and helps keep the sauce from diluting. Also, these chunks of chopped tomatoes should be big, so they are in the sauce more as a vegetable than as a seasoning.

1 tbsp	soy sauce	15 mL
1 tbsp	water	15 mL
2 tsp	cornstarch	10 mL
8 oz	lean boneless beef, thinly sliced	250 g
2 tbsp	oyster sauce	25 mL
2 tbsp	chicken stock or water	25 mL
1 tbsp	dry sherry or Shaoxing rice wine	15 mL
½ tsp	salt or to taste	2 mL
½ tsp	granulated sugar	2 mL
3 tbsp	vegetable oil, divided	45 mL
2 tsp	chopped fresh gingerroot	10 mL
1 tsp	chopped garlic	5 mL
1½ lbs	plum (Roma) tomatoes (about 8), chopped into large chunks and drained (see Tip, left)	750 g
⅓ cup	chopped green onions	75 mL
1 tsp	Asian sesame oil	5 mL

1. In a bowl, combine soy sauce, water and cornstarch and stir well into a smooth sauce. Add beef and stir to coat well. Set aside for 10 minutes.

2. In a small bowl, combine oyster sauce, chicken stock, sherry, salt and sugar and stir to mix well. Set aside. Place a bowl next to the stove to hold beef after its initial cooking.

3. Heat a wok or a large deep skillet over high heat. Add 2 tbsp (25 mL) of the vegetable oil and swirl to coat pan. Add ginger and garlic and toss well, until fragrant, about 15 seconds.

4. Add beef mixture and spread into a single layer. Cook, undisturbed, until edges change color, about 1 minute. Toss well. Cook, tossing occasionally, until no longer pink, 1 to 2 minutes more. Transfer to reserved bowl, leaving behind as much oil and cooking liquid as possible.

5. Add remaining vegetable oil and swirl to coat pan. Add tomatoes and cook, undisturbed, for 1 minute. Toss gently. Add green onions and toss well.

6. Return beef to pan, along with any accumulated juices, and toss well. Cook, tossing occasionally, until beef is cooked through and tomatoes are tender but still firm, 1 to 2 minutes more. Add sesame oil and toss once. Transfer to a serving plate. Serve hot or warm.

Beef with Peppery Garlic Sauce and Cilantro

2 tbsp	chopped garlic	25 mL
2 tsp	soy sauce	10 mL
2 tsp	oyster sauce	10 mL
2 tsp	granulated sugar	10 mL
1 tsp	freshly ground pepper	5 mL
1/2 tsp	salt or to taste	2 mL
12 oz	lean boneless beef, thinly sliced	375 g
3 tbsp	vegetable oil	45 mL
2 tbsp	chopped fresh cilantro	25 mL

Serves 4

I like to serve this rustic dish with a spicy sauce on the side, to be mixed in as we eat it with rice, or used as a dip. Thai-style Sriracha chile sauce makes a fiery accompaniment. This dish needs at least an hour of marinating time so plan ahead.

1. In a bowl, combine garlic, soy sauce, oyster sauce, sugar, pepper and salt and stir well. Add beef and stir to coat well. Cover and refrigerate for at least 1 hour or for up to 8 hours.

2. Heat a wok or a large deep skillet over high heat. Add oil and swirl to coat pan. Add beef mixture and spread into a single layer. Cook, undisturbed, until edges change color, about 1 minute. Toss well. Cook, tossing often, until most pieces have changed color, about 1 minute more.

3. Reduce the heat to medium-high. Cook, tossing occasionally, until beef is cooked through. Add cilantro and toss well. Transfer to a serving plate. Serve hot or warm.

Asparagus and Beef Toss

Serves 4

Fresh asparagus stir-fries beautifully, and goes especially well with beef. I love big, sturdy stalks, but tender small ones work nicely here as well. Adjust cooking time as needed, keeping in mind that pencil-thin spears will cook more quickly.

2 tbsp	fish sauce, divided	25 mL
1 tbsp	soy sauce	15 mL
½ tsp	freshly ground pepper	2 mL
½ tsp	granulated sugar	2 mL
8 oz	lean boneless beef, thinly sliced	250 g
2 tbsp	water	25 mL
2 tbsp	chopped green onions	25 mL
8 oz	fresh asparagus	250 g
2 tbsp	vegetable oil	25 mL
1 tbsp	chopped garlic	15 mL

1. In a bowl, combine 1 tbsp (15 mL) of the fish sauce with soy sauce, pepper and sugar and stir well. Add beef and stir to coat well. Set aside for 10 minutes.

2. In a small bowl, combine remaining fish sauce, water and green onions. Set aside.

3. Trim asparagus by snapping off ends. Cut each asparagus spear on the diagonal into 2-inch (5 cm) lengths, leaving tips whole.

4. Heat a wok or a large deep skillet over high heat. Add oil and swirl to coat pan. Add garlic and toss well, until fragrant, about 15 seconds.

5. Add beef mixture and spread into a single layer. Cook, undisturbed, until edges change color, about 30 seconds. Toss well. Cook, tossing occasionally, until no longer pink, about 1 minute.

6. Add asparagus and toss well. Add fish sauce mixture and toss well. Cook, tossing occasionally, until asparagus is tender-crisp and beef is cooked through, about 2 minutes. Transfer to a serving plate. Serve hot or warm.

Chicken with Sweet and Hot Peppers (page 31)
Overleaf: Chicken and Cherry Tomato Toss (page 33)

Beef and Onion Sauté

2 tbsp	soy sauce	25 mL
1 tbsp	water	15 mL
1 tbsp	granulated sugar	15 mL
½ tsp	salt or to taste	2 mL
8 oz	lean boneless beef, thinly sliced (see Tip, right)	250 g
2 tbsp	vegetable oil	25 mL
2 tbsp	chopped fresh gingerroot	25 mL
2 cups	thinly sliced onions	500 mL
1 tsp	Asian sesame oil	5 mL

1. In a bowl, combine soy sauce, water, sugar and salt and stir well. Add beef and stir to coat well. Set aside for 10 minutes.

2. Heat a wok or a large deep skillet over high heat. Add vegetable oil and swirl to coat pan. Add ginger and toss well, until fragrant, about 15 seconds.

3. Add onions and spread into a single layer. Cook, undisturbed, for 1 minute. Toss well. Cook, tossing occasionally, until fragrant and softened, 1 minute more.

4. Push onions to one side of pan. Add beef mixture and spread into a single layer. Cook, undisturbed, until edges change color, about 30 seconds. Toss well. Cook, tossing occasionally, until no longer pink, about 1 minute. Add sesame oil and toss well. Transfer to a serving plate. Serve hot or warm.

Serves 4

Hearty and satisfying, this dish puts the most accessible ingredients to extraordinary use. A green salad with a citrus-kissed dressing would be a perfect match, along with rice or noodles on which to savor the dish.

TIP

To make it easier to cut thin slices, place the meat in the freezer for up to 1 hour before you plan to cut it. Partially frozen, it will be easier to slice into thin strips. If you use flank steak, cut it lengthwise into strips about 2 inches (5 cm) wide. This will make crosswise slices just the right dimension for slicing.

Overleaf: Fiery Thai-Style Chicken with Cashews and Chiles (page 51)

Beef with Broccoli in Oyster Sauce (page 56)

Five-Spice Beef with Zucchini

Serves 4

An aromatic and delicious seasoning once found only in Asian markets, five-spice powder is often available amongst the spice jars in supermarkets. Popular throughout Asia, this traditional Chinese spice mixture of ground peppercorns, cloves, cinnamon, fennel seeds and star anise bestows a rich, soothing flavor on beef and pork dishes. Steamed spinach makes a fine companion to this dish, along with rice or Green Onions and Noodles with Sesame Oil (see recipe, page 323).

2 tbsp	soy sauce	25 mL
1 tbsp	water	15 mL
2 tsp	cornstarch	10 mL
1 tsp	five-spice powder	5 mL
12 oz	lean boneless beef, thinly sliced	375 g
1	medium zucchini (or 2 or 3 small)	1
3 tbsp	chicken stock or water	45 mL
½ tsp	salt or to taste	2 mL
2 tbsp	vegetable oil	25 mL
2 tbsp	chopped green onions	25 mL

1. In a bowl, combine soy sauce, water, cornstarch and five-spice powder and stir well into a smooth sauce. Add beef and stir to coat well. Set aside for 10 minutes.

2. Cut zucchini in half lengthwise and then thinly crosswise into half-moon shapes. You should have about 2 cups (500 mL). Set aside.

3. In a small bowl, combine chicken stock and salt and stir well. Set aside.

4. Heat a wok or a large deep skillet over high heat. Add oil and swirl to coat pan. Add beef mixture and spread into a single layer. Cook, undisturbed, until edges change color, about 30 seconds. Toss well. Cook, tossing occasionally, until no longer pink, 1 to 2 minutes.

5. Add zucchini and toss well. Add chicken stock mixture and toss well. Cook, tossing occasionally, until zucchini is tender-crisp and beef is cooked through, 1 to 2 minutes more. Add green onions and toss well. Transfer to a serving plate. Serve hot or warm.

Tangy Orange Beef

1 tbsp	soy sauce	15 mL
2 tsp	white or cider vinegar	10 mL
2 tsp	cornstarch	10 mL
1 tsp	salt or to taste	5 mL
12 oz	lean boneless beef, thinly sliced	375 g
1 tsp	grated orange zest, optional	5 mL
3 tbsp	orange juice	45 mL
1 tbsp	granulated sugar	15 mL
2 tbsp	vegetable oil	25 mL
1 tbsp	chopped fresh gingerroot	15 mL
½ cup	shredded carrot	125 mL
¼ cup	chopped green onions	50 mL

Serves 4

This hearty dish has a light, bright flavor, thanks to the inclusion of orange juice and orange zest. You can omit the zest if you don't have an orange handy, and still have a tasty dish. A green salad and rice make it a meal.

1. In a bowl, combine soy sauce, vinegar, cornstarch and salt and mix well into a smooth sauce. Add beef and stir to coat well. Set aside.

2. In a small bowl, combine orange zest, if using, orange juice and sugar and stir well. Set aside.

3. Heat a wok or a large deep skillet over high heat. Add oil and swirl to coat pan. Add ginger and carrot and toss well, until ginger is fragrant and carrots are beginning to soften, about 30 seconds.

4. Push carrots to the side and add beef mixture. Spread into a single layer and cook, undisturbed, until edges change color, about 1 minute. Toss well. Cook, tossing occasionally, until beef is cooked through, 1 to 2 minutes more.

5. Add orange juice mixture, pouring in around sides of pan. When it begins to sizzle, toss well to season beef evenly. Add green onions and toss well. Transfer to a serving plate. Serve hot or warm.

Stir-Fried Tangerine Beef

Serves 4

The classic version of tangerine beef involves deep-frying and then braising. This is my speedy stir-fry version and it is wonderful with lots of rice.

TIP

Dried tangerine peel is available in Asian markets and Chinese herbal medicine shops. You could also make your own: simply peel a tangerine, working the peel off in a long, spiral strip for easy handling. Leave it out to air-dry completely for about 3 days and then store in a jar until needed. If you want to use fresh tangerine peel, use only the bright orange zest. Use a zester or a grater to remove the zest; or carefully make thin strips using a vegetable peeler and then finely chop these strips. You'll need 1 tbsp (15 mL) of fresh tangerine zest, which you will add directly to the pan after the garlic and ginger; no need to soak it.

3	chunks dried tangerine peel (1-inch/2.5 cm chunks) (see Tip, left)	3
½ cup	cold water	125 mL
2 tbsp	dry sherry or Shaoxing rice wine	25 mL
1 tbsp	water	15 mL
2 tsp	dark soy sauce, molasses or honey	10 mL
2 tsp	cornstarch	10 mL
8 oz	lean boneless beef, thinly sliced	250 g
1 tbsp	chicken stock or water	15 mL
2 tsp	soy sauce	10 mL
1 tsp	salt or to taste	5 mL
1 tsp	granulated sugar	5 mL
2 tbsp	vegetable oil	25 mL
1 tbsp	chopped fresh gingerroot	15 mL
2 tsp	chopped garlic	10 mL
⅓ cup	chopped green onions	75 mL
1 tsp	Asian sesame oil	5 mL

1. In a small bowl, combine tangerine peel and cold water. Set aside until peel is softened, about 15 minutes.

2. In a bowl, combine sherry, water, dark soy sauce and cornstarch and stir well into a smooth sauce. Add beef and stir to coat well. Set aside for 10 minutes.

3. In a small bowl, combine chicken stock, soy sauce, salt and sugar and stir well. Set aside.

4. When tangerine peel is softened, drain and slice into very thin strips.

5. Heat a wok or a large deep skillet over high heat. Add oil and swirl to coat pan. Add ginger and garlic and toss well, until fragrant, about 15 seconds. Add tangerine peel and toss well. Cook, tossing once, until it releases its aroma, about 15 seconds.

6. Add beef mixture and spread into a single layer. Cook, undisturbed, until edges change color, about 1 minute. Toss well.

7. Add soy sauce mixture, pouring in around sides of pan. Toss well. Cook, tossing occasionally, until beef is cooked through and evenly coated with a slightly thickened sauce, 1 to 2 minutes more. Add green onions and sesame oil and toss well. Transfer to a serving plate. Serve hot or warm.

Lemongrass Beef in Garlic-Ginger Sauce

2 tbsp	fish sauce	25 mL
1 tbsp	soy sauce	15 mL
2 tsp	granulated sugar	10 mL
1 tsp	cornstarch	5 mL
12 oz	lean boneless beef, thinly sliced	375 g
2	stalks fresh lemongrass	2
1/4 cup	chopped onion	50 mL
1/2 cup	chicken stock or water	125 mL
3 tbsp	vegetable oil	45 mL
1 tbsp	chopped garlic	15 mL
2 tsp	chopped fresh gingerroot	10 mL
1/2 tsp	salt or to taste	2 mL
1/2 tsp	hot pepper flakes	2 mL
1/3 cup	chopped green onions	75 mL

Serves 4

In this recipe, fresh lemongrass is chopped into small chunks and then ground into a seasoning paste that cooks with garlic and ginger to create a delicious sauce. Double the chiles or add a generous splash of hot pepper sauce if you want a little extra kick of chile heat.

1. In a bowl, combine fish sauce, soy sauce, sugar and cornstarch and stir well into a smooth sauce. Add beef and stir to coat well. Set aside for 15 minutes.

2. Meanwhile, trim lemongrass stalks, cutting away top half leaving about a 6-inch (15 cm) base. Cut away the dry root ends leaving a smooth base just under the bulb, and remove any dry outer leaves. Cut stalks in half lengthwise and then crosswise into 1-inch (2.5 cm) pieces.

3. In a blender or mini-food processor, combine chopped lemongrass, onion and chicken stock. Grind well, stopping to scrape sides as necessary, to make a fairly smooth paste.

4. Heat a wok or a large deep skillet over high heat. Add oil and swirl to coat pan. Add garlic and ginger and toss well, until fragrant, about 15 seconds. Add beef mixture and spread into a single layer. Cook, undisturbed, until edges change color, about 1 minute.

5. Add lemongrass paste and toss well. Add salt and hot pepper flakes and cook, tossing occasionally, until beef is cooked through and all ingredients have combined into a fairly smooth sauce, 2 to 3 minutes. Add green onions and toss well. Transfer to a serving plate. Serve hot or warm.

Vietnamese-Style Shaking Beef with Peppery Watercress

Serves 4

Absolutely gorgeous and delicious, this Vietnamese take on steak is a perfect choice when you want a special dish which can be prepared in advance and sizzled up just before serving time. A simple salad of watercress and red onions serves as the foundation for tender steak, cut into chunks for maximum flavor and easy eating.

1 tbsp	fish sauce	15 mL
2 tsp	soy sauce	10 mL
1½ tsp	granulated sugar, divided	7 mL
1 tsp	freshly ground pepper, divided	5 mL
¾ tsp	salt, divided	4 mL
12 oz	thick-cut tender steak (rib-eye, New York strip), cut into 1-inch (2.5 cm) chunks	375 g
2 tbsp	white or cider vinegar	25 mL
1 tsp	vegetable oil	5 mL
½ cup	very thinly sliced purple onion	125 mL
2 cups	very coarsely chopped watercress (bite-size pieces)	500 mL
2 tbsp	vegetable oil	25 mL
2 tbsp	chopped garlic	25 mL

1. In a bowl, combine fish sauce, soy sauce, ½ tsp (2 mL) sugar, ½ tsp (2 mL) pepper and ¼ tsp (1 mL) salt and stir well. Add steak and stir to coat well. Set aside for 20 minutes.

2. Meanwhile, in a bowl, combine vinegar, 1 tsp (5 mL) oil and remaining sugar, pepper and salt.

3. Add onion and toss well to separate into thin strips and mix evenly with dressing. Add watercress but leave it on top of onions and dressing (you will toss it just before serving).

4. Heat a wok or a large deep skillet over high heat. Add 2 tbsp (25 mL) oil and swirl to coat pan. Add steak mixture and spread into a single layer. Cook, undisturbed, until nicely browned, for 1 to 2 minutes. Shake pan to turn meat and start browning on other side; use a spatula or slotted spoon if needed.

5. Add garlic, scattering over beef, and cook, undisturbed, for 1 minute more. Shake pan again. Cook, shaking and scooping as needed, until meat is brown and cooked to desired doneness, 1 to 2 minutes more.

6. Remove pan from heat and set aside while you finish salad. Toss watercress well to dress it and mix with onions. Spread salad on a serving plate. Place beef on top. Serve hot or warm.

Variation: If you can't find watercress, use spinach leaves or a mix of salad greens instead.

Zesty Korean Beef
with Cucumbers

1 tbsp	soy sauce	15 mL
1 tbsp	chicken stock or water	15 mL
1 tsp	salt or to taste	5 mL
1/2 tsp	granulated sugar	2 mL
8 oz	lean boneless beef, thinly sliced	250 g
1 1/2 cups	sliced cucumbers (1/2-inch/1 cm chunks) (see Tip, right)	375 mL
2 tbsp	vegetable oil	25 mL
2 tsp	chopped garlic	10 mL
1/4 cup	chopped green onions	50 mL
1/2 tsp	hot pepper flakes	2 mL
1 tsp	Asian sesame oil	5 mL

1. In a small bowl, combine soy sauce, chicken stock, salt and sugar and stir well. Add beef and stir to coat well.

2. Heat a wok or a large deep skillet over high heat. Add oil and swirl to coat pan. Add garlic and toss well, until fragrant, about 15 seconds.

3. Add beef mixture and spread into a single layer. Cook, undisturbed, until edges change color, about 1 minute. Toss well. Cook, tossing occasionally, until no longer pink, about 1 minute more.

4. Add cucumbers and toss well. Cook, tossing occasionally, until beef is cooked through and cucumbers are tender-crisp, 1 to 2 minutes more.

5. Remove from heat and add green onions, hot pepper flakes and sesame oil. Toss well. Transfer to a serving plate. Serve hot or warm.

Serves 4

This is quick and delicious, especially if you can find small pickling cucumbers or big tender-skinned English cucumbers.

TIP
If using English cucumbers or small Kirby or pickling cucumbers, simply trim away ends and chop them up — seeds, peel and all. If these types of cucumbers are unavailable, simply peel field cucumbers, halve them lengthwise, scoop out and discard the seeds, and cut crosswise into 1/4-inch (0.5 cm) thick slices.

Beef with Dry-Roasted Cashews

Serves 4

Traditional recipes call for frying raw cashews just before cooking them into a stir-fry dish. Using dry-roasted cashews makes this an everyday dish, albeit an extraordinarily tasty one.

2 tbsp	dry sherry or Shaoxing rice wine	25 mL
2 tbsp	water	25 mL
1 tbsp	soy sauce	15 mL
2 tsp	cornstarch	10 mL
½ tsp	granulated sugar	2 mL
½ tsp	salt or to taste	2 mL
12 oz	lean boneless beef, thinly sliced	375 g
2 tbsp	vegetable oil	25 mL
2 tsp	finely chopped garlic	10 mL
2 tsp	finely chopped fresh gingerroot	10 mL
¾ cup	thickly sliced celery (½-inch/1 cm chunks)	175 mL
1 cup	dry-roasted salted cashews	250 mL
3 tbsp	chopped green onions	45 mL

1. In a bowl, combine sherry, water, soy sauce, cornstarch, sugar and salt and stir well into a smooth sauce. Add beef and stir to coat well. Set aside for 10 minutes.

2. Heat a wok or a large deep skillet over high heat. Add oil and swirl to coat pan. Add garlic and ginger and toss well, until fragrant, about 15 seconds.

3. Add beef mixture and spread into a single layer. Cook, undisturbed, until edges change color, about 1 minute. Toss well. Cook, tossing occasionally, until no longer pink, about 1 minute more. Add celery and cook, tossing occasionally, until beef is cooked through and celery is bright green, about 2 minutes more.

4. Stir soy sauce mixture well and add to pan, pouring in around sides. When it begins to sizzle, add cashews and green onions and toss well. Cook, tossing once, for 30 seconds more. Transfer to a serving plate. Serve hot or warm.

Seasoned Beef with Shiitakes and Crunchy Carrots

1 tbsp	soy sauce	15 mL
1 tbsp	fish sauce	15 mL
1 tbsp	dry sherry or Shaoxing rice wine	15 mL
½ tsp	salt or to taste	2 mL
½ tsp	granulated sugar	2 mL
¼ tsp	freshly ground pepper	1 mL
8 oz	lean boneless beef, thinly sliced	250 g
2 tbsp	vegetable oil	25 mL
1 tbsp	chopped garlic	15 mL
1 tbsp	chopped fresh gingerroot	15 mL
6 oz	shiitake mushrooms, stems removed (about 2 cups/500 mL)	175 g
¼ cup	shredded carrots	50 mL
¼ cup	chopped green onions	50 mL

Serves 4

This robust dish of beef and earthy shiitake mushrooms has a handful of shredded carrots for color and crunch. I like to slice the shiitake mushrooms crosswise here to display their light and dark colors, but you could also quarter large caps and leave smaller ones whole.

1. In a bowl, combine soy sauce, fish sauce, sherry, salt, sugar and pepper and stir well. Add beef and stir to coat well. Set aside for 10 minutes.

2. Heat a wok or a large deep skillet over high heat. Add oil and swirl to coat pan. Add garlic and gingerroot, toss well, until fragrant, about 15 seconds.

3. Add beef mixture and spread into a single layer. Cook, undisturbed, until edges change color, about 30 seconds. Toss well. Cook, tossing occasionally, until no longer pink, about 1 minute more.

4. Add mushrooms and carrots and toss well. Cook, tossing occasionally, until mushrooms are tender and beef is cooked through, about 2 minutes.

5. Add green onions and toss well. Transfer to a serving plate. Serve hot or warm.

Beef with Vibrant Vegetables

Serves 4

Look for snow peas on the small side, as they are tender and will cook quickly. If you can only find big flat ones, not to worry. You can prepare them according to the Tip (see below) and then cut each pea diagonally in half to help them cook more quickly and make them easy to eat.

TIPS

To keep ingredients from sticking and burning, be sure to reduce heat to medium after the beef gets a good start. Add more water, 1 tbsp (15 mL) at a time, toward the end of cooking, if you need more time and find the mixture sticking to the pan.

To trim snow peas, cut off and discard tip and cut stem end partway, pulling it down along the straight side of each snow pea to remove any strings.

1 tbsp	soy sauce	15 mL
1 tbsp	dry sherry or Shaoxing rice wine	15 mL
1 tbsp	water	15 mL
1 tsp	salt or to taste	5 mL
½ tsp	granulated sugar	2 mL
2 tsp	cornstarch	10 mL
8 oz	lean boneless beef, thinly sliced	250 g
2 tbsp	vegetable oil	25 mL
1 tbsp	chopped garlic	15 mL
1 tbsp	chopped fresh gingerroot	15 mL
1¼ cups	trimmed snow peas (see Tips, left)	300 mL
¾ cup	halved cherry tomatoes	175 mL

1. In a bowl, combine soy sauce, sherry, water, salt, sugar and cornstarch and stir well into a smooth sauce. Add beef and stir to coat well. Set aside for 10 minutes.

2. Heat a wok or a large deep skillet over high heat. Add oil and swirl to coat pan. Add garlic and ginger and toss well, until fragrant, about 15 seconds.

3. Add beef mixture and spread into a single layer. Cook, undisturbed, until edges change color, about 1 minute. Toss well. Cook, tossing occasionally, until no longer pink, about 1 minute more.

4. Push beef to side of pan. Add snow peas to center of pan and then spread them out so as many as possible are in contact with hot pan. Cook, tossing occasionally, for 1 minute. Reduce heat to medium (see Tips, left).

5. Add tomatoes and toss well. Add soy sauce mixture, pouring in around sides of pan. Cook, tossing occasionally, until beef is cooked through, snow peas are tender-crisp, and both are coated with a slightly thickened sauce, 1 to 2 minutes more. Transfer to a serving plate. Serve hot or warm.

Colorful Beef Combo

1 tbsp	dry sherry or Shaoxing rice wine	15 mL
1 tbsp	water	15 mL
2 tsp	cornstarch	10 mL
12 oz	lean boneless beef, thinly sliced	375 g
2	stalks celery	2
2 tbsp	chicken stock or water	25 mL
1 tbsp	soy sauce	15 mL
1 tsp	granulated sugar	5 mL
1 tsp	salt or to taste	5 mL
2 tbsp	vegetable oil	25 mL
1 tbsp	chopped garlic	15 mL
1 cup	halved cherry tomatoes	250 mL
3 tbsp	thinly sliced green onions	45 mL
1 tsp	Asian sesame oil	5 mL

Serves 4

Enjoy this colorful dish over rice or noodles for a hearty one-dish meal. It makes a great centerpiece dish for a multi-course Asian feast.

1. In a bowl, combine sherry, water and cornstarch and stir well into a smooth sauce. Add beef and stir to coat evenly. Set aside for 10 minutes.

2. Trim the celery, removing the ends and pulling away the strings on the outside of each stalk. Slice on the diagonal into thin pieces and transfer to a plate. You should have about 1 cup (250 mL). Set aside.

3. In a small bowl, combine chicken stock, soy sauce, sugar and salt and stir well. Set aside.

4. Heat a wok or a large deep skillet over high heat. Add oil and swirl to coat pan. Add garlic and celery and cook, tossing occasionally, until garlic is fragrant and celery brightens in color, about 1 minute.

5. Push celery to one side of pan. Add beef mixture and spread into a single layer. Cook, undisturbed, until edges change color, about 1 minute. Toss well. Add chicken stock mixture, pouring in around sides of pan. Cook, tossing once or twice, until beef is cooked through and celery is tender-crisp, about 2 minutes.

6. Add cherry tomatoes, green onions and sesame oil and toss well. Transfer to a serving plate. Serve hot or warm.

Speedy Beef Stir-Fry with Chunky Vegetables

Make this dish when you want something hearty in a hurry. You'll need to do a few tasks — chopping the garlic and ginger and slicing the meat — but the baby corn, water chestnuts and peas need no attention beyond measuring. With rice or noodles, it's a lively one-dish meal.

TIP

To freshen the flavor of canned baby corn cobs, drain well, cover with cold water and drain again. Transfer leftover baby corn to a jar with water to cover. You can slice baby corn cobs crosswise into 3 or 4 chunks or into thin rounds, and add them to soups and salads just before serving.

1 tbsp	dry sherry or Shaoxing rice wine	15 mL
1 tbsp	water	15 mL
½ tsp	dark soy sauce, optional	2 mL
2 tsp	cornstarch	10 mL
8 oz	lean boneless beef, thinly sliced	250 g
3 tbsp	chicken stock	45 mL
2 tsp	soy sauce	10 mL
½ tsp	granulated sugar	2 mL
½ tsp	salt or to taste	2 mL
2 tbsp	vegetable oil	25 mL
2 tsp	chopped garlic	10 mL
2 tsp	finely chopped fresh gingerroot	10 mL
1½ cups	baby corn (about 5 oz/150 g) (see Tip, left)	375 mL
½ cup	sliced water chestnuts	125 mL
½ cup	frozen tiny peas (see Tip, page 47)	125 mL

1. In a bowl, combine sherry, water, dark soy sauce, if using, and cornstarch and stir well into a smooth paste. Add beef and stir to coat well. Set aside for 10 minutes.

2. In a small bowl, combine chicken stock, soy sauce, sugar and salt and stir well.

3. Heat a wok or a large deep skillet over high heat. Add oil and swirl to coat pan. Add garlic and ginger and toss well, until fragrant, about 15 seconds. Add beef mixture and spread into a single layer. Cook, undisturbed, until edges change color, about 1 minute. Toss well.

4. Add chicken stock mixture, baby corn and water chestnuts. Cook, tossing occasionally, until beef is cooked through, about 2 minutes more. Add peas and cook, tossing once, for 1 minute more. Transfer to a serving plate. Serve hot or warm.

Sesame-Flavored Beef with Vegetables

2 tbsp	soy sauce	25 mL
1 tbsp	chicken stock or water	15 mL
2 tsp	cornstarch	10 mL
1 tsp	salt or to taste	5 mL
½ tsp	granulated sugar	2 mL
8 oz	lean boneless beef, thinly sliced	250 g
2 tbsp	vegetable oil	25 mL
2 tsp	chopped garlic	10 mL
2 tsp	chopped fresh gingerroot	10 mL
1 cup	shredded carrots	250 mL
1½ cups	thinly sliced zucchini (about 2 medium or 3 small) (see Tip, right)	375 mL
2 tbsp	chopped green onions	25 mL
2 tsp	Asian sesame oil	10 mL

1. In a bowl, combine soy sauce, chicken stock, cornstarch, salt and sugar and stir well into a smooth sauce. Add beef and stir to coat well.

2. Heat a wok or a large deep skillet over high heat. Add oil and swirl to coat pan. Add garlic and gingerroot and toss well, until fragrant, about 15 seconds.

3. Add beef mixture and spread into a single layer. Cook, undisturbed, until edges change color, about 1 minute.

4. Add carrots and toss well. Cook, tossing occasionally, until carrots have softened a bit and beef is no longer pink, about 1 minute more.

5. Add zucchini and toss well. Cook, tossing occasionally, until beef is cooked through and zucchini and carrots are tender-crisp, 1 to 2 minutes more. Add green onions and sesame oil and toss well. Transfer to a serving plate. Serve hot or warm.

Serves 4

Lots of color and flavor make this dish an inviting choice for supper, with or without company coming.

TIP

If zucchini are small, simply slice them into rounds about ⅛-inch (0.25 cm) thick. If they are on the larger side, trim ends and halve lengthwise. Then slice them crosswise into half-moon shapes.

Gingery Beef with Spinach

Serves 4

Perfect over cooked pasta or paired with rice, this classic Asian sauté of thinly sliced beef with tender spinach is a weeknight treat.

2 tsp	soy sauce	10 mL
2 tsp	dry sherry or Shaoxing rice wine	10 mL
2 tsp	cornstarch	10 mL
1 tsp	water	5 mL
½ tsp	salt or to taste	2 mL
8 oz	lean boneless beef, thinly sliced	250 g
2 tbsp	vegetable oil	25 mL
1 tbsp	chopped fresh gingerroot	15 mL
3 to 4 cups	loosely packed fresh spinach leaves (about 8 oz/250 g)	750 mL to 1 L
3 tbsp	chopped green onions	45 mL

1. In a bowl, combine soy sauce, sherry, cornstarch, water and salt and stir well into a smooth sauce. Add beef and stir to coat well. Set aside for 10 minutes.

2. Heat a wok or a large deep skillet over high heat. Add oil and swirl to coat pan. Add ginger and toss, until fragrant, about 15 seconds.

3. Add beef mixture and spread into a single layer. Cook, undisturbed, until edges change color, about 1 minute. Toss well. Cook, tossing occasionally, until no longer pink, about 1 minute more.

4. Add spinach and green onions and toss well. Cook, tossing often, until spinach softens, green onions release their fragrance and meat is cooked through, about 1 minute more. Transfer to a serving plate. Serve hot or warm.

> **Variation:** You could substitute shredded napa cabbage or chopped watercress for the spinach. If you do, add 1 to 2 tbsp (15 to 25 mL) of water, and allow a little extra cooking time after adding the greens to the hot pan since both these vegetables have a sturdier texture than spinach.

Spicy Basil Beef

3 tbsp	chicken stock or water	45 mL
1 tbsp	soy sauce	15 mL
1 tbsp	granulated sugar	15 mL
1 tsp	salt or to taste	5 mL
2 tbsp	vegetable oil	25 mL
1 tbsp	coarsely chopped garlic	15 mL
½ cup	coarsely chopped onion	125 mL
8 oz	lean boneless beef, thinly sliced	250 g
1 tsp	hot pepper flakes or hot pepper sauce (see Tips, right)	5 mL
1 cup	fresh basil or mint leaves	250 mL

1. In a small bowl, combine chicken stock, soy sauce, sugar and salt and stir well. Set aside.
2. Heat a wok or large deep skillet over high heat. Add oil and swirl to coat pan. Add garlic and onion and cook, tossing once, until fragrant, about 15 seconds.
3. Add beef and spread into a single layer. Cook, undisturbed, until edges change color, about 30 seconds. Cook, tossing occasionally, until no longer pink, about 1 minute.
4. Add chicken stock mixture, pouring in around sides of pan. Cook, tossing occasionally, until beef is cooked through and coated with a thin, smooth sauce (see Tips, right), 1 to 2 minutes more.
5. Add hot pepper flakes and basil and toss well. Transfer to a serving plate. Serve hot or warm.

Serves 4

Enjoy this Thai-style dish with brown rice and a cooling salad of iceberg lettuce, cherry tomatoes and shredded carrots.

TIPS

For a hotter dish, add more hot pepper flakes. If you prefer less heat, add only ½ tsp (2 mL).

You'll have a pleasing amount of dark, delicious sauce, perfect for spooning over rice along with the spicy beef. The sauce will be thin, Thai-style, since no cornstarch is used to thicken it.

Zesty Beef with Minted Green Beans

Fresh green chile peppers heat this dish up, and a final flourish of mint leaves cool it down. Make it a rice bowl or serve it with an array of dishes and a salad with a sweet-and-tangy dressing.

TIP

You could use frozen green beans instead of fresh ones, adjusting the cooking time so that they are done before you add the red peppers.

2 tbsp	fish sauce	25 mL
1 tbsp	water	15 mL
2 tsp	white vinegar	10 mL
2 tsp	granulated sugar	10 mL
1 tbsp	chopped garlic	15 mL
1 tbsp	chopped fresh gingerroot	15 mL
2 tbsp	chopped shallots or onion	25 mL
1 tbsp	coarsely chopped serrano or jalapeño peppers	15 mL
2 tbsp	vegetable oil	25 mL
12 oz	lean boneless beef, thinly sliced	375 g
½ cup	chopped fresh green beans (1 inch/2.5 cm lengths) (see Tip, left)	125 mL
⅓ cup	chopped red bell pepper (½ inch/1 cm pieces)	75 mL
⅓ cup	fresh mint leaves	75 mL

1. In a small bowl, combine fish sauce, water, vinegar and sugar and stir to mix well.

2. In a mini-food processor or a blender, combine garlic, ginger, shallots and serrano pepper. Grind, pulsing and stopping to scrape sides as necessary to a fairly smooth paste. Add 1 to 2 tbsp (15 to 25 mL) water if needed to help move the blades.

3. Heat a wok or a large deep skillet over medium-high heat. Add oil and swirl to coat pan. Carefully add garlic paste, it will sizzle wildly. Reduce heat to maintain a lively sizzle but avoid burning and popping. Cook, stirring and pressing, until fragrant and softened, 1 to 2 minutes.

4. Add beef and spread into a single layer. Cook, undisturbed, until edges have changed color, about 1 minute. Toss well. Add green beans and toss again. Cook, tossing occasionally, until beef is cooked through and beans are bright green, 2 to 3 minutes.

5. Add red peppers and toss well. Add fish sauce mixture, pouring in around sides of pan. Cook, tossing occasionally, for 1 minute more.

6. Add mint leaves and toss well. Transfer to a serving plate. Serve hot or warm.

Peppery Beef with Shiitakes and Bamboo

2 tbsp	dry sherry or Shaoxing rice wine	25 mL
2 tbsp	chicken stock or water	25 mL
1 tsp	dark soy sauce, molasses or honey	5 mL
8 oz	lean boneless beef, thinly sliced	250 g
2 tbsp	soy sauce	25 mL
1 tbsp	water	15 mL
1 tsp	granulated sugar	5 mL
1 tsp	salt or to taste	5 mL
1 tsp	hot pepper flakes	5 mL
2 tbsp	vegetable oil	25 mL
1 tbsp	chopped garlic	15 mL
1 cup	shiitake mushrooms (see Tip, right)	250 mL
½ cup	drained canned sliced bamboo shoots (see Tips, page 90)	125 mL
2 tsp	Asian sesame oil	10 mL

Serves 4

This Hunan-style dish with its hot pepper flakes will add a little heat on a cool winter night.

TIP

To prepare shiitake mushrooms, trim off stems and slice larger caps into thick strips. Cut smaller ones in half or leave them whole.

1. In a bowl, combine sherry, chicken stock and dark soy sauce and stir well. Add beef and stir to coat well. Set aside for 10 minutes.

2. In a small bowl, combine soy sauce, water, sugar, salt and hot pepper flakes and stir well. Set aside.

3. Heat a wok or a large deep skillet over high heat. Add oil and swirl to coat pan. Add garlic and toss well, until fragrant, about 15 seconds. Add beef mixture and spread into a single layer. Cook, undisturbed, until edges change color, about 1 minute. Toss well. Cook, tossing occasionally, until no longer pink, 1 to 2 minutes.

4. Add mushrooms and bamboo shoots and cook, tossing often, until mushrooms are beginning to wilt, about 1 minute more.

5. Add sherry mixture, pouring in around sides of pan. Cook, tossing often, until beef is cooked through and everything is evenly coated with a thin sauce, about 1 minute more. Add sesame oil and toss well. Transfer to serving plate. Serve hot or warm.

Variation: You could use button mushrooms or oyster mushrooms in place of shiitake mushrooms with very tasty results.

Fiery Beef with Zucchini in Fragrant Curry Sauce

Serves 4

Hot and hearty, this dish tastes great over brown rice with sliced cucumbers and a dollop of salsa on the side.

TIPS

Use any Thai-style curry paste in this recipe, or substitute an Indian-style curry paste for lots of spice with less heat.

Cut zucchini into bite-size pieces. I halve them lengthwise and then slice crosswise into ½-inch (1 cm) chunks.

½ cup	chicken stock or water	125 mL
2 tbsp	fish sauce	25 mL
1 tbsp	brown sugar or palm sugar	15 mL
2 tbsp	vegetable oil	25 mL
1 tbsp	chopped garlic	15 mL
2 tbsp	Thai-style red curry paste (see Tips, left)	25 mL
8 oz	lean boneless beef, thinly sliced	250 g
1½ cups	sliced zucchini (about 2 medium or 3 small) (see Tips, left)	375 mL
¼ cup	fresh basil leaves	50 mL

1. In a small bowl, combine chicken stock, fish sauce and brown sugar and stir to mix well. Set aside.
2. Heat a wok or a large deep skillet over medium-high heat. Add oil and swirl to coat pan. Add garlic and toss once. Add curry paste and cook, pressing and mashing to soften and dissolve into the oil, about 1 minute.
3. Add beef and spread into a single layer. Cook, undisturbed, until edges change color, about 30 seconds. Toss well to coat it with curry paste.
4. Add zucchini and toss once. Add chicken stock mixture, pouring in around sides of pan. Cook, tossing occasionally, until zucchini is tender and beef is cooked through, 2 to 3 minutes. Add basil leaves and toss once. Transfer to a serving plate. Serve hot or warm.

> **Variation:** If you don't have fresh basil, you can use mint, cilantro or chopped green onions, or simply omit the herbs altogether.

Little Meatballs in Red Curry Peanut Sauce

8 oz	ground beef	250 g
½ tsp	salt or to taste	2 mL
¼ tsp	freshly ground pepper	1 mL
1 tsp	vegetable oil	5 mL
½ cup	coconut milk	125 mL
1 tbsp	Thai-style red curry paste	15 mL
1 tbsp	smooth peanut butter	15 mL
1 tbsp	fish sauce	15 mL
1 tbsp	brown sugar	15 mL
⅓ cup	frozen tiny peas (see Tip, page 47)	75 mL

Serves 4

This Thai-style dish makes a wonderful anchor for a rice-centered meal, adding a luscious, spicy note without a lot of effort. The deliciously hot sauce works nicely over noodles. Accompany with sliced cucumbers or tomato and cucumber salad for a simple meal.

1. In a bowl, combine ground beef, salt and pepper. Shape into 1-inch (2.5 cm) meatballs, rolling them gently just enough to hold their shape. You should have around 25 petite meatballs. Place a bowl next to stove to hold meatballs after their initial cooking.

2. Heat a wok or a large deep skillet over medium-high heat. Add oil and swirl to coat pan.

3. Add meatballs and arrange in a single layer. Cook on one side, shaking pan gently to keep them from sticking, for 1 minute. Carefully turn meatballs to cook on other side, shaking the pan gently to roll them over. Or turn them over gently using a spatula or a large spoon. Cook, shaking occasionally, until meatballs are fairly evenly browned and firm enough to keep their shape, about 1 minute more. Transfer meatballs into reserved bowl and set aside, leaving their juices behind.

4. Add coconut milk to pan and bring to a gentle boil, stirring to mix well. Boil, stirring occasionally, adjusting heat to maintain an active but gentle boil, for 1 minute. Add curry paste, peanut butter, fish sauce and brown sugar. Stir well to dissolve everything into a fairly smooth, gently boiling sauce. Add peas and toss gently to heat in sauce.

5. Return meatballs to pan, along with any juices from the bowl. Toss gently to coat with sauce. Cook, until meatballs are no longer pink inside and peas are tender, about 1 minute more. Transfer to serving bowl. Serve hot or warm.

Szechwan-Style Spicy Beef in Lettuce Cups

Serves 4

This is quite delicious, quick to prepare and fun to eat. You can make it ahead of time, but be sure to let it warm up before serving, or reheat it gently in the microwave or steamer, as its flavor and texture are not at their best when cold. Served in small lettuce cups, it's an easy-to-eat starter when guests arrive.

TIP

In addition to enjoying this as a lettuce wrap for a party finger-food or on a picnic, you could also serve it hot or warm with rice as part of a meal.

3 tbsp	soy sauce	45 mL
2 tbsp	dry sherry or Shaoxing rice wine	25 mL
2 tsp	cornstarch	10 mL
1/2 tsp	granulated sugar	2 mL
1/2 tsp	salt or to taste	2 mL
8 oz	ground beef	250 g
2 tbsp	vegetable oil	25 mL
2 tbsp	chopped fresh gingerroot	25 mL
1 tbsp	chopped garlic	15 mL
1 tsp	hot pepper flakes	5 mL
3 tbsp	finely chopped green onions	45 mL
1 tbsp	Asian sesame oil	15 mL
	Cup-shaped lettuce leaves, such as Bibb, Boston or iceberg	

1. In a small bowl, combine soy sauce, sherry, cornstarch, sugar and salt and stir well into a smooth sauce.

2. Place ground beef in a separate bowl, and using a spoon, separate into five or six big clumps. Add about half of the soy sauce mixture and mix into ground beef. Set aside for 10 to 15 minutes. Place remaining soy sauce mixture next to stove.

3. Heat a wok or a large deep skillet over medium-high heat. Add oil and swirl to coat pan. Add ginger and garlic and toss once, until fragrant, about 30 seconds.

4. Add ground beef and using your spatula or a large spoon break up meat, spreading out to cook evenly. Cook, gently tossing once or twice, until no longer pink, 1 to 2 minutes.

5. Add remaining soy sauce mixture and hot pepper flakes and cook, tossing occasionally, until beef is no longer pink inside, 1 to 2 minutes more. Add green onions and sesame oil and toss once more. Transfer to a plate.

6. Arrange lettuce cups on another plate and fill each one with a spoonful or two of the cooked beef. Or provide lettuce cups and a serving platter of beef and invite guests to make up the lettuce packets themselves.

Thai-Style Ground Beef with Chiles and Fresh Basil

2 tbsp	fish sauce	25 mL
2 tbsp	chicken stock or water	25 mL
1 tsp	dark soy sauce or molasses, optional	5 mL
1 tbsp	granulated sugar	15 mL
1/4 tsp	salt or to taste	1 mL
2 tbsp	vegetable oil	25 mL
1 tbsp	chopped garlic	15 mL
1 tbsp	chopped fresh hot green chile (serrano or Thai)	15 mL
12 oz	ground beef	375 g
1 cup	fresh basil leaves	250 mL
1/4 cup	long thin strips red bell pepper (see Tip, right)	50 mL

Serves 4

Thai cooks make this dish with *bai gra-prao* or holy basil, a deliciously pungent variety of basil which is difficult to find in the West. Fresh basil, both Asian basil and Italian varieties, make very good substitutes, as does fresh mint. Don't expect much sauce with this dish, but do expect great flavor.

TIP

If you can find red fresh chiles, which are big and several inches long, cut them crosswise on the diagonal into thin ovals, and use these instead of the red bell pepper strips.

1. In a small bowl, combine fish sauce, chicken stock, dark soy sauce, if using, sugar and salt and stir well. Set aside.

2. Heat a wok or a large deep skillet over high heat. Add oil and swirl to coat pan. Add garlic, toss once, and add hot green chile. Toss well. Cook, undisturbed, about 15 seconds.

3. Add ground beef and using your spatula or a large spoon break up meat, spreading out to cook evenly. Cook, gently tossing occasionally and continuing to "chop" the meat into small pieces as it cooks, until no longer pink outside, about 1 minute.

4. Add fish sauce mixture and toss well. Cook, tossing occasionally, until beef is no longer pink inside and cooked through and ingredients form a thin dark sauce.

5. Add basil and toss well. Season with more salt, if desired. Transfer to serving plate. Sprinkle with red peppers. Serve hot or warm.

Gingery Ground Beef with Peas

Serves 4

Since this flavorful dish has very little sauce, you can scoop some into a pita bread, adding shredded lettuce and some cherry tomatoes or cucumbers to make it a meal. I love it Asian-style, with lots of rice and an untraditional bowl of spicy salsa on the side.

2 tbsp	soy sauce	25 mL
1 tsp	granulated sugar	5 mL
½ tsp	salt or to taste	2 mL
¼ cup	chicken stock or water	50 mL
2 tbsp	vegetable oil	25 mL
2 tbsp	chopped fresh gingerroot	25 mL
2 tsp	chopped garlic	10 mL
8 oz	ground beef	250 g
½ cup	frozen peas	125 mL

1. In a small bowl, combine soy sauce, sugar, salt and chicken stock and stir well. Set aside.

2. Heat a wok or a large deep skillet over high heat. Add oil and swirl to coat pan. Add ginger and garlic and toss well, until fragrant, about 15 seconds.

3. Add ground beef and using your spatula or a large spoon break up meat, spreading out to cook evenly. Cook, tossing once or twice, until no longer pink, about 1 minute.

4. Add soy sauce mixture, pouring in around sides of pan. Add peas and cook, tossing occasionally, until beef is cooked through and peas are hot, 1 to 2 minutes. Transfer to serving plate. Serve hot or warm.

Pork

Pork Slices with Bursting Peas

Serves 4

Sugar snap peas look like little snow peas inflated to just-before-the-bursting point. Though the two vegetables differ in a number of ways, they both offer a fresh, intense flavor and delightful crunch and can be used interchangeably in many stir-fried dishes. Sugar snaps need a little more liquid and a slightly longer cooking time than snow peas.

1 tbsp	soy sauce	15 mL
½ tsp	salt or to taste	2 mL
8 oz	boneless pork (such as loin or tenderloin), thinly sliced	250 g
1 tbsp	fish sauce	15 mL
1 tbsp	chicken stock or water	15 mL
1 tsp	granulated sugar	5 mL
¾ tsp	freshly ground pepper	4 mL
2 cups	sugar snap peas	500 mL
2 tbsp	vegetable oil	25 mL
1 tbsp	chopped garlic	15 mL
2 tbsp	chopped green onions	25 mL

1. In a bowl, combine soy sauce and salt and stir well. Add pork and stir to coat well. Set aside for 10 minutes.
2. In a small bowl, combine fish sauce, chicken stock, sugar and pepper and stir well. Set aside.
3. Trim sugar snap peas, cutting off stem and pulling it along straight edge to remove any strings. Set aside.
4. Heat a wok or a large deep skillet over high heat. Add oil and swirl to coat pan. Add garlic and toss well, until fragrant, about 15 seconds. Add pork mixture and spread into a single layer. Cook, undisturbed, until edges change color, about 30 seconds.
5. Toss well. Cook, tossing occasionally, until most of the pork is no longer pink, about 1 minute more. Add sugar snap peas and toss well.
6. Add fish sauce mixture, pouring in around sides of pan. Toss well. Cook, tossing often, until pork is cooked through and sugar snap peas are tender-crisp, 2 to 3 minutes. Add green onions and toss well. Transfer to a serving plate. Serve hot or warm.

Pork with Fragrant Black Beans

1 tbsp	soy sauce	15 mL
2 tsp	cornstarch	10 mL
1 tsp	granulated sugar	5 mL
12 oz	boneless pork (such as loin or tenderloin), thinly sliced	375 g
3 tbsp	chicken stock or water	45 mL
2 tbsp	dry sherry	25 mL
1 tbsp	water	15 mL
2 tbsp	chopped salted black beans (see Tips, page 125)	25 mL
2 tbsp	chopped fresh gingerroot	25 mL
2 tsp	chopped garlic	10 mL
2 tbsp	vegetable oil	25 mL
½ cup	chopped green bell pepper	125 mL
2 tbsp	chopped green onions	25 mL
2 tsp	Asian sesame oil	10 mL

Serves 4

This recipe shows off beautifully atop a mound of rice or noodles. It comes together quickly, once you've put together its three simple seasoning components: Soy sauce flavors the pork, black beans mashed with ginger and garlic are the main flavor notes and a chicken stock-sherry mixture expands the sauce.

1. In a bowl, combine soy sauce, cornstarch and sugar and stir well into a smooth sauce. Add pork and stir to coat evenly. Set aside for 10 minutes.

2. In a small bowl, combine chicken stock, sherry and water and stir well. Set aside.

3. In another small bowl, combine black beans, ginger and garlic and using a spoon, stir and mash gently, just enough to mix together a bit, but not into a smooth paste. Set aside.

4. Heat a wok or a large deep skillet over high heat. Add vegetable oil and swirl to coat pan. Add pork mixture and spread into a single layer. Cook, undisturbed, until edges change color, about 30 seconds. Toss well. Cook, tossing occasionally, until most of pork is no longer pink, about 1 minute more.

5. Add green pepper and black bean sauce mixture and toss well. Add chicken stock mixture and toss again to mix everything well. Allow sauce to come to a gentle boil. Cook, tossing occasionally, until pork is cooked through and coated in a smooth brown sauce, 1 to 2 minutes more.

6. Add green onions and sesame oil and toss well. Transfer to a serving plate. Serve hot or warm.

Hoisin Shredded Pork
with Gingery Vegetables

Serves 4

Based on a Northern Chinese-style classic, this pork dish boasts crunchy bamboo shoots and a deep sweet hoisin flavor. It's perfect for a cool-weather meal with rice and spinach or peas. You could also serve it with lettuce cups or Mandarin Pancakes (see recipe, page 330) as a tasty wrap.

TIPS

Sizes for canned bamboo shoots seem to vary a bit. Some give the weight of the entire can; others of the drained contents and still others give both. One small can of sliced bamboo in the 6 oz (175 g) range should be just fine, giving you between ¾ cup (175 mL) and 1 cup (250 mL) of bamboo shoots.

If you don't have time to shred the pork and bamboo shoots, simply leave them whole and add a little extra cooking time.

8 oz	boneless pork (such as loin or tenderloin)	250 g
1 tbsp	soy sauce	15 mL
1 tbsp	dry sherry or Shaoxing rice wine	15 mL
2 tsp	cornstarch	10 mL
1 tbsp	hoisin sauce	15 mL
1 tbsp	chicken stock or water	15 mL
½ tsp	salt or to taste	2 mL
¾ cup	drained rinsed canned sliced bamboo shoots (see Tips, left)	175 mL
2 tbsp	vegetable oil	25 mL
1 tbsp	chopped garlic	15 mL
2 tsp	chopped fresh gingerroot	10 mL
1 cup	shredded carrots	250 mL
⅓ cup	chopped green onions	75 mL

1. Slice pork crosswise into thin slices, about ¼ inch (0.5 cm) thick. Place 2 or 3 slices into a little stack and slice lengthwise into thin little strips.

2. In a bowl, combine soy sauce, sherry and cornstarch and stir well into a smooth sauce. Add shredded pork and stir to coat evenly. Set aside for 10 minutes.

3. In a small bowl, combine hoisin sauce, chicken stock and salt and stir well. Set aside.

4. Place 2 or 3 bamboo shoots into a little stack and carefully slice lengthwise along the grain into thin shreds. Set aside.

5. Heat a wok or a large deep skillet over high heat. Add oil and swirl to coat pan. Add garlic and ginger and toss well, until fragrant, about 15 seconds.

6. Add pork mixture and spread into a single layer. Cook, undisturbed, until edges change color, about 15 seconds. Toss well and add shredded carrots. Cook, tossing occasionally, until carrots are beginning to wilt and pork is no longer pink, about 30 seconds.

7. Add hoisin sauce mixture and bamboo shoots and toss well. Cook, tossing occasionally, until pork is cooked through, carrots are tender-crisp and everything is coated with a smooth sauce. Add green onions and toss well. Transfer to a serving plate. Serve hot or warm.

Five-Spice Pork with Bok Choy and Green Onions

1 tbsp	soy sauce	15 mL
1 tbsp	dry sherry or Shaoxing rice wine	15 mL
1 tsp	five-spice powder	5 mL
1 tsp	cornstarch	5 mL
8 oz	boneless pork (such as loin or tenderloin), thinly sliced	250 g
1 tbsp	chicken stock or water	15 mL
1 tsp	brown sugar or granulated sugar	5 mL
1 tsp	salt or to taste	5 mL
2 tbsp	vegetable oil	25 mL
2 tbsp	chopped garlic	25 mL
1 cup	chopped bok choy (see Tip, right)	250 mL
3 tbsp	chopped green onions	45 mL

1. In a bowl, combine soy sauce, sherry, five-spice powder and cornstarch and stir well into a smooth sauce. Add pork and stir to coat evenly. Set aside for 10 minutes.

2. In a small bowl, combine chicken stock, sugar and salt and stir well. Set aside.

3. Heat a wok or a large deep skillet over high heat. Add oil and swirl to coat the pan. Add garlic and toss well, until fragrant, about 15 seconds.

4. Add pork mixture and spread into a single layer. Cook, undisturbed, until edges change color, about 30 seconds. Toss well. Cook, tossing occasionally, until no longer pink, about 1 minute more.

5. Add bok choy and toss well. Add chicken stock mixture and cook, tossing occasionally, until pork is cooked through, 1 to 2 minutes more. Add green onions and toss well. Transfer to a serving plate. Serve hot or warm.

Serves 4

Five-spice powder is an extraordinary mélange of aromatic spices that brings marvelous flavor to meat dishes all across Asia. Made from star anise, Szechwan peppercorns, fennel seeds, cinnamon and cloves, it is often available among the spices on supermarket shelves or in Asian markets. Enjoy this richly flavored stir-fry with a salad of spinach, dried cranberries and thinly sliced almonds, tossed with a citrus dressing.

TIP

For 1 cup (250 mL) chopped bok choy, you'll need about 3 leafy stalks. Trim 1 inch (2.5 cm) from the base of each stalk and then halve it lengthwise. Chop resulting strips crosswise into 1-inch (2.5 cm) lengths. You'll have bite-size pieces, roughly 1½ inches-by-1-inch (4 cm by 2.5 cm). If bok choy leaves are very large, cut them lengthwise into 3 or 4 pieces, rather than in half.

Sweet-and-Sour Pork Slices

Serves 4

The classic version of this dish varies in its sweetness, ingredients and the level of red color in its signature sauce. Two things we can say with certainty: It is very popular and its central ingredient is crisp-fried chunks of pork. Here I've followed the Thai practice of using thin slices of stir-fried pork in the dish with the yummy, pineapple-studded Chinese-style sauce I adore.

TIPS

If you long for the pretty red color typical of this dish, add a few drops of red food coloring, or increase the amount of ketchup, or try tomato paste. Adjust the sugar and salt as needed for the latter two options, since they may change the taste a bit.

If you use fresh pineapple, substitute canned pineapple juice or apple juice instead.

2 tbsp	soy sauce	25 mL
1 tbsp	dry sherry or Shaoxing rice wine	15 mL
2 tsp	cornstarch	10 mL
¼ tsp	salt or to taste	1 mL
8 oz	boneless pork (such as loin or tenderloin), thinly sliced	250 g
1 tbsp	ketchup	15 mL
⅔ cup	pineapple chunks (2 tbsp/25 mL reserved juice if canned) (see Tips, left)	150 mL
1 tbsp	white or cider vinegar	15 mL
1 tbsp	granulated sugar	15 mL
2 tbsp	vegetable oil	25 mL
1 tbsp	chopped garlic	15 mL
1 tbsp	chopped fresh gingerroot	15 mL
½ cup	chopped onion (1-inch/2.5 cm chunks)	125 mL
½ cup	chopped red bell pepper (1-inch/2.5 cm chunks)	125 mL
½ cup	chopped green bell pepper (1-inch/2.5 cm chunks)	125 mL
¾ cup	drained rinsed canned sliced bamboo shoots (see Tips, page 90)	175 mL

1. In a bowl, combine soy sauce, sherry, cornstarch and salt and stir well into a smooth sauce. Add pork and stir to coat well. Set aside for 10 minutes.

2. In a small saucepan over medium heat, combine ketchup, 2 tbsp (25 mL) reserved pineapple juice, vinegar and sugar and bring to a gentle boil. Cook, stirring often, until it forms a smooth sauce, 2 to 3 minutes. Set aside.

3. Heat a wok or a large deep skillet over high heat. Add oil and swirl to coat pan. Add garlic and ginger and toss well, until fragrant, about 15 seconds.

4. Add pork mixture and spread into a single layer. Cook, undisturbed, until edges change color, about 30 seconds. Toss well. Cook, tossing occasionally, until no longer pink, about 1 minute more.

5. Add onion, red and green peppers and pineapple chunks and toss well. Cook, tossing often, until meat is cooked through and onion and peppers are tender-crisp, 2 to 3 minutes.

6. Add bamboo shoots and ketchup sauce and toss well. Cook, tossing gently, until everything is combined, about 1 minute. Transfer to a serving plate. Serve hot or warm.

Variation: If you would like a traditional crispy-pork version, chop pork into chunks a little smaller than 1 inch (2.5 cm) and roll them in cornstarch seasoned with a little salt. Set aside to dry for a few minutes and then cook them in about a 3-inch (7.5 cm) depth of very hot oil in a wok or saucepan, turning often, until golden brown and cooked through. Drain well and add them to the sauce while they are hot and very shortly before serving time.

Thai-Style Sweet-and-Sour Pork with Vegetables

Serves 4

Thailand's version of sweet-and-sour pork provides abundant color from tomatoes and cucumbers and a tangy sauce. I love to use pickling cucumbers or a long English cucumber if I can find it.

TIP

If you can't find an English cucumber, peel a field cuke, cut in half lengthwise, scoop out seeds and cut crosswise into half-moon chunks.

3 tbsp	fish sauce	45 mL
2 tbsp	granulated sugar	25 mL
1 tbsp	white or cider vinegar	15 mL
½ tsp	salt or to taste	2 mL
2 tbsp	vegetable oil	25 mL
1 tbsp	chopped garlic	15 mL
8 oz	boneless pork (such as loin or tenderloin), thinly sliced	250 g
1 cup	small cauliflower florets	250 mL
1 cup	coarsely chopped onion	250 mL
2 tbsp	chicken stock or water	25 mL
1 cup	peeled cucumber chunks (see Tip, left)	250 mL
¾ cup	halved cherry tomatoes	175 mL

1. In a small bowl, combine fish sauce, sugar, vinegar and salt and stir well. Set aside.

2. Heat a work or a large deep skillet over high heat. Add oil and swirl to coat pan. Add garlic and toss well, until fragrant, about 15 seconds.

3. Add pork and spread into a single layer. Cook, undisturbed, until edges change color, about 30 seconds. Toss well. Cook, tossing occasionally, until no longer pink, 1 to 2 minutes more.

4. Add cauliflower and onions and toss well. Add chicken stock and cook, tossing occasionally, until onions are softened, about 1 minute.

5. Add cucumber and fish sauce mixture, pouring in around sides of pan. Toss well. Cook, tossing often, until pork is cooked through and vegetables are tender-crisp, about 1 minute more.

6. Add tomatoes and toss well. Transfer to a serving plate. Serve hot or warm.

Garlicky Pork in Lemongrass Paste

2 tbsp	fish sauce	25 mL
1 tbsp	soy sauce	15 mL
2 tsp	granulated sugar	10 mL
1 tsp	cornstarch	5 mL
12 oz	boneless pork (such as loin or tenderloin), thinly sliced	375 g
2	stalks fresh lemongrass	2
1/4 cup	chopped onion	50 mL
1/2 cup	chicken stock or water	125 mL
2 tbsp	vegetable oil	25 mL
1 tbsp	chopped garlic	15 mL
2 tsp	chopped fresh gingerroot	10 mL
1/2 tsp	salt or to taste	2 mL
1/2 tsp	hot pepper flakes	2 mL
1/3 cup	chopped green onions	75 mL

Serves 4

This is a quick take on a *ga xao xa ot*, a Vietnamese dish made with chicken. I use a blender to quickly grind the fibrous chunks of lemongrass, making them smooth enough to add to the marinade.

1. In a bowl, combine fish sauce, soy sauce, sugar and cornstarch and stir well into a smooth sauce. Add pork and stir to coat well evenly. Set aside for 10 minutes.

2. Meanwhile, trim lemongrass stalks, cutting away top half leaving about a 6-inch (15 cm) base. Cut away the dry root ends leaving a smooth base just under the bulb, and remove any dry outer leaves. Cut stalks in half lengthwise and then crosswise into 1-inch (2.5 cm) pieces.

3. In a blender or mini-food processor, combine chopped lemongrass, onion and chicken stock. Grind well, stopping to scrape sides as necessary, to a fairly smooth paste. Set aside.

4. Heat a wok or a large deep skillet over high heat. Add oil and swirl to coat pan. Add garlic and ginger and toss well, until fragrant, about 15 seconds.

5. Add pork mixture and spread into a single layer. Cook, undisturbed, until edges change color, about 1 minute.

6. Reduce heat to medium. Add lemongrass paste and toss well. Cook, tossing occasionally, until most of pork is no longer pink, about 1 minute.

7. Add salt and hot pepper flakes. Cook, tossing occasionally, until pork is cooked through and everything combines into a fairly smooth sauce, 1 to 2 minutes. Add green onions and toss well. Transfer to a serving plate. Serve hot or warm.

Sesame-Scented Pork with Crispy Peas

Serves 4

Fresh snow peas take a few minutes to trim, but their brilliant color and crisp, fresh flavor make it worth your time. You'll be finished in the time it takes the pork to marinate before cooking.

TIPS

I often use boneless thin-cut pork chops in stir-fry recipes like this, but you'll get good results with other cuts, such as pork tenderloin, pork butt or thick-cut pork chops.

To trim snow peas, cut off and discard tip and cut stem end partway, pulling it down along the straight side of each snow pea to remove any strings.

2 tbsp	soy sauce	25 mL
1 tbsp	dry sherry or Shaoxing rice wine	15 mL
2 tsp	cornstarch	10 mL
1 tsp	granulated sugar	5 mL
1/2 tsp	salt or to taste	2 mL
1/2 tsp	freshly ground pepper	2 mL
8 oz	thinly sliced pork (see Tips, left)	250 g
2 tbsp	vegetable oil	25 mL
2 tsp	chopped garlic	10 mL
8 oz	trimmed snow peas (see Tips, left)	250 g
2 tsp	Asian sesame oil	10 mL

1. In a bowl, combine soy sauce, sherry, cornstarch, sugar, salt and pepper and stir well into a smooth sauce. Add pork and stir to coat evenly. Set aside for 10 minutes. (You can cover and refrigerate for several hours if preparing in advance.)

2. Heat a wok or a large deep skillet over high heat. Add vegetable oil and swirl to coat pan. Add garlic and toss well, until fragrant, about 15 seconds.

3. Add pork mixture and spread into a single layer. Cook, undisturbed, until edges change color, about 30 seconds. Toss well. Cook, tossing occasionally, until no longer pink, about 1 minute more.

4. Add snow peas and toss well. Cook, undisturbed, for 1 minute. Toss again. Cook, tossing occasionally, until pork is cooked through and snow peas are brilliant green and tender-crisp, 1 to 2 minutes more. Add sesame oil and toss once. Transfer to a serving plate. Serve hot or warm.

Variation: Substitute 8 oz (250 g) sugar snap peas for the snow peas and add 1 tbsp (15 mL) water after putting them into the pan to cook. Allow an extra minute of cooking time as well.

Vietnamese-Style Shaking Beef with Peppery Watercress (page 70)

Overleaf: Speedy Beef Stir-Fry with Chunky Vegetables (page 76)

Peppery Pork with Garlic and Shallots

2 tbsp	dry sherry or Shaoxing rice wine	25 mL
2 tsp	soy sauce	10 mL
2 tsp	granulated sugar	10 mL
1 tsp	salt or to taste	5 mL
1 tsp	freshly ground pepper	5 mL
12 oz	boneless pork (such as loin or tenderloin), thinly sliced	375 g
2 tbsp	vegetable oil	25 mL
2 tbsp	chopped garlic	25 mL
3 tbsp	chopped shallots or onion	45 mL
2 tbsp	fish sauce	25 mL
3 tbsp	chopped fresh cilantro	45 mL

1. In a small bowl, combine sherry, soy sauce, sugar, salt and pepper and stir well. Add pork and stir to coat evenly. Set aside for 10 minutes.

2. Heat a wok or a large deep skillet over high heat. Add oil and swirl to coat pan. Add garlic and shallots and cook, tossing often, until fragrant, about 1 minute.

3. Add pork mixture and spread into a single layer. Cook, undisturbed, until edges change color, about 1 minute. Toss well. Cook, tossing occasionally, until no longer pink, about 1 minute more.

4. Add fish sauce and toss well. Cook, tossing occasionally, until pork is cooked through, 1 to 2 minutes more. Add cilantro and toss well. Transfer to a serving plate. Serve hot or warm.

Serves 4

Thai people love spareribs cut into small sections, seasoned with garlic and pepper and then deep-fried until lusciously crispy. This stir-fry captures those flavors in a speedier dish. Try it Thai-style, served with rice and two accompaniments: A little bowl of Thai-style Sriracha sauce or any hot pepper sauce that you like for heating things up, and a plate of cucumber slices for cooling things back down.

Overleaf: Little Meatballs in Red Curry Peanut Sauce (page 83)
Pork Slices with Bursting Peas (page 88)

Thai-Style Pork Slices
with Oyster Mushrooms

Serves 4

Oyster mushrooms work wonderfully here, but whether you use fresh shiitakes or button mushrooms, this is a great dish. With buttered peas or a salad of apples, raisins and crispy greens, this makes a fine meal with rice or warm bread.

2 tbsp	fish sauce	25 mL
3 tbsp	chicken stock or water	45 mL
½ tsp	freshly ground pepper	2 mL
8 oz	fresh oyster or button mushrooms	250 g
2 tbsp	vegetable oil	25 mL
2 tbsp	chopped garlic	25 mL
2 tbsp	chopped shallots or green onions	25 mL
½ cup	thinly sliced onion	125 mL
8 oz	boneless pork (such as loin or tenderloin), thinly sliced	250 g
2 tbsp	chopped cilantro leaves	25 mL

1. In a small bowl, combine fish sauce, chicken stock and pepper and stir well. Set aside.

2. Cut oyster mushrooms in half lengthwise. (Cut into thirds if very large and leave whole if very small.) Thinly slice button mushrooms lengthwise as well. Set aside.

3. Heat a wok or a large skillet over medium-high heat. Add oil and swirl to coat pan. Add garlic and toss well, until fragrant, about 15 seconds. Add shallots and onion and cook, tossing occasionally, until softened, about 1 minute.

4. Add pork and spread into a single layer. Cook, undisturbed, until edges change color, about 1 minute. Toss well. Cook, tossing occasionally, until no longer pink, about 1 minute more.

5. Add mushrooms and toss well. Cook, tossing occasionally, until beginning to soften, about 1 minute.

6. Add fish sauce mixture, pouring in around sides of pan and toss well. Cook, tossing occasionally, until mushrooms are tender and pork is cooked through, about 1 minute more. Add cilantro and toss well. Transfer to a serving plate. Serve hot or warm.

Sliced Pork with Ginger Strips and Mushrooms

1 tbsp	fish sauce	15 mL
1 tbsp	soy sauce	15 mL
1 tbsp	chicken stock or water	15 mL
1 tsp	granulated sugar	5 mL
2 tbsp	vegetable oil	25 mL
1 tbsp	chopped garlic	15 mL
8 oz	boneless pork (such as loin or tenderloin), thinly sliced	250 g
1/3 cup	long thin strips peeled fresh gingerroot	75 mL
1/2 cup	chopped onion	125 mL
1 cup	thinly sliced mushrooms	250 mL
1/4 cup	chopped red bell pepper	50 mL

1. In a small bowl, combine fish sauce, soy sauce, chicken stock and sugar and stir well. Set aside.

2. Heat a wok or a large deep skillet over high heat. Add oil and swirl to coat pan. Add garlic and toss well, until fragrant, about 15 seconds.

3. Add pork and spread into a single layer. Cook, undisturbed, until edges change color, about 30 seconds. Toss well. Cook, tossing occasionally, until no longer pink, 1 to 2 minutes.

4. Add ginger and toss well. Cook, undisturbed, for 1 minute. Add onion and mushrooms and toss well. Cook, tossing occasionally, until onion is fragrant and mushrooms are softened, about 1 minute.

5. Add fish sauce mixture, pouring in around sides of pan. Toss well. Add red peppers and toss once more to mix well. Transfer to a serving plate. Serve hot or warm.

Serves 4

I keep gingerroot on hand so that I can add it to stir-fries anytime I want a little burst of bright Asian flavor. I leave it out at room temperature in a basket with garlic and shallots. If you want to keep it longer, peel it and place it in a jar of sherry. It keeps this way in the refrigerator for two months. And the sherry can be used in stir-fries as well.

Stir-Fried Pork with Cauliflower Florets

Cauliflower is an ideal stir-fry vegetable, sturdy enough to take the heat and sweet enough to blossom in flavor while retaining a pleasing little crunch.

TIP

This recipe uses about half a head of cauliflower. Wrap the remaining half and keep it in the crisper, to steam or stir-fry for an upcoming meal. You can also use prepared cauliflower florets found packaged in the produce section. These work well here too, as long as you trim any very large florets to bite-size pieces before you start to cook.

2 tbsp	fish sauce	25 mL
2 tbsp	chicken stock or water	25 mL
1 tsp	granulated sugar	5 mL
½ tsp	freshly ground pepper	2 mL
2 tbsp	vegetable oil	25 mL
1 tbsp	chopped garlic	15 mL
8 oz	boneless pork (such as loin or tenderloin), thinly sliced	250 g
3 cups	small cauliflower florets (about ½ head) (see Tip, left)	750 mL
⅓ cup	chopped green onions	75 mL
3 tbsp	chopped fresh cilantro or dill	45 mL

1. In a small bowl, combine fish sauce, chicken stock, sugar and pepper and stir well. Set aside.

2. Heat a wok or a large deep skillet over high heat. Add oil and swirl to coat pan. Add garlic and toss well, until fragrant, about 15 seconds.

3. Add pork and spread into a single layer. Cook, undisturbed, until edges change color, about 1 minute. Toss well. Cook, tossing occasionally, until no longer pink, about 1 minute more.

4. Add cauliflower and toss well. Cook, tossing once, until cauliflower is beginning to wilt, about 1 minute.

5. Add fish sauce mixture, pouring in around sides of pan. Toss well. Cook, tossing often, until pork is cooked through and cauliflower is tender-crisp, 1 to 2 minutes more. Add green onions and cilantro and toss well. Transfer to a serving plate. Serve hot or warm.

Flavorful Pork with Limas and Corn

1 tbsp	soy sauce	15 mL
1 tsp	salt or to taste	5 mL
¼ tsp	freshly ground pepper	1 mL
8 oz	boneless pork (such as loin or tenderloin), thinly sliced	250 g
2 tbsp	fish sauce	25 mL
1 tbsp	dry sherry or Shaoxing rice wine	15 mL
2 tsp	granulated sugar	10 mL
2 tbsp	vegetable oil	25 mL
¾ cup	frozen lima beans (see Tip, right)	175 mL
¾ cup	frozen corn kernels	175 mL
3 tbsp	chopped fresh cilantro or Italian parsley	45 mL

Serves 4

Colorful and tasty, this quick stir-fry dish relies on vegetables I keep handy in my freezer. Full-size Fordhook limas work well or you can use baby limas if you watch the time and get them out of the pan as soon as they are tender to avoid overcooking them.

1. In a bowl, combine soy sauce, salt and pepper and stir well. Add pork and stir to coat evenly. Set aside for 10 minutes.

2. In a small bowl, combine fish sauce, sherry and sugar and stir well. Set aside.

3. Heat a wok or a large deep skillet over high heat. Add oil and swirl to coat pan. Add pork mixture and spread into a single layer. Cook, undisturbed, until edges change color, about 30 seconds. Toss well. Cook, tossing occasionally, until no longer pink, about 1 minute more.

4. Add lima beans and corn and cook, tossing occasionally, until all ingredients are thawed and well combined, 1 minute more.

5. Add fish sauce mixture, pouring in around sides of pan. Toss well. Cook, tossing often, until pork is cooked through and vegetables are hot and tender, 1 to 2 minutes more. Add cilantro and toss well. Transfer to a serving plate. Serve hot or warm.

TIP

If you have time and want exceptionally beautiful lima beans to adorn your dish, you can peel them. Place frozen limas on a plate in a single layer to thaw at room temperature for about 20 minutes. Squeeze a lima bean gently until the double-lobed inner bean pops out of its little hull. Transfer the bean to another plate and continue until all the beans are done. Discard hulls. Beans will cook very quickly now, so adjust time to merely heat them through, adding after the fish sauce mixture. If they don't pop right out easily, have a paring knife handy and make a quick little cut to give the bean an easy out.

Pork with Shredded Brussels Sprouts

Serves 4

Yes, overcooked Brussels sprouts can be a sad sight on the plate and less than delightful to eat. But treated with care and a little seasoning they make a delicious cool-weather treat. Stir-frying suits them, if you shred them finely and cook them fast.

1 tbsp	soy sauce	15 mL
1 tbsp	dry sherry or Shaoxing rice wine	15 mL
1 tsp	cornstarch	5 mL
8 oz	boneless pork (such as loin or tenderloin), thinly sliced	250 g
3 tbsp	chicken stock or water	45 mL
2 tsp	granulated sugar	10 mL
1 tsp	salt or to taste	5 mL
½ tsp	freshly ground pepper	2 mL
8 oz	Brussels sprouts (about 12)	250 g
2 tbsp	vegetable oil	25 mL
2 tbsp	chopped garlic	25 mL
2 tbsp	chopped green onions	25 mL

1. In a bowl, combine soy sauce, sherry and cornstarch and stir well into a smooth sauce. Add pork and stir to coat evenly. Set aside for 10 minutes.

2. In a small bowl, combine chicken stock, sugar, salt and pepper and stir well. Set aside.

3. Trim Brussels sprouts ¼-inch (0.5 cm) from the base of each sprout and then halve lengthwise. Slice crosswise very thinly into delicate shreds, chopping harder stem ends into little chunks. Set aside.

4. Heat a wok or a large deep skillet over high heat. Add oil and swirl to coat pan. Add garlic and toss well, until fragrant, about 15 seconds.

5. Add pork mixture and spread into a single layer. Cook, undisturbed, until edges change color, about 30 seconds. Toss well. Cook, tossing occasionally, until no longer pink, about 1 minute more.

6. Add Brussels sprouts and toss well. Cook, tossing often, until brighten to a vivid green, about 1 minute more.

7. Add chicken stock mixture, pouring in around sides of pan. Toss well. Cook, tossing occasionally, until pork is cooked through and Brussels sprouts are tender but still bright green, 1 to 2 minutes more. Add green onions and toss well. Transfer to a serving plate. Serve hot or warm.

Apple Cider Pork with Sweet Potatoes and Sesame Oil

1 tbsp	dry sherry or Shaoxing rice wine	15 mL
1 tbsp	apple cider vinegar or red wine vinegar	15 mL
2 tsp	dark brown sugar	10 mL
2 tsp	granulated sugar	10 mL
1 tsp	salt or to taste	5 mL
8 oz	boneless pork (such as loin or tenderloin), thinly sliced	250 g
1 tbsp	soy sauce	15 mL
2 tbsp	vegetable oil	25 mL
1 tbsp	chopped garlic	15 mL
2 tsp	chopped fresh gingerroot	10 mL
1½ cups	chunks cooked sweet potatoes	375 mL
3 tbsp	chopped green onions	45 mL
2 tsp	Asian sesame oil	10 mL

Serves 4

This satisfying dish can be made with cooked sweet potatoes or with canned sweet potatoes that have been rinsed and drained well. A good dash of hot pepper sauce makes a dandy addition to the finished dish if you like chile heat.

TIP
Toss sweet potatoes gently and only occasionally because they are soft and are easily mashed if tossed too often.

1. In a small bowl, combine sherry, vinegar, brown sugar, granulated sugar and salt and stir well. Set aside.

2. In another bowl, combine pork and soy sauce and stir well. Set aside for 10 minutes.

3. Heat a wok or a large deep skillet over high heat. Add oil and swirl to coat pan. Add garlic and ginger and toss well, until fragrant, about 15 seconds.

4. Add pork mixture and spread into a single layer. Cook, undisturbed, until edges change color, about 30 seconds. Toss well. Cook, tossing occasionally, until no longer pink, about 1 minute more.

5. Add sweet potatoes and toss gently (see Tip, right). Cook, tossing once, until pork is cooked through and sweet potatoes are hot, 1 to 2 minutes.

6. Add sherry-vinegar mixture, pouring in around sides of pan. Toss well. Cook, tossing occasionally, until pork and sweet potatoes are evenly coated with the sauce. Add green onions and sesame oil and toss well. Transfer to a serving plate. Serve hot or warm.

Colorful Sweet-and-Sour Pork Stir-Fry

Serves 4

Pineapple chunks brighten this stir-fry dish, with carrot shreds and peas napped in a sweet-sharp sauce.

TIPS

If you are using fresh pineapple, you can use the juice or syrup from a can of pineapple chunks or pineapple or orange juice.

Frozen tiny peas are also referred to as "petite" and "baby." You can also use regular-size frozen peas, if you allow a little extra cooking time to heat them through.

1 tbsp	dry sherry or Shaoxing rice wine	15 mL
1 tbsp	chicken stock or water	15 mL
2 tsp	cornstarch	10 mL
8 oz	boneless pork (such as loin or tenderloin), thinly sliced	250 g
1 cup	pineapple chunks (1/3 cup/75 mL reserved juice if canned) (see Tips, left)	250 mL
2 tbsp	red wine vinegar or apple cider vinegar	25 mL
2 tbsp	fish sauce	25 mL
1 tbsp	granulated sugar	15 mL
1 tsp	soy sauce	5 mL
1 tsp	salt or to taste	5 mL
1/2 tsp	freshly ground pepper	2 mL
2 tbsp	vegetable oil	25 mL
1 tbsp	chopped garlic	15 mL
2/3 cup	shredded carrot	150 mL
1/2 cup	frozen tiny peas (see Tips, left)	125 mL

1. In a bowl, combine sherry, chicken stock and cornstarch and stir well into a smooth sauce. Add pork and stir to coat evenly. Set aside for 10 minutes.

2. In a small bowl, combine 1/3 cup (75 mL) reserved pineapple juice, vinegar, fish sauce, sugar, soy sauce, salt and pepper and stir well. Set aside.

3. Heat a wok or a large deep skillet over high heat. Add oil and swirl to coat pan. Add garlic and toss well, until fragrant, about 15 seconds.

4. Add pork mixture and spread into a single layer. Cook, undisturbed, until edges change color, about 30 seconds. Toss well. Cook, tossing occasionally, until no longer pink, 1 to 2 minutes more.

5. Add pineapple chunks and carrot and toss well. Cook, tossing occasionally, until pork is cooked through and carrots are beginning to wilt, about 1 minute more.

6. Add pineapple juice mixture, pouring in around sides of pan. Toss well. Add peas and continue cooking, tossing often, until pork is cooked through and vegetables are hot about 1 minute more. Transfer to a serving plate. Serve hot or warm.

Balsamic-Spiked Pork with Cherry Tomatoes and Spinach

8 oz	boneless pork (such as loin or tenderloin), thinly sliced	250 g
1 tbsp	soy sauce	15 mL
1 tbsp	chicken stock or water	15 mL
1 tbsp	balsamic vinegar or red wine vinegar	15 mL
1 tsp	salt or to taste	5 mL
½ tsp	granulated sugar	2 mL
¼ tsp	freshly ground pepper	1 mL
2 tbsp	vegetable oil	25 mL
1 tbsp	chopped garlic	15 mL
6 cups	fresh baby spinach (10 oz/300 g)	1.5 L
1 cup	halved cherry tomatoes (see Tip, right)	250 mL

Serves 4

Radiant red, gorgeous green and packed with vitamins and flavor, this dish is delicious. With rice or noodles it's a one-dish meal on a busy day.

TIP

You could use ripe tomatoes chopped into big bite-size chunks instead of cherry tomatoes. Leave behind any juices and seeds released onto the cutting board and give the tomatoes just the briefest turn in the hot pan at the end of cooking time.

1. In a bowl, combine pork and soy sauce and stir well. Set aside for 10 minutes.

2. In a small bowl, combine chicken stock, balsamic vinegar, salt, sugar and pepper and stir well. Set aside.

3. Heat a wok or a large deep skillet over high heat. Add oil and swirl to coat pan. Add garlic and toss well, until fragrant, about 15 seconds.

4. Add pork mixture and spread into a single layer. Cook, undisturbed, until edges change color, about 30 seconds. Toss well. Cook, tossing often, until no longer pink, 1 to 2 minutes more.

5. Add spinach and cook, tossing occasionally, until beginning to wilt, about 1 minute.

6. Add vinegar mixture, pouring in around sides of pan. Toss well. Add tomatoes and cook, tossing twice, until beginning to wilt and pork is cooked through, about 30 seconds more. Transfer to a serving plate. Serve hot or warm.

Pork with Escarole, Cherry Tomatoes and Pine Nuts

Serves 4

This dish over rice makes for a flavorful supper. We like it tossed with angel hair pasta, too. Escarole is a sturdy and delicious cruciferous vegetable, which walks a fine line between being a lettuce and a cabbage.

TIP

To prepare escarole, halve or quarter a head lengthwise and then chop it crosswise into approximately 2-inch (5 cm) chunks.

2 tbsp	vegetable oil	25 mL
2 tbsp	chopped garlic	25 mL
8 oz	boneless pork (such as loin or tenderloin), thinly sliced	250 g
1	head escarole, cut into 2-inch (5 cm) chunks (about 7 cups/1.75 mL) (see Tip, left)	1
1 tsp	salt or to taste	5 mL
½ tsp	freshly ground pepper	2 mL
¾ cup	halved cherry tomatoes	175 mL
¼ cup	pine nuts	50 mL

1. Heat a wok or large skillet over high heat. Add oil and swirl to coat the pan. Add garlic and toss well, until fragrant, about 15 seconds.

2. Add pork and spread into a single layer. Cook, undisturbed, until edges change color, about 30 seconds.

3. Add escarole and toss again. Add salt and pepper. Continue cooking, tossing occasionally, until escarole is softened but still retains a pleasing crunch, 2 to 3 minutes.

4. Add cherry tomatoes and pine nuts and toss well. Cook, tossing occasionally, until tomatoes are beginning to wilt, about 1 minute. Transfer to a serving plate. Serve hot or warm.

Soy-Seasoned Pork with Eggplant and Cilantro

2 tsp	soy sauce	10 mL
1 tsp	dark soy sauce or molasses, optional	5 mL
8 oz	boneless pork (such as loin or tenderloin), thinly sliced	250 g
2 tbsp	chicken stock or water	25 mL
1 tbsp	granulated sugar	15 mL
2 tsp	dry sherry or Shaoxing rice wine	10 mL
1/2 tsp	salt or to taste	2 mL
2 tbsp	vegetable oil	25 mL
1 tbsp	chopped garlic	15 mL
2 tsp	chopped fresh gingerroot	10 mL
1 cup	cubed (1/2 inch/1 cm) eggplant (see Tip, right)	250 mL
1/4 cup	chopped green onions	50 mL
2 tbsp	chopped fresh cilantro	25 mL

Serves 4

Eggplant can work wonderfully in stir-fried dishes, provided it is cut small enough or thinly enough to cook quickly. In this robust dish small chunks take on the dark rich color and flavor of the sauce.

TIP

You can use long thin Asian-style eggplants or big plump eggplants, as long as you cut them down to size.

1. In a bowl, combine soy sauce and dark soy sauce, if using, and stir well. Add pork and stir to coat evenly. Set aside for 10 minutes.

2. In a small bowl, combine chicken stock, sugar, sherry and salt and stir well.

3. Heat a work or a large deep skillet over high heat. Add oil and swirl to coat pan. Add garlic and ginger and toss well, until fragrant, about 15 seconds.

4. Add pork mixture and spread into a single layer. Cook, undisturbed, until edges change color, about 30 seconds. Toss well. Cook, tossing occasionally, until no longer pink, about 1 minute more.

5. Add eggplant and toss well. Cook, tossing often, until eggplant is tender and pork is cooked through, 1 to 2 minutes more.

6. Add chicken stock mixture, pouring in around sides of pan and toss well. Add green onions and cilantro and toss once to mix well. Transfer to a serving plate. Serve hot or warm.

Garlic Pork with Arugula and Sweet Peppers

Serves 4

This recipe will make the family happy on a busy weeknight with its robust flavors and good looks. This is also pretty and tasty enough for a gathering.

TIPS

If you like heat, increase the hot pepper flakes.

To make bell pepper strips, halve one pepper lengthwise and discard the stem section and seeds. Cut off the rounded top and bottom portions and reserve for salad or other dishes. Cut the remaining portion lengthwise into 2-inch (5 cm) long strips. You'll need about half of a small pepper.

8 oz	boneless pork (such as loin or tenderloin), thinly sliced	250 g
1 tbsp	soy sauce	15 mL
2 tbsp	chicken stock or water	25 mL
½ tsp	granulated sugar	2 mL
½ tsp	salt or to taste	2 mL
½ tsp	hot pepper flakes or to taste	2 mL
2 tbsp	vegetable oil	25 mL
2 tbsp	chopped garlic	25 mL
½ cup	thin strips red bell pepper (see Tips, left)	125 mL
2 cups	arugula leaves	500 mL
1 tsp	Asian sesame oil	5 mL

1. In a bowl, combine pork and soy sauce and mix well. Set aside for 10 minutes.

2. In a small bowl, combine chicken stock, sugar, salt and hot pepper flakes and stir well.

3. Heat a wok or a large deep skillet over high heat. Add oil and swirl to coat pan. Add garlic and toss well, until fragrant, about 15 seconds.

4. Add pork mixture and spread into a single layer. Cook, undisturbed, until edges change color, about 30 seconds. Toss well. Cook, tossing occasionally, until no longer pink, about 1 minute more.

5. Add red pepper and cook, tossing occasionally, until peppers are softened and pork is cooked through, about 2 minutes more.

6. Add chicken stock mixture, pouring in around sides of pan. Toss well. Cook, tossing occasionally, 2 minutes more. Add arugula and cook, tossing often, until arugula is wilted, about 1 minute more. Add sesame oil and toss well. Transfer to a serving plate. Serve hot or warm.

Orange-Splashed Pork with Cumin, Tomatoes and Mint

1 tbsp	soy sauce	15 mL
1 tbsp	chicken stock or water	15 mL
1 tsp	cornstarch	5 mL
8 oz	boneless pork (such as loin or tenderloin), thinly sliced	250 g
3 tbsp	orange juice	45 mL
1 tsp	ground cumin	5 mL
1 tsp	salt or to taste	5 mL
½ tsp	freshly ground pepper	2 mL
½ tsp	ground cinnamon	2 mL
2 tbsp	vegetable oil	25 mL
2 tsp	chopped garlic	10 mL
¾ cup	coarsely chopped tomatoes (see Tip, right)	175 mL
2 tbsp	chopped green onions	25 mL
2 tbsp	chopped fresh mint or cilantro	25 mL

Serves 4

This quick dish counts on the rustic flavor of ground cumin and a splash of orange juice for its delicious sauce.

TIP

Plum (Roma) tomatoes work well here and 2 medium ones or 3 small ones should be just the right amount (4 oz/125 g) to yield ¾ cup (175 mL) once they're trimmed and chopped. Cut away stem end, halve them lengthwise and then cut crosswise into 4 chunks. Leave behind any juices and seeds that spill onto your cutting board.

1. In a bowl, combine soy sauce, chicken stock and cornstarch and stir well into a smooth sauce. Add pork and stir to coat evenly. Set aside for 10 minutes.

2. In a small bowl, combine orange juice, cumin, salt, pepper and cinnamon and stir well. Set aside.

3. Heat a wok or a large deep skillet over high heat. Add oil and swirl to coat pan. Add garlic and toss well, until fragrant, about 15 seconds.

4. Add pork mixture and spread into a single layer. Cook, undisturbed, until edges change color, about 30 seconds. Toss again. Cook, tossing occasionally, until no longer pink, about 1 minute more.

5. Add orange juice mixture, pouring in around sides of pan. Toss well. Cook, tossing often, until pork is cooked through, 1 to 2 minutes more.

6. Add tomatoes, green onions and mint. Toss well. Cook, tossing occasionally, until tomatoes begin to soften, about 30 seconds. Transfer to a serving plate. Serve hot or warm.

Variation: If you'd like a more intense flavor note, add 1 tsp (5 mL) orange zest along with the spices and replace the pepper with hot pepper flakes for a little heat.

Peppery Pork with Salsa and Corn

Serves 4

You can use your favorite prepared salsa to create bright, satisfying flavor in this quick stir-fried dish. If you like chile heat, choose a spicy salsa, or add a spoonful of chopped fresh serrano chiles or hot pepper flakes to the pan along with the bell peppers.

TIP

It's fine to use 1/2 cup (125 mL) of either green or red bell peppers, or go for yellow and orange ones if you want a little sunshine in the dish.

1 tbsp	soy sauce	15 mL
1 tbsp	dry sherry or Shaoxing rice wine	15 mL
1/2 tsp	salt or to taste	2 mL
1/2 tsp	granulated sugar	2 mL
8 oz	boneless pork (such as loin or tenderloin), thinly sliced	250 g
2 tbsp	vegetable oil	25 mL
2 tbsp	chopped garlic	25 mL
2 tbsp	chopped onion	25 mL
1/2 cup	chopped red and/or green bell peppers (see Tip, left)	125 mL
2/3 cup	frozen corn	150 mL
2 tbsp	chicken stock or water	25 mL
1/4 cup	chunky tomato salsa	50 mL
1/4 cup	chopped fresh cilantro	50 mL
1/4 cup	chopped green onions	50 mL

1. In a bowl, combine soy sauce, sherry, salt and sugar and stir well. Add pork and stir to coat evenly. Set aside for 10 minutes.

2. Heat a wok or a large deep skillet over high heat. Add oil and swirl to coat pan. Add garlic and onion and toss well, until fragrant, about 15 seconds. Add bell peppers. Toss well. Cook, tossing occasionally, until fragrant and softened, about 1 minute.

3. Add pork mixture and spread into a single layer. Cook, undisturbed, until edges change color, about 30 seconds. Toss well. Cook, tossing occasionally, until no longer pink, 1 to 2 minutes more.

4. Add corn and chicken stock and toss well. Cook, tossing occasionally, until corn is hot and pork is cooked through, 1 to 2 minutes more.

5. Add salsa and toss well. Add cilantro and green onions and toss once to mix well. Transfer to a serving plate. Serve hot or warm.

Green Chile Pork with Hominy, Cilantro and Lime

1 tsp	ground cumin	5 mL
½ tsp	dried oregano leaves	2 mL
1 tsp	salt or to taste	5 mL
¼ tsp	freshly ground pepper	1 mL
8 oz	boneless pork (such as loin or tenderloin), thinly sliced	250 g
3 tbsp	chicken stock or water (see Tips, right)	45 mL
2 tbsp	freshly squeezed lime or lemon juice	25 mL
2 tbsp	vegetable oil	25 mL
1 tbsp	chopped garlic	15 mL
¼ cup	chopped onion	50 mL
¾ cup	hominy, (see Tips, right)	175 mL
1	can (4 oz/113 g) diced roasted green chiles (about ½ cup/125 mL)	1
⅓ cup	loosely packed fresh cilantro	75 mL

1. In a bowl, combine cumin, oregano, salt and pepper and stir well. Add pork and toss to coat evenly. Set aside for 10 minutes.

2. In a small bowl, combine chicken stock and lime juice. Set aside.

3. Heat a wok or a large deep skillet over high heat. Add oil and swirl to coat pan. Add garlic and onion and cook, tossing occasionally, until onion is softened and just beginning to brown, about 1 minute.

4. Add pork mixture and spread into a single layer. Cook, undisturbed, until edges change color, about 30 seconds. Toss well. Cook, tossing occasionally, until no longer pink, 1 to 2 minutes more.

5. Add hominy and toss well. Cook, undisturbed, for 1 minute. Toss well. Add green chiles and chicken broth mixture. Toss well.

6. Cook, tossing occasionally, until pork is cooked through and all ingredients are hot and well combined, about 1 minute more. Add cilantro and toss well. Transfer to a deep serving platter or shallow bowl to hold the sauce. Serve hot or warm.

Serves 4

This recipe celebrates some of New Mexico's signature ingredients and flavors, including roasted green chile peppers, cilantro and hominy. This extraordinarily tasty dish happens to be ready to eat in just a few minutes time. It is especially tasty with warm tortillas, as well as rice, polenta or warm bread.

TIPS

If you buy canned hominy rather than frozen, it will be packed in a pleasing salty juice which is full of hominy's corn flavor. I like to use this in place of some or all of the chicken broth called for in this recipe.

Look for cans of both hominy and roasted green chiles on supermarket shelves.

Stir-Fried "Piccata" with Pork and Peas

Serves 4

You will love this stir-fry spin on the classic Italian dish, veal piccata. It tastes absolutely delicious, which it is; it also tastes rich, which it is not. It is lovely with couscous, rice or a crusty loaf of Italian bread for savoring every little drop of sauce. If you adore lemon's bright flavor, you'll need two here, one to squeeze for cooking and another to cut into wedges for garnishing and enjoying with the finished dish.

3 tbsp	freshly squeezed lemon juice (about 1 lemon)	45 mL
2 tbsp	chicken stock or water	25 mL
1 tbsp	cornstarch	15 mL
½ tsp	salt or to taste	2 mL
¼ tsp	freshly ground pepper	1 mL
¼ tsp	dried thyme leaves	1 mL
12 oz	boneless pork (such as loin or tenderloin), thinly sliced	375 g
2 tbsp	vegetable oil	25 mL
2 tsp	finely chopped garlic	10 mL
1 tbsp	finely chopped shallots or onion	15 mL
½ cup	frozen peas, thawed	125 mL
1 tsp	butter	5 mL
1 tbsp	chopped Italian parsley	15 mL
	Lemon wedges	

1. In a bowl, combine lemon juice, chicken stock, cornstarch, salt, pepper and thyme and stir into a smooth sauce. Add pork and stir to coat evenly. Set aside 10 minutes.

2. Heat a wok or a large skillet over high heat. Add oil and swirl to coat pan. Add garlic and shallots and toss well, until fragrant and golden, about 15 seconds.

3. Add pork mixture and spread into a single layer. Cook, undisturbed, until edges change color, about 30 seconds. Toss well. Cook, tossing occasionally, until no longer pink, 1 to 2 minutes more.

4. Add peas and cook, tossing occasionally, until pork is cooked through and peas are hot, 1 to 2 minutes more.

5. Remove from heat and add butter and parsley and toss well. Transfer to a serving plate and garnish with a few lemon wedges. Serve hot or warm.

Pork with Baby Corn and Tomatoes in Cilantro Sauce

½ cup	loosely packed fresh cilantro, divided	125 mL
2 tbsp	coarsely chopped shallots or onion	25 mL
1 tbsp	coarsely chopped garlic	15 mL
1 tbsp	coarsely chopped gingerroot	15 mL
1 tbsp	coarsely chopped serrano or jalapeño pepper	15 mL
2 tbsp	water	25 mL
8	cobs canned baby corn, drained	8
2 tbsp	fish sauce	25 mL
2 tsp	white or cider vinegar	10 mL
2 tsp	granulated sugar	10 mL
½ tsp	salt or to taste	2 mL
2 tbsp	vegetable oil	25 mL
8 oz	boneless pork (such as loin or tenderloin), thinly sliced	250 g
½ cup	halved cherry tomatoes	125 mL

Serves 4

This dish issues an aromatic invitation to the table while it cooks. It fulfills that promise deliciously with vibrant, hearty flavors and a tasty Thai-style sauce to enjoy over rice or another grain.

1. In a blender, combine ¼ cup (50 mL) of the cilantro leaves, shallots, garlic, ginger, serrano pepper and water. Grind well, stopping to scrape sides as necessary, to a fairly smooth paste. Transfer to a small bowl.

2. Chop each cob of baby corn into 4 pieces. Chop remaining cilantro leaves coarsely. Set both aside separately.

3. In a small bowl, combine fish sauce, vinegar, sugar and salt and stir well. Set aside.

4. Heat a wok or a large deep skillet over medium-high heat. Add oil and swirl to coat pan. Add pork and spread into a single layer. Cook, undisturbed, until edges change color, about 30 seconds. Toss well.

5. Carefully add cilantro paste to pan, it will sizzle wildly. Reduce heat to maintain a lively sizzle but avoid burning and popping. Cook, stirring and pressing, until fragrant and softened, 1 to 2 minutes. Toss well.

6. Add baby corn and toss again. Cook, tossing often, until pork is no longer pink, 1 to 2 minutes. Add fish sauce mixture, pouring in around sides of pan. Toss well. Cook, tossing occasionally, until pork is cooked through and coated with a smooth sauce, about 1 minute more.

7. Add cherry tomatoes and remaining chopped cilantro leaves and toss well. Transfer to a serving plate. Serve hot or warm.

Fiery Thai-Style Pork with Green Beans

Serves 4

Spicy-hot and hearty, my streamlined version of Thailand's *moo paht prik king* makes an outstanding one-dish meal over rice.

TIP

For this dish, you can cut pork tenderloin or a thick pork chop across the grain into thin slices, or cut a thin pork chop or two into 1-inch (2.5 cm) pieces.

8 oz	fresh green beans or Asian long beans, trimmed and chopped into 2-inch (5 cm) lengths	250 g
⅓ cup	chicken stock or water	75 mL
2 tbsp	Thai fish sauce	25 mL
1 tbsp	palm sugar or brown sugar	15 mL
3 tbsp	vegetable oil	45 mL
2 tbsp	Thai-style red curry paste	25 mL
8 oz	thinly sliced pork (see Tip, left)	250 g

1. In a small saucepan of boiling water, cook green beans until tender-crisp, about 3 minutes. Drain and set aside.

2. Meanwhile, in a small bowl, combine chicken stock, fish sauce and palm sugar and stir well.

3. Heat a wok or a large deep skillet over medium heat. Add oil and swirl to coat pan. Add curry paste and cook, mixing it gently into the oil with a spatula to soften the paste and season the oil, 2 to 3 minutes.

4. Increase heat to medium-high. As soon as curry paste begins to bubble up, add pork and spread into a single layer. Cook, undisturbed, for 1 minute. Toss well.

5. Add green beans and fish sauce mixture. Toss well and bring to a boil. Cook, tossing occasionally, until pork is cooked through, 2 to 3 minutes more. Transfer to a serving dish. Serve hot or warm.

Pork with Thai Red Curry Paste

1	medium Asian eggplant (about 8 oz/250 g)	1
2 tbsp	fish sauce	25 mL
1/4 cup	chicken stock or water	50 mL
2 tsp	granulated sugar	10 mL
3 tbsp	vegetable oil	45 mL
3 tbsp	Thai-style red curry paste	45 mL
8 oz	boneless pork (such as loin or tenderloin), thinly sliced	250 g
1/2 cup	frozen green beans (see Tips, right)	125 mL
6	fresh makrut lime leaves, optional	6
1/4 cup	chopped red bell pepper	50 mL
1/2 cup	fresh basil or mint leaves	125 mL

1. Trim both ends from eggplant, halve it lengthwise and then cut crosswise into 1/2-inch (1 cm) chunks.

2. In a small bowl, combine fish sauce, chicken stock and sugar and stir well. Set aside.

3. Heat a wok or a large deep skillet over medium heat. Add oil and swirl to coat pan. Add curry paste and cook, mixing it gently into the oil with a spatula to soften the paste and season the oil, 2 to 3 minutes.

4. Add pork and spread into a single layer. Add eggplant and toss again. Cook, tossing occasionally, until pork is evenly seasoned with curry paste sauce and is no longer pink, 1 to 2 minutes.

5. Add green beans, fish sauce mixture and lime leaves, if using, and toss gently to mix well. Cook, gently tossing occasionally, until vegetables are tender and pork is cooked through, 2 to 3 minutes more. Add 2 to 4 tbsp (25 to 60 mL) water if needed to keep from sticking.

6. Remove from heat and stir in red peppers and fresh basil leaves. Transfer to a serving plate. Serve hot or warm.

Serves 4

Thai people adore *moo paht peht*, a dish of pork cooked quickly in a simple sauce based on fiery red curry paste. Rice is the ideal companion for the chile-based sauce. I like to round out the meal with a salad of field greens tossed with raisins and chunks of apple with a sweet-and-tangy dressing. Wild lime leaves are a lovely addition, but don't worry if you can't find them. It will still be a delicious dish.

TIPS

This dish cooks at a medium level of heat, rather than high heat like so many stir-fry dishes. This keeps the curry paste from sticking and burning.

To use fresh green beans instead of frozen ones, trim and cut into 1-inch (2.5 cm) lengths. Cook them in boiling water, until they are bright green and becoming tender, but are still tender-crisp, 3 to 4 minutes. Rinse with cold water, drain well and set aside to add to this dish. You'll need 12 to 15 green beans to make up the amount you need here.

Pork in Red Curry Peanut Sauce

Serves 4

This saucy dish is delicious served over noodles and equally tasty with its traditional companion, rice.

TIPS

If you like things spicy, increase the curry paste to 2 tbsp (25 mL).

For the optional flourish of herbs at the end of cooking, you could use either Asian basil, with its purple stems and pointed leaves, or the widely available Italian basil. If you use the latter and the leaves are large, tear or cut into small pieces shortly before serving time. This provides the maximum flavor and aroma in the finished dish.

2 tbsp	fish sauce	25 mL
2 tbsp	brown sugar	25 mL
2 tbsp	smooth peanut butter	25 mL
1 tbsp	vegetable oil	15 mL
1 tbsp	finely chopped garlic	15 mL
8 oz	boneless pork (such as loin or tenderloin), thinly sliced	250 g
½ cup	unsweetened coconut milk	125 mL
1 tbsp	Thai-style red curry paste (see Tips, left)	15 mL
½ cup	frozen tiny peas (see Tips, page 104)	125 mL
½ cup	fresh basil leaves, optional (see Tips, left)	125 mL

1. In a small bowl, combine fish sauce and brown sugar and stir well. Add peanut butter, but don't stir it in; it will melt into the sauce when it is added to the hot pan. Place a bowl next to the stove.

2. Heat a wok or a large deep skillet over high heat. Add oil and swirl to coat pan. Add garlic and toss well, until fragrant, about 15 seconds.

3. Add pork and spread into a single layer. Cook, undisturbed, until edges change color, about 30 seconds. Toss well. Cook, tossing occasionally, until no longer pink, 1 to 2 minutes more. Transfer to reserved bowl and set aside.

4. Reduce heat to medium-high. Add coconut milk to pan and bring to a gentle boil, stirring well to keep it from sticking around sides of pan, about 1 minute.

5. When coconut milk is bubbling gently, add curry paste, mixing it gently into the oil with a spatula to soften the paste, about 1 minute.

6. Return pork to pan with any juices. Add fish sauce mixture and frozen peas. Toss well. Cook, gently tossing occasionally, until pork is cooked through, peanut butter is dissolved into the sauce and peas are hot, about 2 minutes more.

7. Add basil leaves, if using, and toss well. Transfer to a small deep serving platter or a shallow bowl to hold the sauce. Serve hot or warm.

Peppery Pork Slices with Bamboo Shoots and Mint

3 tbsp	fish sauce	45 mL
1 tbsp	chicken stock or water	15 mL
1 tsp	hot pepper flakes	5 mL
1/2 tsp	granulated sugar	2 mL
1/2 tsp	freshly ground pepper	2 mL
2 tbsp	vegetable oil	25 mL
1 tbsp	chopped garlic	15 mL
1/2 cup	chopped onion	125 mL
8 oz	boneless pork (such as loin or tenderloin), thinly sliced	250 g
1 cup	drained rinsed canned sliced bamboo shoots (see Tips, page 90)	250 mL
3 tbsp	chopped fresh mint or cilantro leaves	45 mL
2 tbsp	chopped green onions	25 mL

Serves 4

This combination of pork with bamboo shoots and hot pepper flakes is popular throughout Asia. Cooks in Northeastern Thailand season it with fish sauce and a handful of fresh mint, a perfect counterpoint to the strong, salty flavors central to the dish. I love it with chilled asparagus spears and a bowl of salsa.

1. In a small bowl, combine fish sauce, chicken stock, hot pepper flakes, sugar and pepper and stir well. Set aside.

2. Heat a wok or a large deep skillet over medium-high heat. Add oil and swirl to coat pan. Add garlic and toss well, until fragrant, about 30 seconds. Add onion and cook, tossing well, until beginning to wilt, about 1 minute.

3. Add pork and spread into a single layer. Cook, undisturbed, until edges change color, about 1 minute. Toss well. Cook, tossing occasionally, until no longer pink, about 1 minute.

4. Add bamboo shoots and toss well. Add fish sauce mixture, pouring in around sides of pan. Toss well. Cook, tossing often, until pork is cooked through, 1 to 2 minutes more. Remove from heat and add fresh mint leaves and green onions and toss well. Transfer to a serving plate. Serve hot or warm.

Spicy Garlic Pork with Mushrooms and Bamboo

Serves 4

Rustic flavors and a mixture of textures make this dish a hearty centerpiece to an Asian-style meal with rice. I like a small bowl of cucumber slices and cherry tomatoes on the side to cool things off in a refreshing way.

1 tbsp	dry sherry or Shaoxing rice wine	15 mL
1 tsp	Asian sesame oil	5 mL
1 tsp	dark soy sauce, molasses or honey, optional	5 mL
8 oz	boneless pork (such as loin or tenderloin), thinly sliced	250 g
1 tbsp	soy sauce	15 mL
1 tbsp	chicken stock or water	15 mL
1 tsp	granulated sugar	5 mL
1 tsp	salt or to taste	5 mL
1 tsp	hot pepper flakes	5 mL
2 tbsp	vegetable oil	25 mL
1 tbsp	chopped garlic	15 mL
1 cup	thinly sliced mushrooms	250 mL
½ cup	drained rinsed canned sliced bamboo shoots	125 mL
¼ cup	chopped green onions	50 mL

1. In a bowl, combine sherry, sesame oil and dark soy sauce, if using, and stir well. Add pork and stir to coat well. Set aside for 10 minutes.
2. In a small bowl, combine soy sauce, chicken stock, sugar, salt and hot pepper flakes and stir well. Set aside.
3. Heat a wok or a large deep skillet over high heat. Add oil and swirl to coat pan. Add garlic and toss well, until fragrant, about 15 seconds.
4. Add pork mixture and spread into a single layer. Cook, undisturbed, until edges change color, about 1 minute. Toss well. Cook, tossing occasionally, until no longer pink, 1 to 2 minutes.
5. Add mushrooms and bamboo shoots and cook, tossing often, until mushrooms are softened, about 1 minute more.
6. Add soy sauce mixture, pouring in around sides of pan. Toss well. Cook, tossing often, until pork is cooked through and everything is evenly seasoned, about 1 minute more. Add green onions and toss well. Transfer to a serving plate. Serve hot or warm.

Ground Pork with Chiles and Holy Basil

2 tbsp	fish sauce	25 mL
2 tbsp	chicken stock	25 mL
2 tbsp	soy sauce	25 mL
1 tbsp	granulated sugar	15 mL
1 tsp	salt or to taste	5 mL
1 tsp	minced hot green chiles or hot pepper flakes	5 mL
2 tbsp	vegetable oil	25 mL
½ cup	coarsely chopped onion	125 mL
1 tbsp	coarsely chopped garlic	15 mL
8 oz	ground pork	250 g
1 cup	fresh holy basil or mint leaves	250 mL

Serves 4

This classic Thai dish is served over rice for a simple and delicious lunch. It's also good over couscous or noodles. Finding fresh holy basil is a challenge in the West, but you can use any fresh basil or fresh mint leaves in its place with delicious results. Thai cooks make this dish with very finely chopped chicken as well as with pork.

1. In a small bowl, combine fish sauce, chicken stock, soy sauce, sugar, salt and hot pepper flakes and stir well. Set aside.

2. Heat a wok or a large deep skillet over high heat. Add oil and swirl to coat pan. Add onion and garlic and toss well, until fragrant, about 30 seconds.

3. Add ground pork and using your spatula or a large spoon break up meat, spreading out to cook evenly. Cook, tossing occasionally, until almost all the meat has changed color, about 1 minute.

4. Add fish sauce mixture, pouring in around sides of pan. Cook, tossing often, until pork is cooked through and the seasonings form a thin, smooth sauce, 2 to 3 minutes more.

5. Add basil and toss well. Transfer to a serving plate. Serve hot or warm.

Variation: You could use ground chicken or turkey instead of pork. Add an extra tablespoon (15 mL) of oil to keep the meat from sticking to the pan

Crumbly Pork with Peas

Serves 4

This tastes wonderful, cooks fast and uses ingredients which are easy to find and keep on hand. You could jazz it up with frozen edamame beans instead of peas, or a handful of chopped cilantro, green onions or frozen corn.

TIP

Resist the urge to toss and stir this dish too often. Ground meat needs time to cook directly on the hot surface of the pan, so use your spatula to turn it and chop as it cooks.

2 tbsp	soy sauce	25 mL
1 tsp	granulated sugar	5 mL
½ tsp	salt or to taste	2 mL
¼ cup	chicken stock or water	50 mL
2 tbsp	vegetable oil	25 mL
2 tbsp	chopped fresh gingerroot	25 mL
2 tsp	chopped garlic	10 mL
8 oz	ground pork	250 g
½ cup	frozen peas	125 mL

1. In a small bowl, combine soy sauce, sugar, salt and chicken stock and stir well. Set aside.

2. Heat a wok or a large deep skillet over high heat. Add oil and swirl to coat pan. Add ginger and garlic and toss well, until fragrant, about 15 seconds.

3. Add ground pork and using your spatula or a large spoon break up meat, spreading out to cook evenly. Cook, tossing occasionally, until no longer pink, about 1 minute.

4. Add soy sauce mixture, pouring in around sides of pan. Toss well. Add peas. Cook, tossing occasionally, until pork is cooked through and peas are hot, 1 to 2 minutes. Transfer to a serving plate. Serve hot or warm.

Shrimp

Shrimp and Broccoli in Oyster Sauce

Pink and green and tasty, this basic stir-fry can top a plate of rice, couscous, quinoa or a side of noodles with Asian sesame oil, as a one-dish meal. I like this with a mixture of broccoli and cauliflower florets.

TIP

You'll need about one generous bunch of broccoli to make enough florets for this dish.

2 tbsp	oyster sauce	25 mL
2 tbsp	dry sherry or Shaoxing rice wine	25 mL
1 tbsp	soy sauce	15 mL
1 tsp	honey or granulated sugar	5 mL
3 tbsp	chicken stock or water	45 mL
2 tsp	cornstarch	10 mL
2 tbsp	vegetable oil	25 mL
1 tbsp	chopped shallots or onion	15 mL
1 tbsp	chopped garlic	15 mL
2 tsp	chopped fresh gingerroot	10 mL
3 cups	very small (1 inch/2.5 cm) broccoli florets (see Tip, left)	750 mL
12 oz	medium shrimp, peeled and deveined	375 g

1. In small bowl, combine oyster sauce, sherry, soy sauce and honey and stir well. Set aside.

2. In another small bowl, combine chicken stock and cornstarch and stir well into a smooth sauce. Set aside.

3. Heat a wok or a large deep skillet over high heat. Add oil and swirl to coat pan. Add shallots, garlic and ginger and toss well, until fragrant, about 15 seconds.

4. Add broccoli and cook, tossing well, until bright green, about 2 minutes more. Add shrimp and cook, tossing occasionally, until most of the edges turn pink, 1 to 2 minutes.

5. Add oyster sauce mixture, pouring in around sides of pan. Toss well. Cook, tossing occasionally, until broccoli is tender-crisp and shrimp are cooked through, 1 to 2 minutes more.

6. Stir chicken stock mixture and pour into pan. Cook, tossing occasionally, until sauce is slightly thickened and coats everything evenly, about 1 minute more. Transfer to a serving plate. Serve hot or warm.

Seared Shrimp with Sweet Tiny Peas

1 tbsp	soy sauce	15 mL
1 tbsp	dry sherry or Shaoxing rice wine	15 mL
1 tsp	granulated sugar	5 mL
1 tsp	salt or to taste	5 mL
2 tbsp	vegetable oil	25 mL
1 tbsp	coarsely chopped garlic	15 mL
¼ cup	coarsely chopped onion	50 mL
12 oz	medium shrimp, peeled and deveined	375 g
1 cup	frozen tiny peas (see Tip, right)	250 mL
¼ cup	chicken stock or water	50 mL
2 tbsp	thinly sliced green onions	25 mL

Serves 4

This simple dish of plump pink shrimp dotted with green peas is simple, delicious and ready fast. Served over rice, with a salad on the side, it makes a fine meal for a busy night.

TIP

Frozen tiny peas are also referred to as "petite" and "baby." You can also use regular-size frozen peas, if you allow a little extra cooking time to heat them through.

1. In a small bowl, combine soy sauce, sherry, sugar and salt and stir well. Set aside.

2. Heat a wok or a large deep skillet over medium-high heat. Add oil and swirl to coat pan. Add garlic and toss well, until fragrant, about 30 seconds. Add onion and cook, tossing occasionally, for 1 minute.

3. Add shrimp and spread into a single layer. Cook, undisturbed, until most of the edges turn pink, about 1 minute. Toss well. Cook other side, about 30 seconds more.

4. Add soy sauce mixture, pouring in around sides of pan. Toss well. Add peas and toss well. Add chicken stock and cook, tossing occasionally, until shrimp are just cooked through, 1 to 2 minutes more. Add green onions and toss once more. Transfer to a serving plate. Serve hot or warm.

Variation: You can use cooked fresh peas in this dish, adding them to the pan at the same point as the frozen tiny peas, and cooking them just until they are heated through. You can also use regular-size frozen peas or frozen edamame beans, if you allow a little extra cooking time to heat the edamame beans through.

Rainbow Pepper Shrimp

This combination of shrimp and a rainbow of sweet pepper chunks makes for a beautiful invitation to the table.

TIPS

Chop the peppers into chunks, about 1 1/2 inches (4 cm) in diameter; I like to aim for a triangle shape, but anything bite-size will work.

The shrimp will absorb the seasonings and glisten with flavor; the dish will have very little sauce.

2 tbsp	dry sherry or Shaoxing rice wine	25 mL
2 tbsp	water	25 mL
1 tbsp	soy sauce	15 mL
2 tsp	cornstarch	10 mL
1 tsp	granulated sugar	5 mL
1/2 tsp	salt or to taste	2 mL
2 tbsp	vegetable oil	25 mL
1 tbsp	finely chopped garlic	15 mL
2 tsp	finely chopped fresh gingerroot	10 mL
1 1/2 cups	chunks red, green and yellow bell peppers (see Tips, left)	375 mL
12 oz	medium shrimp, peeled and deveined	375 g

1. In a small bowl, combine sherry, water, soy sauce, cornstarch, sugar and salt and stir well into a smooth sauce. Set aside.

2. Heat a wok or a large deep skillet over medium-high heat. Add oil and swirl to coat pan. Add garlic and ginger and toss well, until fragrant, about 15 seconds. Add bell peppers and cook, tossing twice, for 1 minute.

3. Add shrimp and spread into a single layer. Cook, undisturbed, until most of the edges turn pink, about 1 to 2 minutes. Toss well. Cook other side, about 30 seconds more.

4. Stir soy sauce mixture and pour in around sides of pan. Toss well. Cook, tossing occasionally, until peppers are tender-crisp and shrimp are cooked through, 1 to 2 minutes more. Transfer to a serving plate. Serve hot or warm.

Cantonese-Style Shrimp with Black Bean Sauce

2 tbsp	salted black beans (see Tips, right)	25 mL
2 tbsp	finely chopped fresh gingerroot	25 mL
2 tsp	finely chopped garlic	10 mL
¼ cup	chicken stock	50 mL
1 tsp	cornstarch	5 mL
2 tbsp	vegetable oil	25 mL
12 oz	medium shrimp, peeled and deveined	375 g
3 tbsp	finely chopped green onions	45 mL

1. In a small bowl, combine black beans, ginger and garlic and mash with the back of a spoon into a rough paste (see Tips, right). Set aside.

2. In another small bowl, combine chicken stock and cornstarch and stir well into a smooth sauce. Set aside.

3. Heat a wok or a large deep skillet over medium-high heat. Add oil and swirl to coat pan. Add shrimp and spread into a single layer. Cook, undisturbed, until most of the edges turn pink, about 1 minute. Toss well. Cook other side, about 30 seconds more.

4. Scrape black bean mixture onto shrimp and toss well. Stir chicken stock mixture and pour in around sides of pan. Toss well. Cook, tossing occasionally, until shrimp are cooked through and sauce thickens, about 1 minute more. Add green onions and toss once more. Transfer to a serving plate. Serve hot or warm.

Serves 4

A Cantonese-style classic, this dish delivers intense sharp-and-salty flavor with lots of delectable dark sauce, perfect spooned over rice, noodles or couscous. You can serve it with crusty bread, dipping it in the sauce between bites of shrimp.

TIPS

The salted, fermented black beans used in Chinese cooking (also known as Chinese-style black beans or fermented black beans) provide a deliciously pungent flavor to stir-fried and steamed dishes. After you open a new package, transfer the soft, dark beans to a jar and store them airtight at room temperature for up to 6 months.

To mash the black beans, ginger and garlic, you could also pile them up on your cutting board and chop them together to blend them into a coarse paste.

Hoisin Shrimp
with Celery and Peas

Serves 4

The deep wintry flavor of hoisin sauce provides the melody for this tasty dish, while celery adds a warm-weather note. It anchors a rice meal wonderfully, any time of year.

TIP

For the most pleasing celery texture, trim ends to make even stalks, pull away the strings along the curved outer side, and then slice each stalk on the diagonal to form slender pieces in the shape of the letter "c." You could also trim, string and chop celery stalks into ½-inch (1 cm) chunks.

1 tbsp	soy sauce	15 mL
2 tsp	hoisin sauce	10 mL
1 tsp	white or cider vinegar	5 mL
½ tsp	granulated sugar	2 mL
½ tsp	sesame oil	2 mL
½ tsp	salt or to taste	2 mL
½ tsp	freshly ground pepper	2 mL
2 tbsp	vegetable oil	25 mL
2 tsp	chopped garlic	10 mL
1 tbsp	chopped gingerroot	15 mL
3 tbsp	coarsely chopped green onions	45 mL
1 cup	thinly sliced celery, cut on the diagonal (see Tip, left)	250 mL
12 oz	medium shrimp, peeled and deveined	375 g
½ cup	frozen peas	125 mL
1 tbsp	coarsely chopped fresh cilantro	15 mL

1. In a small bowl, combine soy sauce, hoisin sauce, vinegar, sugar, sesame oil, salt and pepper and stir well. Set aside.
2. Heat a wok or a large deep skillet over medium-high heat. Add oil and swirl to coat pan. Add garlic, ginger and green onions and cook, tossing often, until softened and fragrant, about 1 minute. Add celery and cook, tossing well, for 1 minute more.
3. Add shrimp and spread into a single layer. Cook, undisturbed, until most of the edges turn pink, about 1 minute. Toss well. Cook other side, about 30 seconds more.
4. Add peas. Add soy sauce mixture, pouring in around sides of pan. Toss well. Cook, tossing occasionally, until shrimp are cooked through and peas are hot, 1 to 2 minutes more. Add cilantro and toss well. Transfer to a serving plate. Serve hot or warm.

Sherry-Scented Shrimp with Candied Walnuts

2 tbsp	dry sherry or Shaoxing rice wine	25 mL
2 tbsp	water	25 mL
1 tbsp	soy sauce	15 mL
2 tsp	cornstarch	10 mL
1 tsp	granulated sugar	5 mL
½ tsp	salt or to taste	2 mL
2 tbsp	vegetable oil	25 mL
2 tsp	finely chopped garlic	10 mL
1 tsp	finely chopped fresh gingerroot	5 mL
12 oz	medium shrimp, peeled and deveined	375 g
1 cup	Candied Walnuts (see recipe, page 341) or toasted walnut halves (see Tips, right)	250 mL

1. In a small bowl, combine sherry, water, soy sauce, cornstarch, sugar and salt and stir well into a smooth sauce. Set aside.

2. Heat a wok or a large deep skillet over medium-high heat. Add oil and swirl to coat pan. Add garlic and ginger and toss well, until fragrant, about 30 seconds.

3. Add shrimp and spread into a single layer. Cook, undisturbed, until most of the edges turn pink, about 1 minute. Toss well. Cook other side, about 30 seconds more.

4. Stir soy sauce mixture and pour in over shrimp. Toss well. Add walnuts and cook, tossing once or twice, until shrimp are cooked through, for 1 minute more. Transfer to a serving plate. Serve hot or warm.

Serves 4

This beautiful and tasty dish features candied walnuts, which you can make in advance and keep on hand as a snack as well as a component of this elegant dish.

TIPS

The shrimp will absorb the seasonings and glisten with flavor; the dish will have very little sauce.

If you don't have candied walnuts, you can use walnut halves instead. Toast them in a 350°F (180°C) oven for about 15 minutes or until fragrant to heighten their flavor.

Sweet-and-Salty Shrimp
with Pineapple and Carrots

Serves 4

This Thai-style stir-fry provides sweet, salty and tangy flavors all in one dish. You can add a splash of hot pepper sauce at the end if you want to fire up the sauce with a little chile heat.

TIP

Canned or fresh pineapple chunks work equally well here.

3 tbsp	fish sauce	45 mL
1 tbsp	soy sauce	15 mL
1 tbsp	oyster sauce	15 mL
1 tsp	granulated sugar	5 mL
1/4 tsp	freshly ground pepper	1 mL
2 tbsp	vegetable oil	25 mL
2 tsp	chopped garlic	10 mL
8 oz	medium shrimp, peeled and deveined	250 g
2 tbsp	chopped onion	25 mL
3/4 cup	pineapple chunks (see Tip, left)	175 mL
1/3 cup	shredded carrots	75 mL
2 tbsp	chopped green onions	25 mL
2 tbsp	chopped fresh cilantro	25 mL

1. In a small bowl, combine fish sauce, soy sauce, oyster sauce, sugar and pepper and stir well. Set aside.

2. Heat a wok or a large deep skillet over high heat. Add oil and swirl to coat pan.

3. Add garlic and toss well, until fragrant, about 15 seconds.

4. Add shrimp and spread into a single layer. Cook, undisturbed, until most of the edges turn pink, about 1 minute. Toss well. Cook other side, about 30 seconds more.

5. Add onion, pineapple and carrots and toss well. Cook, tossing occasionally, until onion is fragrant, about 1 minute.

6. Add fish sauce mixture, pouring in around sides of pan. Toss well. Cook, tossing occasionally, until pineapple is hot, carrots are tender and shrimp are cooked through, 1 to 2 minutes more.

7. Add green onions and cilantro and toss well. Transfer to a serving plate. Serve hot or warm.

Five-Spice Pork with Bok Choy and Green Onions (page 91)

Overleaf: Garlic Pork with Arugula and Sweet Peppers (page 108)

Seared Shrimp with Summer Squash and Dill Confetti

1	small zucchini	1
1	small yellow summer squash	1
1 tbsp	dry sherry or Shaoxing rice wine	15 mL
2 tsp	soy sauce	10 mL
1 tsp	granulated sugar	5 mL
1 tsp	salt or to taste	5 mL
2 tbsp	vegetable oil	25 mL
1 tbsp	chopped garlic	15 mL
1/4 cup	chopped onion	50 mL
8 oz	medium shrimp, peeled and deveined	250 g
2 tbsp	chopped fresh dill	25 mL
1 tsp	Asian sesame oil	5 mL

Serves 4

You can use all zucchini or all yellow squash for this dish, which is full of flavors as bright as its array of colors would suggest. With green and yellow squash, pink shrimp and a confetti of dill, you have an almost irresistible invitation to the table. Rice is always wonderful with a stir-fry like this, but couscous makes a particularly pleasing alternative here.

1. Trim both ends from zucchini and yellow squash and quarter each lengthwise. Slice each quarter crosswise into little triangles, about 1/4-inch (0.5 cm) thick. Set aside.

2. In a small bowl, combine sherry, soy sauce, sugar and salt and stir well. Set aside.

3. Heat a wok or a large deep skillet over high heat. Add vegetable oil and swirl to coat pan. Add garlic and onion and toss well, until fragrant, about 15 seconds.

4. Add shrimp and spread into a single layer. Cook, undisturbed, until most of the edges turn pink, about 1 minute. Toss well. Cook other side, about 30 seconds more.

5. Add zucchini and squash and toss well. Cook, tossing occasionally, until squash has begun to wilt, about 1 minute more.

6. Add sherry mixture, pouring in around sides of pan. Cook, tossing occasionally, until zucchini and squash are tender-crisp and shrimp are cooked through, about 1 minute more. Add dill and sesame oil. Toss well. Transfer to a serving plate. Serve hot or warm.

Overleaf: Shrimp with Tomatoes, Lemon and Parsley (page 133)

Stir-Fried Shrimp with Olives and Smoked Paprika (page 135)

Shrimp in Sweet-and-Spicy Garlic Sauce

Serves 4

This dish cooks fast and delivers a fabulously tasty little sauce to savor with rice or noodles. You could boost the amount of chiles for a hotter note.

2 tbsp	fish sauce	25 mL
1 tbsp	granulated sugar	15 mL
½ tsp	hot pepper flakes	2 mL
½ cup	water	125 mL
2 tbsp	vegetable oil	25 mL
1 tbsp	finely chopped garlic	15 mL
½ cup	finely chopped onion	125 mL
12 oz	medium shrimp, peeled and deveined	375 g
2 tbsp	chopped green onions	25 mL
2 tbsp	chopped fresh cilantro	25 mL

1. In a bowl, combine fish sauce, sugar, hot pepper flakes and water and stir well. Set aside.

2. Heat a wok or a large deep skillet over medium-high heat. Add oil and swirl to coat pan. Add garlic and onion and toss well, until fragrant, about 30 seconds.

3. Add shrimp and spread into a single layer. Cook, undisturbed, until most of the edges turn pink, about 1 minute. Toss well. Cook other side, about 30 seconds more.

4. Add fish sauce mixture, pouring in around sides of pan. Toss well. Cook, tossing occasionally, until shrimp are cooked through and other ingredients combine to make a thin sauce, 2 to 3 minutes more.

5. Add green onion and cilantro and toss well. Transfer to a serving plate. Serve hot or warm.

Stir-Fried Shrimp with Lima Beans and Garlic Galore

2 tbsp	fish sauce	25 mL
2 tsp	granulated sugar	10 mL
¼ tsp	freshly ground pepper	1 mL
2 tbsp	vegetable oil	25 mL
2 tbsp	chopped garlic	25 mL
12 oz	medium shrimp, peeled and deveined	375 g
1	package (10 oz/300 g) frozen lima beans (see Tip, page 101)	1

1. In a small bowl, combine fish sauce, sugar and pepper and stir well.

2. Heat a wok or a large deep skillet over medium-high heat. Add oil and swirl to coat pan. Add garlic and toss well, until fragrant, about 30 seconds.

3. Add shrimp and spread into a single layer. Cook, undisturbed, until most of the edges turn pink, about 1 minute. Toss well. Cook other side, about 30 seconds more.

4. Toss well. Add lima beans and cook, tossing often, until heated through, about 1 minute.

5. Add fish sauce mixture, pouring in around sides of pan. Toss well. Cook, until shrimp are cooked through and lima beans are tender, about 1 minute more. Transfer to a serving dish. Serve hot or warm.

Serves 4

This is my version of a Southern Thai dish, *goong paht sataw*, which combines shrimp with the sataw bean — a big, beautiful and flavorful legume. You might find sataw beans frozen in Asian markets if you'd like to try them. Allow a little extra cooking time for them to become tender. This speedy stir-fry with lots of garlic is quick and tasty, with just enough thin, Southeast Asian-style sauce to flavor your serving of jasmine rice.

Cajun-Style Shrimp Stir-Fry

Serves 4

This streamlined version of *maque choux* tastes as wonderful as it looks with its sunny tumble of corn, plump pink shrimp, crimson tomatoes and cool green peppers in a delectable mélange. Its roots are in the Cajun kitchens of South Louisiana, where cooks make beautiful use of the bounty of their summertime gardens. I love this with a spinach salad and a big bowl of couscous or a basket of warm garlic bread.

TIP

You could use fresh corn cut from the cob in place of frozen corn, cooking a little longer at a lower heat, so that it doesn't burn.

1 tbsp	chopped garlic	15 mL
½ cup	chopped onion	125 mL
½ cup	chopped green bell pepper	125 mL
¾ cup	coarsely chopped plum (Roma) tomatoes (see Tip, page 133)	175 mL
2 tbsp	chopped green onions	25 mL
½ tsp	salt or to taste	2 mL
½ tsp	freshly ground pepper	2 mL
½ tsp	hot pepper sauce	2 mL
2 tbsp	vegetable oil	25 mL
8 oz	medium shrimp, peeled and deveined	250 g
2 cups	frozen corn kernels (see Tip, left)	500 mL
2 tbsp	half-and-half (10%) cream or evaporated milk	25 mL

1. In a bowl, combine garlic, onion and green pepper. Set aside. In another bowl, combine tomatoes, green onions, salt, pepper and hot sauce. Set aside.

2. Heat a wok or a large deep skillet over high heat. Add oil and swirl to coat pan. Add garlic mixture and toss well. Cook, tossing occasionally, until tender and fragrant, about 1 minute.

3. Add shrimp and toss well. Spread shrimp into a single layer and cook, tossing occasionally, until most of the edges turn pink, about 1 minute.

4. Add corn and toss well. Cook, tossing occasionally, until shrimp are cooked through and corn is hot and tender, 1 to 2 minutes more. Add tomato mixture and toss well.

5. Add cream and toss again. Cook, undisturbed, until tomatoes have softened and a creamy sauce has been created, about 1 minute more. Transfer to a serving bowl. Serve hot or warm.

Variation: You could use butter in place of the vegetable oil.

Shrimp with Tomatoes, Lemon and Parsley

1 tbsp	freshly squeezed lemon juice	15 mL
1 tbsp	dry sherry or Shaoxing rice wine	15 mL
2 tsp	soy sauce	10 mL
1 tsp	salt or to taste	5 mL
½ tsp	granulated sugar	2 mL
2 tbsp	vegetable oil	25 mL
1 tbsp	chopped garlic	15 mL
2 tbsp	chopped onion	25 mL
⅓ cup	chopped green bell pepper	75 mL
8 oz	medium shrimp, peeled and deveined	250 g
2	plum (Roma) tomatoes, chopped into large chunks and drained (1 cup/250 mL) (see Tip, right)	2
3 tbsp	chopped Italian parsley	45 mL
3 tbsp	chopped green onions	45 mL

1. In a small bowl, combine lemon juice, sherry, soy sauce, salt and sugar and stir well. Set aside.

2. Heat a wok or a large deep skillet over high heat. Add oil and swirl to coat pan. Add garlic and onion and toss well. Add green pepper and toss well. Cook, tossing occasionally, until fragrant, about 30 seconds.

3. Push peppers and onions aside. Add shrimp and spread into a single layer. Cook, undisturbed, until most of the edges turn pink, about 1 minute. Toss well. Cook other side, about 30 seconds more.

4. Add lemon juice mixture and toss well. Cook, tossing occasionally, until shrimp are cooked through, 1 to 2 minutes more.

5. Add tomatoes and toss well. Cook, tossing once, for 1 minute. Add parsley and green onions and toss well. Transfer to a serving plate. Serve hot or warm.

Variation: Use cilantro in place of parsley, or try it with 2 tbsp (25 mL) dill and 2 tsp (10 mL) chopped fresh hot green chiles at the end of cooking time.

Serves 4

This recipe puts summery flavors on your table with vibrant colors as an inviting feast for your eyes.

TIP

To chop plum tomatoes, trim off stem end, and cut each tomato lengthwise into quarters. Cut each piece crosswise into 3 or 4 big chunks and transfer to a small bowl, leaving the juice and any easily released seeds behind on cutting board. Chopping the tomatoes in this way removes some of the juices and seeds and helps keep the sauce from diluting. These chopped tomatoes should be big, so they are in the sauce more as a vegetable than as a seasoning.

Greek-Style Shrimp with Tomatoes and Lemon

Serves 4

This is a quick version of *garides saganaki*, which is oven-baked and finished with flaming ouzo just before serving time. Toss in feta cheese if you have it, but don't worry if you don't. It's delicious either way. Plan on lots of crusty bread, rice or couscous to enjoy every drop of its sunny-flavored sauce.

12 oz	medium shrimp, peeled and deveined	375 g
1 tbsp	freshly squeezed lemon juice	15 mL
2 tbsp	olive oil or vegetable oil	25 mL
¼ cup	chopped green onions	50 mL
1 tbsp	chopped garlic	15 mL
¼ cup	dry white wine	50 mL
1	can (14 oz/400 mL) diced tomatoes, drained	1
2 tbsp	chopped Italian parsley	25 mL
1 cup	feta cheese, crumbled, about 4 oz (125 g), optional	250 mL

1. In a bowl, combine shrimp and lemon juice and toss well. Set aside.

2. Heat a wok or a large deep skillet over medium-high heat. Add oil and swirl to coat pan. Add green onions and garlic and toss well, until fragrant and just beginning to brown, about 1 minute. Add wine and cook for 1 minute.

3. Add tomatoes and cook, tossing occasionally, until everything softens into a chunky sauce, 1 to 2 minutes.

4. Add shrimp mixture and cook, tossing occasionally, until shrimp become pink and firm, for 2 minutes more. Add parsley and feta cheese, if using, and cook, tossing once, until shrimp are cooked through, about 1 more minute. Transfer to a serving dish. Serve hot or warm.

Stir-Fried Shrimp with Olives and Smoked Paprika

1 tbsp	soy sauce	15 mL
1 tbsp	dry sherry or Shaoxing rice wine	15 mL
1 tsp	paprika, preferably smoked Spanish paprika	5 mL
1/2 tsp	granulated sugar	2 mL
1/2 tsp	salt or to taste	2 mL
2 tbsp	vegetable oil	25 mL
1 tbsp	chopped garlic	15 mL
2 tbsp	chopped onion or shallots	25 mL
1/4 cup	chopped celery	50 mL
12 oz	medium shrimp, peeled and deveined	375 g
2 tbsp	coarsely chopped kalamata olives or sliced black olives	25 mL
2 tbsp	chopped green onions	25 mL
2 tbsp	chopped Italian parsley	25 mL

1. In a small bowl, combine soy sauce, sherry, paprika, sugar and salt and stir well. Set aside.

2. Heat a wok or a large deep skillet over high heat. Add oil and swirl to coat pan. Add garlic and onion and toss well, until fragrant, about 15 seconds. Add celery and toss well. Cook, tossing once, for 30 seconds.

3. Add shrimp and spread into a single layer. Cook, undisturbed, until most of the edges turn pink, about 1 minute. Toss well. Cook other side, about 30 seconds more.

4. Add soy sauce mixture, pouring in around sides of pan. Toss well. Cook, tossing occasionally, until shrimp are cooked through and everything combines to make a thin, dark sauce, about 1 minute more.

5. Add olives and toss well. Remove from heat and add green onions and parsley. Toss once more. Transfer to a serving plate. Serve hot or warm.

Serves 4

Make this rustic dish when you crave intense flavors with Mediterranean roots. Paprika gives it magnificent depth of color. If you have smoked Spanish paprika, you will enjoy its extraordinary taste.

Sicilian-Style Shrimp Stir-Fry with Fennel

Serves 4

This Italian-inspired dish is a window into the kitchens of Sicily, where sunshine is abundant and fennel grows wild. I find fennel in my supermarket's produce section, tucked between the lettuces and cabbages and in close proximity to the celery. Fennel has a large, rounded white base sprouting slender green stalks festooned with delicate green leaves, which remind me of fresh dill. You can enjoy it chopped up and tossed into a salad, as well as in garlic-infused dishes like this one.

TIP

Toasting slivered almonds or pine nuts heightens their flavor and aroma. To toast them on top of the stove, heat a wok or large skillet on medium-low heat. When hot, add nuts and toss until fragrant and barely toasted, 15 to 30 seconds. Remove from wok and set aside. Or toast them in the oven or a toaster oven, spread out on a baking pan, at 300°F (150°C), until fragrant and just beginning to brown, about 5 minutes.

½ cup	chicken stock, clam juice or water	125 mL
1 tbsp	zante currants or raisins	15 mL
½ tsp	hot pepper flakes	2 mL
Pinch	saffron threads, optional	Pinch
3 tbsp	olive oil or vegetable oil	45 mL
1 tbsp	chopped garlic	15 mL
½ cup	thinly sliced onion	125 mL
1½ cups	finely chopped fennel (about ½ a medium bulb)	375 mL
12 oz	medium shrimp, peeled and deveined	375 g
½ tsp	freshly ground pepper	2 mL
1 tbsp	slivered almonds or pine nuts (see Tip, left)	15 mL

1. In a small bowl, combine chicken stock, currants, hot pepper flakes and saffron threads, if using, and stir well. Set aside for 10 minutes.

2. Heat a wok or a large deep skillet over medium-high heat. Add oil and swirl to coat pan. Add garlic and toss well, until fragrant, about 30 seconds.

3. Add onion and fennel and cook, tossing occasionally, until softened and fragrant, 1 to 2 minutes. Add shrimp and cook, tossing occasionally, until pink all over, about 2 minutes.

4. Add chicken stock mixture and cook, tossing often, until shrimp are cooked through and fennel is tender-crisp, about 1 minute more.

5. Remove from heat. Add pepper and almonds and toss well. Transfer to a serving plate. Serve hot or warm.

Shrimp Scampi with Zucchini

¼ cup	freshly squeezed lemon juice (about 1 lemon)	50 mL
1 tbsp	water	15 mL
½ tsp	salt or to taste	2 mL
¼ tsp	freshly ground pepper	1 mL
2 tbsp	olive oil or vegetable oil	25 mL
2 tbsp	chopped garlic	25 mL
3 cups	chopped zucchini (see Tip, right)	750 mL
12 oz	medium shrimp, peeled and deveined	375 g
1 tbsp	chopped Italian parsley	15 mL
1 tbsp	unsalted butter or olive oil	15 mL

1. In a small bowl, combine lemon juice, water, salt and pepper and stir well.
2. Heat a wok or a large skillet over medium-high heat. Add oil and swirl to coat pan. Add garlic and toss well, until fragrant, about 30 seconds.
3. Add zucchini and toss well. Cook, tossing occasionally, until softened and bright green, 1 to 2 minutes.
4. Add shrimp and toss well. Cook, tossing often, until they are pink, firm and almost done, about 2 minutes.
5. Add lemon juice mixture, pouring in around sides of pan. Toss well. Cook, tossing occasionally, until shrimp are evenly seasoned and cooked through, about 1 minute more.
6. Remove from heat. Add parsley and butter and toss well. Transfer to a serving plate. Serve hot or warm.

Serves 4

Though vibrant and tasty as part of a meal with rice, this sunny, Italian-inspired dish works wonderfully over bowtie pasta, spaghetti or linguine. Crusty bread means that you won't miss out on any remaining sauce, and you will want to get every garlicky drop.

TIP

Trim both ends from zucchini and quarter lengthwise. Slice each quarter crosswise into little triangles, about ¼-inch (0.5 cm) thick. You'll need about 2 zucchini to make 3 cups (750 mL).

Peppery Shrimp with Onion and Mushrooms

Serves 4

Shrimp can be delicate and sweet, but they also shine with strong flavors when tossed with such peppery seasonings as in this dish. Rice should be part of the plan here as a way to moderate the intense flavors of the pungent sauce.

½ tsp	salt or to taste	2 mL
¼ tsp	freshly ground pepper	1 mL
¼ tsp	ground coriander	1 mL
Pinch	hot pepper flakes	Pinch
1 tbsp	soy sauce	15 mL
1 tbsp	dry sherry, white wine or Shaoxing rice wine	15 mL
2 tsp	granulated sugar	10 mL
2 tbsp	vegetable oil	25 mL
2 tbsp	chopped shallots or onion	25 mL
1 tbsp	chopped garlic	15 mL
1 cup	quartered and thinly sliced mushrooms	250 mL
8 oz	medium shrimp, peeled and deveined	250 g
3 tbsp	chopped green onions	45 mL
2 tbsp	chopped Italian parsley	25 mL

1. In a small bowl, combine salt, pepper, coriander and hot pepper flakes and stir well. In another small bowl, combine soy sauce, sherry and sugar and stir well. Set aside.

2. Heat a wok or a large deep skillet over high heat. Add oil and swirl to coat pan. Add shallots and garlic and toss well, until fragrant, about 15 seconds. Add mushrooms and toss well.

3. Add shrimp and spread into a single layer. Cook, undisturbed, until most of the edges turn pink, about 1 minute.

4. Add salt-and-pepper mixture and toss well. Cook, tossing occasionally, until shrimp are pink, firm and almost done, about 1 minute.

5. Add soy sauce mixture, pouring in around sides of pan. Toss well. Cook, tossing occasionally, until shrimp are cooked through and evenly seasoned, about 1 minute more. Add green onions and parsley and toss well. Transfer to a serving plate. Serve hot or warm.

Tangy Shrimp with Curry and Tomatoes

1 tbsp	freshly squeezed lime or lemon juice	15 mL
2 tsp	soy sauce	10 mL
1 tsp	light or dark brown sugar	5 mL
1 tsp	salt or to taste	5 mL
2 tbsp	vegetable oil	25 mL
2 tbsp	chopped onion	25 mL
1 tbsp	curry powder (see Tip, right)	15 mL
12 oz	medium shrimp, peeled and deveined	375 g
⅔ cup	sliced button mushrooms	150 mL
½ cup	halved cherry tomatoes (about 3 oz/90 g)	125 mL
3 tbsp	chopped green onions	45 mL
2 tbsp	chopped fresh cilantro	25 mL

Serves 4

This dish can bring some sunshine to your table, even on a damp and foggy day. The colors alone are fabulous, and the flavors are bright and complex. The sauce complements both couscous and crusty bread, while making a perfect partner for rice.

TIP

If you love chile heat, use a hot curry powder, and add some sliced or chopped fresh hot green chiles, or a dash or two of hot pepper sauce.

1. In a small bowl, combine lime juice, soy sauce, sugar and salt and stir well. Set aside.

2. Heat a wok or a large deep skillet over high heat. Add oil and swirl to coat pan. Add onion and toss well, until fragrant, about 15 seconds. Add curry powder and cook, tossing occasionally, for 1 minute.

3. Add shrimp and spread into a single layer. Cook, undisturbed, until most of the edges turn pink, about 1 minute. Toss well. Cook other side, about 30 seconds more.

4. Add mushrooms over shrimp. Cook, undisturbed, for about 30 seconds more. Toss well. Cook, tossing occasionally, until mushrooms are softened and shrimp are cooked through, 1 to 2 minutes more.

5. Add lime juice mixture and cherry tomatoes and toss well. Add green onions and cilantro and toss well. Transfer to a serving plate. Serve hot or warm.

Curried Shrimp with Onions and Peas

I like this dish spooned over jasmine rice, with a side of steamed spinach or a simple salad. I love hot curry powder, but any kind you like will do nicely.

TIP

If you have an old jar of curry powder in the cupboard, treat yourself to a fresh batch. It makes a world of difference in flavor and that alone is worth the price. Old spices are tired and flat and that is no bargain!

1 tbsp	dry sherry or Shaoxing rice wine	15 mL
2 tsp	soy sauce	10 mL
1 tsp	curry powder (see Tip, left)	5 mL
½ tsp	granulated sugar	2 mL
2 tbsp	water	25 mL
1 tsp	cornstarch	5 mL
½ tsp	salt or to taste	2 mL
2 tbsp	vegetable oil	25 mL
1 tbsp	chopped garlic	15 mL
¾ cup	thinly sliced onion	175 mL
12 oz	medium shrimp, peeled and deveined	375 g
½ cup	frozen peas, thawed	125 mL
2 tbsp	chopped fresh cilantro	25 mL

1. In a small bowl, combine sherry, soy sauce, curry powder and sugar and stir well. In another small bowl, combine water, cornstarch and salt and stir well into a smooth sauce. Set aside.

2. Heat a wok or a large skillet over medium-high heat. Add oil and swirl to coat pan. Add garlic and toss well, until fragrant, about 30 seconds. Add onion and toss well. Cook, tossing often, until beginning to wilt, about 1 minute.

3. Add shrimp and spread into a single layer. Cook, until most of the edges turn pink, about 1 minute. Toss well. Add sherry mixture, pouring in around sides of pan. Cook, tossing often, until shrimp turn pink, 1 minute more.

4. Stir cornstarch mixture and add to pan with peas and toss well. Cook, tossing occasionally, until shrimp are cooked through, peas are hot and everything is evenly seasoned, 1 to 2 minutes more. Add cilantro and toss well. Transfer to a serving plate. Serve hot or warm.

Thai Shrimp
with Roasted Chile Paste

3 tbsp	roasted chile paste (see Tips, right)	45 mL
2 tbsp	fish sauce	25 mL
½ cup	water or chicken stock	125 mL
1 tsp	granulated sugar	5 mL
½ tsp	salt or to taste	2 mL
3 tbsp	vegetable oil	45 mL
1 tbsp	chopped garlic	15 mL
1 lb	medium shrimp, peeled and deveined	500 g
¼ cup	long thin strips red bell pepper, optional	50 mL
1 cup	fresh basil or mint leaves, optional (see Tips, right)	250 mL

1. In a small bowl, combine chile paste, fish sauce, water, sugar and salt and stir well. Set aside.
2. Heat a wok or a large deep skillet over medium-high heat. Add oil and swirl to coat pan. Add garlic and toss well, until fragrant, about 30 seconds.
3. Add shrimp and spread into a single layer. Cook, until most of the edges turn pink, about 1 minute. Toss well.
4. Add chili paste mixture and toss well. Cook, tossing occasionally, until shrimp are cooked through and coated with a thin dark sauce, 1 to 2 minutes more.
5. Add red pepper and basil leaves, if using, and toss well. Transfer to a serving plate. Serve hot or warm.

Serves 4

Roasted chile paste, made from dried red chiles, garlic and shallots bestows rustic flavor and handsome color on an array of Thai dishes. Here it is added to the pan near the end of cooking time, and accented with sweet red peppers and aromatic basil leaves.

TIPS

Look for roasted chile paste in Asian markets, often enigmatically labeled "chilies in soya bean oil." You can make a batch to have on hand, using the recipe on page 337.

If using basil or mint leaves that are large, tear them or chop them coarsely just before you begin making the dish. This helps maintain their color and aroma prior to cooking.

Shrimp with Pepper and Onions

Serves 4

Here big chunks of onion cooked with two kinds of pepper add a robust, sweet-and-salty flavor to a panful of shrimp. A cool green salad makes a welcome accompaniment, along with lots of rice.

1 tbsp	soy sauce	15 mL
1 tbsp	dry sherry or Shaoxing rice wine	15 mL
2 tsp	Asian sesame oil	10 mL
2 tsp	granulated sugar	10 mL
½ tsp	salt or to taste	2 mL
½ tsp	hot pepper flakes	2 mL
¼ tsp	freshly ground pepper	1 mL
2 tbsp	vegetable oil	25 mL
1 tbsp	chopped garlic	15 mL
1 tbsp	chopped gingerroot	15 mL
¾ cup	onion wedges (½ inch/1 cm)	175 mL
8 oz	medium shrimp, peeled and deveined	250 g
½ cup	frozen tiny peas	125 mL
¼ cup	chopped green onions	50 mL

1. In a small bowl, combine soy sauce, sherry, sesame oil, sugar, salt, hot pepper flakes and pepper and stir well. Set aside.

2. Heat a wok or a large deep skillet over high heat. Add oil and swirl to coat pan. Add garlic and ginger and toss well. Add onion and toss well. Cook, tossing occasionally, until onion and garlic are fragrant, about 1 minute.

3. Push onions aside. Add shrimp and spread into a single layer. Cook, undisturbed, until most of the edges turn pink, about 1 minute. Toss well. Cook other side, about 30 seconds more.

4. Add peas and soy sauce mixture, pouring in around the sides of pan. Cook, tossing occasionally, until peas are hot and shrimp are cooked through, 1 to 2 minutes more. Add green onions and toss well. Transfer to a serving plate. Serve hot or warm.

Cajun-Spiced Shrimp

½ tsp	white pepper	2 mL
½ tsp	black pepper	2 mL
½ tsp	cayenne pepper	2 mL
½ tsp	paprika	2 mL
½ tsp	dried thyme	2 mL
½ tsp	garlic powder	2 mL
½ tsp	onion powder	2 mL
12 oz	medium shrimp, peeled and deveined	375 g
1 tbsp	dry sherry, white wine or chicken broth	15 mL
2 tsp	soy sauce	10 mL
2 tsp	water	10 mL
½ tsp	granulated sugar	2 mL
2 tbsp	vegetable oil	25 mL
¾ cup	chopped celery (see Tip, right)	175 mL
3 tbsp	chopped green onions	45 mL
3 tbsp	chopped Italian parsley	45 mL

1. In a bowl, combine white pepper, black pepper, cayenne, paprika, thyme, garlic powder and onion powder and stir well. Add shrimp and coat well. Set aside for 10 minutes.
2. In a small bowl, combine sherry, soy sauce, water and sugar and stir well. Set aside.
3. Heat a wok or a large deep skillet over high heat. Add oil and swirl to coat pan.
4. Add shrimp mixture and spread into a single layer. Cook, undisturbed, until most of the edges turn pink, about 1 minute. Toss well. Cook other side, about 30 seconds more.
5. Add celery. Cook, tossing occasionally, until shrimp are pink, firm and almost done, about 1 minute more.
6. Add sherry mixture, pouring in around sides of pan. Toss well. Cook, tossing occasionally, until shrimp are cooked through, 1 to 2 minutes more. Add green onions and parsley and toss once more. Transfer to a serving plate. Serve hot or warm.

Serves 4

Stir together a handful of spices and you have the key to a fantastically delicious dish that your fiery-food loving family and friends will adore. You can adjust the seasonings to create a milder version, with more paprika and less cayenne, but leave some heat in there and cool things off by mixing the sauce with rice as you eat it. You could also use a prepared Cajun seasoning mix and simply add it in place of the spices combined here.

TIP

To prepare the celery, I like to trim ends to make even stalks, pull away the strings along the curved outer side, and then slice each stalk on the diagonal to form slender pieces in the shape of the letter "c." You could also trim, string and chop celery stalks into ½-inch (1 cm) chunks.

Red Curry Shrimp with Pineapple and Asian Basil

Serves 4

A little Thai curry paste, some coconut milk, pineapple chunks and fresh shrimp, and in a flash you're ready to serve up an extraordinary main course. Serve this beautiful and luscious curry with rice or long thin noodles and a cucumber salad. Add a few small sprigs of fresh basil if you have them, to garnish the finished dish.

TIP

If you have makrut lime leaves, tear each leaf into quarters, discarding the stem, or cut them into quarters, leaving the stem intact. If you can't find lime leaves, simply omit them.

1 ½ cups	unsweetened coconut milk, divided	375 mL
2 tbsp	Thai red curry paste	25 mL
½ cup	water	125 mL
2 tbsp	fish sauce	25 mL
1 tbsp	palm sugar or brown sugar	15 mL
1 cup	drained canned pineapple chunks	250 mL
6	makrut lime leaves, optional (see Tip, left)	6
12 oz	medium shrimp, peeled and deveined	375 g
⅓ cup	fresh Asian basil or Italian basil leaves	75 mL

1. In a wok or a large deep skillet, bring ½ cup (125 mL) of the coconut milk to a gentle boil over medium-high heat. Boil gently, until thickened and fragrant, about 2 minutes.

2. Add curry paste. Press and mash to help it dissolve, creating a rusty red sauce.

3. Add remaining coconut milk, water, fish sauce, sugar and pineapple. Add lime leaves, if using, and return to a gentle boil.

4. Add shrimp and basil and cook, stirring gently once or twice, until shrimp are pink and cooked through, 2 to 3 minutes. Transfer to a serving dish. Serve hot or warm.

Shrimp with Zucchini and Mushrooms in Curry Sauce

¼ cup	unsweetened coconut milk (see Tip, right)	50 mL
2 tbsp	fish sauce	25 mL
2 tbsp	brown sugar or granulated sugar	25 mL
2 tbsp	vegetable oil	25 mL
3 tbsp	chopped onion	45 mL
2 tbsp	Thai-style green curry paste	25 mL
8 oz	medium shrimp, peeled and deveined	250 g
½ cup	sliced zucchini (see Tip, page 137)	125 mL
½ cup	quartered button mushrooms	125 mL
¼ cup	fresh basil leaves, optional	50 mL

1. In a bowl, combine coconut milk, fish sauce and sugar and stir well. Set aside.
2. Heat a wok or a large deep skillet over medium-high heat. Add oil and swirl to coat pan. Add onion and toss well, until fragrant, about 30 seconds.
3. Reduce heat to medium. Add curry paste and cook, mashing and stirring it to soften in the hot oil, about 30 seconds. Reduce heat if the mixture spatters and pops.
4. Add shrimp and spread into a single layer. Cook, undisturbed, for 30 seconds. Toss gently to mix shrimp with curry paste.
5. Add zucchini and mushrooms and toss well. Cook, tossing occasionally, until zucchini and mushrooms have softened a little and most of the shrimp have turned pink, about 1 minute more.
6. Add coconut milk mixture. Toss gently and bring to a gentle boil. Cook, tossing occasionally, until vegetables are tender but still firm and shrimp are cooked through, about 2 minutes more.
7. Meanwhile, slice basil leaves crosswise into thin ribbons and add to pan. Toss gently. Transfer to a small deep serving platter or a shallow bowl. Serve hot or warm.

Serves 4

This is a hot one, and nothing beats rice to help moderate the heat as you savor its explosion of flavors. The flourish of basil at serving time is a plus, but you'll still have a memorable dish without it.

TIP

In cooler weather, canned unsweetened coconut milk naturally separates into a very thick, creamy essence at the top and a very thin juice at the bottom of the can. You want everything mixed together into a smooth liquid with the texture of very rich cream. To do so, open the can, insert a fork into the center of the thick, white top cream, and begin stirring gently, working both textures together into a single, rich liquid.

Spiced Shrimp with Green Onions

Serves 4

Stir together this round-up of ground spices and watch a batch of shrimp light up with gorgeous color and extraordinary flavor. No need for a long marinade here. Simply tumble the shrimp with the spices, set out the remaining ingredients and a serving plate, and you're ready to cook. Serve with rice or noodles.

TIP

If you want to season the shrimp ahead of time, toss them with the spices, cover and refrigerate for up to 1 day. If you don't have the spices called for, use 2 tbsp (25 mL) of your favorite curry powder or another savory spice mixture in place of the spices and sugar, but do add the salt.

2 tsp	paprika	10 mL
2 tsp	granulated sugar	10 mL
½ tsp	salt or to taste	2 mL
½ tsp	ground cumin	2 mL
¼ tsp	ground coriander	1 mL
¼ tsp	freshly ground pepper	1 mL
12 oz	medium shrimp, peeled and deveined	375 g
3	green onions	3
2 tbsp	vegetable oil	25 mL
1 tbsp	coarsely chopped garlic	15 mL
⅓ cup	water or chicken broth	75 mL

1. In a bowl, combine paprika, sugar, salt, cumin, coriander and pepper and stir well. Add shrimp and toss to coat well. Set aside for 10 minutes.

2. Divide the green onions into green and white parts, chopping the white parts coarsely, and cutting the green tops into 2-inch (5 cm) lengths. Set aside.

3. Heat a wok or a large deep skillet over medium-high heat. Add oil and swirl to coat pan. Add garlic and toss well, until fragrant, about 30 seconds. Add shrimp mixture and cook, tossing occasionally, until shrimp are pink and firm, 2 to 3 minutes.

4. Add water and stir once. As soon as the water comes to a boil, add green onions and toss well. Transfer to a serving plate. Serve hot or warm.

> **Variation:** If you want a little heat, add up to 1 tbsp (15 mL) coarsely chopped fresh hot green chiles or 1 to 2 tsp (5 to 10 mL) hot pepper flakes to the wok along with the green onions.

Shrimp with Tomatoes and Eggs

2 tbsp	fish sauce	25 mL
1 tbsp	water	15 mL
½ tsp	salt or to taste	2 mL
½ tsp	granulated sugar	2 mL
2 tbsp	vegetable oil	25 mL
1 tbsp	chopped garlic	15 mL
12 oz	medium shrimp, peeled and deveined	375 g
⅓ cup	coarsely chopped onion	75 mL
⅓ cup	chopped green onions	75 mL
4	eggs, well beaten	4
2	plum (Roma) tomatoes, chopped into large chunks and drained (1 cup/250 mL) (see Tip, page 133)	2
3 tbsp	chopped fresh cilantro	45 mL

1. In a small bowl, combine fish sauce, water, salt and sugar and stir well. Set aside.

2. Heat a wok or large deep skillet over high heat. Add oil and swirl to coat pan. Add garlic and toss well, until fragrant, about 15 seconds.

3. Add shrimp and spread into a single layer. Cook, until most of the edges turn pink, for 1 minute. Toss well. Add onion and green onions. Cook, tossing occasionally, until shrimp have turned pink and onions are fragrant, about 1 minute more. Add fish sauce mixture and cook, tossing occasionally, for 30 seconds to season everything well.

4. Pour eggs in around sides of pan, and cook, undisturbed, until they begin to set, about 30 seconds. Toss gently. Cook, tossing often, for 1 minute more.

5. Add tomatoes and toss again, gently breaking up large chunks of egg and letting tomatoes heat up just a little on the pan. Add cilantro and toss gently. Transfer to a serving plate. Serve hot or warm.

Serves 4

This is a satisfying and handsome dish, whether you eat it with rice, Asian-style, or as a deconstructed omelet, along with toast and orange juice for a spin on brunch. Shrimp at breakfast time are part of the cuisine of the American South, and in this recipe would go just fine with biscuits and grits. Thais love hot pepper sauce with any egg dish, and that option is particularly a good match with this dish.

Shrimp in the Shell with Green Onions and Fresh Ginger

Serves 4

This recipe will give you an extraordinarily delicious plate of shrimp, worth every bit of time and mess involved in preparing and eating them. The only effort of cooking would be cutting open the shells along the back, so that they can absorb the sauce as they cook. The other challenge is eating them. These are hands-on, with lots of sauce to enjoy throughout the process. Make this a picnic take-along, or a meal to share on a take-it-easy evening with family and friends. Be sure to offer bowls or plates where guests can deposit the shells as they eat. Pass lemon wedges and extra napkins when everyone has finished their hands-on feast.

TIP

If you have kitchen shears, the task of cutting the shrimp shells is simple and goes quickly. You can also buy shell-on shrimp, which have been split open for cleaning, and this means all you have to do is remove the legs and devein.

2 tbsp	dry sherry	25 mL
1 tbsp	soy sauce	15 mL
½ tsp	granulated sugar	2 mL
12 oz	medium shrimp, shell on (see Tip, left)	375 mL
3 tbsp	vegetable oil	45 mL
2 tsp	chopped garlic	10 mL
1 tsp	salt or to taste	5 mL
3 tbsp	chopped green onions	45 mL
2 tbsp	finely chopped fresh gingerroot	25 mL

1. In a small bowl, combine sherry, soy sauce and sugar and stir well. Set aside.

2. To prepare the shrimp, pull off and discard the legs, leaving shell on shrimp. Using a pair of kitchen scissors, cut along the curving back of each shrimp, to where the tail begins. Remove and discard any dark veins you find, and carefully break off or cut away the small, sharp point extending out over the tail. You should now have a shrimp that is open along the back, and trimmed of everything except the split shell and the tail.

3. Heat a wok or a large deep skillet over high heat. Add oil and swirl to coat pan. Add garlic and salt and toss well, until fragrant, about 15 seconds.

4. Add shrimp, green onions and ginger and spread into a single layer. Cook, undisturbed, until most of the shrimp turn pink around the edges, about 1 minute. Toss well. Cook other side, about 30 seconds more.

5. Add soy sauce mixture, pouring in around sides of pan. Cook, tossing occasionally, until shrimp are cooked through, 1 to 2 minutes more. Transfer to a serving plate. Serve hot or warm.

Ham, Sausage, Lamb & Roasted Meats

Sesame-Scented Crispy Bean Sprouts with Ham

Asian cooks love fresh bean sprouts as a cool, crisp component in salads, and a refreshing textural note in stir-fries and soups. Look for fresh, bright sprouts, which are firm and white. Use them within a day or two once you've brought them home.

2 tbsp	soy sauce	25 mL
1 tsp	granulated sugar	5 mL
½ tsp	salt or to taste	2 mL
2 tbsp	vegetable oil	25 mL
2 tbsp	chopped onion	25 mL
1 tbsp	chopped garlic	15 mL
8 oz	chopped baked ham (2 cups/500 mL) (½-inch/1 cm chunks)	250 g
3 cups	fresh bean sprouts	750 mL
2 tbsp	chopped green onions	25 mL
1 tsp	Asian sesame oil	5 mL

1. In a small bowl, combine soy sauce, sugar and salt and stir well. Set aside.

2. Heat a wok or a large deep skillet over high heat. Add oil and swirl to coat pan. Add onion and garlic and toss well, until fragrant, about 15 seconds.

3. Add ham and toss well. Spread into a single layer and cook, undisturbed, for 30 seconds. Toss well.

4. Add bean sprouts, spreading into a single layer and exposing them to the hot pan. Cook, tossing once, for 1 minute.

5. Add soy sauce mixture, pouring in around sides of pan and toss again. Cook, tossing occasionally, until bean sprouts have wilted but are still tender-crisp, about 1 minute more.

6. Add green onions and sesame oil and toss well. Transfer to a serving plate. Serve hot or warm.

Ham with Chunky Salsa and Corn

1 tbsp	soy sauce	15 mL
1 tbsp	water	15 mL
½ tsp	salt or to taste	2 mL
½ tsp	granulated sugar	2 mL
2 tbsp	vegetable oil	25 mL
2 tbsp	chopped onion	25 mL
1 tbsp	chopped garlic	15 mL
8 oz	chopped baked ham (2 cups/500 mL) (½-inch/1 cm chunks)	250 g
½ cup	fresh, frozen or canned corn (see Tip, right)	125 mL
3 tbsp	chunky tomato salsa	45 mL
¼ cup	chopped green onions	50 mL
¼ cup	chopped fresh cilantro	50 mL

1. In a small bowl, combine soy sauce, water, salt and sugar and stir well. Set aside.

2. Heat a wok or a large deep skillet over high heat. Add oil and swirl to coat pan. Add onion and garlic and toss well, until fragrant, about 15 seconds.

3. Add ham and toss well. Spread into a single layer and cook, undisturbed, for 30 seconds. Toss well. Add corn and toss well. Cook, tossing occasionally, for 1 minute.

4. Add soy sauce mixture, pouring in around sides of pan. Cook, tossing occasionally, until ham is hot and corn is heated through and tender-crisp, 1 to 2 minutes more.

5. Add salsa, green onions and cilantro and toss well. Transfer to a serving plate. Serve hot or warm.

Serves 4

Chunky tomato salsa is a staple in my refrigerator. I love it with eggs at breakfast, soft tacos at lunchtime or grilled salmon at supper. Here I add a generous dollop to the pan just before everything is done, resulting in a fast and flavorful little sauce to enjoy with rice or couscous.

TIP

If you're using fresh or frozen corn, you may need a little extra cooking time before adding the salsa, green onions and cilantro and finishing the dish. Taste and add an extra 1 to 2 tbsp (15 to 25 mL) of water if the corn needs more cooking time, to keep everything from drying out or burning.

Black-Eyed Peas 'n' Greens

Serves 4

This is a little stir-fry tribute to Hoppin' John, a classic Southern dish made with black-eyed peas or field peas, ham hocks and rice. Here I've used chopped ham and cooked black-eyed peas to make a speedy stir-fry version. Since the real thing is often served with collards or turnip greens, I've included spinach here in place of those longer-cooking greens. Rice would be lovely, but either noodles or cornbread would be delicious as well.

1 tbsp	soy sauce	15 mL
1 tbsp	water	15mL
1 tsp	salt or to taste	5 mL
½ tsp	freshly ground pepper	2 mL
½ tsp	granulated sugar	2 mL
½ tsp	hot pepper flakes, optional	2 mL
2 tbsp	vegetable oil	25 mL
8 oz	chopped baked ham (2 cups/500 mL) (½-inch/1 cm chunks)	250 g
3 tbsp	chopped onion	45 mL
1 tbsp	chopped garlic	15 mL
1½ cups	spinach, trimmed	375 mL
2 cups	canned or cooked black-eyed peas, drained and rinsed	500 mL
3 tbsp	chopped green onions	45 mL
3 tbsp	chopped Italian parsley	45 mL

1. In a small bowl, combine soy sauce, water, salt, pepper, sugar and hot pepper flakes, if using, and stir well. Set aside.
2. Heat a wok or a large deep skillet over high heat. Add oil and swirl to coat pan.
3. Add ham and toss well. Spread into a single layer and cook, undisturbed, for 30 seconds. Toss well. Add onion and garlic and toss well, until fragrant, about 15 seconds. Cook, tossing often, until ham is lightly browned and heated through, about 1 minute more.
4. Add spinach and black-eyed peas and toss well. Add soy sauce mixture, pouring in around sides of pan. Toss well and cook until everything is evenly seasoned and black-eyed peas are hot, about 1 minute more.
5. Add green onions and parsley and toss well. Transfer to a serving plate. Serve hot or warm.

Ham with Zucchini and Colorful Carrot Shreds

1 tbsp	soy sauce	15 mL
1 tbsp	water	15 mL
½ tsp	salt or to taste	2 mL
½ tsp	granulated sugar	2 mL
2 tbsp	vegetable oil	25 mL
1 tbsp	chopped garlic	15 ml
2 tsp	chopped fresh gingerroot	10 mL
8 oz	chopped ham (2 cups/500 mL) (see Tip, right)	250 g
2 cups	sliced zucchini (¼-inch/0.5 cm rounds)	500 mL
¾ cup	shredded carrots	175 mL
3 tbsp	chopped green onions	45 mL
2 tsp	sesame oil	10 mL

1. In a small bowl, combine soy sauce, water, salt and sugar and stir well. Set aside.

2. Heat a wok or a large deep skillet over high heat. Add oil and swirl to coat pan. Add garlic and ginger and toss well, until fragrant, about 15 seconds.

3. Add ham and toss well. Add zucchini and spread into a single layer. Cook, undisturbed, for 30 seconds. Toss well.

4. Add carrots and toss well. Add soy sauce mixture, pouring in around sides of pan. Cook, tossing occasionally, until zucchini are tender-crisp and everything is evenly seasoned, about 1 to 2 minutes longer.

5. Add green onions and sesame oil and toss well. Transfer to a serving plate. Serve hot or warm.

Serves 4

Since the ham needs only to be chopped and heated up, and the carrots can be purchased in shredded form in the produce section, the main task here is slicing zucchini and chopping the garlic and ginger. I like this tossed with angel hair pasta or rice.

TIP

For this recipe I like to cut the ham into strips, about 2-inches by ¼-inch (5 cm by 0.5 cm), giving me strips of carrots and ham with rounds of zucchini. But any way you chop it will work fine.

BLT Stir-Fry

Serves 4

BLT is shorthand for the classic sandwich of bacon, lettuce and tomato on white bread spread with mayonnaise. It holds iconic status in the South. Here we skip the bread and mayo, allowing escarole to stand in for lettuce and tiny tomatoes to substitute for slices. The fabulous flavors remain and make a wonderful accompaniment to rice or pasta. You could even tuck some into a pita bread or a warm tortilla if you want that hand-held quality of a true BLT.

TIP

About half a head of escarole is needed to make 4 packed cups (1 L). To chop escarole, trim away outer leaves and then cut lengthwise into 1-inch (2.5 cm) strips, and then crosswise to make pieces which are roughly 1 inch (2.5 cm) square.

1 tbsp	chicken stock or water	15 mL
1 tsp	cornstarch	5 mL
1 tsp	soy sauce	5 mL
½ tsp	granulated sugar	2 mL
¼ tsp	freshly ground pepper	1 mL
1 tbsp	vegetable oil	15 mL
1 tbsp	chopped garlic	15 mL
3	strips smoked bacon, cut into 1-inch (2.5 cm) pieces	3
¾ cup	thinly sliced onion, preferably red	175 mL
½ cup	thinly sliced button mushrooms	125 mL
4 cups	packed chopped escarole (1-inch/2.5 cm pieces) (see Tip, left)	1 L
¾ cup	halved cherry tomatoes	175 mL

1. In a small bowl, combine stock, cornstarch, soy sauce, sugar and pepper and stir well. Set aside.
2. Heat a wok or large skillet over medium-high heat. Add oil and swirl to coat pan. Add garlic and toss well, until fragrant, about 30 seconds. Add bacon and cook, tossing often, until it curls and begins to brown, 1 to 2 minutes.
3. Add onions and toss well. Add mushrooms and cook, tossing occasionally, until both have wilted and onions are fragrant, about 1 minute more.
4. Increase heat to high. Add escarole and toss well. Cook, stirring, until escarole wilts, about 3 minutes.
5. Stir cornstarch mixture and add to pan, pouring in around sides. Add cherry tomatoes. Toss well. Cook, tossing twice, until sauce is thickened, about 1 minute more. Transfer to a serving plate. Serve hot or warm.

Aromatic Bacon with Cauliflower and Chives

2 tbsp	fish sauce	25 mL
2 tbsp	water	25 mL
1 tsp	granulated sugar	5 mL
½ tsp	freshly ground pepper	2 mL
2 tbsp	vegetable oil	25 mL
1 tbsp	chopped garlic	15 mL
3	slices meaty bacon, cut into ½-inch (1 cm) pieces	3
3 cups	small cauliflower florets (see Tips, right)	750 mL
3 tbsp	chopped chives or green onions (½-inch/1 cm lengths)	45 mL
2 tbsp	chopped fresh cilantro	25 mL

1. In a small bowl, combine fish sauce, water, sugar and pepper and stir well. Set aside.

2. Heat a wok or a large deep skillet over high heat. Add oil and swirl to coat pan.

3. Add garlic and toss well, until fragrant, about 15 seconds. Add bacon and spread into a single layer. Cook, undisturbed, until it curls and begins to brown, about 30 seconds. Toss well. Cook, tossing occasionally, until bacon has browned nicely and is cooked through, 1 to 2 minutes.

4. Add cauliflower florets and toss well. Cook, undisturbed, for 30 seconds. Toss well. Add fish sauce mixture, pouring in around sides of pan. Cook, tossing occasionally, until cauliflower is tender-crisp, 1 to 2 minutes more.

5. Add chives and cilantro and toss well. Transfer to a serving plate. Serve hot or warm.

Serves 4

If you use thick-cut peppery bacon for this dish, it will cook up with the texture of ham. If you use thinly sliced smoky bacon, it will curl and brown and add a crispy note. Both are delicious and a fine counterpoint to cauliflower.

TIPS

To save a little time, you can often purchase trimmed cauliflower florets in the produce section. You will need to cut them down to bite-size pieces, which means quartering big clusters lengthwise, and halving medium-size ones.

Chives are lovely, but green onions will work just fine in this dish.

Corn-Spiked Hominy with Bacon and Tomatoes

Serves 4

I love corn and here I get to enjoy it two ways, pairing corn kernels with old-fashioned hominy. I keep corn, hominy and bacon on hand in the pantry or freezer, so that this dish can be supper on short notice. For me, it delivers the taste of supper on my grandparents' dairy farm.

TIPS

If cherry tomatoes are large, more like walnuts than marbles, cut each one lengthwise into quarters rather than halves. You could also use coarsely chopped tomatoes, but don't add any of the seeds and juice that end up on your cutting board as you chop them; just the tomato chunks.

If you're using fresh or frozen corn, you may need a little extra cooking time before adding the cherry tomatoes and finishing the dish. Add an extra 1 to 2 tbsp (15 to 25 mL) of water if the corn needs more cooking time, to keep everything from drying out or burning.

2 tbsp	chicken stock or water	25 mL
1 tbsp	soy sauce	15 mL
½ tsp	salt or to taste	2 mL
½ tsp	granulated sugar	2 mL
1 tbsp	vegetable oil	15 mL
4 oz	chopped meaty bacon (½-inch/1 cm pieces)	125 g
2 tbsp	chopped onion	25 mL
2 tsp	chopped garlic	10 mL
1 cup	drained, canned hominy or thawed frozen hominy	250 mL
¾ cup	fresh, frozen or canned corn (see Tips, left)	175 mL
1 cup	halved cherry tomatoes (see Tips, left)	250 mL
½ cup	chopped green onions	125 mL
¼ cup	chopped fresh cilantro	50 mL

1. In a small bowl, combine chicken stock, soy sauce, salt and sugar and stir well. Set aside.

2. Heat a wok or a large deep skillet over high heat. Add oil and swirl to coat pan. Add bacon, spreading around pan as best you can. Cook, undisturbed, for 30 seconds. Toss well. Cook, tossing often, until bacon separates into pieces and becomes fragrant, about 1 minute.

3. Add onion and garlic and toss well, until fragrant, about 15 seconds. Cook, tossing often, until bacon has curled and browned, about 1 minute more.

4. Add hominy and toss well. Add corn and toss well. Cook, tossing occasionally, until bacon is cooked through and hominy is hot and corn is tender-crisp, 1 to 2 minutes.

5. Add chicken stock mixture, pouring in around sides of pan. Toss well. Cook, tossing occasionally, for 30 seconds. Add cherry tomatoes and green onions. Toss well and cook for 30 seconds more. Add cilantro and toss once. Transfer to a serving plate. Serve hot or warm.

Down-Home Sausage with Apples

3 tbsp	chicken stock or water	45 mL
1 tbsp	soy sauce	15 mL
1 tsp	granulated sugar	5 mL
¼ tsp	ground cinnamon	1 mL
2 tbsp	vegetable oil	25 mL
12 oz	country-style pork sausage (bulk or removed from casings)	375 g
⅓ cup	coarsely chopped onion	75 mL
1	sweet red unpeeled apple, cut into very thin wedges (see Tip, right)	1
1	tart green unpeeled apple, cut into very thin wedges (see Tip, right)	1
1 tbsp	chopped fresh parsley or cilantro	15 mL

1. In a small bowl, combine stock, soy sauce, sugar and cinnamon and stir well. Set aside.

2. Heat a wok or a large deep skillet over high heat. Add oil and swirl to coat pan. Add sausage and using a spatula or slotted spoon begin breaking up the meat into small chunks. Cook, tossing gently and continuing to break the meat into small pieces, until it has changed color, for 1 minute.

3. Add onion and cook, tossing occasionally, until onion is wilted and sausage is no longer pink, 1 to 2 minutes more.

4. Add red and green apple wedges and cook, tossing occasionally, until apples are lightly browned and sausage is cooked through, 1 to 2 minutes more.

5. Add chicken stock mixture and cook, tossing occasionally, until apples are tender and the ingredients make a smooth sauce, about 1 more minute. Add parsley and toss well. Transfer to a serving plate. Serve hot or warm.

> **Variation:** Instead of country-style pork sausage, use 12 oz (375 g) ground pork mixed with 1 tsp (5 mL) sage leaves or dried thyme, 1 tsp (5 mL) packed light or dark brown sugar, ½ tsp (2 mL) salt, ¼ tsp (1 mL) freshly ground pepper and ¼ tsp (1 mL) cayenne pepper. Let stand for 15 minutes and then continue with the recipe.

Serves 4

This classic Southern combination of sausage and apples is a pleasure with rice, but cornbread would be an excellent option as well. You could also serve this with omelets or potato pancakes for a hearty breakfast on a wintry weekend morning.

TIP

You will need about ¾ cup (175 mL) of each kind of sliced unpeeled apples for this recipe, or about 1½ cups (375 mL) of one kind of apple.

Country-Style Sausage with Cabbage and Peppers

Sausage and cabbage make great partners in this hearty dish, and red peppers add a bright note both in color and in taste. Hot, chile-spiked sausage is my favorite here, but if I'm using a milder sausage, I put the hot pepper sauce on the table at serving time for those of us who like some heat.

TIP

For this recipe, you want only the thin, soft portions of cabbage leaves, shredded into thin strips. Remove any thick rib or core sections before you measure out the 2 cups (500 mL) you need here.

2 tbsp	soy sauce	25 mL
2 tbsp	chicken stock or water	25 mL
2 tsp	brown sugar or granulated sugar	10 mL
2 tsp	red wine vinegar or cider vinegar	10 mL
1 tsp	salt or to taste	5 mL
2 tbsp	vegetable oil	25 mL
8 oz	country-style pork sausage (bulk or removed from casings)	250 g
2 tbsp	chopped onion	25 mL
2 tsp	chopped fresh gingerroot	10 mL
2 cups	finely shredded cabbage (see Tip, left)	500 mL
½ cup	thinly sliced red bell pepper	125 mL
¼ cup	chopped green onions	50 mL

1. In a small bowl, combine soy sauce, stock, brown sugar, vinegar and salt and stir well. Set aside.

2. Heat a wok or a large deep skillet over high heat. Add oil and swirl to coat pan. Add sausage and using a spatula or slotted spoon begin breaking up the meat into small chunks. Cook, tossing gently and continuing to break the meat into small pieces, until it has changed color, about 1 minute.

3. Add onion and ginger and toss well, until fragrant, about 30 seconds more.

4. Add cabbage and toss well. Cook, tossing occasionally, until cabbage has softened, about 1 minute. Add soy sauce mixture, pouring in around sides of pan and toss well. Cook, tossing occasionally, until sausage is no longer pink and cabbage is tender-crisp, about 2 minutes more, adding 1 to 2 tbsp (15 to 25 mL) of water if the pan becomes too dry.

5. Add red pepper and green onions. Toss well and cook for 1 minute more. Transfer to a serving plate. Serve hot or warm.

Green Beans and Hominy
with Country-Style Sausage

1 tbsp	soy sauce	15 mL
1 tbsp	chicken stock or water	15 mL
½ tsp	granulated sugar	2 mL
½ tsp	salt or to taste	2 mL
2 tbsp	vegetable oil	25 mL
8 oz	country-style pork sausage (bulk or removed from casings)	250 g
3 tbsp	chopped onion	45 mL
1 tbsp	chopped garlic	15 mL
1 cup	chopped green beans (1-inch/2.5 cm lengths) (see Tip, right)	250 mL
¾ cup	drained, canned hominy or thawed frozen hominy	175 mL
3 tbsp	chopped green onions	45 mL

Serves 4

Cornbread would be marvelous with this dish, as would rice. Have hot pepper sauce on the table so that fans of fiery food can heat things up as they wish.

TIP

You could use frozen green beans in place of fresh ones, taking care to see that they are cooked through before you add the hominy.

1. In a small bowl, combine soy sauce, stock, sugar and salt and stir well. Set aside.

2. Heat a wok or large deep skillet over high heat. Add oil and swirl to coat pan. Add sausage and using a spatula or slotted spoon begin breaking up the meat into small chunks. Cook, tossing gently and continuing to break the meat into small pieces, until it has changed color, for 1 minute.

3. Add onion and garlic and toss well, until fragrant, about 15 seconds. Add green beans and hominy and toss well. Cook, tossing occasionally, until beans are bright green and beginning to wilt and hominy is hot, about 1 minute more.

4. Add soy sauce mixture, pouring in around sides of pan. Cook, tossing occasionally, until meat is no longer pink and green beans are tender-crisp, 2 to 3 minutes. Add green onions and toss well. Transfer to a serving plate. Serve hot or warm.

Stir-Fried Italian Sausage with Peppers

Serves 4

With a few ingredients and a little prep, you can have a hearty stir-fry version of Italian sausage and peppers on your table any night of the week. Use grilled Italian sausage from last night's cookout or cook sausage in a small skillet shortly before you plan to make this dish. This is great in a hero sandwich, but also wonderful over pasta or with rice — a plate of cucumbers and a spicy salsa on the side.

TIP

To cook Italian sausage for this dish, place about 3 links in a small skillet over medium-high heat. Add ½ cup (125 mL) water and bring to a boil. Cover, reduce heat to medium and cook, turning once or twice, until sausages are no longer pink inside and firm enough to slice, about 10 minutes. Set aside until cool enough to handle.

2 tbsp	soy sauce	25 mL
2 tbsp	chicken stock or water	25 mL
1 tsp	salt or to taste	5 mL
½ tsp	granulated sugar	2 mL
2 tbsp	vegetable oil	25 mL
1 tbsp	chopped garlic	15 mL
1½ cups	bite-size chunks red and green bell peppers	375 mL
¾ cup	coarsely chopped onion	175 mL
1½ lbs	Italian sausage, cooked, cut diagonally into ½-inch (1 cm) slices (see Tip, left)	750 g
2 tbsp	finely chopped Italian parsley	25 mL

1. In a small bowl, combine soy sauce, stock, salt and sugar and stir well. Set aside.

2. Heat a wok or a large deep skillet over high heat. Add oil and swirl to coat pan. Add garlic and toss well, until fragrant, about 15 seconds. Add red and green peppers and onion. Cook, tossing once or twice, until vegetables are fragrant, about 1 minute.

3. Add sausage and toss once. Add soy sauce mixture, pouring in around sides of pan. Cook, tossing occasionally, until sausage is hot and peppers and onions are tender-crisp, 1 to 2 minutes more.

4. Add parsley and toss once. Transfer to a serving plate. Serve hot or warm.

Thai Shrimp with Roasted Chile Paste
(page 141)

Overleaf: Chinese Sausage with Cucumber (page 164)

Garlic-Scented Sausage with Bok Choy and Pine Nuts

1 tbsp	soy sauce	15 mL
1 tbsp	water	15 mL
½ tsp	granulated sugar	2 mL
½ tsp	salt or to taste	2 mL
¼ tsp	freshly ground pepper	1 mL
2 tbsp	vegetable oil	25 mL
2 tbsp	chopped garlic	25 mL
8 oz	Italian sausage, hot or mild (bulk or casings removed)	250 g
5 cups	chopped bok choy (2-inch/5 cm squares) (see Tip, right)	1.25 L
¼ cup	pine nuts or chopped walnuts, optional	50 mL

1. In a small bowl, combine soy sauce, water, sugar, salt and pepper and stir well. Set aside.

2. Heat a wok or large deep skillet over high heat. Add oil and swirl to coat pan. Add garlic and toss well, until fragrant, about 15 seconds.

3. Add sausage and using a spatula or slotted spoon begin breaking up the meat into small chunks. Cook, tossing gently and continuing to break the meat into small pieces, until it has changed color, about 1 minute.

4. Add bok choy and toss well. Cook, tossing occasionally, until bok choy leaves are wilted and sausage is no longer pink, 2 to 3 minutes.

5. Add soy sauce mixture, pouring in around sides of pan. Add pine nuts, if using. Cook, tossing occasionally, until everything is evenly seasoned and bok choy is tender-crisp, about 1 minute more. Transfer to a serving plate. Serve hot or warm.

Serves 4

I like to make this with spicy-hot Italian sausage, but you could use any kind of ground pork sausage with tasty results. With the deep green and white colors of bok choy leaves and stalks, this dish looks inviting and sausage makes a wonderful partner.

TIP

To prepare the bok choy, halve a head of it lengthwise, and then chop it crosswise into 2-inch (5 cm) squarish chunks. For larger heads of bok choy, quarter it lengthwise, so that each long piece is about 2 inches (5 cm) wide.

Overleaf: Spicy Lamb with Tomatoes and Edamame Beans (page 167)

Chinese-Style Roast Duck with Hoisin Sauce and Cabbage (page 168)

Italian Sausage with Smoked Paprika and Tiny Peas

Serves 4

Spicy or mild, Italian sausage rises to new heights when seasoned with smoked Spanish paprika. This is tasty tossed with bowtie pasta or spaghetti.

1 tbsp	soy sauce	15 mL
1 tbsp	water	15 mL
2 tsp	smoked Spanish or sweet paprika	10 mL
½ tsp	freshly ground pepper	2 mL
½ tsp	salt or to taste	2 mL
½ tsp	granulated sugar	2 mL
2 tbsp	vegetable oil	25 mL
3 tbsp	chopped onion	45 mL
1 tbsp	chopped garlic	15 mL
12 oz	Italian sausage (bulk or removed from casing)	375 g
1 cup	frozen tiny peas	250 mL
3 tbsp	chopped Italian parsley	45 mL
3 tbsp	chopped green onions	45 mL

1. In a small bowl, combine soy sauce, water, paprika, pepper, salt and sugar and stir well.

2. Heat a wok or a large deep skillet over high heat. Add oil and swirl to coat pan. Add onion and garlic and toss well, until fragrant, about 15 seconds.

3. Add sausage and using a spatula or slotted spoon begin breaking up the meat into small chunks. Cook, tossing gently and continuing to break the meat into small pieces, until it has changed color, about 1 minute. Add peas and toss well.

4. Add soy sauce mixture, pouring in around sides of pan. Cook, tossing occasionally, until meat is no longer pink and peas are tender and hot, 1 to 2 minutes.

5. Add parsley and green onions and toss well. Transfer to a serving plate. Serve hot or warm.

Kielbasa with Home Fries and Peppers

2 tbsp	soy sauce	25 mL
1 tbsp	water	15 mL
½ tsp	granulated sugar	2 mL
2 tbsp	vegetable oil	25 mL
2 tsp	chopped garlic	10 mL
12 oz	chopped kielbasa (½-inch/1 cm chunks)	375 g
½ cup	chopped green bell pepper	125 mL
½ cup	chopped red bell pepper	125 mL
2 cups	frozen home fries-style potatoes	500 mL
¼ cup	chopped green onions	50 mL

Serves 4

Kielbasa is a Polish-style cooked sausage found in supermarkets. With its rich, salty notes and the ease it is to dice, toss in and heat up, kielbasa is a staple item for my stir-fry kitchen. You can use it in place of ham in any of these recipes.

1. In a small bowl, combine soy sauce, water and sugar and stir well. Set aside.

2. Heat a wok or a large deep skillet over high heat. Add oil and swirl to coat pan. Add garlic and toss well, until fragrant, about 15 seconds. Add kielbasa. Toss well and spread into a single layer. Cook, undisturbed, for 30 seconds. Toss again. Add green and red peppers and toss well.

3. Cook, tossing often, until kielbasa is lightly browned all over and peppers are tender-crisp, about 1 minute.

4. Add potatoes, tossing well, and cook until heated through and lightly browned, 1 to 2 minutes more.

5. Add soy sauce mixture, pouring in around sides of pan. Add green onions. Cook, tossing often, until everything is evenly combined, about 30 seconds more. Transfer to a serving plate. Serve hot or warm.

Chinese Sausage with Cucumber

Serves 4

This rich Chinese sausage is firm and dried like pepperoni, but has the richness of bacon and the sweetness of sugar-cured ham to turn your expectations in a different direction. Cooks in Thailand slice it up and stir-fry it quickly as in this recipe, while in China, it is often chopped up and added to fried rice or noodle stir-fries.

TIP

Chinese sausage is widely available in Asian markets. Usually it is sold in shelf-stable plastic packages, sometimes labeled *lap cheong*, the Cantonese name for them. They are dark red in color and shaped into very firm links, a little shorter and smaller than hot dogs, with about 6 links to a 16 oz (500 g) package. They should be transferred to a resealable package and refrigerated after opening.

1 tbsp	soy sauce	15 mL
2 tsp	dry sherry or Shaoxing rice wine	10 mL
1 tsp	sesame oil	5 mL
½ tsp	granulated sugar	2 mL
½ tsp	salt or to taste	2 mL
¼ tsp	freshly ground pepper	1 mL
2 tbsp	vegetable oil	25 mL
1 tbsp	chopped garlic	15 mL
2 cups	diagonally sliced Chinese sausage (¼ inch/0.5 cm slices) (see Tip, left)	500 mL
1½ cups	chopped peeled cucumber (½-inch/1 cm chunks)	375 mL
3 tbsp	chopped green onions	45 mL
3 tbsp	chopped fresh cilantro	45 mL

1. In a small bowl, combine soy sauce, sherry, sesame oil, sugar, salt and pepper and stir well. Set aside.

2. Heat a wok or large deep skillet over high heat. Add oil and swirl to coat pan. Add garlic and toss well, until fragrant, about 15 seconds.

3. Add sausage, toss well, and spread into a single layer. Cook, undisturbed, for 1 minute. Toss well and cook until lightly and evenly browned, about 1 minute more.

4. Add cucumbers, toss well, and cook, until they begin to soften, 1 minute.

5. Add soy sauce mixture, pouring in around sides of pan. Cook, tossing often, until everything is evenly seasoned and sausage is heated through, 1 to 2 minutes more. Add green onions and cilantro and toss well. Transfer to a serving plate. Serve hot or warm.

> **Variation:** You could use diced ham or kielbasa instead of Chinese sausage with tasty results.

Curry-Spiced Lamb with Cauliflower

2 tbsp	chicken stock or water	25 mL
1 tbsp	fish sauce	15 mL
2 tsp	freshly squeezed lime juice	10 mL
1 tsp	granulated sugar	5 mL
1 tsp	cornstarch	5 mL
1 tsp	soy sauce	5 mL
1/4 tsp	freshly ground pepper	1 mL
2 tbsp	vegetable oil	25 mL
1 tbsp	chopped garlic	15 mL
1 tbsp	chopped fresh gingerroot	15 mL
1/2 cup	chopped onion	125 mL
1 tbsp	chopped green onions	15 mL
1 tbsp	curry powder	15 mL
12 oz	thinly sliced boneless lamb shoulder	375 g
3 cups	thinly sliced cauliflower florets (see Tip, right)	750 mL

1. In a small bowl, combine stock, fish sauce, lime juice, sugar, cornstarch, soy sauce and pepper and stir well into a smooth sauce. Set aside.

2. Heat a wok or a large deep skillet over high heat. Add oil and swirl to coat pan. Add garlic and ginger and toss well. Add onion and green onions and cook, tossing occasionally, until fragrant, about 1 minute.

3. Add curry powder and cook, tossing often, until everything is wilted and evenly combined, about 1 minute more.

4. Push onion mixture to one side and add lamb, spreading into a single layer. Cook on one side, undisturbed, until edges have changed color, about 1 minute. Toss well and cook until most of the meat is no longer pink, about 30 seconds.

5. Add cauliflower and toss well. Cook, tossing often, until cauliflower is tender-crisp and lamb is cooked through, 2 to 3 minutes more.

6. Stir chicken stock mixture and add to pan, pouring in around sides. Cook, tossing occasionally, to combine everything well, 1 minute more. Transfer to a serving plate. Serve hot or warm.

TIP

For this dish, you need large, thin cauliflower slices, which I cut in cross sections rather than rounded florets. Trim a head of cauliflower and cut it lengthwise in half. Place one half cut side down, and then slice thinly into large flat pieces that are about 1/4-inch (0.5 cm) thick. Cut these tree-like slabs into pieces that are about 1 1/2 inches (4 cm) in diameter.

Mongolian-Style Lamb with Shredded Carrots

Serves 4

This satisfying dish works nicely with a green salad to contrast with the rich-flavored sauce and lots of rice on which to enjoy it.

TIP

You could use lamb loin, lamb shoulder or leg of lamb for this recipe.

1 tbsp	chicken stock or water	15 mL
1 tbsp	water	15 mL
2 tsp	dark soy sauce or molasses, optional	10 mL
2 tsp	cornstarch	10 mL
12 oz	thinly sliced boneless lamb (see Tip, left)	375 g
2 tbsp	dry sherry or Shaoxing rice wine	25 mL
1 tbsp	red wine vinegar	15 mL
2 tsp	sesame oil	10 mL
½ tsp	granulated sugar	2 mL
2 tbsp	vegetable oil	25 mL
2 tbsp	chopped onion	25 mL
1 tbsp	chopped garlic	15 mL
¾ cup	shredded carrots	175 mL
¼ cup	chopped green onions	50 mL

1. In a bowl, combine chicken stock, water, dark soy sauce, if using, and cornstarch and stir well to make a smooth sauce. Add lamb and stir to coat evenly and mix well. Set aside for 10 minutes.

2. In a small bowl, combine sherry, vinegar, sesame oil and sugar and stir well. Set aside.

3. Heat a wok or a large deep skillet over high heat. Add oil and swirl to coat pan. Add onion and garlic and toss well, until fragrant, about 15 seconds.

4. Add lamb mixture and spread into a single layer. Cook, undisturbed, for 30 seconds. Toss well. Cook, tossing occasionally, until lamb has changed color, about 1 minute. Add carrots and toss well.

5. Add sherry mixture, pouring in around sides of pan. Toss well. Add green onions. Cook, tossing occasionally, until lamb is cooked through and everything is evenly seasoned and well combined, about 1 minute more. Transfer to a serving plate. Serve hot or warm.

Spicy Lamb with Tomatoes and Edamame Beans

2 tbsp	soy sauce	25 mL
2 tbsp	dry sherry or Shaoxing rice wine	25 mL
2 tsp	curry powder	10 mL
1 tsp	ground cumin	5 mL
1 tsp	granulated sugar	5 mL
½ tsp	salt or to taste	2 mL
½ tsp	hot pepper flakes	2 mL
2 tbsp	vegetable oil	25 mL
1 tbsp	chopped garlic	15 mL
8 oz	ground lamb	250 g
¾ cup	frozen edamame beans	175 mL
3 tbsp	water	45 mL
½ cup	halved cherry tomatoes	125 mL
¼ cup	chopped fresh cilantro	50 mL

Serves 4

This recipe can be tossed with pasta or tucked into warm tortillas.

1. In a small bowl, combine soy sauce, sherry, curry powder, cumin, sugar, salt and hot pepper flakes and stir well. Set aside.

2. Heat a wok or a large deep skillet over high heat. Add oil and swirl to coat pan. Add garlic and toss well, until fragrant, about 15 seconds.

3. Add ground lamb and using a spatula break up meat and spread into a single layer. Toss well. Cook, tossing occasionally, until no longer pink on the outside, about 1 minute.

4. Add soy sauce mixture and toss well. Add edamame beans and water. Cook, tossing occasionally, until lamb is no longer pink and edamame beans are hot, about 1 to 2 minutes more.

5. Add cherry tomatoes and cilantro and toss well. Transfer to a serving plate. Serve hot or warm.

Chinese-Style Roast Duck with Hoisin Sauce and Cabbage

Serves 4

If you are lucky enough to live where Chinese-style roast duck is available, you will enjoy this dish often. But it's also quite delicious made with rotisserie chicken, which many supermarkets now carry. Rice is always right here, but you can also try this with mandarin pancakes or tortillas.

2 tbsp	hoisin sauce	25 mL
1 tbsp	water	15 mL
1 tbsp	dry sherry or Shaoxing rice wine	15 mL
1 tsp	salt or to taste	5 mL
2 tbsp	vegetable oil	25 mL
1 tbsp	chopped garlic	15 mL
2½ cups	shredded roast duck or roast chicken (about 12 oz/375 g)	625 mL
1 cup	shredded napa cabbage or spinach leaves	250 mL
¼ cup	chopped green onions	50 mL

1. In a small bowl, combine hoisin sauce, water, sherry and salt and stir well. Set aside.

2. Heat a wok or a large heavy skillet over high heat. Add oil and swirl to coat pan. Add garlic and toss well, until fragrant, about 15 seconds.

3. Add roast duck and toss well. Add cabbage and cook, tossing often, until duck is heated through and napa cabbage is bright green and tender-crisp, about 1 minute.

4. Add hoisin sauce mixture, pouring in around sides of pan. Cook, tossing often, until everything is evenly seasoned, about 1 minute more. Add green onions and toss well. Transfer to a serving plate. Serve hot or warm.

Next-Day Turkey Stir-Fry

2 tbsp	dry sherry	25 mL
1 tbsp	soy sauce	15 mL
1 tbsp	water	15 mL
1/2 tsp	salt or to taste	2 mL
2 tbsp	vegetable oil	25 mL
2 tbsp	chopped onion	25 mL
1 tbsp	chopped garlic	15 mL
1 1/2 cups	diced celery	375 mL
3 cups	chopped cooked turkey or chicken (big bite-size chunks)	750 mL
3 tbsp	chunky cranberry sauce	45 mL
2 tbsp	chopped Italian parsley	25 mL

1. In a small bowl, combine sherry, soy sauce, water and salt and stir well. Set aside.

2. Heat a wok or large heavy skillet over high heat. Add oil and swirl to coat pan. Add onion and garlic and toss well, until fragrant, about 15 seconds.

3. Add celery and toss well. Add turkey and toss well. Cook, undisturbed, for 30 seconds. Toss well. Cook, tossing occasionally, until turkey is heated through and celery is bright green and tender-crisp, about 1 minute more.

4. Add sherry mixture, pouring in around sides of pan. Toss well. Add cranberry sauce and cook, tossing twice, until everything is evenly seasoned. Add parsley and toss well. Transfer to a serving plate. Serve hot or warm.

Serves 4

If turkey with cranberry sauce is on your holiday menu, turn what's left after the big meal into a quick, tasty supper. You could use roast chicken as well as roast turkey with tasty results.

Just Jerky Caribbean-Style Chicken Stir-Fry

Serves 4

Jazz up rotisserie chicken in this speedy, spice-kissed dish. Shred or chop the chicken and you're ready to stir-fry it into a filling for warm tortillas as well as a tasty companion to rice. Add hot pepper sauce at the table if you like.

1 tsp	ground cumin	5 mL
½ tsp	ground coriander	2 mL
¼ tsp	ground allspice	1 mL
1 tsp	salt or to taste	5 mL
½ tsp	granulated sugar	2 mL
¼ tsp	freshly ground pepper	1 mL
2 tbsp	soy sauce	25 mL
1 tbsp	freshly squeezed lime juice or vinegar	15 mL
1 tbsp	water	15 mL.
2 tbsp	vegetable oil	25 mL
¼ cup	chopped onion	50 mL
1 tbsp	chopped garlic	15 mL
3 cups	chopped roast chicken (big bite-size chunks)	750 mL
¾ cup	halved cherry tomatoes	175 mL
¼ cup	chopped green onions	50 mL
3 tbsp	chopped fresh cilantro	45 mL

1. In a small bowl, combine cumin, coriander, allspice, salt, sugar and pepper and stir well. Set aside.

2. In another small bowl, combine soy sauce, lime juice and water. Set aside.

3. Heat a wok or a large deep skillet over high heat. Add oil and swirl to coat pan. Add onion and garlic and toss well, until fragrant, about 15 seconds.

4. Add cumin mixture and toss well. Add chicken and toss well. Cook, tossing once or twice, until evenly seasoned and heated through, about 1 minute.

5. Add soy sauce mixture, pouring in around sides of pan. Toss well. Add cherry tomatoes, green onions and cilantro and toss to mix well. Transfer to a serving plate. Serve hot or warm.

Fish & Seafood

Pretty Pink Salmon Chunks with Green Pea and Dill Accents

Serves 4

Pink salmon chunks tumble with vivid green peas and fresh dill in a delightful contrast of colors in this decorative dish.

TIP

Use thick portions of salmon for this dish, so that they are sturdy enough to hold up during the cooking process.

1 tbsp	soy sauce	15 mL
1 tbsp	dry sherry or Shaoxing rice wine	15 mL
1 tbsp	water	15 mL
½ tsp	salt or to taste	2 mL
½ tsp	granulated sugar	2 mL
2 tbsp	vegetable oil	25 mL
2 tsp	chopped fresh gingerroot	10 mL
2 tsp	chopped garlic	10 mL
12 oz	skinless salmon, cut into 2-inch (5 cm) chunks (see Tip, left)	375 g
¾ cup	frozen tiny peas	175 mL
2 tbsp	chopped green onions	25 mL
2 tbsp	chopped fresh dill	25 mL

1. In a small bowl, combine soy sauce, sherry, water, salt and sugar and stir well. Set aside.

2. Heat a wok or large deep skillet over medium-high heat. Add oil and swirl to coat pan. Add ginger and garlic and toss well, until fragrant, about 15 seconds.

3. Add salmon and spread into a single layer. Cook, undisturbed, until edges change color, about 1 minute. Gently turn and cook other side, undisturbed, for 30 seconds more. Add peas and toss gently.

4. Add soy sauce mixture, pouring in around sides of pan. Cook, tossing gently once or twice, until salmon is cooked through and peas are hot, 1 to 2 minutes more.

5. Add green onions and dill and toss gently to mix well. Transfer to a serving plate. Serve hot or warm.

Lime-Splashed Salmon with Chiles and Cilantro

12 oz	skinless salmon fillets, cut into 2-inch (5 cm) chunks	375 g
2 tbsp	soy sauce	25 mL
2 tbsp	fish sauce	25 mL
2 tbsp	freshly squeezed lime juice	25 mL
2 tsp	granulated sugar	10 mL
1 tsp	chopped fresh hot green chiles	5 mL
½ tsp	salt or to taste	2 mL
2 tbsp	vegetable oil	25 mL
2 tbsp	chopped garlic	25 mL
2 tbsp	chopped onion	25 mL
2 tbsp	chopped green onions	25 mL
2 tbsp	chopped fresh cilantro	25 mL

Serves 4

Thai flavors take the stage here, with a splash of lime and a flare of chiles to season a quick and delicious dish.

1. In a bowl, combine salmon and soy sauce. Toss gently to season the salmon evenly. Set aside for 10 minutes.

2. In a small bowl, combine fish sauce, lime juice, sugar, chiles and salt and stir well. Set aside.

3. Heat a wok or a large deep skillet over medium-high heat. Add oil and swirl to coat pan. Add garlic and onion and toss well. Cook, tossing often, until softened and fragrant, about 1 minute.

4. Add salmon mixture and spread into a single layer. Cook, undisturbed, until edges change color, about 1 minute. Gently turn and cook other side, undisturbed, for 30 seconds

5. Toss gently. Add fish sauce mixture, pouring in around sides of pan. Cook, tossing gently once or twice, until salmon is cooked through and evenly seasoned with sauce, 1 to 2 minutes more.

6. Add green onions and cilantro and toss to mix well. Transfer to a serving plate. Serve hot or warm.

Thai-Style Salmon with Green Curry Sauce and Fresh Basil

Serves 4

Salmon's signature color makes for a particularly pleasing presentation here. The lime leaves and basil contribute lovely flavor and aroma to this dish, but can be omitted if they are difficult to find. You will still have a delicious dish.

TIP

If basil leaves are small, add them whole to the curry. If they are large, tear them into 1-inch (2.5 cm) pieces right after you add coconut milk to the pan.

12 oz	skinless salmon fillets, cut into 2-inch (5 cm) chunks	375 g
1 tbsp	soy sauce	15 mL
1 cup	unsweetened coconut milk	250 mL
2 tbsp	fish sauce	25 mL
1 tbsp	brown sugar	15 mL
½ tsp	salt or to taste	2 mL
6	makrut lime leaves, quartered, optional	6
2 tbsp	vegetable oil	25 mL
¾ cup	frozen peeled edamame beans or tiny peas	175 mL
2 tbsp	Thai-style green curry paste	25 mL
2 tbsp	water	25 mL
¼ cup	fresh basil leaves, optional (see Tip, left)	50 mL

1. In a bowl, combine salmon and soy sauce. Toss gently to season the salmon evenly. Set aside for 10 minutes.

2. In a bowl, combine coconut milk, fish sauce, brown sugar, salt and lime leaves, if using, and stir well. Set aside.

3. Heat a wok or a large deep skillet over medium-high heat. Add oil and swirl to coat pan. Add salmon mixture and spread into a single layer. Cook, undisturbed, until edges change color, about 1 minute. Gently turn and cook other side, undisturbed, for 15 seconds more.

4. Add edamame beans, curry paste and water. Cook, tossing gently once or twice, until curry paste dissolves into a thin sauce, about 30 seconds.

5. Add coconut milk mixture, pouring in around sides of pan. Cook, tossing gently once or twice, until curry has reached a gentle boil and salmon and edamame beans are cooked through, 1 to 2 minutes more. Stir well and add basil leaves, if using. Transfer to a shallow serving bowl or deep serving plate. Serve hot or warm.

Tuna Chunks with White Beans and Flavorful Greens

12 oz	tuna steaks, cut into 2-inch (5 cm) chunks	375 g
2 tbsp	soy sauce	25 mL
2 tbsp	freshly squeezed lemon juice	25 mL
1 tbsp	water	15 mL
1 tsp	granulated sugar	5 mL
1 tsp	salt or to taste	5 mL
½ tsp	freshly ground pepper	2 mL
2 tbsp	vegetable oil	25 mL
1 tbsp	chopped garlic	15 mL
2 tbsp	chopped shallots or onion	25 mL
3 cups	arugula or coarsely chopped watercress leaves	750 mL
¾ cup	halved cherry tomatoes	175 mL
2 tbsp	chopped green onions	25 mL

Serves 4

Tuna steaks cut into chunks and stir-fried with garlic, white beans and flavorful greens make for a delicious Asian-style approach to Mediterranean ingredients. Serve this with couscous and a colorful mix of olives.

1. In a bowl, combine tuna and soy sauce. Toss gently to season tuna evenly. Set aside for 10 minutes.

2. In a small bowl, combine lemon juice, water, sugar, salt and pepper and stir well. Set aside.

3. Heat a wok or a large deep skillet over medium-high heat. Add oil and swirl to coat pan. Add tuna mixture and spread into a single layer. Cook, undisturbed, until edges change color, about 1 minute. Gently turn and cook other side, undisturbed, for 30 seconds more.

4. Toss gently. Add garlic and shallots and toss well. Cook, tossing gently once, until fragrant and softened, about 30 seconds more.

5. Add lemon juice mixture, pouring in around sides of pan. Cook, tossing once or twice, until tuna is almost cooked to desired doneness.

6. Add arugula, cherry tomatoes and green onions. Toss well and cook until arugula is just wilted, about 1 minute more. Transfer to a serving plate. Serve hot or warm.

Mediterranean-Inspired Tuna Stir-Fry

Serves 4

Serve this dish with couscous or rice and a crusty loaf of warm bread. You could also toss it with roughly torn romaine lettuce leaves and enjoy it as a hearty warm salad.

TIPS

You could use kalamata olives or black olives or a mix of your favorites.

Drizzle a little of a favorite fruity olive oil over the dish at serving time for an extra flavor note.

2 tbsp	balsamic vinegar	25 mL
1 tbsp	freshly squeezed lemon juice	15 mL
1 tsp	granulated sugar	5 mL
1 tsp	salt or to taste	5 mL
2 tbsp	vegetable oil	25 mL
3 tbsp	chopped green onions	45 mL
1 tbsp	chopped garlic	15 mL
12 oz	tuna steaks, cut into 2-inch (5 cm) chunks	375 g
¾ cup	halved cherry tomatoes	175 mL
2 tbsp	chopped pitted ripe olives (see Tips, left)	25 mL
1 tbsp	chopped capers	15 mL
2 tbsp	chopped fresh oregano or cilantro	25 mL

1. In a small bowl, combine vinegar, lemon juice, sugar and salt and stir well. Set aside.
2. Heat a wok or a large deep skillet over medium-high heat. Add oil and swirl to coat pan. Add green onions and garlic and toss well, until fragrant, about 20 seconds.
3. Add tuna and spread into a single layer. Cook, undisturbed, until edges change color, about 1 minute. Gently turn and cook other side, undisturbed, for 30 seconds more.
4. Add vinegar mixture, pouring in around sides of pan. Cook, tossing once or twice, until tuna is cooked through (or to your liking), 1 to 2 minutes.
5. Add cherry tomatoes, olives, capers and oregano and toss well. Cook, tossing gently, until tomatoes just begin to wilt and everything is seasoned evenly, about 30 seconds more. Transfer to a serving plate. Serve hot or warm.

Cod with Black Bean Sauce

2 tbsp	coarsely chopped salted black beans (see Tips, right and page 125)	25 mL
2 tbsp	chopped fresh gingerroot	25 mL
2 tsp	chopped garlic	10 mL
2 tbsp	dry sherry or Shaoxing rice wine	25 mL
1 tbsp	soy sauce	15 mL
¼ cup	water	50 mL
2 tsp	cornstarch	10 mL
2 tbsp	vegetable oil	25 mL
½ cup	chopped onion	125 mL
½ cup	chopped green bell pepper	125 mL
12 oz	cod, cut into 2-inch (5 cm) chunks	375 g
2 tbsp	chopped green onions	25 mL

1. In a small bowl, combine salted black beans, ginger and garlic. Using the back of a spoon, mash everything together to make a rough paste. Set aside.

2. In another small bowl, combine sherry, soy sauce, water and cornstarch and stir well to make a smooth paste. Set aside.

3. Heat a wok or a large deep skillet over high heat. Add oil and swirl to coat pan. Add onion and green pepper and toss well. Cook, tossing occasionally, until fragrant and softened, about 1 minute.

4. Push onion and pepper to one side and add cod, spreading into a single layer. Cook, undisturbed, until edges change color, about 1 minute. Gently turn and cook other side, undisturbed, for 30 seconds more. Add black bean mixture, tossing gently to mix with cod.

5. Stir sherry mixture and add to pan, tossing gently to mix everything well. Add green onions and cook, tossing gently once or twice, until cod is just cooked through and everything is nicely combined in a dark, smooth sauce, about 1 minute more. Transfer to a deep serving plate or a shallow serving bowl. Serve hot or warm.

Serves 4

In Cantonese cuisine, black bean sauce with chunks of meaty fish is a classic pairing and it makes an outstanding dish. Soft, small and very salted black beans keep well if you transfer them to a glass jar after opening the package. Rice is the perfect partner for this saucy dish.

TIPS

Because fish has such a delicate texture, it receives a gentler treatment in stir-fry cooking than many other ingredients. Toss it less and with greater care, so that pieces stay intact for the most part and be sure not to overcook it.

To mash the black beans, ginger and garlic, you could also pile them up on your cutting board and chop them together to blend them into a coarse paste.

Miso-Soaked Cod
with Edamame

Serves 4

I love the deep, rich flavor of miso in this Japanese-inspired dish. You get a triple play with soy as well, since edamame, which are fresh green soybeans, team up with soy sauce and miso, both of which are made from soybeans.

TIP

Look for miso in Asian markets or in some grocery stores and supermarkets. Once you open the package, place it in a resealable bag or container and keep it refrigerated. It keeps well for a long time.

2 tbsp	red miso paste (see Tip, left)	25 mL
1 tbsp	dry sherry or Shaoxing rice wine	15 mL
1 tsp	soy sauce	5 mL
½ tsp	granulated sugar	2 mL
½ tsp	freshly ground pepper	2 mL
12 oz	cod or salmon, cut into 2-inch (5 cm) chunks	375 g
2 tbsp	vegetable oil	25 mL
1 tbsp	chopped garlic	15 mL
¾ cup	frozen edamame beans	175 mL
⅓ cup	chopped green onions	75 mL

1. In bowl, combine miso, 2 tbsp (25 mL) water, sherry, soy sauce, sugar and pepper and stir well. Add cod and toss gently to coat evenly. Set aside for 15 minutes.

2. Heat a wok or large skillet over medium-high heat. Add oil and swirl to coat pan. Add garlic and toss well, until fragrant, about 15 seconds. Add edamame beans and green onions and cook, tossing often, until green onions have softened, about 1 minute.

3. Add cod mixture, spreading into a single layer. Cook, undisturbed, until edges change color, for 1 minute. Turn and cook other side, undisturbed, for 30 seconds more.

4. Add 2 tbsp (25 mL) water and toss gently to mix in with the sauce. Cook, tossing gently, until cod is just cooked through, about 1 minute more. Transfer to a serving plate. Serve hot or warm.

Halibut Provençal

2 tbsp	red or white wine vinegar	25 mL
1 tbsp	dry sherry or Shaoxing rice wine	15 mL
1 tsp	salt or to taste	5 mL
2 tbsp	vegetable oil	25 mL
1 tbsp	chopped garlic	15 mL
2 tbsp	chopped onion	25 mL
12 oz	skinless halibut fillet, cut into 2-inch (5 cm) pieces	375 g
½ cup	coarsely chopped plum (Roma) tomatoes	125 mL
3 tbsp	chopped Italian parsley	45 mL
2 tbsp	extra virgin olive oil, optional	25 mL

1. In a small bowl, combine vinegar, sherry and salt and stir well. Set aside.

2. Heat a wok or a large deep skillet over high heat. Add oil and swirl to coat pan. Add garlic and onion and toss well, until fragrant, about 30 seconds.

3. Add halibut and spread into a single layer. Cook, undisturbed, until edges change color, about 1 minute. Gently turn and cook other side, undisturbed, for 30 seconds.

4. Toss gently. Add vinegar mixture, pouring in around sides of pan. Cook, tossing gently once or twice, until halibut is cooked through, 1 to 2 minutes more.

5. Add tomatoes and toss well. Cook, tossing gently once or twice, until tomatoes have softened a little, 1 minute more. Add parsley and toss gently to mix everything well. Transfer to a serving plate and pour olive oil over the dish, if using. Serve hot or warm.

Serves 4

The warm flavors of the Mediterranean kitchen light up this dish and the colors are a treat for the eye.

Jerk-Style Catfish
with Cherry Tomatoes

Serves 4

Spicy and delicious, this dish could win over anyone who thinks fish can't rule the table as a flashy and feisty dish. Catfish chunks work well, but any thick, firm fish will do nicely, too. A little plate of sliced cucumbers and radishes make a pleasing accompaniment to this dish, along with rice and a salad with a poppy seed or a honey-mustard dressing.

½ tsp	dried thyme	2 mL
¼ tsp	ground allspice	1 mL
¼ tsp	granulated sugar	1 mL
¼ tsp	ground cayenne pepper	1 mL
¼ tsp	salt or to taste	1 mL
¼ tsp	freshly ground pepper	1 mL
12 oz	catfish or other firm fish (such as cod or halibut), cut into 2-inch (5 cm) chunks	375 g
1 tbsp	Worcestershire sauce or soy sauce	15 mL
1 tbsp	dry sherry or Shaoxing rice wine	15 mL
1 tbsp	red wine vinegar or cider vinegar	15 mL
2 tbsp	vegetable oil	25 mL
1 tbsp	chopped garlic	15 mL
½ cup	halved cherry tomatoes	125 mL
¼ cup	chopped green onions	50 mL
2 tbsp	chopped fresh cilantro	25 mL
	Lime wedges	

1. In a bowl, combine thyme, allspice, sugar, cayenne pepper, salt and pepper and stir well. Add catfish and mix gently to season evenly with spice mixture. Set aside for 10 minutes.

2. In a small bowl, combine Worcestershire sauce, sherry and vinegar and stir well. Set aside.

3. Heat a wok or a large deep skillet over medium-high heat. Add oil and swirl to coat pan. Add garlic and toss well, until fragrant, about 15 seconds.

4. Add catfish mixture and spread into a single layer. Cook, undisturbed, until edges change color, about 1 minute. Gently turn and cook other side, undisturbed, for 30 seconds.

5. Add Worcestershire sauce mixture, pouring in around sides of pan. Add tomatoes. Toss well. Cook, tossing gently once or twice, until catfish is cooked through and tomatoes have begun to wilt, about 1 minute more.

6. Add green onions and cilantro and toss gently just to mix everything well. Transfer to a serving plate. Serve hot or warm with lime wedges to squeeze over top.

Vietnamese-Style Curry Catfish with Fresh Dill

1 tbsp	curry powder	15 mL
3 tbsp	vegetable oil, divided	45 mL
12 oz	catfish or tilapia, cut into 2-inch (5 cm) chunks	375 g
2 tbsp	fish sauce	25 mL
1 tbsp	soy sauce	15 mL
½ tsp	salt or to taste	2 mL
½ tsp	granulated sugar	2 mL
1 tbsp	chopped garlic	15 mL
1 tbsp	chopped fresh gingerroot	15 mL
¼ cup	chopped green onions	50 mL
¼ cup	chopped fresh dill	50 mL
3 tbsp	chopped salted peanuts	45 mL

Serves 4

This dish is inspired by the classic Northern-style dish, *Cha Ca La Vong*. It is usually served with rice noodles, but my family loves this fragrant and delicious dish with rice.

1. In a bowl, combine curry powder and 1 tbsp (15 mL) of the oil. Add catfish and mix everything well. Set aside for 10 minutes.

2. In a small bowl, combine fish sauce, soy sauce, salt and sugar and stir well. Set aside.

3. Heat a wok or a large deep skillet over medium-high heat. Add remaining oil and swirl to coat pan. Add garlic and ginger and toss well, until fragrant, about 30 seconds.

4. Add catfish and spread into a single layer. Cook, undisturbed, until edges change color, about 1 minute. Gently turn and cook other side, undisturbed, for 30 seconds.

5. Toss gently and add fish sauce mixture, pouring in around sides of pan. Cook, tossing gently once or twice, until fish is cooked through, about 1 minute more.

6. Add green onions and dill and toss well. Transfer to a serving plate and sprinkle with chopped peanuts. Serve hot or warm.

Turmeric-Brushed Thai-Style Catfish

Serves 4

Turmeric is ginger's first cousin and its warm rich golden color makes this fish dish as beautiful as it is tasty.

2 tbsp	fish sauce	25 mL
2 tsp	soy sauce	10 mL
1 tbsp	water	15 mL
1 tbsp	coarsely minced garlic	15 mL
1 tbsp	coarsely minced shallots	15 mL
1 tsp	ground turmeric	5 mL
½ tsp	granulated sugar	2 mL
½ tsp	salt or to taste	2 mL
¼ tsp	freshly ground pepper	1 mL
3 tbsp	vegetable oil, divided	45 mL
12 oz	catfish or other firm fish (such as cod or halibut), cut into 2-inch (5 cm) chunks	375 g
2 tbsp	chopped green onions	25 mL
2 tbsp	chopped fresh cilantro	25 mL

1. In a small bowl, combine fish sauce, soy sauce and water and stir well. Set aside.

2. In a bowl, combine garlic, shallots, turmeric, sugar, salt, pepper and 1 tbsp (15 mL) of the oil and stir well. Add fish and turn to coat evenly with marinade. Set aside for 15 minutes.

3. Heat a wok or a large deep skillet over medium-high heat. Add remaining oil and swirl to coat pan.

4. Add catfish mixture and spread into a single layer. Cook, undisturbed, until edges change color, for 1 minute. Gently turn and cook other side, undisturbed, for 30 seconds.

5. Toss gently and add fish sauce mixture, pouring in around sides of pan. Cook, tossing gently once or twice, until catfish is cooked through and evenly seasoned and browned, about 1 minute more. Add green onions and cilantro and toss gently. Transfer to a serving plate. Serve hot or warm.

Ginger-Scented Scallops with Snow Peas and Sesame Finish

12 oz	sea scallops (see Tip, right)	375 g
3 tbsp	fish sauce	45 mL
2 tbsp	water	25 mL
2 tsp	granulated sugar	10 mL
½ tsp	salt or to taste	2 mL
2 tbsp	vegetable oil	25 mL
1 tbsp	chopped garlic	15 mL
2 tsp	chopped fresh gingerroot	10 mL
2 cups	trimmed snow peas	500 mL
1 tsp	sesame oil	5 mL

1. Rinse scallops and pat completely dry with paper towels.

2. In a small bowl, combine fish sauce, water, sugar and salt and stir well. Set aside.

3. Heat a wok or a large deep skillet over medium-high heat. Add oil and swirl to coat pan. Add garlic and ginger and toss well, until fragrant, about 30 seconds. Add snow peas and toss well.

4. Push snow peas aside and add scallops. Quickly spread scallops into a single layer. Cook, undisturbed, until edges change color, about 1 minute. Gently turn and cook other side, undisturbed, for 30 seconds more.

5. Toss scallops gently and add fish sauce mixture, pouring in around sides of pan. Cook, tossing once or twice, until scallops are cooked through and snow peas are tender-crisp, 1 to 2 minutes more. Add sesame oil and toss well. Transfer to a serving plate. Serve hot.

Serves 4

Scallops are a splurge, but they cook quickly and take center stage with a minimum of additional ingredients and fuss. We love this dish with a side of angel hair pasta tossed with fresh herbs and sesame oil, as well as in a rice-centered Asian-style meal.

TIP

To cook quickly and evenly, scallops should be about the same size, particularly in terms of thickness. Halve any very large ones crosswise, using a very sharp knife, making them similar in thickness to others. You could also remove smaller ones with tongs when they are done and add a little water to the pan allowing the jumbo ones a little extra time to cook through.

Fragrant Scallops with Tiny Peas

Serves 4

Plump and plush in texture, scallops are a feast. Ginger accents their natural oceanic sweetness perfectly. I love this simple dish with a salad of crisp and tender lettuces tossed with dried cranberries, sliced almonds and chunks of apple in a fruity vinaigrette.

TIP

To quickly thaw frozen peas, place them in a bowl and add warm water to cover. Stir and let stand about 5 minutes and then drain well and continue with the recipe.

12 oz	sea scallops (see Tip, page 183)	375 g
2 tbsp	soy sauce	25 mL
1 tbsp	freshly squeezed lime juice	15 mL
2 tsp	dry sherry or Shaoxing rice wine	10 mL
1 tsp	granulated sugar	5 mL
½ tsp	salt or to taste	2 mL
2 tbsp	vegetable oil	25 mL
1 tbsp	chopped fresh gingerroot	15 mL
½ cup	frozen tiny peas, thawed (see Tip, left)	125 mL
2 tbsp	chopped green onions	25 mL

1. Rinse scallops and pat completely dry with paper towels.
2. In a small bowl, combine soy sauce, lime juice, sherry, sugar and salt and stir well. Set aside.
3. Heat a wok or a large deep skillet over medium-high heat. Add oil and swirl to coat pan. Add ginger and toss well, until fragrant, about 30 seconds.
4. Add scallops and spread into a single layer. Cook, undisturbed, until edges change color, about 1 minute. Gently turn and add peas and cook, undisturbed, for 30 seconds more.
5. Toss gently and add soy sauce mixture, pouring in around sides of pan. Cook, tossing once or twice, until scallops are cooked through and peas are hot, about 1 minute more.
6. Add green onions and toss well. Transfer to a serving plate. Serve hot.

Scallops with Cilantro-Garlic Sauce

12 oz	sea scallops (see Tip, page 183)	375 g
1 tbsp	soy sauce	15 mL
1 tbsp	fish sauce	15 mL
1 tbsp	water (approx.)	15 mL
1 tbsp	chopped garlic	15 mL
1 tbsp	chopped cilantro roots, or stems and leaves	15 mL
1 tsp	granulated sugar	5 mL
½ tsp	freshly ground pepper	2 mL
2 tbsp	vegetable oil	25 mL
½ cup	chopped celery (½-inch/1 cm chunks)	125 mL
3 tbsp	chopped fresh cilantro	45 mL

1. Rinse scallops and pat completely dry with paper towels.

2. In a blender or a mini-food processor, combine soy sauce, fish sauce, water, garlic and cilantro roots. Grind to a smooth paste, stopping to scrape down the sides once or twice and adding 1 to 2 tbsp (15 to 25 mL) more water as needed to help the blades move (see Tip, right). Transfer to a small bowl and add sugar and pepper and stir well. Set aside.

3. Heat a wok or a large deep skillet over medium-high heat. Add oil and swirl to coat pan. Add scallops and spread into a single layer. Cook, undisturbed, until edges change color, about 1 minute. Gently turn and add celery and cook, undisturbed, for 30 seconds more.

4. Toss gently and add seasoning paste. Cook, tossing gently once or twice, until scallops are cooked through and evenly seasoned with sauce and celery is tender-crisp. Add chopped cilantro and toss well. Transfer to a serving plate. Serve hot.

Serves 4

Thai cooks use this simply brilliant seasoning combination in countless ways, all of them delicious. If you can find cilantro with the roots attached, use the chopped roots with a bit of stems and leaves. If you can't find the root on, just use chopped stems with a few leaves and you'll still have a flavorful seasoning paste.

TIP

If you have trouble grinding this small amount of seasoning paste, double or triple it and add enough water to move the blades easily. Transfer half or two-thirds of the mixture (depending on the amount by which you increased the ingredients) to a jar, seal and refrigerate for up to 3 days. Use in this recipe or with shrimp using the same method, or stir into soup or spaghetti sauce.

Cantonese-Style Calamari

This Cantonese-style sauce works wonderfully with calamari. Cutting them this way helps them cook up into adorable little tubes that are perfect for capturing the pungent sauce. You could also slice the cleaned calamari crosswise into rings instead of following the scoring and cutting method in Step 1.

TIP

The salted, fermented black beans used in Chinese cooking provide a deliciously pungent flavor to stir-fried and steamed dishes. After you open a new package, transfer the soft, dark beans to a jar and store them airtight at room temperature.

12 oz	cleaned calamari (see Tip, page 187)	375 g
2 tbsp	dry sherry or Shaoxing rice wine	25 mL
2 tbsp	coarsely chopped salted black beans (see Tips, left)	25 mL
1 tbsp	chopped garlic	15 mL
1 tbsp	chopped fresh gingerroot	15 mL
1/4 cup	chicken stock or water	50 mL
2 tsp	cornstarch	10 mL
1 tsp	soy sauce	5 mL
1/4 tsp	granulated sugar	1 mL
2 tbsp	vegetable oil	25 mL
1/4 cup	chopped green onions, divided	50 mL

1. Rinse calamari, cut off tentacles and set aside. Cut bodies in half lengthwise and open flat. With a very sharp knife, score each piece lightly on the diagonal in a cross-hatch pattern, making lines about 1/2 inch (1 cm) apart. Then cut into pieces about 2 inches-by-1-inch (5 cm by 2.5 cm). Cut any tentacles in half. Set both aside.

2. In a small bowl, combine sherry, black beans, garlic and ginger and stir well. In another small bowl, combine chicken stock, cornstarch, soy sauce and sugar and stir well to make a smooth sauce. Set aside.

3. Heat a wok or a large deep skillet over medium-high heat. Add oil and swirl to coat pan. Add calamari and about 2 tbsp (25 mL) of the green onions and toss well. Cook, tossing often, until calamari roll up into small tubes, about 1 minute.

4. Add black bean mixture and cook, tossing, for 1 minute more. Stir chicken stock mixture and add to pan, pouring in around sides and toss well. Cook, tossing occasionally, until sauce thickens and calamari are tender, about 1 minute more. Add remaining green onions and toss well. Transfer to a serving plate. Serve hot or warm.

Spicy Calamari with Watercress

12 oz	cleaned calamari (see Tip, right)	375 g
1 tbsp	freshly squeezed lime juice	15 mL
1 tbsp	soy sauce	15 mL
2 tsp	water	10 mL
1 tsp	granulated sugar	5 mL
½ tsp	salt or to taste	2 mL
½ tsp	hot pepper flakes	2 mL
2 tbsp	vegetable oil	25 mL
1 tbsp	chopped garlic	15 mL
2½ cups	chopped watercress	625 mL

1. Rinse calamari and slice the tubes crosswise into ½-inch (1 cm) thick rings. Cut tentacles in half if large. Set both aside.

2. In a small bowl, combine lime juice, soy sauce, water, sugar, salt and hot pepper flakes and stir well. Set aside.

3. Heat a wok or large deep skillet over medium-high heat. Add oil and swirl to coat pan. Add garlic and toss well, until fragrant, about 30 seconds. Add calamari and toss well. Cook, tossing often, until calamari becomes firmer and whiter, about 1 minute.

4. Add watercress and toss well. Cook, tossing often, until watercress is tender-crisp and calamari is cooked through, 1 to 2 minutes more. Add lime juice mixture and toss well. Transfer to a serving plate. Serve hot or warm.

Serves 4

Watercress and calamari go together wonderfully, with ample contrasts in color, texture and taste. This dish can work as an Asian-style salad, in addition to being a tasty and unusual centerpiece dish for a meal with rice.

TIP

Sometimes you can find only calamari that has not yet been cleaned and prepared for cooking. In that case, you will need a little more than the recipe calls for. For this recipe, purchase about 1 lb (500 g) to yield 12 oz (375 g). Place in a colander under running water, pull head out of each calamari body and remove the clear internal bone. Peel purple skin off body and scoop insides out with finger. Take each head, cut the tentacles off and squeeze out the two tiny beaks from the center. Proceed with recipe.

Baja-Style Fish Fillets with Cabbage and Lime

This dish is inspired by the simple, delicious fish tacos sold by street vendors. This stir-fry spin gives you a dish with bright flavors from simple ingredients. It's tasty with rice, but naturally, warm tortillas make a fine companion as well.

2 tbsp	white or red wine vinegar	25 mL
1 tbsp	dry sherry or white wine	15 mL
1 tsp	salt or to taste	5 mL
1 tsp	granulated sugar	5 mL
2 tbsp	vegetable oil	25 mL
¼ cup	chopped onion	50 mL
1 tbsp	chopped garlic	15 mL
12 oz	firm fish fillets (such as cod, halibut or catfish), cut into 2-inch (5 cm) chunks	375 g
1 cup	shredded napa cabbage	250 mL
¾ cup	halved cherry tomatoes	175 mL
¼ cup	chopped green onions	50 mL
⅓ cup	chopped fresh cilantro	75 mL
3 tbsp	freshly squeezed lime juice	45 mL
¾ cup	spicy tomato salsa, optional	175 mL

1. In a small bowl, combine vinegar, sherry, salt and sugar and stir well. Set aside.

2. Heat a wok or a large deep skillet over high heat. Add oil and swirl to coat pan. Add onion and garlic and toss well, until softened and fragrant, about 1 minute.

3. Add fish and spread into a single layer. Cook, undisturbed, until edges change color, about 1 minute. Gently turn and cook other side, undisturbed, for 30 seconds more.

4. Add cabbage. Toss gently and add vinegar mixture, pouring in around sides of pan. Cook, tossing gently once or twice, until fish is cooked through and cabbage is tender-crisp, 1 to 2 minutes more.

5. Add cherry tomatoes and green onions and toss well. Remove from heat. Add cilantro and lime juice and toss gently once more to combine everything well. Transfer to a serving plate. Serve salsa on the side, if using. Serve hot or warm.

Fiery Cajun-Style Fish Chunks

½ tsp	ground white pepper	2 mL
½ tsp	ground black pepper	2 mL
½ tsp	ground cayenne pepper	2 mL
½ tsp	paprika	2 mL
½ tsp	dried thyme	2 mL
½ tsp	garlic powder	2 mL
½ tsp	onion powder	2 mL
3 tbsp	vegetable oil, divided	45 mL
12 oz	firm fish fillets (such as cod, halibut or catfish), cut into 2-inch (5 cm) chunks	375 g
2 tbsp	soy sauce	25 mL
1 tbsp	dry sherry or white wine	15 mL
1 tbsp	water	15 mL
½ tsp	granulated sugar	2 mL
½ cup	chopped green bell peppers	125 mL
2 tbsp	chopped green onions	25 mL
2 tbsp	chopped Italian parsley	25 mL

Serves 4

Feisty flavor makes this dish a winner, but do plan to serve a cool green salad alongside it to quench those flames. This recipe looks long, but once you've measured out the spices for seasoning the fish, it's simple, fast and delicious.

1. In a bowl, combine white pepper, black pepper, cayenne, paprika, thyme, garlic powder, onion powder and 1 tbsp (15 mL) of the oil. Stir well. Add fish and stir to coat evenly. Set aside for 10 minutes.

2. In a small bowl, combine soy sauce, sherry, water and sugar and stir well.

3. Heat a wok or a large deep skillet over high heat. Add remaining oil and swirl to coat pan. Add fish mixture, spreading into a single layer. Cook, undisturbed, until edges change color, about 1 minute. Gently turn and cook other side, undisturbed, for 30 seconds more.

4. Add green peppers and toss gently to mix well. Add soy sauce mixture, pouring in around sides of pan. Cook, tossing gently once or twice, until fish is cooked through and peppers are tender-crisp, 1 to 2 minutes more.

5. Add green onions and parsley and toss gently to mix everything well. Transfer to a serving platter. Serve hot or warm.

Stir-Fried Clams
with Chinese Aromatics

Look for small, delicate clams, such as Manila clams, which are about the size of a walnut when closed. Rice is the ideal accompaniment to dishes with Cantonese-style black bean sauce, though it is also tasty tossed with noodles or pasta.

TIP

The salted, fermented black beans used in Chinese cooking provide a deliciously pungent flavor to stir-fried and steamed dishes. After you open a new package, transfer the soft, dark beans to a jar and store them airtight at room temperature.

28	small clams in shell, about 2 ½ lbs (1.25 kg)	28
2 tbsp	coarsely chopped salted black beans (see Tip, left)	25 mL
2 tbsp	dry sherry or Shaoxing rice wine	25 mL
1 tbsp	oyster sauce	15 mL
2 tsp	soy sauce	10 mL
½ tsp	granulated sugar	2 mL
2 tsp	cornstarch	10 mL
1 tsp	sesame oil	5 mL
2 tbsp	vegetable oil	25 mL
1 tbsp	chopped garlic	15 mL
1 tbsp	chopped fresh gingerroot	15 mL
¼ cup	chopped fresh cilantro	50 mL
2 tbsp	chopped green onions	25 mL

1. Scrub clams well with a stiff brush under running water. Discard any clams that remain open when tapped. Set aside.
2. In small bowl, combine ½ cup (125 mL) water, black beans, sherry, oyster sauce, soy sauce and sugar and stir well. Set aside.
3. In another small bowl, combine 2 tbsp (25 mL) water, cornstarch and sesame oil and stir into a smooth sauce. Set aside.
4. Heat a wok or a large deep skillet over medium-high heat. Add oil and swirl to coat pan. Add garlic and ginger and toss well, until fragrant, about 30 seconds.
5. Add black bean mixture and toss well. Add clams and toss well. Increase heat to high. Cook, tossing occasionally, until most of the clams have opened, 5 to 6 minutes. Add 1 to 2 tbsp (15 to 25 mL) of water if pan becomes dry.
6. Stir cornstarch mixture and add to pan, pouring in around sides and toss well. Cook, tossing occasionally, until sauce is thickened and smooth. Toss once more and remove from heat.
7. Add cilantro and green onions and toss again. Discard any clams that still have not opened. Transfer to a serving plate. Serve hot or warm.

Basil-Doused Thai-Style Clams

28	small clams in shell, about 2½ lbs (1.25 kg)	28
¼ cup	chicken stock or water	50 mL
3 tbsp	roasted chile paste (see Tips, right)	45 mL
2 tbsp	fish sauce	25 mL
1 tsp	granulated sugar	5 mL
3 tbsp	vegetable oil	45 mL
1 tbsp	chopped garlic	15 mL
1 cup	fresh basil or mint leaves	250 mL

1. Scrub clams well with a stiff brush under running water. Discard any clams that remain open when tapped. Set aside.

2. In a bowl, combine chicken stock, chile paste, fish sauce and sugar and stir well. Set aside.

3. Add oil and swirl to coat pan. Heat a wok or a large deep skillet over medium-high heat. Add garlic and toss well. Add clams and toss well. Cook, tossing once, for 2 minutes.

4. Add chicken stock mixture and cook, tossing now and then, until most of the clams have opened and seasonings have formed a sauce, 2 to 3 minutes more.

5. Add basil and toss well. Discard any clams that still have not opened. Transfer to a serving platter. Serve hot or warm.

Serves 4

Small, delicate clams, such as Manila clams, are ideal for this dish, since they cook quickly. Rice is the standard accompaniment for this dish, but it's terrific over noodles as well.

TIPS

Thai cooks garnish this dish with thin slices of long, thin hot red chile peppers, known in Thai as *prik chee fah*. You could also use strips of red bell pepper for their fabulous color and cool counterpoint to this piquant dish.

Look for roasted chile paste in Asian markets, or order it (see Sources, page 346).

Fragrant Goan-Style Clams

Serves 4

This stir-fried version of a shellfish dish from India's southwestern coast is fragrant and tasty with rice or over noodles. If you find yourself with freshly grated coconut on hand, toss some over this dish along with the cilantro at serving time for a luscious finishing touch. I make it with canned clams, but if you want to start with fresh clams, see Tip, below.

TIP

To steam fresh clams, buy about 3 lbs (1.5 kg) Manila clams or any other small, delicate clam with a thin shell. Scrub clams well with a stiff brush under running water. Discard any clams that remain open when tapped. Place in a stockpot with about 1 cup (250 mL) water and 1 tsp (5 mL) salt. Bring to a boil over high heat. Cover, reduce heat to maintain a lively simmer and cook for 8 to 10 minutes, until shells open and clams are cooked. Discard any unopened clams and remove clams from their shells.

2 tbsp	water or clam juice	25 mL
1 tbsp	white vinegar	15 mL
1 tbsp	curry powder	15 mL
1 tsp	salt or to taste	5 mL
½ tsp	ground cumin	2 mL
2 tbsp	vegetable oil	25 mL
2 tbsp	chopped garlic	25 mL
2 tbsp	chopped fresh gingerroot	25 mL
2 tsp	chopped serrano or jalapeño peppers, optional	10 mL
1 cup	chopped onion	250 mL
1	can (12 oz/375 g) clams, drained	1
½ cup	chopped fresh cilantro	125 mL
2 tbsp	chopped green onions	25 mL
1 tbsp	freshly squeezed lemon juice	15 mL

1. In a small bowl, combine water, vinegar, curry powder, salt and cumin and stir well. Set aside.

2. Heat a wok or a large deep skillet over high heat. Add oil and swirl to coat pan. Add garlic and ginger and toss well, until fragrant, about 15 seconds.

3. Add serrano pepper and onion and cook, tossing often, until fragrant and softened, about 1 minute.

4. Add clams and toss well. Cook, tossing often, until they are heated through, for 1 minute.

5. Add curry mixture, pouring in around sides of pan and toss well. Cook, tossing often, until clams are evenly seasoned, about 1 minute more.

6. Remove from heat and add cilantro, green onions and lemon juice and toss well. Transfer to a serving plate. Serve hot.

Variation: Use mussels instead of clams and follow the instructions for using fresh clams (see Tip, left). Look for the small blue or black mussel rather than the larger green-tipped variety.

Lime-Splashed Salmon with Chiles and Cilantro (page 173)

Overleaf: Fiery Cajun-Style Fish Chunks (page 189)

Crab with Luscious Mushrooms

4 oz	shiitake mushrooms	125 g
4 oz	oyster mushrooms	125 g
2 tbsp	fish sauce	25 mL
1 tbsp	dry sherry or Shaoxing rice wine	15 mL
1 tbsp	water	15 mL
½ tsp	granulated sugar	2 mL
¼ tsp	salt or to taste	1 mL
2 tbsp	vegetable oil	25 mL
2 tsp	chopped garlic	10 mL
2 tsp	chopped fresh gingerroot	10 mL
12 oz	lump cooked crabmeat, thawed if frozen	375 g
3 tbsp	chopped green onions	45 mL
3 tbsp	chopped fresh cilantro	45 mL

Serves 4

Crabmeat is delicate, so I like to stir-fry it with other ingredients, as a delicious accent in an inviting dish. Two kinds of mushrooms provide luxurious texture and handsome color. Try this with steamed spinach or a crisp green salad and rice. Fresh crabmeat is lovely but canned works well here and makes this an everyday dish.

TIP
You could use button mushrooms for this dish. Slice them thinly crosswise into ¼-inch (0.5 cm) strips, or halve them lengthwise if they are very small.

1. Cut fibrous stems from shiitakes (add to soup stocks or discard) and slice large caps into ¼-inch (0.5 cm) thick strips. Smaller caps can be quartered or halved. For oyster mushrooms, gently separate clusters into individual petal-like mushrooms. Very large ones can be halved lengthwise.

2. In a small bowl, combine fish sauce, sherry, water, sugar and salt and stir well. Set aside.

3. Heat a wok or a large deep skillet over medium-high heat. Add oil and swirl to coat pan. Add garlic and ginger and toss well, until fragrant, about 30 seconds.

4. Add shiitake and oyster mushrooms and spread into a single layer. Cook, undisturbed, for 30 seconds and then toss well. Cook, tossing occasionally, until mushrooms have softened a bit, about 30 seconds more.

5. Add fish sauce mixture, pouring in around sides of pan. Toss well.

6. Add crabmeat and toss very gently just enough to mix with mushrooms. Cook, tossing gently once or twice, until mushrooms are tender and crabmeat is hot, about 1 minute more.

7. Add green onions and cilantro and toss well. Transfer to a serving plate. Serve hot.

Overleaf: Stir-Fried Clams with Chinese Aromatics (page 190)

Tumbled Tofu with Snow Peas and Toasted Walnuts (page 201)

Spicy Oyster and Egg Jumble

Serves 4

You'll find versions of this dish throughout Asia, often in open-air markets where you can watch the chef cook up batch after batch for eager patrons standing in line for a tasty lunch. The flour mixture creates a fresh noodle in the pan and the accompanying salsa or hot pepper sauce makes the perfect accent to a terrific street food dish. A skillet works best for this dish, but you can use a wok if need be (see Tips, right). Pass hot pepper sauce or salsa at the table for those who want a little heat.

¼ cup	all-purpose flour	50 mL
¼ cup	cornstarch	50 mL
1 tsp	salt or to taste	5 mL
½ cup	water	125 mL
2	eggs	2
2 tsp	fish sauce	10 mL
3 tbsp	vegetable oil	45 mL
8 oz	fresh shucked oysters or peeled and deveined medium shrimp	250 g
1½ cups	bean sprouts	375 mL
½ cup	chopped green onions	125 mL
⅓ cup	chopped fresh cilantro	75 mL
1 cup	spicy tomato salsa, optional	250 mL
	Hot pepper sauce, optional	

1. In a small bowl, combine flour, cornstarch and salt and stir well. Add water and stir into a smooth thick sauce. Set aside.

2. In another small bowl, combine eggs and fish sauce and beat with a fork to mix well. Set aside.

3. Heat a large deep skillet over medium-high heat. Add oil and swirl to coat pan.

4. Drizzle in the batter, using just enough to form a large, open and somewhat lacy pancake (you may have excess batter left over). As it begins to set, add oysters over the pancake and cook, undisturbed, until pancake is firm and rather crisp, 2 to 4 minutes.

5. Add egg mixture, splashing gently and unevenly over pancake and oysters. Cook, undisturbed, until eggs are almost set, about 2 minutes more. Using your spatula, cut the big pancake into about six pieces. Toss gently.

6. Push everything aside. Add bean sprouts and green onions to center of pan. Cook, tossing occasionally, until wilting and fragrant, about 1 minute more.

7. Transfer to a serving platter and sprinkle with chopped cilantro. Serve hot, along with small bowls of salsa or hot pepper sauce, if using.

Variation: For a more traditional version, check Asian markets or natural and health food stores for tapioca flour and rice flour and use ¼ cup (50 mL) of each in place of the all-purpose flour and cornstarch used here. Store remaining rice and tapioca flours in glass jars, tightly sealed and labeled; they'll keep indefinitely, but make this often, with oysters or with shrimp and use them up!

TIPS

This dish is traditionally made on a big, flat griddle, so a large flat skillet would be the first choice. You could use a wok, if you lift it and swirl to spread out both the batter and the eggs during their early cooking stages. This lets them spread out into a thin, quick-cooking thin layer as they begin to cook.

If your skillet is too small to accommodate the bean sprouts and green onions in Step 6, use a second smaller skillet and about 1 tsp (5 mL) extra oil to stir-fry them until wilted and fragrant.

The stirring part comes toward the end, so be patient and let it fry. Your time to stir will come!

Cheater's Thai-Style Tuna Curry

Serves 4

This is good fast food, using ingredients from the pantry shelf. Use chopped yellow squash or zucchini in place of peas for a more substantial dish. To me rice is a must here, but it would be very tasty over noodles as wells.

¾ cup	unsweetened coconut milk	175 mL
¼ cup	water	50 mL
2 tbsp	fish sauce	25 mL
2 tsp	granulated sugar	10 mL
2 tbsp	vegetable oil	25 mL
1 tbsp	chopped garlic	15 mL
3 tbsp	chopped onion	45 mL
2 tbsp	Thai-style red curry paste	25 mL
12 oz	canned albacore tuna, drained	375 g
½ cup	frozen tiny peas	125 mL
3 tbsp	chopped green onions	45 mL
2 tbsp	chopped fresh cilantro	25 mL

1. In a bowl, combine coconut milk, water, fish sauce and sugar and stir well. Set aside

2. Heat a wok or a large deep skillet over high heat. Add oil and swirl to coat pan. Add garlic and onion and toss well. Cook, tossing often, until softened and fragrant, about 1 minute.

3. Add curry paste and stir well. Cook, pressing and stirring, until paste dissolves and everything combines into a smooth red sauce, about 1 minute.

4. Add tuna and peas and toss very gently to mix well. Cook, tossing gently once or twice, until tuna and peas are hot and evenly seasoned, 1 to 2 minutes.

5. Add green onions and cilantro and toss gently once more to mix well. Transfer to a serving plate. Serve hot or warm.

Meatless Mains

Tofu and Bok Choy with Gingery Black Beans

Tofu delivers the pungent flavor of Cantonese-style black bean sauce in this zesty dish. I love it over brown rice or barley, along with a salad of butter lettuce tossed with chopped apples and raisins in a sweet-sour dressing.

TIPS

To make soft tofu into firm, drain well and place tofu block on a dinner plate in the sink. Place a second dinner plate on top of tofu. Press down gently on top plate to compress tofu and extract liquid. Tip plates so that liquid drains away. Transfer pressed tofu to a cutting board and pat dry with paper towels or kitchen towels. Cut tofu into $\frac{1}{2}$-inch (1 cm) cubes.

To mash the black beans, ginger and garlic, you could also pile them up on your cutting board and chop them together to blend them into a coarse paste.

2 tbsp	salted black beans (see Tip, page 125)	25 mL
2 tbsp	chopped fresh gingerroot	25 mL
2 tsp	chopped garlic	10 mL
$\frac{1}{4}$ cup	vegetable stock or water	50 mL
2 tbsp	dry sherry or Shaoxing rice wine	25 mL
1 tbsp	soy sauce	15 mL
2 tsp	cornstarch	10 mL
$\frac{1}{2}$ tsp	granulated sugar	2 mL
2 tbsp	vegetable oil	25 mL
$\frac{1}{4}$ cup	chopped onion	50 mL
4 cups	chopped bok choy (2-inch/5 cm pieces)	1 L
16 oz	firm or extra-firm tofu, drained and cut into $\frac{1}{2}$-inch (1 cm) cubes (see Tips, left and page 204)	500 g
2 tbsp	chopped green onions	25 mL
1 tsp	Asian sesame oil	5 mL

1. In a small bowl, combine black beans, ginger and garlic. Using the back of a spoon, mash everything together to make a rough paste (see Tips, left). In another small bowl, combine vegetable stock, sherry, soy sauce, cornstarch and sugar and stir well into a smooth sauce. Set both aside.

2. Heat a wok or a large deep skillet over high heat. Add oil and swirl to coat pan. Add onion and toss well, until fragrant and softened, about 15 seconds.

3. Add bok choy and cook, tossing often, until it begins to wilt, about 30 seconds. Add tofu and toss well.

4. Scrape black bean mixture onto bok choy and tofu and toss well. Stir vegetable stock mixture and add to pan, pouring in around sides. Toss well. Cook, tossing occasionally, until bok choy is tender-crisp and tofu is evenly seasoned with sauce, about 2 minutes. (Add 1 to 2 tbsp/15 to 25 mL of water if needed to keep from burning or sticking to pan.)

5. Add green onions and sesame oil and toss well. Transfer to a serving plate. Serve hot or warm.

Hoisin-Scented Tofu with Zucchini in Peanut Sauce

¼ cup	vegetable stock or water	50 mL
2 tbsp	hoisin sauce	25 mL
1 tbsp	soy sauce	15 mL
1 tsp	granulated sugar	5 mL
3 tbsp	smooth peanut butter	45 mL
½ tsp	Asian sesame oil	2 mL
2 tbsp	vegetable oil	25 mL
2 tbsp	chopped shallot or onion	25 mL
1 tbsp	chopped fresh gingerroot	15 mL
2 tsp	chopped garlic	10 mL
1	medium zucchini (or 2 small), thinly sliced (about 1½ cups/375 mL)	1
8 oz	firm or extra-firm tofu, drained and cut into ½-inch (1 cm) cubes (see Tips, pages 198 and 204)	250 g
3 tbsp	chopped fresh cilantro	45 mL
¼ cup	chopped roasted salted peanuts	50 mL

Serves 4

Enjoy this recipe over bowls of angel hair pasta or Asian noodles, or with a pilaf of jasmine and wild rice. Peas tossed with butter and a squeeze of lemon juice would complement either combination well. Pass a bowl of a fiery salsa or hot sauce to provide heat if you like.

1. In a small saucepan over medium-high heat, combine vegetable stock, hoisin sauce, soy sauce and sugar. Cook, stirring often, to dissolve everything into a smooth sauce. Add peanut butter and sesame oil and stir well into a smooth sauce. Set aside.

2. Heat a wok or a large deep skillet over high heat. Add oil and swirl to coat pan. Add shallot, ginger and garlic and toss well, until fragrant, about 15 seconds.

3. Add zucchini and toss well. Cook, tossing often, until it begins to wilt, about 1 minute. Add tofu and toss well. Cook, tossing gently once or twice, until zucchini is tender-crisp and tofu is heated through, 1 to 2 minutes.

4. Add peanut sauce, pouring in around sides of pan. Toss gently to season everything evenly. Transfer to a serving plate. Sprinkle with cilantro and peanuts. Serve hot or warm.

Wok-Seared Kale with Five-Spice Tofu

Here tofu takes on the rich flavor of Chinese five-spice powder and soy sauce. Paired with kale, it makes a hearty cool-weather dish.

TIP

You will need about 2 cups (500 mL) cubed tofu.

1	small bunch fresh kale (about 8 oz/250 g)	1
2 tbsp	vegetable stock or water	25 mL
1 tbsp	dry sherry or Shaoxing rice wine	15 mL
2 tsp	soy sauce	10 mL
1 tsp	dark soy sauce or molasses, optional	5 mL
2 tsp	granulated sugar	10 mL
1 tsp	salt or to taste	5 mL
½ tsp	five-spice powder	2 mL
2 tsp	cornstarch	10 mL
2 tbsp	vegetable oil	25 mL
1 tbsp	chopped fresh gingerroot	15 mL
2 tsp	chopped garlic	10 mL
⅓ cup	chopped shallot or onion	75 mL
8 oz	firm or extra-firm tofu, drained and cut into ½-inch (1 cm) cubes	250 g
¾ cup	halved cherry tomatoes	175 mL

1. Wash kale well in a bowl of water. Trim and discard the thick stems. Stack leaves and cut into pieces, about 2 inches-by 1-inch (5 by 2.5 cm). Measure out about 6 cups (1.5 L).

2. Bring a saucepan of water to a rolling boil over high heat. Add trimmed kale and cook, stirring gently occasionally, until bright green and tender, 4 to 5 minutes. Drain, rinse in cold water and drain well again. Set aside.

3. In a small bowl, combine vegetable stock, sherry, soy sauce, dark soy sauce, if using, sugar, salt and five-spice powder and stir well into a smooth sauce. Set aside.

4. In another small bowl, combine 2 tbsp (25 mL) of water and cornstarch and stir well into a smooth sauce. Set aside.

5. Heat a wok or a large deep skillet over high heat. Add oil and swirl to coat pan. Add ginger and garlic and toss well, until fragrant, about 15 seconds. Add shallot and cook, tossing often, until fragrant and softened, about 30 seconds more. Add tofu and cook, tossing often, for 1 minute. Add kale and toss to mix well, about 1 minute.

6. Stir cornstarch mixture and add to pan, pouring in around sides. Cook, tossing occasionally, until sauce has thickened a little and everything is evenly seasoned, 1 to 2 minutes more. Add cherry tomatoes and toss well. Transfer to a serving platter or a shallow bowl. Serve hot or warm.

Tumbled Tofu with Snow Peas and Toasted Walnuts

1 cup	orange juice	250 mL
3 tbsp	rice or cider vinegar	45 mL
3 tbsp	soy sauce	45 mL
1 tbsp	brown sugar	15 mL
1 tbsp plus ⅓ cup	cornstarch, divided	15 mL plus 75 mL
16 oz	firm or extra-firm tofu , drained and cut into ½-inch (1 cm) cubes (see Tips, pages 198 and 204)	500 g
2 tbsp	vegetable oil, divided	25 mL
1 tbsp	chopped fresh gingerroot	15 mL
2 tsp	chopped garlic	10 mL
8 oz	snow peas	250 g
1 cup	walnuts, toasted (see Tip, right)	250 mL
2 tbsp	thinly sliced green onions	25 mL

1. In a small bowl, combine orange juice, vinegar, soy sauce, brown sugar and 1 tbsp (15 mL) of the cornstarch and stir well into a smooth sauce. Set aside.

2. Place remaining ⅓ cup (75 mL) of cornstarch in a large resealable plastic bag. Add half the tofu and shake gently to coat. Transfer to a plate. Repeat with remaining tofu. Discard any remaining cornstarch.

3. Heat a wok or a large deep skillet over high heat. Add 1 tbsp (15 mL) of the oil and swirl to coat pan. Add tofu and spread into a single layer. Cook, undisturbed, until bottoms are light golden and crusty, about 2 minutes. Turn carefully and cook, undisturbed, 1 minute more. Cook, tossing gently once or twice, until tofu is light golden all over, 1 to 2 minutes more. Transfer to a large bowl and set aside.

4. Add remaining oil and swirl to coat pan. Add ginger and garlic and toss well, until fragrant, about 15 seconds. Add snow peas and toss well. Cook, tossing often, until tender-crisp, 1 to 2 minutes.

5. Stir orange juice sauce and add to pan, pouring in around sides. Cook, tossing gently, until sauce has thickened.

6. Add reserved tofu, walnuts and green onions. Cook, tossing gently, to combine and season evenly with the sauce, about 1 minute more. Transfer to a serving platter or shallow serving dish. Serve hot or warm.

Serves 4

Coating tofu cubes in cornstarch before browning them creates a light golden, slightly crispy crust, a pleasing contrast to the mellow interior of each cube. This recipe produces lots of zesty sauce, so plan to serve it over rice or noodles.

TIP

To toast walnuts, heat a dry wok or a large deep skillet over medium-high heat. Add walnuts and cook, stirring and tossing often, until fragrant and beginning to brown, 1 to 2 minutes. Transfer to a small plate and set aside.

Tofu with Chickpeas in Spicy Bean Sauce

Serves 4

Hot bean paste and Chinese-style black beans enliven this quickly made dish. Steamed asparagus or broccoli tossed with lemon butter and a bowl of brown rice make this a pleasing busy-day meal.

TIP

When using canned baby corn and chickpeas, drain each well, rinse and drain again. Chop corn cobs into thirds and measure out 1 cup (250 mL).

¼ cup	vegetable stock or water	50 mL
1 tbsp	hot bean paste	15 mL
2 tsp	soy sauce	10 mL
2 tsp	cornstarch	10 mL
1 tsp	granulated sugar	5 mL
1 tbsp	chopped fresh gingerroot	15 mL
2 tsp	chopped salted black beans (see Tip, page 125)	10 mL
2 tsp	chopped garlic	10 mL
2 tbsp	vegetable oil	25 mL
8 oz	firm, baked or fried (Hong Su) tofu, diced	250 g
1½ cups	cooked or canned drained chickpeas	375 mL
1 cup	chopped baby corn (see Tips, left)	250 mL
2 tsp	Asian sesame oil	10 mL
¼ cup	chopped green onions	50 mL
¼ cup	chopped fresh cilantro	50 mL

1. In a bowl, combine vegetable stock, bean paste, soy sauce, cornstarch and sugar and stir well into a smooth sauce. Set aside.

2. In a small bowl, combine ginger, black beans and garlic and stir well. Set aside.

3. Heat a wok or a large deep skillet over high heat. Add oil and swirl to coat pan. Add ginger mixture and toss well, until fragrant, about 15 seconds. Add tofu, chickpeas and baby corn. Toss well to heat and combine them with the seasonings, about 1 minute.

4. Stir stock mixture and add to pan, pouring in around sides. Cook, tossing occasionally, until ingredients are heated through and sauce has thickened a little and coats everything evenly, about 1 minute.

5. Remove from heat and add sesame oil, green onions and cilantro. Toss well. Transfer to a serving plate. Serve hot or warm.

Kung Pao Tofu

16 oz	firm tofu, drained and chopped into 1-inch/2.5 cm chunks	500 g

Marinade

1 tbsp	soy sauce	15 mL
1 tbsp	dry sherry, divided	15 mL
1 tbsp	cornstarch	15 mL
1 tsp	vegetable oil	5 mL

Sauce

1 tbsp	soy sauce	15 mL
1 tbsp	dry sherry	15 mL
1 tbsp	red wine vinegar	15 mL
1 tbsp	granulated sugar	15 mL
1 tsp	cornstarch	5 mL
1 tsp	salt or to taste	5 mL
2 tbsp	vegetable oil	25 mL
5 to 10	small dried hot red chiles	5 to 10
1 tsp	finely ground Szechwan peppercorns, optional	5 mL
1 tbsp	chopped garlic	15 mL
1 tbsp	chopped gingerroot	15 mL
¼ cup	chopped green onions	50 mL
¾ cup	roasted, salted peanuts	175 mL
1 tsp	Asian sesame oil	5 mL

Serves 4

Toss up a crisp green salad to cool your palate as you enjoy these pungent flavors along with rice or noodles.

1. *Marinade:* In a bowl, combine soy sauce, sherry, cornstarch and oil and stir well into a smooth sauce. Add tofu, tossing to coat evenly. Set aside for 30 minutes.

2. *Sauce:* In a bowl, combine soy sauce, sherry, vinegar, sugar, cornstarch and salt and stir into a smooth sauce.

3. Heat a wok or a large deep skillet over medium-high heat. Add 2 tbsp (25 mL) vegetable oil and swirl to coat pan. Add chiles and peppercorns, if using, and toss well.

4. Add garlic, ginger and green onions and toss well. Add tofu mixture and cook, tossing gently, about 1 minute.

5. Stir soy sauce mixture and add to pan, pouring in around sides. Cook, tossing often, for 1 minute more. Add peanuts and sesame oil and toss once. Transfer to a serving plate.

Curry-Scrambled Tofu with Peas

Serves 4

This sunny-colored dish brightens any menu, whether it's a weekend brunch or a weeknight supper. I love it with brown basmati rice or in warm flour tortillas with spicy salsa.

TIPS

To crumble tofu, break into 4 large chunks and then crumble each chunk with your hands into very small pieces. Or cut into 4 sections and chop each section into small dice. Transfer to a bowl and place by the stove.

If you use soft tofu, the cooking process will cause it to scramble up. If you use firm tofu, you need to chop it into small pieces before cooking so it will have the right texture for this dish, since it is too firm to break up during cooking. Drain it, and then cut it up into small bits, about ¼-inch (0.5 cm) dice. It can be roughly chopped rather than precisely chopped.

¼ cup	vegetable stock or water	50 mL
2 tbsp	Indian-style curry paste	25 mL
1 tsp	soy sauce	5 mL
1 tsp	granulated sugar	5 mL
2 tbsp	vegetable oil	25 mL
1 tbsp	chopped fresh gingerroot	15 mL
2 tsp	chopped garlic	10 mL
1 tsp	whole cumin seeds, optional	5 mL
1 cup	red bell pepper, cut into 2-inch (5 cm) lengths	250 mL
½ cup	shredded carrot	125 mL
16 oz	crumbled or finely chopped firm tofu (see Tips, left)	500 g
1 cup	frozen peas	250 mL
2 tbsp	chopped green onions	25 mL

1. In a small bowl, combine vegetable stock, curry paste, soy sauce and sugar and stir well. Set aside.

2. Heat a wok or a large deep skillet over high heat. Add oil and swirl to coat pan. Add ginger, garlic and cumin seeds, if using, and cook, tossing often, until fragrant, about 15 seconds.

3. Add bell pepper and carrot and toss well. Cook, tossing often, until tender-crisp, about 1 minute more.

4. Add tofu, peas and green onions and toss well. Add vegetable stock mixture and toss gently to mix well. Cook, tossing gently, until tofu and peas are hot and everything is evenly seasoned with sauce, 1 to 2 minutes. Transfer to a serving plate. Serve hot or warm.

Crisp Tofu and Cucumbers in Barbecue Sauce

1/3 cup plus 2 tsp	cornstarch, divided	75 mL plus 10 mL
1/2 tsp	five-spice powder	2 mL
16 oz	firm or extra-firm tofu, drained and cut into 2-inch (5 cm) chunks	500 g
2 tbsp	smoky barbecue sauce	25 mL
2 tbsp	dry sherry or Shaoxing rice wine	25 mL
2 tbsp	vegetable stock or water	25 mL
2 tsp	soy sauce	10 mL
3 tbsp	vegetable oil, divided	45 mL
1 tbsp	chopped fresh gingerroot	15 mL
2 tsp	chopped garlic	10 mL
1 1/2 cups	chopped peeled English cucumber (1/2-inch/1 cm chunks)	375 mL
1/2 tsp	salt or to taste	2 mL
3/4 cup	halved cherry tomatoes	175 mL
3 tbsp	chopped green onions	45 mL
2 tbsp	chopped fresh cilantro	25 mL

Serves 4

Barbecue sauce gives this dish a hint of smoky flavor. I love it with plates of jasmine rice and a bowl of steamed broccoli tossed with Asian sesame oil.

TIPS

Tofu is often sold in 14-ounce (438 g) containers. That amount will work fine in this recipe, which calls for 16 ounces (500 g).

To prepare tofu, drain well and place tofu block on a dinner plate in the sink. Place a second dinner plate on top of tofu. Press down gently on top plate to compress tofu and extract liquid. Tip plates so that liquid drains away. Transfer pressed tofu to a cutting board and pat dry with paper towels or kitchen towels. Cut tofu into 2-inch (5 cm) chunks.

1. In a resealable plastic bag, combine 1/3 cup (75 mL) of cornstarch and five-spice powder. Add half the tofu and shake gently to coat. Transfer to a plate. Repeat with remaining tofu. Set aside. Discard any remaining cornstarch.

2. In a small bowl, combine barbecue sauce, sherry, vegetable stock, soy sauce and remaining 2 tsp (10 mL) of cornstarch and stir into a smooth sauce. Set aside.

3. Heat a wok or a large deep skillet over high heat. Add 2 tbsp (25 mL) of oil and swirl to coat pan. Carefully add tofu and spread into a single layer. Cook, undisturbed, until lightly browned on the bottom, 1 to 2 minutes. Turn carefully and cook, undisturbed, 1 minute more. Transfer to a plate.

4. Add remaining oil to pan and swirl to coat well. Add ginger and garlic and toss well, until fragrant, 15 seconds.

5. Add cucumber. Sprinkle with salt and toss well. Cook, tossing often, until cucumbers are heated through and beginning to wilt, 1 to 2 minutes.

6. Stir barbecue sauce mixture and add to pan, pouring in around sides. Cook, tossing often, until sauce thickens, about 1 minute. Add cherry tomatoes and green onions and toss well. Pour cucumbers and sauce over tofu on serving plate. Sprinkle with cilantro leaves. Serve hot or warm.

Honey-Mustard Tempeh with Broccoli

Serves 4

Serve this dish over bowls of brown rice or quinoa and offer a platter of crudités with hummus to round out the meal. Crudités can be baby carrots and cherry tomatoes on a wintry night, or the pick of your garden during the sunnier seasons.

TIP

I especially like Dijon or Creole mustard here, but you can use any kind of prepared mustard that you like. Chinese-style mustard, available in Asian stores, would work as well, adding some heat to the flavors of the dish.

¼ cup	vegetable stock or water	50 mL
3 tbsp	soy sauce	45 mL
2 tbsp	honey	25 mL
1 tbsp	Asian sesame oil	15 mL
2 tsp	prepared mustard, such as Dijon or Creole (see Tip, left)	10 mL
2 tbsp	vegetable oil	25 mL
1 tbsp	chopped fresh gingerroot	15 mL
2 tsp	chopped garlic	10 mL
6 cups	small broccoli florets	1.5 L
¾ cup	chopped onion	175 mL
1 cup	shredded carrot	250 mL
8 oz	diced tempeh	250 g

1. In a small bowl, combine vegetable stock, soy sauce, honey, sesame oil and mustard and stir well. Set aside.

2. Heat a wok or a large deep skillet over high heat. Add oil and swirl to coat pan. Add ginger and garlic and toss well, until fragrant, about 15 seconds.

3. Add broccoli and toss well. Cook, tossing often, until bright green and beginning to wilt, about 1 minute.

4. Add onion and carrot and toss well. Cook, tossing often, until onion is fragrant and carrots are beginning to wilt, about 1 minute. Add tempeh, toss well and cook for 1 minute.

5. Add vegetable stock mixture, pouring in around sides of pan. Toss well. Cook, tossing occasionally, until vegetables are tender-crisp and evenly seasoned with sauce, 1 to 2 minutes more. Transfer to a serving plate. Serve hot or warm.

Bolognese-Style Stir-Fried Tempeh

2 tbsp	dry red wine	25 mL
1 tbsp	vegetable stock	15 mL
1 tsp	granulated sugar	5 mL
1 tsp	salt or to taste	5 mL
2 tbsp	olive oil or vegetable oil	25 mL
½ cup	chopped onion	125 mL
2 tbsp	chopped garlic	25 mL
8 oz	finely chopped tempeh	250 g
1 cup	drained diced canned tomatoes	250 mL
1 tbsp	tomato paste	15 mL
1 tsp	dried oregano	5 mL
1 tsp	hot pepper flakes	5 mL
¼ cup	chopped Italian parsley, divided	50 mL

Serves 4

This saucy stir-fry takes inspiration from hearty Bolognese sauce, but it cooks quickly and is delicious with brown rice, barley or another whole grain. Naturally it's a fine topping for pasta as well. I love it with a platter of roasted vegetables seasoned with extra virgin olive oil and sprinkled with fresh basil.

1. In a small bowl, combine wine, vegetable stock, sugar and salt and stir well. Set aside.

2. Heat a wok or a large deep skillet over high heat. Add oil and swirl to coat pan. Add onion and garlic and toss well, until fragrant and softened, about 1 minute.

3. Add tempeh and toss well. Add wine mixture, pouring in around sides of pan. Cook, tossing often, for 30 seconds.

4. Add tomatoes, tomato paste, oregano, hot pepper flakes and half the parsley and toss well.

5. Reduce heat to medium. Cook, tossing often, until everything is heated through and combines into a chunky sauce, about 2 minutes more.

6. Add remaining parsley and toss well. Transfer to a serving bowl or deep plate. Serve hot or warm.

Sesame-Scented Tempeh with Celery and Radish

Serves 4

Enjoy this flavorful dish over brown rice or couscous. You can serve it alongside steaming bowls of miso soup and a bowl of edamame beans cooked in their pods.

3 tbsp	vegetable stock or water	45 mL
2 tbsp	soy sauce	25 mL
1 tbsp	rice vinegar or cider vinegar	15 mL
1 tbsp	dry sherry or Shaoxing rice wine	15 mL
2 tsp	cornstarch	10 mL
1 tsp	granulated sugar	5 mL
½ tsp	salt or to taste	2 mL
2 tbsp	vegetable oil	25 mL
1 tbsp	chopped garlic	15 mL
1 tbsp	chopped fresh gingerroot	15 mL
2 cups	sliced radishes	500 mL
2 cups	sliced celery	500 mL
1 cup	shredded carrot	250 mL
8 oz	diced tempeh	250 g
2 tbsp	chopped green onions	25 mL
2 tsp	Asian sesame oil	10 mL

1. In a small bowl, combine vegetable stock, soy sauce, vinegar, sherry, cornstarch, sugar and salt and stir well into a smooth sauce. Set aside.

2. Heat a wok or a large deep skillet over high heat. Add oil and swirl to coat pan. Add garlic and ginger and toss well, until fragrant, about 15 seconds.

3. Add radishes, celery and carrot and toss well. Cook, tossing often, until softened, 1 to 2 minutes.

4. Add tempeh and toss well. Stir vegetable stock mixture and add to pan, pouring in around sides. Toss well. Cook, tossing occasionally, until sauce has thickened, vegetables are tender-crisp and tempeh is heated through, 1 to 2 minutes more. Add green onions and sesame oil and toss well. Transfer to a serving plate. Serve hot or warm.

Sliced Seitan with Mushrooms in Five-Spice Sauce

1 tbsp	soy sauce	15 mL
1 tbsp	dry sherry or Shaoxing rice wine	15 mL
2 tsp	cornstarch	10 mL
1/2 tsp	five-spice powder	2 mL
1/2 tsp	salt or to taste	2 mL
1/2 tsp	granulated sugar	2 mL
2 tbsp	vegetable oil	25 mL
3 tbsp	chopped onion	45 mL
2 tsp	chopped garlic	10 mL
2 tsp	chopped fresh gingerroot	10 mL
8 oz	sliced mushrooms (1 1/2 cups/375 mL)	250 g
8 oz	seitan, drained and sliced into 1/2-inch (1 cm) slices	250 g
3/4 cup	frozen tiny peas	175 mL
3 tbsp	chopped fresh cilantro	45 mL

Serves 4

Seitan is an ancient kind of "wheat meat," made from the gluten in flour. It is a chewy, high-protein vegetarian substitute for meat, available in natural and health food stores and some grocery stores as well as in Asian markets.

1. In a small bowl, combine soy sauce, sherry, cornstarch, five-spice powder, salt and sugar and stir well into a smooth sauce. Set aside.

2. Heat a wok or a large deep skillet over high heat. Add oil and swirl to coat pan. Add onion, garlic and ginger and toss well, until fragrant and softened, about 15 seconds.

3. Add mushrooms and toss well. Spread into a single layer and cook, undisturbed, for 30 seconds. Toss well. Cook, tossing occasionally, until softened and tender, 2 minutes more.

4. Add seitan and peas and toss well. Stir soy sauce mixture and add to pan, pouring in around sides. Cook, tossing often, until seitan and peas are hot and sauce thickens and seasons everything evenly, about 1 minute more.

5. Add cilantro and toss well. Transfer to a serving plate. Serve hot or warm.

Curried Cabbage with Edamame Beans

Serves 4

Cabbage shines as a last-minute dinner ingredient, since it keeps well and cooks quickly. Carrot shreds and edamame beans add color and crunch to this tasty busy-night dish.

TIP

To prepare cabbage, quarter it lengthwise. Cut away and discard most of the thick, pale core from each section, leaving just enough to hold the section together in one piece. Cut each quarter crosswise into thin shreds, until you have 6 cups (1.5 L). Transfer unused portion to resealable bag and store in the refrigerator for another use.

⅓ cup	vegetable stock or water	75 mL
3 tbsp	mild Indian-style curry paste	45 mL
2 tsp	brown sugar	10 mL
1 tsp	prepared mustard, such as Dijon or Creole (see Tip, page 206)	5 mL
½ tsp	salt or to taste	2 mL
2 tbsp	vegetable oil	25 mL
½ cup	chopped onion	125 mL
2 tbsp	chopped fresh gingerroot	25 mL
¾ cup	chopped red bell pepper	175 mL
1 cup	shredded carrots	250 mL
6 cups	shredded cabbage, divided (see Tip, left)	1.5 L
¾ cup	frozen edamame beans	175 mL
3 tbsp	chopped fresh cilantro	45 mL

1. In a bowl, combine vegetable stock, curry paste, sugar, mustard and salt and stir well. Set aside.

2. Heat a wok or a large deep skillet over high heat. Add oil and swirl to coat pan. Add onion and ginger and toss well, until fragrant, about 15 seconds.

3. Add red pepper and carrots and cook, tossing often, until peppers are fragrant and carrots have begun to wilt, about 1 minute more.

4. Add half the cabbage and toss well. Cook, tossing once or twice, until it begins to wilt, about 1 minute. Stir in remaining cabbage and edamame beans and toss well. Cook, tossing often, until cabbage and edamame beans are tender-crisp, 1 to 2 minutes more. (Add 1 to 2 tbsp/ 15 to 25 mL of water if needed to keep cabbage from burning as it cooks.)

5. Add vegetable stock mixture, pouring in around sides of pan. Toss well. Cook, tossing often, until everything is evenly seasoned with curry mixture, about 1 minute more. Transfer to a serving plate. Sprinkle with cilantro and serve hot or warm.

Mushroom, Tomato and Asparagus Toss

3 tbsp	dry sherry or Shaoxing rice wine	45 mL
2 tbsp	soy sauce	25 mL
1 tbsp	vegetable stock or water	15 mL
½ tsp	granulated sugar	2 mL
½ tsp	salt or to taste	2 mL
1 lb	fresh asparagus	500 g
8 oz	portobello mushroom caps (see Tip, right)	250 g
2 tbsp	vegetable oil	25 mL
1 tbsp	chopped onion	15 mL
1 tbsp	chopped fresh gingerroot	15 mL
2 tsp	chopped garlic	10 mL
¾ cup	halved cherry tomatoes	175 mL
3 tbsp	chopped fresh cilantro	45 mL
2 tsp	Asian sesame oil	10 mL

Serves 4

Colorful and delicious, this dish is especially fine served over grilled or fried polenta, buttered grits or a rice pilaf. A salad of colorful lettuce leaves tossed with mandarin orange sections and thinly sliced almonds would fill out the plate nicely.

TIP

Before slicing portobello mushroom caps for this recipe, scrape out the dark gills lining the cap. I use a spoon to scoop them out, starting at the stem area and pulling outward to the edge of the cap.

1. In a small bowl, combine sherry, soy sauce, stock, sugar and salt and stir well. Set aside.

2. Trim asparagus by snapping off ends. Cut each asparagus spear on the diagonal into ¼-inch (0.5 cm) pieces, leaving the tips whole. You should have about 3 cups (750 mL) chopped asparagus. Set aside.

3. Quarter mushrooms and then thinly slice each section into ¼-inch (0.5 cm) thick pieces. Set aside.

4. Heat a wok or a large deep skillet over high heat. Add vegetable oil and swirl to coat pan. Add onion, ginger and garlic and toss well, until fragrant, about 15 seconds.

5. Add mushrooms and toss well. Spread into a single layer and cook, undisturbed, for 30 seconds. Add asparagus and toss well. Cook, tossing often, until both vegetables have begun to wilt, 1 minute.

6. Add sherry mixture, pouring in around sides of pan. Toss well. Cook, tossing occasionally, until asparagus is tender-crisp, 1 to 2 minutes more.

7. Add cherry tomatoes, cilantro and sesame oil and toss well. Transfer to a serving plate. Serve hot or warm.

Moo Shu Vegetables

Enjoy this dish tucked into Mandarin Pancakes (see recipe, page 330) or warm tortillas. It's equally delicious with rice or noodles and garlicky sautéed greens.

TIP

To make soft tofu into firm, drain well and place tofu block on a dinner plate in the sink. Place a second dinner plate on top of tofu. Press down gently on top plate to compress tofu and extract liquid. Tip plates so that liquid drains away. Transfer pressed tofu to a cutting board and pat dry with paper towels or kitchen towels. Cut tofu into ½-inch (1 cm) cubes.

2 tbsp	soy sauce	25 mL
1 tbsp	dry sherry or Shaoxing rice wine	15 mL
2 tsp	cornstarch	10 mL
½ tsp	granulated sugar	2 mL
½ tsp	salt or to taste	2 mL
2	large eggs	2
¾ cup	drained canned sliced bamboo shoots	175 mL
2 tbsp	vegetable oil	25 mL
1 tbsp	chopped fresh gingerroot	15 mL
1 tbsp	chopped garlic	15 mL
8 oz	sliced mushrooms (1½ cups/375 mL)	250 g
1 cup	shredded carrots	250 mL
4 oz	firm or extra-firm tofu, drained and cut in ½-inch (1 cm) cubes (see Tip, left)	125 g
3 cups	shredded napa cabbage	750 mL
3 tbsp	chopped green onions	45 mL
2 tsp	Asian sesame oil	10 mL

1. In a small bowl, combine soy sauce, sherry, cornstarch, sugar and salt and stir well into a smooth sauce. Set aside. In another bowl, lightly beat eggs. Set aside.

2. Stack bamboo shoots two or three high and then cut them lengthwise into strips. Set aside.

3. Heat a wok or a large deep skillet over high heat. Add vegetable oil and swirl to coat pan. Add ginger and garlic and toss well, until fragrant, about 15 seconds.

4. Add mushrooms and toss well. Spread into a single layer and cook, undisturbed, for 30 seconds. Add carrots, tofu and bamboo shoots and toss well. Cook, tossing occasionally, until carrots and mushrooms are softened, about 1 minute. Add cabbage and toss well. Cook, tossing often, until tender-crisp, 1 to 2 minutes. (Add 1 to 2 tbsp/15 to 25 mL of water as needed to avoid burning.)

5. Push vegetables aside and pour beaten eggs into center of pan. Swirl pan to spread as much as possible and cook, undisturbed, for 30 seconds. Toss well to scramble eggs and gently combine everything well.

6. Stir soy sauce mixture and add to pan. Toss well and cook, about 1 minute. Add green onions and sesame oil and toss well. Transfer to a plate. Serve hot or warm.

Luscious Eggplant in Thai Red Curry Sauce

¼ cup	vegetable stock or water	50 mL
1 tbsp	granulated sugar	15 mL
2 tsp	soy sauce	10 mL
1 tsp	salt or to taste	5 mL
3 tbsp	vegetable oil	45 mL
1 tbsp	chopped fresh gingerroot	15 mL
2 tbsp	Thai-style red curry paste	25 mL
1 cup	thickly sliced onion strips	250 mL
3½ cups	chopped unpeeled Asian eggplant (¾-inch/2 cm chunks) (2 or 3 medium eggplants) (see Tip, right)	875 mL
8	makrut lime leaves, quartered, optional	8
½ cup	frozen tiny peas	125 mL
3 tbsp	unsweetened coconut milk, evaporated milk or cream	45 mL
¼ cup	fresh basil leaves, optional	50 mL

1. In a small bowl, combine vegetable stock, sugar, soy sauce and salt and stir well. Set aside.

2. Heat a wok or a large deep skillet over medium-high heat. Add oil and swirl to coat pan. Add ginger and toss well, until fragrant, about 15 seconds.

3. Add curry paste, pressing and scooping to soften and help melt into oil. Reduce heat if it pops or splashes as it heats up. Cook, stirring often, until fragrant and dissolved into oil, 1 to 2 minutes.

4. Add onion and eggplant and toss gently to mix with curry sauce. Cook, tossing often, until vegetables begin to wilt and are evenly coated with sauce.

5. Add vegetable stock mixture and lime leaves, if using, and toss gently to mix into sauce. Bring to a gentle boil. Cook, tossing occasionally, until eggplant is tender, 3 to 4 minutes. Reduce heat to medium or as needed to maintain a gentle boil.

6. Add peas and coconut milk and toss gently to combine with sauce. Cook, tossing occasionally, until peas are hot, about 1 minute. Add basil, if using, tearing any large leaves in half and reserving a sprig or two for garnish, if you like. Transfer to a shallow serving bowl. Serve hot or warm.

Serves 4

The luscious texture of eggplant can take the heat of Thai curry paste. The sauce lights up jasmine rice beautifully. A bowl of fresh pineapple chunks and a batch of steamed snow peas would work wonderfully to make this a meal.

TIP

Look for long slender Asian eggplants, which could be dark or pale purple in hue. One way to chop them is to halve them lengthwise and then chop them crosswise into chunks. You could also use globe eggplant here, if you salt first to remove some of its bitterness. Cut it crosswise into 1-inch (2.5 cm) rounds. Stack them in batches and cut away most of the peeling. Arrange them on a platter in a single layer. Sprinkle with salt and set aside for about 30 minutes, until they release some of their liquid and soften a little. Rinse and pat dry and then chop into chunks.

Swirled Eggs with Tomatoes and Onions

Serves 4

In Asia, eggs appear on the table throughout the day, not simply as a breakfast favorite. This delicious dish served with rice and a salad makes a fine, fast supper. In Thailand, hot sauce is often served on the side with main course egg dishes and I think it is the perfect accompaniment.

TIP

For this dish, firm tomatoes, such as plum (Roma) tomatoes, are ideal. If you have only lush ripe tomatoes, cut them in half crosswise, gently squeeze out the seeds and juice and then chop them into bite-size chunks. You can use cherry tomatoes, halving them and adding them just before the dish is ready so that they get just a little heat.

4	large eggs	4
2 tsp	Asian sesame oil	10 mL
1 tsp	salt or to taste	5 mL
2 tbsp	vegetable oil	25 mL
2 tbsp	chopped onion	25 mL
1 tbsp	chopped garlic	15 mL
¾ cup	very coarsely chopped plum (Roma) tomatoes (see Tip, left)	175 mL
¼ cup	chopped green onions	50 mL
3 tbsp	chopped fresh cilantro	45 mL

1. In a bowl, whisk together eggs, sesame oil and salt. Set aside.
2. Heat a wok or a large deep skillet over high heat. Add vegetable oil and swirl to coat pan. Add onion and garlic and toss well, until fragrant, about 15 seconds.
3. Stir in egg mixture and swirl gently to spread around pan. Cook, undisturbed, for 30 seconds. Gently but quickly stir and scoop to scramble eggs until almost done but still very moist, about 1 minute.
4. Add tomatoes and toss well. Add green onions and toss again, so eggs finish cooking and tomatoes soften and cook just a bit, about 15 seconds more.
5. Transfer to a serving plate. Sprinkle with cilantro. Serve hot or warm.

Stir-Fried Eggs with Mushrooms and Zucchini

6	large eggs	6
2 tsp	soy sauce	10 mL
1 tsp	Asian sesame oil	5 mL
½ tsp	salt or to taste	2 mL
½ tsp	freshly ground pepper	2 mL
2 tbsp	vegetable oil	25 mL
2 tbsp	chopped onion	25 mL
2 tsp	chopped garlic	10 mL
8 oz	sliced mushrooms (1 cup/250 mL)	250 g
2	medium zucchini, halved lengthwise and sliced (about 3 cups)	2
½ cup	red bell pepper strips	125 mL
3 tbsp	chopped green onions	45 mL
2 tbsp	chopped fresh dill	25 mL

Serves 4

Make this for brunch, along with cheese grits or polenta, or serve it for supper with jasmine rice and a platter of roasted vegetables tossed with extra virgin olive oil and chopped fresh dill.

1. In a bowl, whisk together eggs, soy sauce, sesame oil, salt and pepper. Set aside.

2. Heat a wok or a large deep skillet over high heat. Add vegetable oil and swirl to coat pan. Add onion and garlic and toss well, until fragrant, about 15 seconds.

3. Add mushrooms and toss well. Spread into a single layer and cook, undisturbed, for 30 seconds. Toss well. Cook, undisturbed, until beginning to wilt, about 1 minute.

4. Add zucchini and red pepper and toss well. Cook, tossing often, until mushrooms are tender and zucchini and pepper are tender-crisp, 1 to 2 minutes more.

5. Push vegetables aside. Stir in egg mixture and swirl gently to spread around pan. Cook, undisturbed, for 30 seconds. Gently but quickly stir and scoop to scramble eggs until almost done, about 1 minute. Mix vegetables into eggs as you scramble them, tossing more quickly when they are almost done. When eggs are just cooked, but not dry, remove from heat. Add green onions and dill and toss well. Transfer to a serving plate. Serve hot or warm.

Fried Rice with Edamame and Corn

Satisfying for lunch or supper, this dish is delicious with miso soup and a bowl of spinach or collard greens cooked with olive oil and garlic. I love it with aromatic Thai-style jasmine rice or delicate South Asian basmati rice, but you could use any kind of cooked rice, white or brown.

TIP

Edamame are a flavorful variety of soybean picked when young and green. An excellent source of protein, they are available shelled and frozen in many supermarkets as well as health food stores and Asian groceries.

4	large eggs	4
1 tsp	soy sauce	5 mL
1 tsp	Asian sesame oil	5 mL
2 tbsp	vegetable oil	25 mL
1 tbsp	chopped fresh gingerroot	15 mL
1 tbsp	chopped garlic	15 mL
3/4 cup	frozen shelled edamame or peas (see Tip, left)	175 mL
3/4 cup	frozen corn	175 mL
2 1/2 cups	cooked basmati or jasmine rice, preferably cold (see pages, 316 and 317)	625 mL
3 tbsp	chopped fresh cilantro or dill, divided	45 mL
3 tbsp	chopped green onions, divided	45 mL

1. In a bowl, whisk together eggs, soy sauce and sesame oil.

2. Heat a wok or a large deep skillet over high heat. Add vegetable oil and swirl to coat pan. Add ginger and garlic and toss well, until fragrant, about 15 seconds. Add edamame and corn and cook, tossing often, for 30 seconds.

3. Push vegetables aside. Stir in egg mixture and swirl gently to spread around pan. Cook, undisturbed, for 30 seconds. Gently but quickly stir and scoop to scramble eggs until almost done, about 1 minute.

4. Add rice and toss well. Cook, tossing occasionally, until rice is heated through, edamame and corn are tender-crisp and everything is evenly combined. Add half the cilantro and green onions and toss well. Transfer to a serving plate. Sprinkle with remaining green onions and cilantro. Serve hot or warm.

Hoisin-Seasoned Fried Rice with Chickpeas and Corn

2 tbsp	hoisin sauce	25 mL
2 tbsp	vegetable stock or water	25 mL
1 tbsp	soy sauce	15 mL
2 tsp	Chinese-style mustard or Dijon mustard (see Tip, page 206)	10 mL
1 tsp	granulated sugar	5 mL
½ tsp	salt or to taste	2 mL
2 tbsp	vegetable oil	25 mL
2 tbsp	chopped fresh gingerroot	25 mL
2 tsp	chopped garlic	10 mL
¼ cup	chopped onion	50 mL
1 cup	drained cooked or canned chickpeas	250 mL
1 cup	shredded carrot	250 mL
1	can (14 oz/398 mL) baby corn, drained	1
3½ cups	cooked brown rice, preferably chilled (see page 316)	825 mL
3 tbsp	chopped green onions	45 mL
2 tsp	Asian sesame oil	10 mL
3 tbsp	white sesame seeds, toasted, optional (see page 342)	45 mL

Serves 4

You will need cooked brown rice for this recipe. Hoisin sauce provides a deep, sweet note to this dish, which is a perfect choice when you want a hearty meal fast. I love it with steamed spinach and lentil soup.

TIP

To prepare the brown rice, transfer it to a large bowl and use your hands to break up chunks and crumble it into loose, individual grains.

1. In a small bowl, combine hoisin sauce, vegetable stock, soy sauce, mustard, sugar and salt and stir well. Set aside.

2. Heat a wok or large deep skillet over high heat. Add oil and swirl to coat pan. Add ginger, garlic and onion. Toss well and cook until fragrant, about 15 seconds. Add chickpeas, carrots and baby corn. Cook, tossing often, until carrots have softened, about 1 minute.

3. Add brown rice and toss well. Cook, tossing often, until rice is heated through and tender and everything is well combined, about 2 minutes.

4. Add hoisin sauce mixture, pouring in around sides of pan. Cook, tossing often, until everything is evenly seasoned and combined well. Add green onions, sesame oil and sesame seeds, if using, and toss well, about 1 minute more. Transfer to a serving plate. Serve hot or warm.

Fragrant Brown Rice with Shanghai Bok Choy and Tofu

Serves 4

Soft green with smooth, rounded leaves and short, plump stalks, Shanghai bok choy is available in many supermarkets as well as in Asian markets. It offers flavor and beauty, making it an ideal stir-fry choice.

2 tbsp	soy sauce	25 mL
2 tbsp	dry sherry or Shaoxing rice wine	25 mL
2 tsp	Asian sesame oil	10 mL
1 tsp	granulated sugar	5 mL
½ tsp	salt or to taste	2 mL
½ tsp	hot pepper flakes	2 mL
1¼ lbs	Shanghai bok choy (about 3 stalks)	625 g
1 cup	shiitake mushrooms (4 oz/125 g)	250 mL
2 tbsp	vegetable oil	25 mL
1 tbsp	chopped fresh gingerroot	15 mL
2 tsp	chopped garlic	10 mL
8 oz	firm or extra-firm tofu, drained and diced (see Tips, page 198)	250 g
3½ cups	cooked brown rice, preferably chilled (see page 316)	825 mL
3 tbsp	chopped green onions	45 mL

1. In a small bowl, combine soy sauce, sherry, sesame oil, sugar, salt and hot pepper flakes and stir well. Set aside.

2. To prepare bok choy, trim away the root end of each stalk. Quarter each stalk lengthwise. Separate into individual leaves. Stack the leaves and halve them lengthwise to make long slender strips. Set aside.

3. Cut away and discard stems of shiitake mushrooms. Cut large caps into quarters, halve medium ones, and leave small ones whole. Set aside.

4. Heat a wok or a large deep skillet over high heat. Add vegetable oil and swirl to coat pan. Add ginger and garlic and toss well, until fragrant, about 15 seconds.

5. Add bok choy and toss well. Cook, tossing often, until they begin to wilt, about 30 seconds. Add shiitake mushrooms and toss well. Cook, tossing occasionally, until bok choy is tender-crisp and shiitakes have softened, about 2 minutes.

6. Add tofu and brown rice and toss well. Cook, tossing occasionally, until rice and tofu are heated through, 1 to 2 minutes.

7. Add soy sauce mixture, pouring in around sides of pan. Toss well and cook until everything is evenly seasoned, about 1 minute more. Add green onions and toss well. Transfer to a serving plate. Serve hot or warm.

Soy-Scented Rice and Peas with Crunchy Cashews

1 tbsp	soy sauce	15 mL
1 tbsp	dry sherry or Shaoxing rice wine	15 mL
½ tsp	granulated sugar	2 mL
½ tsp	salt or to taste	2 mL
2 tbsp	vegetable oil	25 mL
1 tbsp	chopped fresh gingerroot	15 mL
2 tsp	chopped garlic	10 mL
8 oz	sliced mushrooms (1 cup/250 mL)	250 g
1 cup	thinly sliced celery (cut on the diagonal)	250 mL
3½ cups	cooked brown rice, preferably chilled (see page 316)	825 mL
1 cup	frozen tiny peas	250 mL
¾ cup	halved cherry tomatoes	175 mL
1 cup	roasted salted cashews	250 mL
2 tbsp	chopped fresh cilantro	25 mL
2 tsp	Asian sesame oil	10 mL

1. In a small bowl, combine soy sauce, sherry, sugar and salt and stir well. Set aside.

2. Heat a wok or a large deep skillet over high heat. Add oil and swirl to coat pan. Add ginger and garlic and toss well, until fragrant, about 15 seconds.

3. Add mushrooms, toss well and spread out into a single layer. Cook, undisturbed, for 30 seconds. Add celery and toss well. Cook, tossing often, until mushrooms and celery are beginning to wilt, about 1 minute.

4. Add brown rice and peas and toss well. Cook, tossing often, until rice is heated through and tender and peas are hot, 1 to 2 minutes.

5. Add soy sauce mixture, pouring in around sides of pan. Toss well to season rice and mix everything together well, about 1 minute more. Add cherry tomatoes, cashews, cilantro and sesame oil and toss well. Transfer to a serving plate. Serve hot or warm.

Serves 4

You will need cooked brown rice for this recipe. Pair this satisfying main course with chilled cream of cucumber or asparagus soup in warm weather and with steaming cream of mushroom soup when it's cold outside. Or serve it with herb-and-cheese omelets anytime of year.

TIP

To prepare the cooked chilled brown rice for this recipe, transfer it to a large bowl and use your hands to break up chunks and crumble it into loose, individual grains.

Vegetarian Pad Thai

Serves 2 to 4

The top favorite Thai restaurant dish for many people can be made at home, especially when you have helping hands to organize the preparation. Slender dried rice noodles, about the size of linguine, are the standard noodle choice, but wider ones will work as well.

TIPS

If you want the crispy tofu used in traditional pad Thai, fry the tofu in about 2 inches (5 cm) of hot vegetable oil until golden brown, drain well and add along with the green onions toward the end of cooking time.

Brown bean sauce is one kind of fermented soybean condiment widely used in Asian cooking. Made from soybeans that are salted and fermented, it provides a sharp, tangy flavor (see Ingredient Glossary, page 12, for more details). You could substitute Chinese-style bean paste or hot bean paste (see Tips, page 287).

4 oz	dried rice noodles	125 g
½ cup	vegetable stock	125 mL
2 tbsp	tamarind liquid, optional (see recipe, page 339)	25 mL
1 tbsp	soy sauce	15 mL
1 tbsp	brown bean sauce or bean paste (see Tips, left)	15 mL
1 tbsp	granulated sugar	15 mL
1 tsp	salt or to taste	5 mL
1 tsp	hot pepper flakes	5 mL
1⅓ cups	fresh shiitakes or other mushrooms	325 mL
3 tbsp	vegetable oil, divided	45 mL
1 tbsp	chopped garlic	15 mL
8 oz	firm or extra-firm tofu, drained and diced	250 g
¾ cup	shredded carrots	175 mL
2	large eggs, beaten	2
½ cup	chopped green onions	125 mL
2 cups	bean sprouts, divided	500 mL
½ cup	chopped roasted salted peanuts	125 mL
2 tbsp	freshly squeezed lime juice	25 mL
4	lime wedges	4

1. Bring a large pot of water to a rolling boil over high heat. Add rice noodles and remove from heat. Stir gently to separate the noodles. Let stand for 5 to 7 minutes, stirring occasionally, until noodles are softened but still firm. Drain, rinse well in cold water. Drain and set aside.

2. In another bowl, combine vegetable stock, tamarind liquid, if using, soy sauce, bean sauce, sugar, salt and hot pepper flakes and stir well. Set aside.

3. Cut away and discard stems of shiitake mushrooms. Cut caps into thin strips, about ⅛ inch (0.25 cm) wide. Set aside.

4. Heat a wok or a large deep skillet over medium heat. Add 2 tbsp (25 mL) of the oil and swirl to coat pan. Add garlic and toss well, until fragrant, about 15 seconds.

5. Add shiitake mushrooms and toss well. Add tofu and carrots and cook, tossing often, until shiitakes are softened and carrots are tender-crisp, 1 to 2 minutes.

6. Add noodles to the pan and toss well. Add vegetable stock mixture, pouring in around sides of pan. Cook, tossing often, until noodles are seasoned and tender, 1 to 2 minutes more. (Add 1 to 2 tbsp/15 to 25 mL of water as needed to prevent sticking or burning).

7. Push noodles aside. Add remaining oil to pan. Add eggs, swirling the pan to spread eggs out into a thin sheet. When it is almost set, break egg up into small chunks.

8. Add green onions and half of the bean sprouts and cook, tossing often, until sprouts are starting to wilt, about 1 minute more. Add peanuts and the lime juice and toss to combine everything well. Transfer to a serving platter and place the remaining bean sprouts and the lime wedges on one side. Serve hot or warm.

> **Variation:** You could use other noodles in place of dried rice noodles, such as linguine, spaghetti or fettuccine. Cook the noodles according to package directions until just barely tender, rinse in cold water and drain well. You will need about 2½ cups (625 mL) of cooked noodles.

Slurpy Thai-Style Noodles

Serves 4

This Thai noodle-shop standard, *pad si-yu*, is one to put into your repertoire. Hearty and delicious, it is one of my favorite dishes, both to order in Thai restaurants and to cook in my kitchen at home. Thai people eat this from a plate using a spoon and fork, but you could serve it in individual bowls and serve it with chopsticks, too.

TIP

Fresh wide rice noodles are the classic choice for this dish, but I make it with dried rice noodles about the width of fettuccine since fresh are unavailable where I live. You could make this with the thinner dried rice noodles, which are typically used for pad Thai, or with another long slender pasta such as spaghetti or linguine, cooked al dente.

8 oz	dried rice noodles (see Tip, left)	250 g
3 tbsp	vegetable stock or water	45 mL
2 tbsp	dark soy sauce (see Tip, right)	25 mL
1 tbsp	molasses or dark brown sugar	15 mL
1 tbsp	soy sauce	15 mL
1 tsp	salt or to taste	5 mL
½ tsp	freshly ground pepper	2 mL
1 cup	fresh shiitake mushrooms (4 oz/125 g)	250 g
3 tbsp	vegetable oil, divided	45 mL
1 tbsp	chopped garlic	15 mL
3 cups	small broccoli florets	750 mL
2	large eggs, lightly beaten	2

1. Bring a large pot of water to a rolling boil over high heat. Add rice noodles and remove from heat. Stir gently to separate the noodles. Let stand for 5 to 7 minutes, stirring occasionally, until noodles are softened but still firm. Drain, rinse well in cold water. Drain and set aside.

2. In a bowl, combine vegetable stock, dark soy sauce, molasses, soy sauce, salt and pepper and stir well. Set aside.

3. Cut away and discard stems of shiitake mushrooms. Cut large caps into quarters, halve medium ones and leave small ones whole. Set aside.

4. Heat a wok or a large deep skillet over medium-high heat. Add 1 tbsp (15 mL) of the oil and swirl to coat pan. Add garlic and toss, until fragrant, about 15 seconds. Add mushrooms, toss well and spread into a single layer. Cook, undisturbed, for 30 seconds and then toss well.

5. Add broccoli and cook, tossing often, until bright green and tender-crisp, about 2 minutes. (Add 1 to 2 tbsp/15 to 25 mL water if the pan becomes dry or the broccoli starts to burn.) Transfer the broccoli and shiitakes to serving platter and set aside.

6. Add remaining oil to the pan and swirl to coat. Add noodles and toss well. Cook, tossing often, until they have softened and curled up into tender separate strands, 1 to 2 minutes. (Add 1 to 2 tbsp/15 to 25 mL water if needed to prevent sticking or burning.)

7. Push the noodles aside. Add eggs, swirling the pan to spread eggs out into a thin sheet and cook, undisturbed, for 30 seconds. When almost set, toss well to break egg up into small chunks. Return shiitakes and broccoli to the pan, with any accumulated juices and toss well.

8. Add soy sauce mixture, pouring in around sides of pan. Toss well to coat everything evenly with the sauce. Transfer to the serving platter. Serve hot.

> **Variation:** Serve the noodles with a small bowl of tangy-hot seasoning sauce. In a small bowl, combine ½ cup (125 mL) white vinegar or cider vinegar with 2 tsp (10 mL) granulated sugar. Stir well to dissolve the sugar. Sprinkle with 1 tsp (5 mL) finely chopped hot green chiles and stir well. Pass at the table, inviting guests to sprinkle a spoonful or two onto their noodles before they eat.

TIP

This dish traditionally uses the Thai condiment, *si-yu wahn*, a dark sweet soy sauce made with dark soy sauce and molasses. It is very similar to the Indonesian condiment, kecap (or kejap) manis, which can be substituted for it. These condiments give a deep, mild and sweet flavor and handsome color to the noodles. Both are widely available in Asian markets. If you want to use one of them in this recipe, replace both the 2 tbsp dark soy sauce and the 1 tbsp molasses called for with a total of 3 tbsp (45 mL) of Thai-style dark sweet soy sauce (*si-yu wahn*) or kecap manis.

Singapore-Style Noodles with Vegetables in Curry Sauce

Serves 4

This terrific noodle dish is often served in Chinese restaurants specializing in the dumplings, noodles and other special tea lunch treats known as dim sum. The very thin rice noodles traditionally used in this dish are often available in supermarkets as well as Asian grocery stores; cooked angel hair pasta would also work in this recipe.

6 oz	very thin dried rice noodles	175 g
2/3 cup	vegetable stock or water	150 mL
2 tbsp	curry powder	25 mL
1 tbsp	soy sauce	15 mL
1 tsp	salt or to taste	5 mL
1/2 tsp	granulated sugar	2 mL
1 cup	shiitake mushrooms (4 oz/125 g)	250 mL
2 tbsp	vegetable oil	25 mL
1 tbsp	chopped garlic	15 mL
1 cup	chopped onion	250 mL
1 1/4 cups	sliced green bell peppers	300 mL
8 oz	firm or extra-firm tofu, drained and pressed (see Tips, page 198)	250 g
1/4 cup	chopped green onions	50 mL
3 tbsp	chopped fresh cilantro	45 mL

1. Bring a large pot of water to a rolling boil over high heat. Add rice noodles and remove from heat. Stir gently to separate the noodles. Let stand for 5 to 7 minutes, stirring occasionally, until noodles are softened but still firm. Drain, rinse well in cold water. Drain and set aside.

2. In a small bowl, combine vegetable stock, curry powder, soy sauce, salt and sugar and stir well. Set aside.

3. Cut away and discard stems of shiitake mushrooms. Slice the caps into 1/4-inch (0.5 cm) strips. Set aside.

4. Heat a wok or a large deep skillet over high heat. Add oil and swirl to coat pan. Add garlic and toss well, until fragrant, about 15 seconds.

5. Add onion, green peppers and shiitake mushrooms and toss well. Cook, tossing often, until onion is fragrant, mushrooms are softened and peppers are tender-crisp, 1 to 2 minutes.

6. Add tofu and noodles and toss well. Add vegetable stock mixture, pouring in around sides of pan. Cook, tossing often, until noodles and other ingredients are hot, evenly seasoned and well combined, about 1 minute more. Add green onions and cilantro and toss well. Transfer to a serving plate. Serve hot.

Mushroom, Tomato and Asparagus Toss (page 211)

Overleaf: Stir-Fried Eggs with Mushrooms and Zucchini (page 215)

Vegetable Sides

Overleaf: Shanghai-Style Bok Choy
(page 228)

Butternut Stir-Fry with Peppers and Peas
(page 238)

Broccoli Florets with Ginger and Sesame

Serves 4

Cooked this way, florets of broccoli become tender and inviting, brilliant green and enlivened with a small burst of ginger-sesame flavor.

TIP

Use trimmed broccoli florets found packaged in the produce section of supermarkets. Chop large florets into 2 or 3 pieces so that they cook quickly and evenly. Or buy a crown or head or two of broccoli and chop the florets into bite-size pieces. You can peel the stalk and slice it crosswise into coins, and include it in this or other stir-fry dishes, allowing just enough time for it to become tender-crisp.

2 tbsp	water	25 mL
1 tsp	salt or to taste	5 mL
½ tsp	granulated sugar	2 mL
2 tbsp	vegetable oil	25 mL
1 tbsp	chopped fresh gingerroot	15 mL
8 cups	bite-size broccoli florets (about 12 oz/375 g) (see Tip, left)	2 L
1 tsp	Asian sesame oil	5 mL

1. In a small bowl, combine water, salt and sugar and stir well. Set aside.
2. Heat a wok or a large deep skillet over high heat. Add vegetable oil and swirl to coat pan. Add ginger and toss well, until fragrant, about 15 seconds.
3. Add broccoli and spread into a single layer. Cook, undisturbed, for 1 minute. Toss well.
4. Add water mixture and toss well. Cook, tossing occasionally, until broccoli is brilliant green and tender-crisp, 2 to 3 minutes more. Add sesame oil and toss once. Transfer to a serving plate. Serve hot, cold or at room temperature.

Peppery Tumbled Spinach

2 tbsp	fish sauce	25 mL
2 tsp	granulated sugar	10 mL
½ tsp	freshly ground pepper	2 mL
2 tbsp	vegetable oil	25 mL
1 tbsp	chopped garlic	15 mL
8 to 10 cups	loosely packed fresh spinach leaves, about 20 oz (600 g), (see Tip, right)	2 to 2.5 L
¼ cup	water	50 mL

1. In a small bowl, combine fish sauce, sugar and pepper.

2. Heat a wok or a large deep skillet over medium-high heat. Add oil and swirl to coat pan. Add garlic and toss well, until fragrant, about 30 seconds.

3. Add spinach, spreading around pan, and cook for 15 seconds. Turn the pile of spinach leaves and cook, until spinach is mostly wilted, another 30 seconds.

4. Stir in fish sauce mixture. Add water and continue stir-frying gently, until spinach is tender, dark green and seasoned well, 1 to 2 minutes more.

5. Transfer mixture to a serving platter deep enough to hold the cooking liquid along with the spinach. Serve hot or warm.

Serves 4

This quickly cooked dish is a favorite at my house, thanks to its deep peppery flavor and simple speedy preparation. A set of metal tongs or two utensils, such as a big spatula and a slotted spoon, will help you manage the pile of spinach leaves as they cook down.

TIP

If you are using a large deep skillet, you can add the spinach leaves in two or three batches, allowing each portion to cook down before adding the next one. A wok should hold all the leaves at once.

Shanghai-Style Bok Choy

Serves 4

Baby bok choy is a cousin of regular bok choy. It has soft green stems and smooth, oval leaves, and it is often sold in sets of three or four plump little stalks. It cooks quickly and can be quartered lengthwise with stalks left intact for an elegant presentation.

1 lb	baby bok choy (about 3 small stalks)	500 g
2 tbsp	vegetable oil	25 mL
1 tbsp	chopped garlic	15 mL
1 tbsp	chopped fresh gingerroot	15 mL
1 tsp	salt or to taste	5 mL
2 tbsp	water	25 mL

1. Trim each bok choy stalk, cutting away about ¾ inches (2 cm) from the base of each. Then slice crosswise on the diagonal into 1½-inch (4 cm) pieces. Keep stems and leaves in separate piles.

2. Heat a wok or a large deep skillet over high heat. Add oil and swirl to coat pan. Add garlic and ginger and toss well, until fragrant, about 15 seconds.

3. Add bok choy stems and spread into a single layer. Cook for 1 minute. Toss well and add leaves. Cook, undisturbed, for 1 minute. Toss once.

4. Add salt and water, pouring in slowly around sides of pan. Cook, tossing occasionally, until bok choy is tender-crisp, 1 to 2 minutes more. Transfer to a serving plate. Serve hot or warm.

Classic Stir-Fried Napa Cabbage

1	small head napa cabbage (about 12 oz/375 g) (see Tip, right)	1
2 tbsp	vegetable oil	25 mL
1 tbsp	chopped garlic	15 mL
1 tbsp	water	15 mL
1 tsp	salt or to taste	5 mL
2 tbsp	chopped green onions	25 mL

1. Trim about 2 inches (5 cm) from the base of cabbage (discard any wilted outer leaves). Halve cabbage lengthwise and place each half cut side down on a cutting board. Cut crosswise into 2-inch (5 cm) pieces. Transfer to a bowl and toss with your hands to separate into individual pieces. (You will need about 6 cups/1.5 L.)

2. Heat a wok or a large deep skillet over medium-high heat. Add oil and swirl to coat pan. Add garlic and toss once, until fragrant, about 30 seconds.

3. Add cabbage and toss well. Cook, undisturbed, for 1 minute. Toss again and add water and salt, pouring in slowly around sides of pan. Cook, tossing occasionally, until fairly crisp, 1 to 2 minutes more.

4. Add green onions and toss once. Transfer to a serving plate. Serve hot, warm or at room temperature.

Serves 4

This classic stir-fry is elementary, featuring one vegetable that is lightly seasoned and quickly cooked. The result is a nourishing and satisfying dish, providing great flavor with very little sauce. I love this over rice, with grilled salmon, roast chicken or Swirled Eggs with Tomatoes and Onions (see recipe, page 214) to round out the meal.

TIP

If you are using a large head of napa cabbage, quarter it lengthwise, so that the pieces you cut will measure approximately 3-by 2-inches (7.5 by 5 cm) before cooking. Then measure out about 6 cups (1.5 L).

Szechwan-Seasoned Napa Cabbage

Serves 4

I love the strange, wonderful flavor imparted by Szechwan peppercorns. If you can't find them, simply omit them, and add 1 tsp (5 mL) hot pepper flakes to the pan in their place. It won't be the same, but you'll still have a tasty and tangy dish.

1	small head napa cabbage (about 12 oz/375 g) (see Tip, page 229)	1
½ tsp	whole Szechwan peppercorns	2 mL
½ tsp	hot pepper flakes	2 mL
½ tsp	salt or to taste	2 mL
1 tbsp	granulated sugar	15 mL
1 tbsp	white vinegar	15 mL
2 tsp	soy sauce	10 mL
2 tbsp	vegetable oil	25 mL
1 tsp	Asian sesame oil	5 mL

1. Trim about 2 inches (5 cm) from the base of cabbage (discard any wilted outer leaves). Halve cabbage lengthwise and place each half cut side down on a cutting board. Cut crosswise into 2-inch (5 cm) pieces. Transfer to a bowl and toss with your hands to separate into individual pieces. (You will need about 6 cups/1.5 L.)

2. In a small bowl, combine peppercorns, hot pepper flakes and salt. Set aside. In another bowl, combine sugar, vinegar and soy sauce and stir well. Set aside.

3. Heat a wok or large deep skillet over high heat. Add oil and swirl to coat pan.

4. Add peppercorn mixture and toss well. Add cabbage and toss well. Spread into a single layer and cook, undisturbed, for 1 minute. Toss well and cook, until brightened in color and beginning to wilt a little, 1 minute more.

5. Stir vinegar-soy sauce mixture and pour in around sides of pan. Cook, tossing often, until cabbage is evenly seasoned and tender-crisp, 1 minute more.

6. Add sesame oil and toss once. Transfer to a serving plate. Serve hot or warm.

Gingery Chinese Broccoli

12 oz	Chinese broccoli (about 3 to 4 stalks)	375 g
2 tbsp	vegetable oil	25 mL
1 tbsp	chopped fresh gingerroot	15 mL
1 tsp	salt or to taste	5 mL
½ tsp	granulated sugar	2 mL
2 tbsp	water	25 mL

1. Trim about ½ inch (1 cm) from broccoli stalks. Chop off leaves and set aside. Peel stems, halve lengthwise and cut on the diagonal into 2-inch (5 cm) pieces. Stack leaves and cut in half lengthwise, and then crosswise into 2-inch (5 cm) pieces. Keep stems and leaves in separate piles.

2. Heat a wok or large deep skillet over high heat. Add oil and swirl to coat pan. Add ginger and toss well, until fragrant, about 15 seconds.

3. Add broccoli stems and toss well. Cook, tossing often, until bright green and beginning to soften, about 1 minute. Add leaves and cook, tossing twice, for 1 minute more.

4. Add salt and sugar and toss once. Add water, pouring in around sides of pan. Cook, tossing occasionally, until broccoli is vivid green and tender-crisp, about 2 minutes more. Transfer to a serving plate. Serve hot, warm or at room temperature.

Serves 4

Chinese broccoli, known as *gai lan* in Cantonese and *pahk kah-nah* in Thai, has thick, sturdy leaves and slender stems. Its bold flavor has a bitter note, but cooked with fresh ginger and salt, it brightens to a vivid color and taste that goes wonderfully with rice or noodles. Cook it within a day or so after purchase, as it ages quickly, despite its sturdy appearance.

Asian Eggplant with Peppers and Peas

Serves 4

Use long, slender Asian eggplant for this dish, and enjoy their lush flavor, brightened with sweet peppers and a dash of sesame oil. Asian eggplants are smaller in size with a more tender texture compared to eggplants used in Western cooking, so they do not need to be salted or peeled before cooking.

TIP

Frozen tiny peas are also referred to as "petite" and "baby." You can also use regular-size frozen peas, if you allow a little extra cooking time to heat them through.

1 lb	Asian eggplant (about 3)	500 g
2 tbsp	vegetable oil, divided	25 mL
½ cup	thinly sliced red bell pepper	125 mL
⅓ cup	frozen tiny peas (see Tip, left)	75 mL
1 tsp	salt or to taste	5 mL
1 tsp	Asian sesame oil	5 mL

1. Trim both ends from each eggplant and slice crosswise into thin rounds.
2. Heat a wok or a large deep skillet over high heat. Add 1 tablespoon (15 mL) of the vegetable oil and swirl to coat pan.
3. Add eggplant and spread into an even layer. Cook, tossing often, for 2 minutes.
4. Push eggplant aside and add remaining tablespoon (15 mL) of the vegetable oil to center of pan. When hot, add red pepper and peas. Toss well. Cook, tossing occasionally, until eggplant is tender and red pepper and peas are tender-crisp, about 2 minutes more. Add salt and sesame oil and toss well. Transfer to a serving plate. Serve hot or warm.

Variations: Use green bell peppers instead of red. And regular frozen peas instead of tiny ones.

Garlic-Scented Zucchini

1 lb	small zucchini (about 4) (see Tip, right)	500 g
2 tbsp	vegetable oil	25 mL
2 tsp	chopped garlic	10 mL
1 tsp	salt or to taste	5 mL
½ tsp	granulated sugar	2 mL

1. Trim both ends from each zucchini and slice into thin rounds. You will need about 3 cups (750 mL).

2. Heat a wok or a large deep skillet over high heat. Add oil and swirl to coat pan. Add garlic and toss well, until fragrant, about 15 seconds.

3. Add zucchini and spread into a single layer. Cook, undisturbed, for 1 minute. Toss once.

4. Add salt and sugar and toss well. Reduce heat to medium and cook, tossing occasionally, until zucchini are tender-crisp, 2 to 3 minutes more. Transfer to a serving plate. Serve hot or warm.

Serves 4

Slender zucchini sliced into thin rounds cook down to a beautiful pile of pale green, flavorful summer squash. This dish is delicious hot, and even tastier about 5 minutes after it comes out of the pan.

TIP
Cut large zucchini in half lengthwise, and then slice them into half-moon shapes.

Stir-Fried Celery Hearts

1	bunch celery	1
1 tbsp	vegetable oil	15 mL
½ tsp	salt or to taste	2 mL
½ tsp	granulated sugar	2 mL
1 tbsp	thinly sliced green onions	15 mL

1. Discard the outermost stalks of celery and choose about 4 nice stalks from the core portion of the bunch. Trim each stalk, removing the ends and pulling away the strings on the outside of each stalk. Slice on the diagonal into thin pieces. You should have about 3 cups (750 mL).

2. Heat a wok or a large deep skillet over high heat. Add oil and swirl to coat pan. Add celery and spread into a single layer. Cook, undisturbed, for 1 minute. Toss well.

3. Add salt and sugar and toss. Cook, tossing occasionally, until celery is tender-crisp, 1 to 2 minutes.

4. Add green onions and toss well. Transfer to a small bowl.

Serves 4

Celery cooks fast and adds a crunchy note to a hearty main dish. Here I've used celery hearts, the inner rib of the celery stalk. Enjoy this dish hot as a side or cold as a salad.

Fragrant Iceberg Lettuce

Serves 4

Iceberg lettuce is a stand out when cooked this way. It quickly cooks and its refreshing crunch tastes wonderful.

2 tbsp	vegetable oil	25 mL
1 tbsp	chopped garlic	15 mL
3 cups	2-inch (5 cm) chunks iceberg lettuce	750 mL
½ tsp	salt or to taste	2 mL
½ tsp	granulated sugar	2 mL
1 tsp	Asian sesame oil	5 mL

1. Heat a wok or a large deep skillet over high heat. Add oil and swirl to coat pan. Add garlic and toss well, until fragrant, about 30 seconds.

2. Add lettuce and spread into a single layer. Cook, tossing twice, for 1 minute. Add salt and sugar and toss well. Cook, tossing once, for 1 minute more.

3. Add sesame oil and toss once. Transfer to a serving plate.

Garlic-Spiked Bok Choy

Serves 4

This simple, traditional stir-fry might inspire you to include bok choy on your weekly grocery list. Its bright white stalks and lush green leaves cook up into a remarkably delicious dish that tastes great with rice, steak and baked potatoes, tossed with pasta or tucked into a BLT for tomorrow's lunch.

1	head bok choy (about 1¼ lbs/625 g)	1
2 tbsp	vegetable oil	25 mL
1 tbsp	chopped garlic	15 mL
1 tsp	salt or to taste	5 mL
2 tbsp	water	25 mL

1. Trim 2 to 3 inches (5 to 7.5 cm) from the base of bok choy (discard any wilted outer leaves). Halve bok choy lengthwise and place each half cut side down on a cutting board. Cut it crosswise into 2-inch (5 cm) pieces. Transfer to a large bowl and toss with your hands to separate into individual pieces. (You will need about 6 cups/1.5 L.)

2. Heat a wok or a large deep skillet over medium-high heat. Add oil and swirl to coat pan. Add garlic and salt and toss well, until garlic is fragrant, about 30 seconds. Add bok choy and cook, undisturbed, about 1 minute. Toss well.

3. Add water and continue cooking, tossing occasionally, until bok choy is tender-crisp, 1 to 2 minutes more. Transfer to a serving plate. Serve hot, warm or at room temperature.

Sesame-Kissed Asparagus

• Wok or large deep skillet with lid

1 lb	fresh asparagus	500 g
2 tbsp	vegetable oil	25 mL
1 tsp	salt or to taste	5 mL
½ tsp	granulated sugar	2 mL
3 tbsp	water	45 mL
1 tsp	Asian sesame oil	5 mL

1. Trim asparagus by snapping off ends. Cut each asparagus spear on the diagonal into 1-inch (2.5 cm) lengths, leaving tips a little longer. Discard ends.

2. Heat a wok or a large deep skillet over high heat. Add vegetable oil and swirl to coat pan.

3. Add asparagus and toss well. Spread into a single layer and cook, undisturbed, for 1 minute. Toss well.

4. Add salt, sugar and water. Cover pan with a large lid and cook, undisturbed, for 3 minutes.

5. Uncover and toss well. Cook, tossing occasionally, until asparagus is tender-crisp, 1 to 2 minutes more. Add sesame oil and toss well. Transfer to a serving plate. Serve hot or warm.

Serves 4

Elegant and easy to prepare, stir-fried asparagus work beautifully on busy weeknights and for special-occasion menus. I like sturdy, finger-size stalks best, but you can use pencil-thin ones if you shorten the cooking time by a minute or so. You will need to cover the pan for this recipe, using either a large wok-size lid or a stockpot lid big enough to rest fairly high up on the sides of the wok. You want a lid that will cover the asparagus with room to spare.

Vietnamese-Style Cauliflower with Herbs

Stir-fried with garlic, green onions and fresh herbs, the sometimes-maligned cauliflower shows off its sweet notes and a pleasing crunch in this simple and fast recipe. It's perfect with grilled salmon or roast chicken and a big cool salad.

2 tbsp	fish sauce (or 1 tbsp water/15 mL plus 1 tsp /5 mL salt)	25 mL
2 tbsp	water	25 mL
1 tsp	granulated sugar	5 mL
½ tsp	freshly ground pepper	2 mL
2 tbsp	vegetable oil	25 mL
1 tbsp	chopped garlic	15 mL
½	head cauliflower, trimmed and chopped into small florets (about 4 cups/1 L)	½
2	green onions, cut into 1-inch (5 cm) lengths	2
3 tbsp	chopped fresh cilantro	45 mL

1. In a small bowl, combine fish sauce, water, sugar and pepper and stir well.
2. Heat a wok or a large heavy skillet over high heat. Add oil and swirl to coat pan. Add garlic and toss well, until fragrant, about 15 seconds.
3. Add cauliflower and spread into a single layer. Cook, undisturbed, for 1 minute. Toss well.
4. Add fish sauce mixture and green onions and toss again. Cook, tossing occasionally, until cauliflower is tender-crisp, about 2 minutes more.
5. Add cilantro and toss again. Transfer to a shallow bowl or a small serving platter large enough to accommodate the sauce. Serve hot or warm.

Fragrant Beans with Cherry Tomatoes

10 oz	French green beans	300 g
1 tbsp	vegetable oil	15 mL
2 tsp	chopped fresh gingerroot	10 mL
1 tsp	salt or to taste	5 mL
1/3 cup	halved cherry tomatoes	75 mL

Serves 4

This way of cooking delicate French-style beans is pleasing and speedy on a busy day.

1. Trim ends from green beans and cut on the diagonal into 2-inch (5 cm) lengths.

2. Heat a wok or a large deep skillet over high heat. Add oil and swirl to coat pan. Add ginger and salt and toss well, until ginger is fragrant, about 15 seconds.

3. Add green beans and toss well. Cook, tossing twice, for 1 minute. Add 1/4 cup (50 mL) water and toss well. Cook, tossing occasionally, until beans are tender-crisp, 1 to 2 minutes more. Add cherry tomatoes and toss once. Transfer to a serving plate. Serve hot or warm.

Gingery Carrots

2 to 3	medium carrots (about 8 oz/250 g)	2 to 3
2 tbsp	vegetable oil	25 mL
1 tbsp	chopped fresh gingerroot	15 mL
1 tsp	salt or to taste	5 mL
1 tsp	granulated sugar	5 mL
1/2 tsp	Asian sesame oil	2 mL

Serves 4

Here's a way to cook carrots that brings out their natural sweetness. Ginger complements them perfectly, and they taste great cold the next day.

1. Peel carrots and trim both ends. Chop crosswise on the diagonal into 1/4-inch (0.5 cm) thick slices.

2. Heat a wok or large deep skillet over high heat. Add vegetable oil and swirl to coat pan. Add ginger and toss well, until fragrant, about 15 seconds. Add carrots and spread into a single layer. Cook, undisturbed, for 1 minute. Toss well.

3. Add salt, sugar and 3 tbsp (45 mL) water and toss. Cover and cook, undisturbed, for 3 minutes. Uncover and cook, tossing twice, for 1 minute. Add sesame oil and toss well. Transfer to a serving plate. Serve hot, warm or cold.

Butternut Stir-Fry with Peppers and Peas

Chopped into small chunks, butternut squash cooks quickly into a lush texture and gorgeous color — perfect with bell peppers and peas in a sweet and tangy barbecue sauce.

2 tbsp	vegetable oil	25 mL
1 tbsp	chopped fresh gingerroot	15 mL
2 cups	cubed peeled butternut squash (1/2-inch/1 cm cubes)	500 mL
1/3 cup	diced red bell pepper	75 mL
1/3 cup	frozen tiny peas (see Tip, page 232)	75 mL
2 tbsp	water	25 mL
3 tbsp	barbecue sauce	45 mL
1 tsp	salt	5 mL

1. Heat a wok or a large deep skillet over high heat. Add oil and swirl to coat pan. Add ginger and toss well, until fragrant, about 15 seconds.

2. Add squash and spread into a single layer. Cook, undisturbed, for 1 minute. Toss well. Cook, tossing often, until squash is browning lightly around edges, 2 minutes more.

3. Push squash aside and add red pepper and peas. Scoop squash on top of vegetables. Add water, pouring in around sides of pan.

4. When everything is sizzling away, add barbecue sauce and salt. Cook, tossing once or twice, until vegetables are tender and evenly coated with sauce, 1 to 2 minutes more. Transfer to a serving plate. Serve hot or warm.

Bean Sprouts with Ginger and Garlic

2 tbsp	vegetable oil	25 mL
1 tbsp	each chopped garlic and gingerroot	15 mL
5 cups	bean sprouts (see Tip, right)	1.25 L
1 tsp	salt or to taste	5 mL
½ tsp	granulated sugar	2 mL
1 tsp	Asian sesame oil	5 mL
2 tbsp	chopped green onions	25 mL

1. Heat a wok or a large deep skillet over high heat. Add vegetable oil and swirl to coat pan. Add garlic and ginger and toss well, until fragrant, about 15 seconds.

2. Add bean sprouts and spread into a single layer. Cook, undisturbed, for 1 minute. Toss well. Add salt and sugar. Cook, tossing twice, 1 minute more. Add sesame oil and green onions and toss well. Serve hot or warm.

Serves 4

Look for crisp, bright white bean sprouts and use them within a day, as they wilt fast.

TIP

The bean sprouts most commonly found at grocery stores are the tender young shoot of the mung bean.

Limas with Sesame Oil

- Wok or large deep skillet with lid

2 tbsp	vegetable oil	25 mL
1	package (10 oz/300 g) frozen lima beans (see Tip, right)	1
¾ tsp	salt or to taste	4 mL
½ tsp	granulated sugar	2 mL
1 tsp	Asian sesame oil	5 mL

1. Heat a wok or a large deep skillet over high heat. Add vegetable oil and swirl to coat pan.

2. Add lima beans and toss once. Spread into a single layer and cook, undisturbed, for 1 minute.

3. Add salt, sugar and ⅓ cup (75 mL) water. Cover with a large lid and let lima beans cook, undisturbed, for 2 minutes. Uncover and toss well. Cook for 1 minute more. Add sesame oil and toss once. Transfer to a serving plate. Serve hot, warm or cold.

Serves 4

Frozen lima beans make a fine, satisfying side dish — tasty when hot and equally good cold. You can use any variety of frozen lima beans.

TIP

Fordhook lima beans are a larger variety of lima beans. Use them in this dish or baby lima beans, adjusting the cooking time accordingly. Fordhooks may need more time and baby limas cook more quickly; just test to see when they are tender.

Stir-Fried Shiitakes with Garlic

Serves 4

I love how mushrooms develop deep flavor and a pleasing texture when stir-fried. This dish goes especially well with a main course of grilled salmon or steak and a salad tossed with a bright and tangy dressing. Use all shiitakes or all button mushrooms if you like.

¼ cup	vegetable stock or water	50 mL
1 tsp	granulated sugar	5 mL
1 tsp	salt or to taste	5 mL
8 oz	fresh shiitake mushrooms	250 g
8 oz	fresh button mushrooms	250 g
3	green onions	3
2 tbsp	vegetable oil	25 mL
2 tbsp	coarsely chopped garlic	25 mL
2 tbsp	thinly sliced shallots or finely chopped onion	25 mL
½ tsp	freshly ground pepper	2 mL

1. In a small bowl, combine vegetable stock, sugar and salt and stir well. Set aside.

2. Prepare shiitakes by removing and discarding stems. Slice caps crosswise into ½-inch (1 cm) strips. Slice button mushrooms, including stems, crosswise into thin slices. Trim green onions and chop white parts coarsely. Chop green tops into 1-inch (2.5 cm) lengths. Set green onions aside separately from mushrooms.

3. Heat a wok or a large deep skillet over high heat. Add oil and swirl to coat pan. Add garlic and shallots and toss well, until garlic is fragrant, about 15 seconds.

4. Add shiitake and button mushrooms and spread into a single layer. Cook, undisturbed, for 1 minute. Toss well. Cook, tossing once or twice, until mushrooms start to release their liquid and soften, 1 minute more.

5. Add vegetable stock mixture and toss well. Cook, tossing once, until mushrooms are tender, 1 to 2 minutes more.

6. Add pepper and green onions and cook for 1 minute more. Toss once. Transfer to a serving plate. Serve hot or warm.

Oyster Mushrooms with Tiny Peas

1 tbsp	soy sauce	15 mL
1 tbsp	water	15 mL
1 tsp	granulated sugar	5 mL
½ tsp	salt or to taste	2 mL
¼ tsp	freshly ground pepper	1 mL
8 oz	oyster mushrooms	250 g
8 oz	button mushrooms	250 g
2 tbsp	vegetable oil	25 mL
2 tbsp	chopped garlic	25 mL
½ cup	frozen tiny peas (see Tip, page 232)	125 mL

1. In a small bowl, combine soy sauce, water, sugar, salt and pepper and stir well. Set aside.

2. Separate clusters of oyster mushrooms into individual pieces. Tear or chop larger ones lengthwise into halves or thirds. Cut button mushrooms lengthwise into thin slices.

3. Heat a wok or a large deep skillet over high heat. Add oil and swirl to coat pan. Add garlic and toss well, until fragrant, about 15 seconds.

4. Add mushrooms and spread into a single layer. Cook, undisturbed, for 1 minute. Toss well.

5. Add soy sauce mixture and toss well. Add peas and cook, tossing often, until mushrooms are tender and evenly seasoned, and peas are hot, tender and brilliant green, 1 to 2 minutes. Transfer to a serving plate. Serve hot or warm.

Serves 4

Soft grey in color and luscious in texture, oyster mushrooms cook up beautifully and take seasonings well. You could use all oyster mushrooms or shiitakes in place of button mushrooms here for a mix of color and texture.

Peppery Corn Kernels with Cherry Tomatoes

Serves 4

This quick stir-fry of corn and tomatoes lights up the table any time of year. In the summer, cut the kernels off two or three ears of fresh corn. Or in cooler weather, keep frozen or canned corn on hand so you can enjoy this recipe whenever you need a quick dish using whatever you have on hand.

2 tbsp	vegetable oil	25 mL
1 tbsp	chopped garlic	15 mL
2½ cups	corn kernels (see Tip, page 243)	625 mL
½ cup	halved cherry tomatoes	125 mL
1 tsp	salt or to taste	5 mL
½ tsp	hot pepper flakes	2 mL
2 tbsp	chopped fresh cilantro	25 mL

1. Heat a wok or a large deep skillet over high heat. Add oil and swirl to coat pan. Add garlic and toss well, until fragrant, about 15 seconds.

2. Add corn and toss well. Spread into a single layer. If using fresh or frozen corn, cook, tossing twice, until hot, brightened in color and tender-crisp, about 2 minutes. If using canned corn, cook, tossing once, until hot, about 1 minute.

3. Push corn aside and add cherry tomatoes to pan, spreading into a single layer. Cook, undisturbed, for 30 seconds. Then cook, tossing twice, until tomatoes are beginning to soften, about 1 minute more.

4. Add salt, hot pepper flakes and cilantro and toss once more. Transfer to a serving plate. Serve hot or warm.

Gorgeous Green and Yellow Stir-Fry

2 tbsp	water	25 mL
1 tsp	salt or to taste	5 mL
½ tsp	freshly ground pepper	2 mL
¼ tsp	granulated sugar	1 mL
2 tbsp	vegetable oil	25 mL
1 tbsp	chopped fresh gingerroot	15 mL
2½ cups	corn kernels, fresh, frozen or canned (see Tip, right)	625 mL
1 cup	frozen shelled edamame beans	250 mL
3 tbsp	finely chopped green onions	45 mL

1. In a small bowl, combine water, salt, pepper and sugar and stir well. Set aside.

2. Heat a wok or a large deep skillet over high heat. Add oil and swirl to coat pan. Add ginger and toss well, until fragrant, about 15 seconds.

3. Add corn and toss well. Spread into a single layer. If using fresh or frozen corn, cook, tossing twice, until hot, brightened in color and tender-crisp, about 2 minutes. If using canned corn, cook, tossing once, until hot, about 1 minute.

4. Push corn aside and add edamame beans to center of pan, spreading into a single layer. Cook, undisturbed, for 1 minute. Add water mixture and toss well. Continue cooking, tossing often, until edamame beans are tender-crisp, 1 to 2 minutes.

5. Add green onions and toss well. Transfer to a serving plate. Serve hot or warm.

Serves 4

Fresh soybeans, often called by their Japanese name, edamame, are firm, delicious and a gorgeous green. You'll find them frozen in their pods as well as shelled. Keep a package in the freezer for an excellent addition to stir-fries, soups, noodles and salads.

TIP

Corn is sturdy and easy to work with in stir-fry cooking. If it's fresh, it needs time to cook, and care to avoid scorching, since it tends to be juicy and sweet when freshly cut off the cob. When frozen, it will be dry and sturdy, but needs a little time to thaw as well as cook. Canned corn needs a good rinse before cooking to freshen it up, and then a good draining so that it doesn't add extra water to the dish. If you're using canned corn in this dish, taste it right after cooking. If you think it needs a little brightening up of flavor, add a squeeze of lemon juice or a small splash of vinegar, and an extra pinch of sugar and toss well.

Sugar Snap Peas with Cherry Tomatoes

Sugar snap peas burst with sweet, juicy flavor. Here they're cooked quickly with ginger and garlic. Cherry tomatoes tossed in at the end of cooking need only a quick turn in the hot pan to complete this pleasing dish.

8 oz	sugar snap peas (about 3 cups/750 mL)	250 g
¼ cup	water	50 mL
2 tsp	soy sauce	10 mL
1 tsp	granulated sugar	5 mL
½ tsp	salt or to taste	2 mL
2 tbsp	vegetable oil	25 mL
2 tsp	finely chopped fresh gingerroot	10 mL
1 tsp	coarsely chopped garlic	5 mL
1 cup	halved cherry tomatoes	250 mL
1 tsp	Asian sesame oil	5 mL

1. Trim sugar snap peas, cutting off stem end and pulling it along straight edge to remove any strings.

2. In a small bowl, combine water, soy sauce, sugar and salt and stir well. Set aside.

3. Heat a wok or a large deep skillet over high heat. Add vegetable oil and swirl to coat pan. Add ginger and garlic and toss well Add sugar snap peas and cook, undisturbed, for 1 minute.

4. Add soy sauce mixture to pan and toss once. Reduce heat to medium. Continue cooking, tossing occasionally, until peas are vivid green and tender-crisp, about 2 minutes more.

5. Add cherry tomatoes and sesame oil and toss once. Transfer to a serving plate. Serve hot or warm.

Stir-Fried Sweet Peppers

1	large green bell pepper (8 oz/250 g)	1
1	large red bell pepper (8 oz/250 g)	1
2 tbsp	vegetable oil	25 mL
½ tsp	salt or to taste	2 mL
¼ tsp	granulated sugar	1 mL
2 tbsp	chopped fresh cilantro	25 mL
1 tsp	Asian sesame oil	5 mL

1. To prepare peppers, cut each one in half lengthwise. Cut away and discard stem portion and seeds. Chop pepper halves into big bite-size pieces, about 1½ inches (4 cm) in size.

2. Heat a wok or a large deep skillet over high heat. Add vegetable oil and swirl to coat pan.

3. Add peppers and toss well. Spread into a single layer and cook, tossing often, for 1 minute.

4. Reduce heat to medium. Add salt and sugar. Cook, tossing often to keep peppers from browning or burning, until tender-crisp, 2 to 3 minutes more. Add cilantro and sesame oil and toss well. Transfer to a serving plate. Serve hot, warm or cold.

Serves 4

Sweet peppers take well to stir-frying, intensifying in sweetness and mellowing to a delicate, juicy texture with just a little crunch. Use all green or all red peppers here, and enjoy them cold as well as hot from the pan.

Sweet-and-Tangy Cabbage

Serves 4

This dish works as a vegetable when hot and as a refreshing pickle when cold. Use regular cabbage, savoy cabbage or napa cabbage.

TIP

Chop cabbage leaves into big bite-size pieces, 1 to 2 inches (2.5 to 5 cm) in diameter.

1 tbsp	white vinegar	15 mL
1 tbsp	granulated sugar	15 mL
1 tsp	soy sauce	5 mL
½ tsp	salt or to taste	2 mL
2 tbsp	vegetable oil	25 mL
2 tsp	chopped garlic	10 mL
1 tsp	chopped fresh gingerroot	5 mL
⅓ cup	thinly sliced green bell pepper	75 mL
3 cups	coarsely chopped cabbage (see Tip, left)	750 mL

1. In a small bowl, combine vinegar, sugar, soy sauce and salt and stir well.

2. Heat a wok or a large deep skillet over high heat. Add oil and swirl to coat pan. Add garlic and ginger and toss well, until fragrant, about 15 seconds.

3. Add green pepper and toss well. Add cabbage and toss well. Spread into a single layer and cook, tossing often, until cabbage is softened but still crisp, about 2 minutes.

4. Add vinegar mixture, pouring in around sides of pan and toss well. Cook, tossing occasionally, for 1 minute more. Transfer to a serving plate. Serve hot, warm or cold.

Fried Rice

Chinese-Style Ham and Eggs with Rice

Serves 4

Enjoy this familiar Western breakfast combination in a new way. Stir-frying cooked rice with diced ham, onions and eggs is a popular Chinese dish, easy to cook and delicious to eat.

TIP

Chilled rice is ideal for making fried rice. Room temperature rice also works well. Hot or warm rice tends to clump together. If you need to start with freshly cooked rice, spread into a thin layer on a baking sheet and let cool as much as possible. The colder and drier the rice, the easier it is to crumble up into separate grains for quick, even cooking.

4 cups	cooked long-grain rice, preferably chilled (see White Rice or Brown Rice, page 316 and Tip, left)	1 L
2 tbsp	vegetable oil	25 mL
3 tbsp	chopped onion	45 mL
1 cup	diced ham (4 oz/125 g)	250 mL
2	eggs, beaten	2
1 tsp	salt or to taste	5 mL
½ tsp	granulated sugar	2 mL
3 tbsp	chopped green onions	45 mL

1. Crumble rice with your fingers, breaking up into individual grains. Set aside.

2. Heat a wok or a large deep skillet over medium-high heat. Add oil and swirl to coat pan. Add onion and toss well, until fragrant, about 30 seconds. Add ham and toss well. Spread into a single layer and cook, undisturbed, for 30 seconds. Toss well.

3. Push ham aside and add eggs. Swirl to expose them to the hot pan and cook, undisturbed, until edges have begun to set, about 30 seconds. Stir, mixing eggs with ham, and scoop to break the cooked portions into soft lumps rather than flat sheets. Continue swirling and scooping until eggs are softly scrambled but still very moist, about 1 minute.

4. Add rice and toss well. Cook, undisturbed, for 30 seconds. Add salt and sugar and toss well. Cook, tossing occasionally, until rice is hot and tender and ham and eggs are mixed in well, 1 to 2 minutes. Add green onions and toss well. Transfer to a serving plate. Serve hot or warm.

Stir-Fried Rice with Chinese Sausage and Cucumbers

4 cups	cooked long-grain rice, preferably chilled (see White Rice or Brown Rice, page 316)	1 L
¾ cup	chopped Chinese sausage or cooked ham (½-inch/1 cm chunks) (4 oz/125 g) (see Tips, right)	175 mL
¼ cup	water	50 mL
2 tbsp	fish sauce	25 mL
2 tsp	soy sauce	10 mL
1 tsp	salt or to taste	5 mL
1 tsp	granulated sugar	5 mL
2 tbsp	vegetable oil	25 mL
1 tbsp	chopped garlic	15 mL
1 tbsp	chopped fresh gingerroot	15 mL
½ cup	chopped cucumber (½-inch/1 cm chunks) (about 2 small pickling or ½ large English cucumber, see Tips, right)	125 mL
¼ cup	thinly sliced green onions	50 mL
¼ cup	chopped fresh cilantro, divided	50 mL

1. Crumble rice with your fingers, breaking up into individual grains. Set aside.

2. In a small saucepan or skillet, combine Chinese sausage and water. Bring to a rolling boil over high heat. Cook, stirring once, for 1 minute. Remove from heat. Pour liquid into a small bowl and set sausage aside.

3. Add fish sauce, soy sauce, salt and sugar to cooking liquid and stir well. Set aside.

4. Heat a wok or a large deep skillet over high heat. Add oil and swirl to coat pan. Add garlic and ginger and toss well, until fragrant, about 15 seconds.

5. Add sausage and cook, tossing often, for 30 seconds. Add cucumber and toss well. Add rice and toss well. Cook, tossing occasionally, until rice is heated through, 1 to 2 minutes.

6. Add cooking liquid mixture, pouring in around sides of pan. Cook, tossing often, until rice is hot and evenly seasoned, about 30 seconds more. Add green onions and half the cilantro. Toss well. Transfer to a serving plate and sprinkle remaining cilantro over top. Serve hot or warm.

Serves 4

Chinese sausages are rich, sweet pork sausages, beloved throughout Asia. They are often used in steamed rice dumplings or sautéed quickly and served over rice. You can substitute ham.

TIPS

Chinese sausage, called *lap cheong* in Cantonese dialect, is a very firm sweet pork sausage widely available in Asian markets. It comes in short, plump links, about 7 to a 1 lb (500 g) package. Usually sold vacuum-packed, it is cured and needs no refrigeration until package is opened. To dice the sausage, cut each link in half crosswise. Quarter each half lengthwise and then gather the long pieces and chop them crosswise into ½-inch (1 cm) chunks.

Use English cucumbers or small pickling cucumbers and leave them unpeeled if they are tender and very fresh. If you use regular field cucumbers, peel them and halve them lengthwise. Scoop out and discard the seeds before chopping. Chop into ½-inch (1 cm) chunks.

Yangchow Fried Rice

Serves 4

This Chinese fried rice dish is a feast of ham, chicken and shrimp. I love this served alongside bowls of egg drop soup and a big salad tossed with chopped apple and raisins.

TIP

If you can't find perfectly crisp fresh bean sprouts, substitute finely shredded napa cabbage, thinly shredded iceberg lettuce, thinly sliced celery or simply omit them.

4 cups	cooked long-grain rice, preferably chilled (see White Rice or Brown Rice, page 316)	1 L
2 tbsp	chicken stock or water	25 mL
2 tsp	soy sauce	10 mL
1 tsp	salt or to taste	5 mL
1/2 tsp	granulated sugar	2 mL
8	cooked medium shrimp	8
2 tbsp	vegetable oil	25 mL
1/2 cup	chopped ham	125 mL
1/2 cup	chopped cooked chicken	125 mL
1/2 cup	frozen tiny peas	125 mL
3/4 cup	bean sprouts (see Tip, left)	175 mL
1/4 cup	chopped green onions	50 mL

1. Crumble rice with your fingers, breaking up into individual grains. Set aside.

2. In a small bowl, combine chicken stock, soy sauce, salt and sugar and stir well. Set aside.

3. Chop each shrimp crosswise into 4 pieces. Set aside.

4. Heat a wok or a large deep skillet over high heat. Add oil and swirl to coat pan. Add ham and chicken and cook, tossing often, for 1 minute. Add shrimp and cook, tossing often, for 30 seconds more. Add rice and toss well. Cook, tossing often, for 1 minute.

5. Add soy sauce mixture, pouring in around sides of pan. Toss well. Add peas and toss well. Cook, tossing often, until rice is hot and tender and evenly seasoned, about 1 minute more. Add bean sprouts and green onions and toss well. Transfer to a serving plate. Serve hot or warm.

Stir-Fried Rice with Roast Duck in Hoisin Sauce

4 cups	cooked long-grain rice, preferably chilled (see White Rice or Brown Rice, page 316)	1 L
2 tbsp	hoisin sauce	25 mL
1 tbsp	soy sauce	15 mL
1 tbsp	water	15 mL
1 tsp	salt or to taste	5 mL
1 tsp	granulated sugar	5 mL
2 tbsp	vegetable oil	25 mL
1 tbsp	chopped garlic	15 mL
2 tsp	chopped fresh gingerroot	10 mL
1 cup	chopped roast duck or roast chicken	250 mL
½ cup	halved cherry tomatoes	125 mL
3 tbsp	chopped green onions	45 mL
3 tbsp	chopped fresh cilantro	45 mL

1. Crumble rice with your fingers, breaking up into individual grains. Set aside.
2. In a small bowl, combine hoisin sauce, soy sauce, water, salt and sugar and stir well. Set aside.
3. Heat a wok or a large deep skillet over high heat. Add oil and swirl to coat pan. Add garlic and ginger and toss well, until fragrant, about 15 seconds.
4. Add roast duck and toss well. Add rice and toss well. Cook, tossing often, for 1 minute. Add hoisin sauce mixture, pouring in around sides of pan. Toss well.
5. Add cherry tomatoes and green onions and toss well. Cook, tossing often, until rice is hot and tender and evenly seasoned, about 1 minute more. Add cilantro and toss well. Transfer to a serving plate. Serve hot or warm.

Serves 4

Chinese-style roast duck is luscious as an ingredient in fried rice, but roast chicken makes a delicious dish as well. Serve this with a green salad with a lemon and olive oil dressing and a fruit salad tossed with fresh mint.

TIP

If you live near a Chinatown, look for shops where Chinese barbecue specialties are made on the premises. You can purchase a whole or half roast duck, or a supply of Chinese-style barbecued pork to enjoy at home. It's fantastic fast food, either as a main course with a stir-fried vegetable dish and rice, or as a component to fried rice, noodles and soups.

Savory Stir-Fried Rice
with Barbecued Pork

Serves 4

Chinese-style barbecued pork has a rich flavor with a touch of sweetness that is perfect for fried rice.

TIP

You can buy Chinese-style barbecued pork, known as *char siu* in Cantonese, in many Asian markets. In areas with a large Asian population, you may find Chinese barbecue shops where roast duck, roast pork and barbecued pork are made in-house. Or make your own barbecued pork using the recipe on page 332.

4 cups	cooked long-grain rice, preferably chilled (see White Rice or Brown Rice, page 316)	1 L
1 tbsp	dry sherry or Shaoxing rice wine	15 mL
1 tbsp	soy sauce	15 mL
1 tsp	salt or to taste	5 mL
2 tbsp	vegetable oil	25 mL
2 tsp	chopped garlic	10 mL
2 tsp	chopped fresh gingerroot	10 mL
1 cup	chopped Chinese barbecued pork or ham (½-inch/1 cm chunks) (see Tip, left)	250 mL
¾ cup	finely diced celery	175 mL
⅓ cup	chopped green onions	75 mL
3 tbsp	chopped fresh cilantro	45 mL

1. Crumble rice with your fingers, breaking up into individual grains. Set aside.

2. In a small bowl, combine sherry, soy sauce and salt and stir well. Set aside.

3. Heat a wok or a large deep skillet over high heat. Add oil and swirl to coat pan. Add garlic and ginger and toss well, until fragrant, about 15 seconds.

4. Add pork and toss well. Add celery and cook, tossing often, until celery is beginning to soften, about 1 minute. Add rice and toss well. Cook, tossing often, for 1 minute.

5. Add sherry mixture, pouring in around sides of pan. Toss well. Cook, tossing often, until rice is hot and tender and evenly seasoned, about 1 minute more. Add green onions and cilantro and toss well. Transfer to a serving plate. Serve hot or warm.

Thai-Style Fried Rice with Pork

4 cups	cooked long-grain rice, preferably chilled (see White Rice or Brown Rice, page 316)	1 L
2 tbsp	fish sauce	25 mL
1 tsp	granulated sugar	5 mL
1/2 tsp	salt or to taste	2 mL
2 tbsp	vegetable oil	25 mL
1/2 cup	chopped onion	125 mL
1 tbsp	chopped garlic	15 mL
8 oz	boneless pork (such as loin or tenderloin), thinly sliced (2-inch/5 cm strips)	250 g
1	large egg, beaten	1
3 tbsp	chopped green onions	45 mL
3 tbsp	chopped fresh cilantro	45 mL
1	lime, cut into 4 wedges, optional (see Tip, right)	1

1. Crumble rice with your fingers, breaking up into individual grains. Set aside.

2. In a small bowl, combine fish sauce, sugar and salt and stir well. Set aside.

3. Heat a wok or large skillet over high heat. Add oil and swirl to coat pan. Add onion and garlic and toss well, until fragrant, about 15 seconds.

4. Add pork and toss well. Spread into a single layer and cook, undisturbed, until edges change color, about 1 minute. Continue cooking, tossing often, until no longer pink, about 1 minute more.

5. Push the pork aside. Add egg and swirl to expose to the hot pan. Cook, undisturbed, until edges have begun to set, about 15 seconds. Stir to mix with pork and scoop to break the cooked portions into soft lumps rather than flat sheets. Continue swirling and scooping until egg is softly scrambled but still very moist, about 1 minute. Add rice and toss well.

6. Add fish sauce mixture and toss well. Cook, tossing often, until rice is hot and tender, pork is cooked through and everything is evenly seasoned, 1 to 2 minutes. Add green onions and cilantro and toss well. Transfer to a serving plate and garnish with lime wedges, if using, for each portion. Serve hot or warm.

Serves 4

This is the classic Thai version of fried rice. Thai cooks accompany each serving with sliced cucumbers and a chunk of lime for squeezing onto the rice just before eating. Also standard is a small bowl of fish sauce fortified with finely chopped Thai chiles, serranos or hot pepper flakes with which to heat up and season the dish throughout the meal.

TIP

Squeezing the lime over the finished dish is standard operating procedure in Thailand, done just before eating to preserve the burst of flavor and aroma of freshly squeezed lime. If you will be taking this dish to a gathering, cut the lime into chunks, and then squeeze them over the rice just before serving time.

Eight-Treasure Fried Rice

Eight-treasure dishes, also called "eight-precious," feature an abundance of luxury ingredients. The ingredients can vary, and there can be a few more or less than eight, as long as the message is delivered that this is a little splurge. Typical are items that are expensive, rare, beloved, or all three. Sweet versions include the classic *ba bao fan*, a steamed dessert of sticky rice enclosing a center of sweet red bean paste and garnished with a mosaic of dried fruits and nuts. Savory versions featuring meat and nuts in auspicious numbers are used as a stuffing for poultry or steamed in lotus leaf packets. My fried-rice version makes a luxurious party dish. The ingredients can be prepared in advance, leaving you with a quick-cooking session just before serving time.

4 cups	cooked long-grain rice, preferably chilled (see White Rice or Brown Rice, page 316)	1 L
2 tbsp	dry sherry or Shaoxing rice wine	25 mL
1 tbsp	soy sauce	15 mL
1 tsp	salt or to taste	5 mL
1 tsp	granulated sugar	5 mL
3 tbsp	vegetable oil, divided	45 mL
2	eggs, beaten	2
2 tbsp	chopped onion	25 mL
2 tsp	chopped garlic	10 mL
2 tsp	chopped fresh gingerroot	10 mL
½ cup	frozen, shelled edamame beans or tiny peas	125 mL
½ cup	diced sweet Chinese sausage or kielbasa (3 oz/90 g)	125 mL
12	medium shrimp, peeled and deveined	12
¾ cup	thickly sliced shiitake mushroom caps	175 mL
½ cup	diced ham	125 mL
½ cup	dry-roasted salted cashews	125 mL
3 tbsp	thinly sliced green onions	45 mL
3 tbsp	chopped fresh cilantro	45 mL
2 tsp	Asian sesame oil	10 mL

1. Crumble rice with your fingers, breaking up into individual grains. Set aside.

2. In a small bowl, combine sherry, soy sauce, salt and sugar and stir well. Set aside.

3. Place a plate next to the stove to hold eggs after you cook them. Heat a wok or a large deep skillet over high heat. Add 1 tbsp (15 mL) of the vegetable oil and swirl to coat pan. Add eggs and swirl to expose them to the hot pan and cook, undisturbed, until edges have begun to set, about 15 seconds. Stir and scoop to break the cooked portions into soft lumps rather than flat sheets. Continue swirling and scooping until eggs are softly scrambled but still very moist, about 1 minute. Transfer to reserved plate.

4. Add remaining oil to pan and swirl to coat well. Add onion, garlic and ginger and toss well, until fragrant about 15 seconds. Add edamame and sausage and toss well. Cook, tossing often, for 30 seconds.

5. Add shrimp, spreading into a single layer. Cook, undisturbed, until most of the edges turn pink, about 1 minute. Toss well. Add mushrooms and ham. Cook, tossing often, until mushrooms have softened and most of the shrimp have turned pink, about 1 minute more. Add rice and toss well. Cook, tossing often, for 1 minute.

6. Add sherry mixture, pouring in around sides of pan and toss well. Cook, tossing often, until shrimp is cooked through and rice is hot and tender and evenly seasoned, about 1 minute more. Add cashews, green onions and scrambled eggs and toss well. Add cilantro and sesame oil and toss well. Transfer to a serving plate. Serve hot or warm.

> **Variation:** You can choose treasures that suit you, substituting a similar amount of a comparable ingredient. Typical ingredients in traditional eight-treasure rice stuffings include sweet Chinese sausage, pork and chicken, bamboo shoots, dried shrimp, lotus seeds, gingko nuts, chestnuts, dried shiitake mushrooms and cloud ear mushrooms. You could use Chinese-style roast duck, grilled chicken, kielbasa, crabmeat, bay scallops, peanuts, pine nuts, chopped asparagus or string beans.

TIP

There's a bit more preparation and assembly for this fried rice recipe, so you may want to handle all the chopping in one preliminary session and then keep the cleaned shrimp, chopped meats and scrambled egg in separate bowls. Cover and refrigerate for up to 1 day before cooking.

Shrimp Fried Rice with Pineapple

Serves 4

This dish makes a lovely impression, with its bright flavors and beautiful colors. I love it with a spinach salad tossed with poppy seed dressing.

TIP

You can substitute 1 cup (250 mL) finely chopped fresh pineapple for the canned crushed pineapple.

4 cups	cooked long-grain rice, preferably chilled (see White Rice or Brown Rice, page 316)	1 L
2 tbsp	fish sauce	25 mL
1/2 tsp	granulated sugar	2 mL
1/2 tsp	salt or to taste	2 mL
2 tbsp	vegetable oil	25 mL
1/4 cup	chopped onion	50 mL
1 tbsp	chopped garlic	15 mL
8 oz	medium shrimp, peeled and deveined	250 g
1	can (8 oz/227 mL) crushed pineapple with juice (about 1 cup/250 mL) (see Tip, left)	1
2 tbsp	thinly sliced green onions	25 mL
3 tbsp	chopped fresh cilantro	45 mL

1. Crumble rice with your fingers, breaking up into individual grains. Set aside.
2. In a small bowl, combine fish sauce, sugar and salt and stir well. Set aside.
3. Heat a wok or a large deep skillet over high heat. Add oil and swirl to coat pan. Add onions and garlic and toss well, until fragrant, about 15 seconds.
4. Add shrimp and spread into a single layer. Cook, undisturbed, until most of the edges turn pink, about 1 minute. Toss well. Cook other side, undisturbed, for 30 seconds more.
5. Add rice and fish sauce mixture and toss well. Add pineapple and green onions and cook, tossing often, until shrimp are cooked through and rice is hot and tender and evenly seasoned, 1 to 2 minutes more. Add cilantro and toss well. Transfer to a serving plate. Serve hot or warm.

Oyster Mushrooms with Tiny Peas (page 241)

Overleaf: Eight-Treasure Fried Rice (page 254)

Crab Fried Rice

4 cups	cooked jasmine rice, chilled (see recipe, page 314)	1 L
2 tbsp	fish sauce	25 mL
1 tsp	soy sauce	5 mL
1 tsp	granulated sugar	5 mL
½ tsp	salt or to taste	2 mL
¼ tsp	freshly ground pepper	1 mL
2 tbsp	vegetable oil	25 mL
2 tbsp	chopped onion	25 mL
2 tsp	chopped garlic	10 mL
2	eggs, beaten	2
1 cup	cooked lump crabmeat (see Tip, right)	250 mL
3 tbsp	chopped green onions	45 mL
3 tbsp	chopped fresh cilantro	45 mL

1. Crumble rice with your fingers, breaking up into individual grains. Set aside.

2. In a small bowl, combine fish sauce, soy sauce, sugar, salt and pepper and stir well. Set aside.

3. Heat a wok or a large deep skillet over medium-high heat. Add oil and swirl to coat pan. Add onion and garlic and toss well, until fragrant, about 15 seconds.

4. Add eggs and swirl to expose them to the hot pan and cook, undisturbed, until edges have begun to set, about 30 seconds. Stir and scoop to break the cooked portions into soft lumps rather than flat sheets. Continue swirling and scooping until eggs are softly scrambled but still very moist, about 1 minute.

5. Add rice and cook, tossing often, for 1 minute. Add fish sauce mixture, pouring in around sides of pan. Toss well.

6. Add crabmeat and green onions. Cook, tossing often, until rice is hot, tender and evenly seasoned, about 1 minute more. Transfer to a serving plate and sprinkle with cilantro. Serve hot or warm.

Serves 4

I first tried crab fried rice in Thailand, where it is a great favorite. Now I keep canned crabmeat on hand in my pantry, so that I can enjoy this delicious dish as an everyday treat. Fresh crabmeat is delicious as well. Serve this with asparagus with lemon butter or grilled vegetables and a Caesar salad.

TIP

If using canned crabmeat, drain before measuring. If using frozen, thaw and drain, very gently pressing or squeezing out excess liquid before measuring. To get 1 cup (250 mL) you'll need about 12 oz (375 g) before draining.

Overleaf: Stir-Fried Rice with Red Curry, Beef and Baby Corn (page 258)

Pork Lo Mein (page 283)

Stir-Fried Rice with Red Curry, Beef and Baby Corn

Serves 4

Spicy hot and robust, this dish calls for cooling accompaniments. Consider a platter of cucumber slices and pineapple chunks sprinkled with lime juice and fresh mint leaves, or a big green salad with sliced almonds and mandarin orange sections tossed with raspberry vinaigrette.

TIP

Thai curry pastes are fiery hot and some are particularly incendiary. If you like milder heat, start with 2 tsp (10 mL). If you like more heat, start with 2 tbsp (25 mL) and add another 1 to 2 tbsp (15 to 25 mL) of water to help dissolve the paste after it goes into the pan. If you don't like much heat at all, use a mild Indian curry paste or curry powder instead of the Thai curry paste.

4 cups	cooked long-grain rice, preferably chilled (see White Rice or Brown Rice, page 316)	1 L
2 tbsp	fish sauce	25 mL
1 tbsp	chicken stock or white wine	15 mL
1 tbsp	granulated sugar	15 mL
1 tsp	salt or to taste	5 mL
10	cobs canned baby corn	10
2 tbsp	vegetable oil	25 mL
2 tbsp	chopped shallots or onion	25 mL
2 tsp	chopped garlic	10 mL
8 oz	lean boneless beef, thinly sliced	250 g
1 tbsp	Thai-style red curry paste (see Tip, left)	15 mL
1 tbsp	water	15 mL
¾ cup	frozen chopped green beans or peas	175 mL
3 tbsp	chopped green onions	45 mL

1. Crumble rice with your fingers, breaking up into individual grains. Set aside.
2. In a small bowl, combine fish sauce, chicken stock, sugar and salt and stir well. Set aside.
3. Chop each baby corn cob crosswise into 4 pieces. Set aside.
4. Heat a wok or a large deep skillet over high heat. Add oil and swirl to coat pan. Add shallots and garlic and toss well, until fragrant, about 15 seconds.
5. Add beef, spreading into a single layer. Cook, undisturbed, until edges change color, about 1 minute. Toss well and cook, until no longer pink, about 30 seconds more.
6. Add curry paste and water and cook, pressing and tossing gently, to soften and mix with beef, about 30 seconds. Add green beans and baby corn and toss well. Add rice and cook, tossing often, for 1 minute.
7. Add fish sauce mixture, pouring in around sides of pan. Toss well. Cook, tossing often, until beef is cooked through and rice is hot, tender and evenly seasoned, about 1 minute more. Add green onions and toss well. Transfer to a serving plate. Serve hot or warm.

Stir-Fried Rice with Green Curry, Shrimp and Tiny Peas

4 cups	cooked long-grain rice, preferably chilled (see White Rice or Brown Rice, page 316)	1 L
2 tbsp	fish sauce	25 mL
1 tbsp	chicken or vegetable stock or white wine	15 mL
1 tbsp	granulated sugar	15 mL
1 tsp	salt or to taste	5 mL
2 tbsp	vegetable oil	25 mL
2 tbsp	chopped shallots or onion	25 mL
2 tsp	chopped garlic	10 mL
12 oz	medium shrimp, peeled and deveined	375 g
1 tbsp	Thai-style green curry paste (see Tip, page 258)	15 mL
1 tbsp	water	15 mL
¾ cup	frozen tiny peas (see Tip, page 232)	175 mL
¼ cup	chopped fresh cilantro	50 mL
3 tbsp	chopped green onions	45 mL

Serves 4

Bright with flavor and color, this spicy dish makes a fine choice as a hot-and-spicy component within a buffet. We love it with a big fruit salad and bowls of soup, such as gingery carrot soup if it's cold outside and cool cucumber soup if the air is sultry and hot.

1. Crumble rice with your fingers, breaking up into individual grains. Set aside.
2. In a small bowl, combine fish sauce, chicken stock, sugar and salt and stir well. Set aside.
3. Heat a wok or a large deep skillet over high heat. Add oil and swirl to coat pan. Add shallots and garlic and toss well, until fragrant, about 15 seconds.
4. Add shrimp and spread into a single layer. Cook, undisturbed, until most of the edges turn pink, about 1 minute. Toss well. Cook other side, undisturbed, for 30 seconds more.
5. Add curry paste and water and cook, pressing and tossing gently, to soften and mix with shrimp, about 30 seconds. Add peas and toss well. Add rice and cook, tossing often, for 1 minute.
6. Add fish sauce mixture, pouring in around sides of pan. Toss well. Cook, tossing often, until shrimp are cooked through and rice is hot, tender and evenly seasoned, about 1 minute more. Add cilantro and green onions and toss well. Transfer to a serving plate. Serve hot or warm.

Thai-Style Shrimp Fried Rice with Chile Paste and Basil

Serves 4

Roasted chile paste lights up a number of Thai stir-fried dishes. You can find it in Asian markets, often labeled "chili paste in soybean oil," or make your own (see recipe, page 336) to keep on hand for an array of great dishes fast.

TIP

For best flavor and aroma, chop the fresh basil leaves at the last minute, just before you begin to cook the dish.

4 cups	cooked long-grain rice, preferably chilled (see White Rice or Brown Rice, page 316)	1 L
2 tbsp	fish sauce	25 mL
1 tbsp	soy sauce	15 mL
2 tsp	granulated sugar	10 mL
1 tsp	salt or to taste	5 mL
2 tbsp	vegetable oil	25 mL
1/3 cup	finely chopped red bell pepper	75 mL
1 tbsp	chopped garlic	15 mL
8 oz	medium shrimp, peeled and deveined	250 g
3 tbsp	Thai-Style Roasted Chile Paste (see recipe, page 336) or store-bought	45 mL
1/4 cup	Thai basil or other fresh basil, chopped (see Tip, left)	50 mL
3 tbsp	chopped green onions	45 mL

1. Crumble rice with your fingers, breaking up into individual grains. Set aside.

2. In a small bowl, combine fish sauce, soy sauce, sugar and salt and stir well. Set aside.

3. Heat a wok or a large deep skillet over high heat. Add oil and swirl to coat pan. Add red peppers and garlic and toss well, until fragrant, about 15 seconds.

4. Add shrimp and spread into a single layer. Cook, undisturbed, until most of the edges turn pink, about 1 minute. Toss well. Cook other side, undisturbed, for 30 seconds more.

5. Add roasted chile paste and cook, tossing often, until shrimp are evenly coated with the paste, about 30 seconds. Add rice and toss well. Cook, tossing often, 1 minute.

6. Add fish sauce mixture, pouring in around sides of pan. Toss well. Cook, tossing often, until rice is hot and tender and evenly seasoned and shrimp are cooked through, about 1 minute more. Add basil and green onions and toss well. Transfer to a serving plate. Serve hot or warm.

Vietnamese-Style Shrimp Fried Rice with Egg Ribbons

3 tbsp	vegetable oil, divided	45 mL
1	egg, beaten	1
4 cups	cooked long-grain rice, preferably chilled (see White Rice or Brown Rice, page 316)	1 L
2 tbsp	fish sauce	25 mL
2 tsp	soy sauce	10 mL
½ tsp	salt or to taste	2 mL
¼ tsp	freshly ground pepper	1 mL
2 tbsp	chopped shallots or onion	25 mL
2 tsp	chopped garlic	10 mL
½ cup	shredded carrot	125 mL
8 oz	medium shrimp, peeled and deveined	250 g
⅓ cup	chopped green onions, divided	75 mL

1. Heat a wok or a large deep skillet over high heat until very hot. Add 1 tbsp (15 mL) of oil and swirl to coat pan.

2. Place a plate by the stove to hold the cooked egg pancake. Add beaten egg to pan and swirl to spread into a thin layer over the pan's surface. Flip over and cook until you have a thin, firm, pale yellow pancake. Remove pan from heat and tip egg pancake onto plate. Set aside to let cool.

3. Meanwhile, using your hands, crumble rice with your fingers, breaking up into individual grains. Set aside.

4. In a small bowl, combine fish sauce, soy sauce, salt and pepper and stir well. Set aside.

5. When egg pancake has cooled, roll into a cylinder. Slice crosswise into slender ribbons, about ⅛ inch (0.25 cm) wide. Toss to separate into threads and set aside.

6. Heat pan over high heat. Add remaining vegetable oil and swirl to coat pan. Add shallots and garlic and toss well, until fragrant, about 15 seconds. Add carrot and toss well.

7. Add shrimp, spreading into a single layer. Cook, undisturbed, until most of the edges turn pink, about 1 minute. Toss well. Cook other side, undisturbed, for 30 seconds more.

8. Add rice and toss well. Cook, tossing often, about 1 minute. Add half the green onions. Add fish sauce mixture, pouring in around sides of pan. Toss well. Cook, tossing often, until shrimp are cooked through and rice is hot, tender and evenly seasoned, about 1 minute more. Add remaining green onions and egg ribbons and toss well. Transfer to a serving plate. Serve hot or warm.

Serves 4

Delicious and pretty with ribbons of omelet and carrot adding color and texture, this version of fried rice makes a handsome centerpiece dish. We love it with a salad of mixed greens and a delicate soup of tofu in chicken stock.

TIP

Making the egg pancake adds an extra step or two to this recipe. If you would like a simpler version, cook the egg this way: Push shrimp to one side as soon as they are cooked and add beaten egg directly to pan. Swirl to expose them to the hot pan and cook, undisturbed, until edges have begun to set, about 30 seconds. Stir and scoop to break the cooked portions into soft lumps rather than flat sheets. Continue swirling and scooping until eggs are softly scrambled but still very moist, about 1 minute. Add rice and continue with the recipe.

Burmese-Style Golden Stir-Fried Rice with Bean Sprouts

Serves 4

This is my version of a Burmese-style fried rice dish, *htamin kyaw*. It is traditionally made with dried garden peas or English peas, which are sprouted and then cooked until tender. Known in Burma as *pepyoat*, they can be found in Indian markets in their dried form, under their Hindi name, *vatana*. I use a combination of green peas and fresh bean sprouts in this beautiful and tasty sunny-colored dish.

4 cups	cooked long-grain rice, preferably chilled (see White Rice or Brown Rice, page 316)	1 L
2 tbsp	fish sauce	25 mL
1 tbsp	water	15 mL
1 tsp	salt or to taste	5 mL
¼ tsp	ground turmeric	1 mL
2 tbsp	vegetable oil	25 mL
2 tbsp	chopped onion	25 mL
2	eggs, beaten	2
1½ cups	bean sprouts	375 mL
¾ cup	frozen tiny peas (see Tip, page 232)	175 mL
3 tbsp	thinly sliced green onions	45 mL

1. Crumble rice with your fingers, breaking up into individual grains. Set aside.

2. In a small bowl, combine fish sauce, water, salt and turmeric and stir well. Set aside.

3. Heat a wok or a large deep skillet over high heat. Add oil and swirl to coat pan. Add onion and toss well, until fragrant, about 15 seconds.

4. Add eggs and swirl to expose them to the hot pan and cook, undisturbed, until edges have begun to set, about 30 seconds. Stir and scoop to break the cooked portions into soft lumps rather than flat sheets. Continue swirling and scooping until eggs are softly scrambled but still very moist, about 1 minute.

5. Add bean sprouts and peas and toss well. Add rice and cook, tossing often, for 1 minute. Add green onions.

6. Add fish sauce mixture, pouring in around sides of pan. Toss well. Cook, tossing often, until rice is hot, tender and evenly seasoned, about 1 minute more. Transfer to a serving plate. Serve hot or warm.

Variations: If you don't have ground turmeric, substitute ½ tsp (2 mL) curry powder.

Substitute an equal amount of shredded napa cabbage or very finely shredded green cabbage for bean sprouts.

For a vegetarian version, omit fish sauce and add 1 tsp (5 mL) soy sauce and another ½ tsp (2 mL) salt.

Korean-Style Fried Rice with Wok-Seared Beef

4 cups	cooked long-grain rice, preferably chilled (see White Rice or Brown Rice, page 316)	1 L
2 tbsp	soy sauce	25 mL
2 tsp	Asian sesame oil	10 mL
1 tsp	granulated sugar	5 mL
6 oz	lean boneless beef, thinly sliced	175 g
2 tbsp	chicken stock or white wine	25 mL
1 tbsp	water	15 mL
1 tsp	salt or to taste	5 mL
½ tsp	hot pepper flakes	2 mL
2 tbsp	vegetable oil	25 mL
2 tbsp	chopped garlic	25 mL
2 tsp	chopped fresh gingerroot	10 mL
½ cup	thinly sliced mushrooms	125 mL
½ cup	shredded carrots	125 mL
¼ cup	chopped green onions	50 mL

Serves 4

This hearty dish goes wonderfully with a cooling spinach salad and a bowl of kimchee, a fiery, crunchy relish. Or serve cucumbers tossed with Asian sesame oil, rice vinegar and sugar for a cooling accompaniment.

1. Crumble rice with your fingers, breaking up into individual grains. Set aside.

2. In a bowl, combine soy sauce, sesame oil and sugar and stir well. Add beef and toss to coat evenly. Set aside for 10 minutes.

3. In a small bowl, combine chicken stock, water, salt and hot pepper flakes and stir well. Set aside.

4. Heat a wok or a large deep skillet over high heat. Add oil and swirl to coat pan. Add garlic and ginger and toss well, until fragrant, about 15 seconds.

5. Add beef mixture, spreading into a single layer. Cook, undisturbed, until edges change color, about 30 seconds. Toss well. Add mushrooms and carrots and toss well. Cook, tossing often, until beef is no longer pink and carrots and mushrooms are beginning to soften, about 1 minute.

6. Add rice and toss well. Cook, tossing often, for 1 minute. Add chicken stock mixture, pouring in around sides of pan. Toss well. Cook, tossing often, until rice is hot and tender and evenly seasoned, about 1 minute more. Add green onions and toss well. Transfer to a serving plate. Serve hot or warm.

Indonesian-Style Stir-Fried Rice with Chicken and Shrimp

Serves 4

Throughout the archipelago of Indonesia, fried rice is a popular everyday dish. Traditional ingredients include the dark sweet soy sauce known as kecap (ketjap) manis, which handsomely deepens both the color and the flavor of the dish. I love it with a platter of sliced fresh vegetables, such as sweet bell peppers, carrots, cherry tomatoes and sliced cucumbers, along with a lemony dressing for dipping. For a more classic version called *nasi goreng* (see Variation, right).

4 cups	cooked long-grain rice, preferably chilled (see White Rice or Brown Rice, page 316)	1 L
3 tbsp	chicken stock or white wine	45 mL
2 tbsp	dark sweet soy sauce (kecap manis) or 2 tbsp (25 mL) soy sauce plus 2 tsp (10 mL) molasses or dark brown sugar (see Tip, right)	25 mL
1 tsp	salt or to taste	5 mL
2 tbsp	vegetable oil	25 mL
3 tbsp	chopped shallots or onion	45 mL
2 tsp	chopped garlic	10 mL
2 tsp	chopped fresh hot red chile or serrano chile	10 mL
8 oz	medium shrimp, peeled and deveined	250 g
2	eggs, beaten	2
1 cup	chopped cooked chicken (bite-size chunks)	250 mL
3 tbsp	chopped green onions	45 mL
½ cup	Crisp-Fried Shallots (see recipe, page 343), optional	125 mL

1. Crumble rice with your fingers, breaking up into individual grains. Set aside.

2. In a small bowl, combine chicken stock, dark sweet soy sauce and salt and stir well. Set aside.

3. Heat a wok or a large deep skillet over high heat. Add oil and swirl to coat pan. Add shallots, garlic and chile and toss well, until fragrant, about 15 seconds.

4. Add shrimp and spread into a single layer. Cook, undisturbed, until most of the edges turn pink, about 1 minute. Toss well. Cook other side, undisturbed, for 30 seconds more.

5. Push the shrimp aside and add eggs. Swirl to expose them to the hot pan and cook, undisturbed, until edges have begun to set, about 30 seconds. Stir and scoop to break the cooked portions into soft lumps rather than flat sheets. Continue swirling and scooping until eggs are softly scrambled but still very moist, about 1 minute.

6. Add cooked chicken and toss well. Add rice and cook, tossing often, for 1 minute. Add green onions.

7. Add chicken stock mixture, pouring in around sides of pan and toss well. Cook, tossing often, until shrimp are cooked through and rice is hot and tender and evenly seasoned, about 1 minute more. Transfer to a serving plate and sprinkle Crisp-Fried Shallots, if using, over the rice. Serve hot or warm.

> **Variation:** For a classic version of *nasi goreng*, you will need 2 tsp (10 mL) of the salty shrimp paste called *trassi*. This is Indonesia's version of an intensely aromatic condiment used throughout Southeast Asia to add flavor and protein to an array of dishes. Mash it in a small bowl with enough hot water to soften it into a paste, mix it with the chopped shallots, garlic and chile and then fry this mixture in Step 3. Omit the 2 eggs scrambled with the rice and instead top each portion with a fried egg.

TIP

Dark sweet soy sauce, popular in Southeast Asia, is a specialty version of dark soy sauce but with a good dose of molasses added. Since it is used in only a few recipes in this book and comes only in huge bottles, I offer the soy sauce plus molasses substitution. *Kecap manis* is the Indonesian name and *si-yu wahn* is the Thai name for the condiment.

Stir-Fried Curried Rice with Chicken, Cashews and Peas

Serves 4

Sunny-colored and delicious, this stir-fry anchors a party menu beautifully. A simple salad of cucumbers, radishes and cherry tomatoes makes a cooling accompaniment, along with steamed broccoli or zucchini dressed with butter and lemon juice.

4 cups	cooked long-grain rice, preferably chilled (see White Rice or Brown Rice, page 316)	1 L
3 tbsp	chicken stock or water	45 mL
1 tsp	salt or to taste	5 mL
2 tbsp	vegetable oil	25 mL
3 tbsp	chopped onion	45 mL
1 tbsp	chopped fresh gingerroot	15 mL
2 tsp	chopped garlic	10 mL
2 tsp	finely chopped fresh hot green chile	10 mL
1 tbsp	curry powder	15 mL
1 tsp	ground cumin, optional	5 mL
12 oz	chopped cooked chicken	375 g
1 cup	frozen tiny peas	250 mL
1 cup	dry-roasted salted cashews	250 mL
¼ cup	thinly sliced green onions	50 mL
¼ cup	chopped fresh cilantro, divided	50 mL

1. Crumble rice with your fingers, breaking up into individual grains. Set aside.

2. In a small bowl, combine chicken stock and salt and stir well. Set aside.

3. Heat a wok or a large deep skillet over high heat. Add oil and swirl to coat pan. Add onion, ginger, garlic and chile and toss well, until fragrant, about 15 seconds. Add curry powder and cumin, if using, and toss well. Cook, tossing often, for 30 seconds.

4. Add chicken and cook, tossing occasionally, for 1 minute. Add rice, toss well and cook for 1 minute.

5. Add peas and chicken stock mixture, pouring in around sides of pan. Cook, tossing often, until rice is hot and tender and evenly seasoned, about 1 minute more. Add cashews, green onions and half the cilantro leaves. Toss well and cook for 1 minute more. Transfer to a serving plate and sprinkle with remaining cilantro leaves. Serve hot or warm.

> **Variation:** For a more lavish version, make any or all of these additions, tossing in along with the cilantro at the end of cooking time: 3 tbsp (45 mL) chopped fresh mint (chopped right before use), 3 tbsp (45 mL) lemon or lime juice, 1 tsp (5 mL) garam masala.

Stir-Fried Rice à la Kedgeree

4 cups	cooked long-grain rice, preferably chilled (see White Rice or Brown Rice, page 316)	1 L
8 oz	smoked trout or mackerel, or cooked or canned salmon or tuna (see Tips, right)	250 g
2 tbsp	chicken stock, white wine or water	25 mL
1 tsp	salt or to taste	5 mL
1/2 tsp	freshly ground pepper	2 mL
2 tbsp	vegetable oil	25 mL
1/3 cup	chopped onion	75 mL
1 tbsp	curry powder	15 mL
3/4 cup	frozen tiny peas	175 mL
1/4 cup	chopped Italian parsley	50 mL
1 tbsp	butter, optional	15 mL
4	hard-boiled eggs, peeled and quartered lengthwise	4

1. Crumble rice with your fingers, breaking up into individual grains. Set aside.
2. Break fish into bite-size chunks, about 1 1/2 inches (4 cm) in diameter, discarding any skin and bones. Set aside.
3. In a small bowl, combine chicken stock, salt and pepper and stir well. Set aside.
4. Heat a wok or a large deep skillet over high heat. Add oil and swirl to coat pan. Add onion and toss well. Add curry powder and cook, tossing often, until onion is fragrant and softened, about 30 seconds.
5. Add rice and cook, tossing often, about 1 minute. Add fish and peas and cook, tossing often, for 1 minute more.
6. Add chicken stock mixture, pouring in around sides of pan. Cook, tossing often, until fish is heated through and rice is hot and tender and evenly seasoned, about 1 minute more. Add parsley and butter, if using, and toss well. Transfer to a serving plate and arrange quartered eggs around sides of plate. Serve hot or warm.

Variations: You can chop the hard-boiled eggs coarsely and toss them gently into the rice just before serving time; or chop two of the eggs and quarter the other two, adding the chopped eggs to the rice and garnishing the platter with the quartered eggs.

Serves 4

This is my stir-fry version of kedgeree, the Victorian breakfast favorite with roots in India's British colonial kitchens. Smoked haddock, also known as Finnan haddie, is the classic choice, but most any smoked or cooked fish makes a very fine and most satisfying dish. I love it with a big fruit salad and bowls of lentil soup.

TIPS

If you want to use smoked haddock, cook gently in milk or water, until tender and moist, about 5 minutes. Remove from cooking liquid. Let cool and then remove skin and bones. Using 2 forks, gently pull fish into big, bite-size chunks.

Some recipes call for a generous squeeze of fresh lemon juice over the rice just before serving, a lovely bright flavor note if you have lemon on hand.

Spicy Fried Rice
with Mexican Chorizo

Spicy and robust in flavor, Mexican-style chorizo lends wonderful flavor and color to fried rice. Unlike Spanish-style chorizo, which is smoked and cured and ready to eat like pepperoni and salami, it is made with freshly ground pork and must be cooked. This recipe takes the standard chorizo and eggs from the breakfast menu to a delicious centerpiece dish perfect for weeknight suppers and potluck gatherings.

TIP

Like Italian sausage, Mexican-style chorizo is often sold in links. If you can't find it in bulk-form, simply cut or slit open the casings and turn the sausage meat out into a medium bowl. Break it up into small chunks prior to cooking. Some versions are more coarsely chopped than Italian and country-style sausage, and all are a handsome rusty red from generous seasoning with Spanish paprika.

4 cups	cooked long-grain rice, preferably chilled (see White Rice or Brown Rice, page 316)	1 L
2 tbsp	chicken stock or water	25 mL
1 tsp	salt or to taste	5 mL
½ tsp	granulated sugar	2 mL
4 oz	Mexican-style chorizo sausage, bulk or casings removed (about 1 cup/250 mL) (see Tip, left)	125 g
1 tbsp	vegetable oil	15 mL
1 tbsp	chopped garlic	15 mL
2	eggs, beaten	2
¾ cup	corn kernels, frozen, canned or fresh (see Tip, page 243)	175 mL
½ cup	frozen tiny peas	125 mL
½ cup	thinly sliced green onions, divided	125 mL
¾ cup	coarsely chopped plum (Roma) tomatoes	175 mL
⅓ cup	coarsely chopped fresh cilantro, divided	75 mL

1. Crumble rice with your fingers, breaking up into individual grains. Set aside.

2. In a small bowl, combine chicken stock, salt and sugar and set aside.

3. Place chorizo in a bowl and using a large spoon or a table knife and fork break and pull into small chunks, about 1 inch (2.5 cm) in diameter. Set aside.

4. Heat a wok or a large deep skillet over medium-high heat. Add oil and swirl to coat pan. Add chorizo and using your spatula or a large spoon spread out as it begins to cook. Adjust heat so that it sizzles actively but not wildly. Cook, scooping and pressing gently and chopping into smaller pieces, until meat is firm and cooked through, about 2 minutes. (Due to chorizo's red color, you will need to depend on timing and texture, rather than visible changes in color, in order to judge doneness.)

5. Increase heat to high. Add garlic and toss well. Push sausage aside and add eggs. Swirl to expose them to the hot pan and cook, undisturbed, until edges have begun to set, about 30 seconds. Stir and scoop to break the cooked portions into soft lumps rather than flat sheets. Continue swirling and scooping until eggs are softly scrambled but still very moist, about 1 minute more.

6. Add corn and peas and toss well. Add rice and cook, tossing often, for 1 minute. Add half the green onions.

7. Add chicken stock mixture, pouring in around sides of pan. Cook, tossing often, until rice and vegetables are hot and tender and evenly seasoned, about 1 minute more. Add tomatoes, remaining green onions and half the cilantro and toss well. Transfer to a serving plate and sprinkle remaining cilantro over rice. Serve hot or warm.

> **Variation:** You can substitute another kind of bulk pork sausage if you can't find Mexican-style chorizo. You could also use Spanish-style chorizo, a hard, cured sausage similar to pepperoni. To use Spanish chorizo, simply chop it into ¼-inch (0.5 cm) chunks, or cut it lengthwise in half and then crosswise into very thin slices. It will not release a significant amount of oil, so ignore references to extra oil in the recipe if you use Spanish-style chorizo.

TIP

Mexican-style chorizo can be high in fat, so start with a smaller amount of oil here than in other fried rice recipes. If there is more than about 2 tbsp (25 mL) of oil after the meat is cooked through in Step 4, spoon out excess before you add garlic and continue cooking.

Stir-Fried Beans and Rice Southwestern-Style

Serves 4

Pretty on the plate and delicious to eat, this dish is especially quick to make. Pair it with bowls of chili and coleslaw with a tangy dressing.

TIP

Look for canned black beans among the Hispanic ingredients in supermarkets, or in Hispanic markets. (Don't confuse these with the Chinese seasoning ingredient known as salted black beans, used in Cantonese-style sauces.) You want whole beans, rinsed and drained.

4 cups	cooked long-grain rice, preferably chilled (see White Rice or Brown Rice, page 316)	1 L
3 tbsp	chicken stock, white wine or water	45 mL
1 tsp	salt or to taste	5 mL
¾ tsp	ground cumin	4 mL
½ tsp	granulated sugar	2 mL
½ tsp	hot pepper flakes	2 mL
2 tbsp	vegetable oil	25 mL
¼ cup	chopped onion	50 mL
1 tbsp	chopped garlic	15 mL
2 cups	chopped ham	500 mL
¾ cup	corn kernels, frozen, canned or fresh (see Tip, page 243)	175 mL
¾ cup	coarsely chopped plum (Roma) tomatoes	175 mL
⅔ cup	canned black beans, rinsed and drained (see Tip, left)	150 mL
⅓ cup	chopped green onions	75 mL
¼ cup	chopped fresh cilantro	50 mL

1. Crumble rice with your fingers, breaking up into individual grains. Set aside.

2. In a small bowl, combine chicken stock, salt, cumin, sugar and hot pepper flakes and stir well. Set aside.

3. Heat a wok or a large deep skillet over high heat. Add oil and swirl to coat pan. Add onion and garlic and toss well, until fragrant, about 15 seconds. Add ham and corn and cook, tossing often, for 1 minute. Add rice and toss well. Cook, tossing often, for 1 minute.

4. Add chicken stock mixture, pouring in around sides of pan. Cook, tossing often, until rice is hot and tender and evenly seasoned, about 1 minute more.

5. Add tomatoes, black beans, green onions and cilantro and toss well. Transfer to a serving plate. Serve hot or warm.

Ham Fried Rice with Caramelized Pineapple

4 cups	cooked long-grain rice, preferably chilled (see White Rice or Brown Rice, page 316)	1 L
1 tbsp	soy sauce	15 mL
1 tbsp	water	15 mL
1 tsp	salt or to taste	5 mL
1 tsp	granulated sugar	5 mL
2 tbsp	vegetable oil	25 mL
1 tbsp	chopped garlic	15 mL
2 tsp	chopped fresh gingerroot	10 mL
¾ cup	drained pineapple tidbits or halved pineapple chunks	175 mL
1 cup	chopped ham	250 mL
½ cup	frozen tiny peas	125 mL
3 tbsp	chopped green onions	45 mL
3 tbsp	chopped Italian parsley	45 mL

Serves 4

Browning the pineapple first flavors this delicious dish with its tangy sweetness. Baked sweet potatoes with butter and cinnamon and a crisp green salad make delicious accompaniments.

1. Crumble rice with your fingers, breaking up into individual grains. Set aside.

2. In a small bowl, combine soy sauce, water, salt and sugar and stir well. Set aside.

3. Heat a wok or a large deep skillet over high heat. Add oil and swirl to coat pan. Add garlic and ginger and toss well, until fragrant, about 15 seconds.

4. Add pineapple, spreading into a single layer. Cook, undisturbed, until nicely browned on the bottom, about 30 seconds. Toss well. Cook, undisturbed, for 30 seconds more. Add ham and toss well. Add rice and toss well. Cook, tossing often, for 1 minute.

5. Add soy sauce mixture, pouring in around sides of pan. Toss well. Add peas and green onions and toss well. Cook, tossing often, until rice is hot and tender and evenly seasoned, about 1 minute more. Transfer to a serving plate and sprinkle with parsley. Serve hot or warm.

Hoppin' John's Stir-Fried Rice

Serves 4

This is a salute to the traditional Southern dish known as Hoppin' John, with its combination of black-eyed peas or field peas and rice. Since it is often served along with greens and hot cornbread, I recommend you consider those accompaniments, or steamed spinach and buttered corn on the cob.

4 cups	cooked long-grain rice, preferably chilled (see White Rice or Brown Rice, page 316)	1 L
1 tbsp	red wine vinegar	15 mL
1 tbsp	water	15 mL
1 tsp	salt or to taste	5 mL
½ tsp	granulated sugar	2 mL
½ tsp	hot pepper flakes, optional	2 mL
2 tbsp	vegetable oil	25 mL
3 tbsp	chopped onion	45 mL
1 cup	chopped ham	250 mL
½ cup	diced celery	125 mL
⅓ cup	chopped green bell pepper	75 mL
¾ cup	cooked black-eyed peas or canned, drained and rinsed, or frozen, thawed	175 mL
¼ cup	thinly sliced green onions	50 mL
2 tbsp	chopped Italian parsley	25 mL

1. Crumble rice with your fingers, breaking up into individual grains. Set aside.

2. In a small bowl, combine vinegar, water, salt, sugar and hot pepper flakes, if using, and stir well. Set aside.

3. Heat a wok or a large deep skillet over high heat. Add oil and swirl to coat pan. Add onion and toss well, until fragrant, about 15 seconds. Add ham, celery and green pepper and toss well. Cook, tossing often, until celery and peppers are softened, about 30 seconds. Add rice and toss well. Cook, tossing often, for 1 minute.

4. Add vinegar mixture, pouring in around sides of pan. Toss well. Add black-eyed peas and green onions and cook, tossing often, until rice is hot and tender and evenly seasoned, 1 to 2 minutes more. Transfer to a serving plate and sprinkle with chopped parsley. Serve hot or warm.

Stir-Fried Rice with Chickpeas and Pineapple

4 cups	cooked long-grain rice, preferably chilled (see White Rice or Brown Rice, page 316)	1 L
1 tbsp	soy sauce	15 mL
1 tbsp	water	15 mL
1 tsp	salt or to taste	5 mL
½ tsp	granulated sugar	2 mL
2 tbsp	vegetable oil	25 mL
½ cup	chopped onion	125 mL
1 tbsp	chopped garlic	15 mL
¾ cup	shredded carrots	175 mL
1 cup	canned chickpeas, rinsed and drained (see Tips, right)	250 mL
1	can (8 oz/227 mL) crushed pineapple, with juices (1 cup/250 mL) (see Tips, right)	1
2 tbsp	thinly sliced green onions	25 mL

1. Crumble rice with your fingers, breaking up into individual grains. Set aside.
2. In a small bowl, combine soy sauce, water, salt and sugar and stir well. Set aside.
3. Heat a wok or a large deep skillet over high heat. Add oil and swirl to coat pan. Add onion and garlic and toss well, until fragrant, about 15 seconds.
4. Add carrots and cook, tossing often, until beginning to wilt, about 30 seconds. Add rice and toss well. Cook, tossing often, for 1 minute.
5. Add soy sauce mixture, pouring in around sides of pan. Toss well. Add chickpeas and pineapple and cook, tossing often, until rice is hot and tender and evenly seasoned, about 1 minute more. Add green onions and toss well. Transfer to a serving plate. Serve hot or warm.

Serves 4

Chickpeas, shredded carrots and pineapple give this dish substance as well as visual appeal. It works nicely as an accompaniment to baked ham or roast chicken, or as the anchor of a vegetarian menu.

TIPS

You can use canned chickpeas that have been rinsed and drained well or dried chickpeas that have been soaked, cooked until tender and cooled to room temperature.

You can substitute 1 cup (250 mL) finely chopped fresh pineapple for the canned crushed pineapple.

Stir-Fried Rice à la BLT

The inspired sandwich combination of bacon, lettuce and tomato translates deliciously into a platter of deliciously seasoned rice. Halved cherry tomatoes provide flavor even when summer garden tomatoes are out of season, and sturdy, nutritious greens, such as escarole, watercress or the leafy portions of bok choy, provide bold flavor and color to a delicious dish. Serve with steamed snow peas and a simple salsa of chopped mangoes or pineapple tossed with lemon juice, sugar, chiles and fresh mint.

4 cups	cooked long-grain rice, preferably chilled (see White Rice or Brown Rice, page 316)	1 L
3 tbsp	chicken stock or white wine	45 mL
1 tsp	salt or to taste	5 mL
1 tsp	granulated sugar	5 mL
1/4 tsp	freshly ground pepper	1 mL
4 oz	thick-cut meaty bacon or chopped ham	125 g
1 tbsp	vegetable oil	15 mL
2 tbsp	chopped onion	25 mL
2 tsp	chopped garlic	10 mL
2 cups	loosely packed chopped escarole or watercress (1-inch/2.5 cm pieces)	500 mL
1/2 cup	halved cherry tomatoes	125 mL
3 tbsp	chopped green onions	45 mL

1. Crumble rice with your fingers, breaking up into individual grains. Set aside.

2. In a small bowl, combine chicken stock, salt, sugar and pepper and stir well. Set aside.

3. Chop bacon slices crosswise into 1/4-inch (0.5 cm) strips. Set aside. Place a medium bowl next to the stove to hold bacon fat.

4. Heat a wok or a large deep skillet over high heat. Add oil and swirl to coat pan. Add bacon and toss well. Spread into a single layer and cook, undisturbed, until fragrant, about 30 seconds. Toss well. Cook, tossing occasionally, until lightly browned and cooked through, 1 to 2 minutes more.

5. Carefully strain hot bacon fat into the reserved bowl, using your spatula to keep the bacon pieces in the pan. Return 2 tbsp (25 mL) of this bacon fat to pan and heat for 15 seconds. (Discard remaining bacon fat in bowl.) Add onion and garlic and toss well, until fragrant, about 15 seconds.

6. Add escarole and cook, tossing often, until bright green and beginning to wilt, about 30 seconds. Add rice and toss well. Cook, tossing often, for 1 minute.

7. Add chicken stock mixture, pouring in around sides of pan. Toss well. Cook, tossing often, until rice is hot and tender and evenly seasoned, about 1 minute more. Add cherry tomatoes and green onions and toss well. Transfer to a serving plate. Serve hot or warm.

Garlic-Scented Stir-Fried Rice with Clams and Parsley

4 cups	cooked long-grain rice, preferably chilled (see White Rice or Brown Rice, page 316)	1 L
2 tbsp	clam juice or chicken stock	25 mL
1 tbsp	white wine	15 mL
1 tsp	salt or to taste	5 mL
½ tsp	granulated sugar	2 mL
2 tbsp	vegetable oil	25 mL
3 tbsp	chopped garlic	45 mL
1 cup	drained canned baby clams	250 mL
2 tbsp	chopped green onions	25 mL
½ cup	frozen tiny peas	125 mL
3 tbsp	chopped Italian parsley	45 mL
2 tbsp	extra virgin olive oil, optional	25 mL

Serves 4

With canned clams and bottled clam juice on the pantry shelf, this dish gives you a little oceanic flavor in record time.

1. Crumble rice with your fingers, breaking up into individual grains. Set aside.
2. In a small bowl, combine clam juice, wine, salt and sugar and stir well. Set aside.
3. Heat a wok or a large deep skillet over high heat. Add oil and swirl to coat pan. Add garlic and toss well, until fragrant, about 15 seconds. Add clams and green onions and toss well. Add rice and toss well. Cook, tossing often, for 1 minute.
4. Add clam juice mixture, pouring in around sides of pan. Toss well. Add peas and parsley and toss well. Cook, tossing often, until rice is hot and tender and evenly seasoned, about 1 minute more. Add olive oil, if using, and toss well. Transfer to a serving plate. Serve hot or warm.

Salmon Fried Rice with Peas and Dill

Serves 4

Salmon is first choice here for its beauty and flavor, but any cooked fish makes a tasty dish. You can add a squeeze of lime or lemon just before serving for a little burst of summer flavor.

TIP

Poached or grilled salmon is ideal here, but you can use canned salmon with tasty results. Buy 2 cans (each 7½ oz/213 g), drain well and remove skin and bones before gently pulling into chunks using 2 forks.

4 cups	cooked long-grain rice, preferably chilled (see White Rice or Brown Rice, page 316)	1 L
2 tbsp	white wine, dry sherry or water	25 mL
1 tbsp	soy sauce	15 mL
1 tsp	salt or to taste	5 mL
½ tsp	granulated sugar	2 mL
2 tbsp	vegetable oil	25 mL
2 tsp	chopped garlic	10 mL
2 tsp	chopped fresh gingerroot	10 mL
8 oz	cooked salmon, cut into 1-inch (2.5 cm) chunks (see Tip, left)	250 g
½ cup	frozen tiny peas	125 mL
3 tbsp	chopped green onions	45 mL
¼ cup	chopped fresh dill, mint or cilantro	50 mL

1. Crumble rice with your fingers, breaking up into individual grains. Set aside.
2. In a small bowl, combine wine, soy sauce, salt and sugar and stir well. Set aside.
3. Heat a wok or a large deep skillet over high heat. Add oil and swirl to coat pan. Add garlic and ginger and toss well, until fragrant, about 15 seconds.
4. Add salmon and peas and toss gently. Add rice and cook, tossing often, for 1 minute. Add green onions and toss well.
5. Add wine mixture, pouring in around sides of pan. Toss well. Cook, tossing often, until rice is hot and tender and evenly seasoned, about 1 minute more. Add dill and toss well. Transfer to a serving plate. Serve hot or warm.

Noodles

Wok-Seared Beef with Broccoli and Spaghetti

Serves 2 to 4

Fast, hearty and made from easy-to-find ingredients, this dish is worthy of a place on your standard weeknight menu. Enjoy it with chopsticks from a small bowl or with a fork from a plate.

TIP

Use trimmed broccoli florets found packaged in the produce section of supermarkets. Chop large florets into 2 or 3 pieces so that they cook quickly and evenly. Or buy a crown or head or two of broccoli and chop the florets into bite-size pieces.

8 oz	spaghetti	250 g
2 tbsp	soy sauce	25 mL
½ tsp	salt or to taste	2 mL
8 oz	lean boneless beef, thinly sliced crosswise into 2-inch (5 cm) long strips (see Tip, 295)	250 g
⅓ cup	chicken stock	75 mL
1 tbsp	oyster sauce	15 mL
1 tsp	granulated sugar	5 mL
2 tbsp	vegetable oil	25 mL
1 tbsp	chopped garlic	15 mL
2 cups	bite-size broccoli florets (see Tip, left)	500 mL

1. In a large pot of boiling salted water, cook spaghetti noodles until just tender, about 9 minutes. Drain, rinse with cold water and drain well again. If you don't plan to cook them right away, toss with 1 tsp (5 mL) vegetable oil or Asian sesame oil to keep noodles soft. (You should have about 3 cups/750 mL cooked spaghetti.)

2. In a bowl, combine soy sauce and salt and stir well. Add beef and stir to coat evenly. Set aside for 10 minutes.

3. In a small bowl, combine chicken stock, oyster sauce and sugar and stir well. Set aside.

4. Heat a wok or a large deep skillet over high heat. Add oil and swirl to coat pan. Add garlic and toss well, until fragrant, about 15 seconds.

5. Add beef mixture, spreading into a single layer. Cook, undisturbed, until edges change color, about 30 seconds. Toss well and cook for 15 seconds more.

6. Add broccoli and toss well. Cook, tossing often, until broccoli is bright green and beginning to wilt and beef is no longer pink, about 1 minute. Add noodles and toss well, turning and scooping to mix everything well.

7. Add chicken stock mixture, pouring in around sides of pan. Toss well. Cook, tossing often, until most of the sauce has been absorbed, broccoli is tender-crisp and beef is cooked through, 1 to 2 minutes more. (The stock will cool the pan down and quiet the cooking, and liquid will pool in the bottom of the wok. As it heats back up, the sauce will be absorbed and sizzling sounds will return.) Transfer to a serving platter. Serve hot or warm.

Asian-Style Spaghetti with Shrimp and Zucchini

12 oz	spaghetti	375 g
12 oz	medium shrimp, peeled and deveined	375 g
1 tbsp	soy sauce	15 mL
1/3 cup	chicken stock	75 mL
1 tbsp	oyster sauce	15 mL
1 tsp	salt or to taste	5 mL
1/2 tsp	granulated sugar	2 mL
2 tbsp	vegetable oil	25 mL
1 tbsp	chopped garlic	15 mL
2 tsp	chopped fresh gingerroot	10 mL
2 cups	chopped zucchini (about 2 medium) (see Tip, right)	500 mL
3 tbsp	chopped green onions	45 mL
2 tsp	Asian sesame oil	10 mL

Serves 2 to 4

Special enough for company, this dish is also simple enough to cook on a busy night when you need a mid-week treat at home. Use a mix of yellow squash and zucchini for an extra splash of color.

TIP
To chop zucchini, quarter lengthwise and then slice crosswise.

1. In a large pot of boiling salted water, cook spaghetti noodles until just tender, about 9 minutes. Drain, rinse with cold water and drain well again. If you don't plan to cook them right away, toss with 1 tsp (5 mL) vegetable oil or Asian sesame oil to keep noodles soft. (You should have about 3 cups/750 mL cooked spaghetti.)

2. In a bowl, combine shrimp and soy sauce and stir well. Set aside for 10 minutes.

3. In a small bowl, combine chicken stock, oyster sauce, salt and sugar and stir well. Set aside.

4. Heat a wok or a large deep skillet over high heat. Add oil and swirl to coat pan. Add garlic and ginger and toss well, until fragrant, about 15 seconds.

5. Add shrimp mixture, spreading into a single layer. Cook, undisturbed, until most of the edges have turned pink, about 1 minute. Toss and cook other side, about 30 seconds more.

6. Add zucchini and toss well. Cook, tossing often, until zucchini brightens in color and begins to wilt and shrimp are pink and firm, about 1 minute. Add noodles and toss well.

7. Add chicken stock mixture, pouring in around sides of pan. Toss well. Cook, tossing often, until most of the sauce has been absorbed, zucchini is tender-crisp and shrimp are cooked through, about 2 minute more. Add green onions and sesame oil and toss well. Transfer to a serving platter. Serve hot or warm.

Egg Noodles with Spicy Ham and Greens

Serves 2 to 4

What a fast feast this makes, perfect for a hearty supper. I use dried pappardelle, which are wide egg noodles, broader than fettuccine. Fresh collard greens or turnip greens work well here, or you could use frozen greens instead.

TIPS

To prepare collard greens or turnip greens, wash them well. Trim away the thick central rib and stack the leaf sections. Cut lengthwise into 2-inch (5 cm) strips and crosswise into 2-inch (5 cm) lengths to make generous pieces.

I use a tasty locally made North Carolina-style barbecue sauce here, but most any kind you like will make a delicious dish.

8 oz	dried pappardelle or fettuccine	250 g
2½ cups	coarsely chopped collard greens or turnip greens (2-inch/5 cm pieces) (see Tips, left)	625 mL
¼ cup	barbecue sauce	50 mL
2 tbsp	chicken stock	25 mL
1 tsp	granulated sugar	5 mL
1 tsp	salt or to taste	5 mL
¼ tsp	freshly ground pepper	1 mL
2 tbsp	vegetable oil	25 mL
2 tbsp	chopped shallots or onion	25 mL
1 tbsp	chopped garlic	15 mL
1¼ cups	chopped ham (6 oz/175 g)	300 mL
¼ cup	chopped green onions	50 mL

1. In a large pot of boiling salted water, cook pappardelle until tender, 4 to 6 minutes. Drain, rinse well in cold water and drain again. Set aside.

2. Bring a small saucepan of water to a rolling boil. Add greens and cook, stirring occasionally, until bright green and almost tender, about 3 minutes. Drain, rinse in cold water and drain well. Set aside.

3. In a small bowl, combine barbecue sauce, chicken stock, sugar, salt and pepper and stir well. Set aside.

4. Heat a wok or a large deep skillet over medium-high heat. Add oil and swirl to coat pan. Add shallots and garlic and toss well, until fragrant, about 15 seconds.

5. Add ham and spread into a single layer. Cook, undisturbed, for 30 seconds. Toss well. Cook, tossing often, until it begins to brown just a little, about 30 seconds more. Add collard greens and noodles and toss well.

6. Add barbecue sauce mixture, pouring in around sides of pan and toss well. Cook, tossing often, until ham is heated through and noodles are evenly seasoned, 1 to 2 minutes more. Add green onions and toss well.

> **Variations:** Use Chinese-Style Barbecued Pork (see recipe, page 332) instead of ham.
>
> Use spinach instead of greens and skip the blanching and add right before serving time.

Linguine with Hot Italian Sausage and Sweet Peppers

9 oz	fresh linguine or fettuccine (see Tip, right)	275 g
3 tbsp	chicken stock or white wine	45 mL
1 tsp	salt or to taste	5 mL
¼ tsp	freshly ground pepper	1 mL
2 tbsp	vegetable oil	25 mL
2 tbsp	chopped garlic	25 mL
8 oz	hot Italian sausage (bulk or removed from casings)	250 g
1 cup	sliced red bell pepper	250 mL
¾ cup	thinly sliced mushrooms	175 mL
¼ cup	chopped Italian parsley	50 mL

1. In a large pot of boiling salted water, cook linguine until just tender, 3 to 5 minutes. Drain well, rinse with cold water and drain again. Set aside.

2. In a small bowl, combine chicken stock, salt and pepper and stir well. Set aside.

3. Heat a wok or a large deep skillet over medium-high heat. Add oil and swirl to coat pan. Add garlic and toss well, until fragrant, about 15 seconds.

4. Add sausage and using a spatula or slotted spoon begin breaking up the meat into small chunks. Cook, tossing often, continuing to break up meat, until sausage is crumbly and no longer pink, about 2 minutes.

5. Add red peppers and mushrooms and toss well. Cook, tossing often, until sausage is cooked through, 1 to 2 minutes. Add linguine and toss well.

6. Add chicken stock mixture, pouring in around sides of pan. Cook, tossing often, until noodles are evenly seasoned and peppers are tender-crisp, 1 to 2 minutes more. Add parsley and toss well. Transfer to a serving platter. Serve hot or warm.

Variation: You could use dried linguine or fettuccine, cooking in boiling salted water until tender, 7 to 9 minutes; or another kind of fresh pasta, cooked according to package directions.

Serves 2 to 4

You could use any ground pork sausage in this satisfying dish. Add a good splash of hot pepper sauce along with the parsley if you want more heat, or use regular Italian sausage if you prefer a milder flavor.

TIP

Several brands of fresh Chinese-style noodles come in 9-oz (275 g) packages and are available in many supermarkets. If you don't find those, simply use about half of a 16 oz (500 g) package and don't worry about exact amounts here.

Egg Noodles with Cabbage and Kielbasa

Serves 4 to 6

Comfort food in any language, this delicious hearty dish goes wonderfully with a big bowl of buttered peas and a salad of crisp greens, chopped apples and raisins with a honey-mustard dressing.

TIP

Dried wide egg noodles can be found in the pasta section of most supermarkets. Wider than fettuccine but shorter than spaghetti noodles, they have a pleasing texture and work well with robust flavors. You could use any other cooked noodle in this recipe.

1 lb	dried wide egg noodles (see Tip, left)	500 g
3 tbsp	chicken stock	45 mL
1 tsp	salt or to taste	5 mL
½ tsp	granulated sugar	2 mL
½ tsp	freshly ground pepper	2 mL
2 tbsp	vegetable oil	25 mL
1 tbsp	butter	15 mL
2 tsp	chopped garlic	10 mL
2 tsp	chopped fresh gingerroot	10 mL
2 cups	diced kielbasa or other smoked sausage or ham (about 8 oz/250 g, ½-inch/1 cm chunks)	500 mL
2¼ cups	shredded green cabbage or savoy cabbage	550 mL
3 tbsp	chopped green onions	45 mL
3 tbsp	chopped Italian parsley	45 mL
2 tsp	caraway seeds, optional	10 mL

1. In a large saucepan of boiling salted water, cook egg noodles, until tender but still firm, 9 to 12 minutes or according to package directions. Drain well, rinse in cold water and drain again. Toss with 1 tsp (5 mL) of vegetable oil if you don't plan to use the noodles right away.

2. In a small bowl, combine chicken stock, salt, sugar and pepper and stir well. Set aside.

3. Heat a wok or a large deep skillet over medium-high heat. Add oil and butter and swirl to coat pan and melt butter. Add garlic and ginger and toss well, until fragrant, about 15 seconds.

4. Add kielbasa and toss well. Cook, tossing often, for 1 minute. Add cabbage and toss well. Cook, tossing often, until cabbage brightens in color and begins to wilt, about 1 minute more.

5. Add chicken stock mixture, pouring in around sides of pan and toss well. Cook, tossing often, until kielbasa is heated through and cabbage is tender-crisp, about 2 minutes more.

6. Add noodles and toss well. Add green onions, parsley and caraway seeds, if using. Toss well. Transfer to a serving platter. Serve hot or warm.

Pork Lo Mein

9 oz	fresh Chinese-style egg noodles (see Tips, right)	275 g
1 tbsp	soy sauce	15 mL
1 tbsp	oyster sauce	15 mL
1 tbsp	dry sherry or Shaoxing rice wine	15 mL
½ tsp	granulated sugar	2 mL
½ tsp	salt or to taste	2 mL
2 tbsp	vegetable oil	25 mL
2 tsp	chopped garlic	10 mL
2 tsp	chopped fresh gingerroot	10 mL
½ cup	shredded carrots	125 mL
1¼ cups	diced Chinese-Style Barbecued Pork (see recipe, page 332) or shredded roast chicken (about 6 oz/175 g)	300 mL
2 cups	bean sprouts (see Tips, right)	500 mL
3 tbsp	chopped green onions	45 mL

1. In a large pot of boiling salted water, cook noodles until just tender, 2 to 4 minutes. Drain, rinse in cold water and drain again. Toss with 1 tsp (5 mL) of vegetable oil or sesame oil if you don't plan to use the noodles right away.

2. In a small bowl, combine soy sauce, oyster sauce, sherry, sugar and salt and stir well. Set aside.

3. Heat a wok or a large deep skillet over medium-high heat. Add oil and swirl to coat pan. Add garlic and ginger and toss well, until fragrant, about 15 seconds. Add carrots and toss well.

4. Add pork and cook, tossing often, until carrots have wilted and pork is heated through, about 1 minute. Add bean sprouts and toss well. Add noodles and toss well, scooping and turning to mix them well.

5. Add soy sauce mixture, pouring in around sides of pan. Cook, tossing often, until noodles are evenly seasoned, 1 to 2 minutes. Add green onions and toss well. Transfer to a serving platter. Serve hot or warm.

> **Variation:** If you don't have fresh bean sprouts, use another cool, crisp component, such as lightly cooked shredded napa cabbage, diced cucumber, shredded lettuce, or snow peas, whole or sliced into strips, or simply leave them out.

Serves 2 to 4

If you love lo-mein dishes at your favorite Chinese restaurant, you'll be happy to see how easy it is to make them at home. Chinese-style egg noodles are tossed with a few savory ingredients. Using cooked ingredients, such as ham, roast chicken or barbecued pork, makes this a quick and simple dish to prepare.

TIPS

Several brands of fresh Chinese-style noodles come in 9-oz (275 g) packages and are available in many supermarkets. If you don't find those, simply use about half of a 16 oz (500 g) package and don't worry about exact amounts here.

Bean sprouts are a delight when fresh, crisp and cool, but they are fragile and must be used within a day or two. If they look sad at the store, don't bring them home. If they are perfectly fresh at the store, don't tuck them away in the crisper and forget you have this treasure to enjoy.

Shrimp Lo Mein

Serves 2 to 4

This recipe lets you enjoy Chinese take-out without leaving home. Broccoli steamed and tossed with a little butter or olive oil and salt goes nicely with this dish. Or make a simple soup of chicken stock with fresh spinach leaves and halved cherry tomatoes tossed in and a handful of cilantro leaves on top.

TIP

You can chop the celery into chunks if you prefer (½ inch/1 cm), but I like to slice it thinly crosswise on the diagonal. This makes delicate pieces which cook quickly and are shaped like the shrimp.

9 oz	fresh Chinese-style egg noodles (see Tips, page 283)	275 g
1 tbsp	dry sherry or Shaoxing rice wine	15 mL
12	medium shrimp, peeled and deveined	12
1 tbsp	soy sauce	15 mL
1 tbsp	oyster sauce	15 mL
1 tbsp	water	15 mL
½ tsp	granulated sugar	2 mL
½ tsp	salt or to taste	2 mL
2 tbsp	vegetable oil	25 mL
2 tsp	chopped garlic	10 mL
2 tsp	chopped fresh gingerroot	10 mL
½ cup	thinly sliced celery (see Tip, left)	125 mL
½ cup	shredded carrots	125 mL
2 cups	fresh bean sprouts or shredded napa cabbage (see Tips, page 283)	500 mL
3 tbsp	chopped green onions	45 mL
2 tsp	Asian sesame oil	10 mL

1. In a large pot of boiling salted water, cook noodles until tender, 2 to 4 minutes. Drain, rinse in cold water and drain again. Toss with 1 tsp (5 mL) of vegetable oil or sesame oil if you don't plan to use the noodles right away.

2. In a bowl, combine sherry and shrimp and mix to coat evenly. Set aside for 10 minutes. In a small bowl, combine soy sauce, oyster sauce, water, sugar and salt and stir well.

3. Heat a wok or a large deep skillet over medium-high heat. Add oil and swirl to coat pan. Add garlic and ginger and toss well, until fragrant, about 15 seconds.

4. Add shrimp mixture, spreading into a single layer. Cook, undisturbed, until edges turn pink, about 30 seconds.

5. Add celery and carrots and toss well. Cook, tossing often, until shrimp are firm and pink all over and celery and carrots begin to soften, about 1 minute. Add bean sprouts and toss well. Add noodles and toss well, scooping and turning to mix them well.

6. Add soy sauce mixture, pouring in around sides of pan. Cook, tossing often, until shrimp are cooked through, vegetables are tender-crisp and noodles are evenly seasoned, 1 to 2 minutes. Add green onions and sesame oil and toss well. Transfer to a serving platter. Serve hot or warm.

Spinach-Studded Noodles with Pork

9 oz	fresh Chinese-style egg noodles (see Tips, page 283)	275 g
2 tbsp	soy sauce	25 mL
2 tsp	cornstarch	10 mL
6 oz	boneless pork (such as loin or tenderloin), thinly sliced	175 g
½ cup	chicken stock	125 mL
1 tbsp	dry sherry or Shaoxing rice wine	15 mL
1 tsp	salt or to taste	5 mL
½ tsp	granulated sugar	2 mL
2 tbsp	vegetable oil	25 mL
2 tsp	chopped garlic	10 mL
2 tsp	chopped fresh gingerroot	10 mL
½ cup	shredded carrots	125 mL
3 cups	baby spinach leaves	750 mL
3 tbsp	chopped green onions	45 mL

Serves 2 to 4

This Chinese-style dish turns a plain pork chop into a delicious noodle feast studded with spinach leaves, carrots and a touch of fresh ginger.

1. In a large pot of boiling salted water, cook noodles until tender, 2 to 4 minutes. Drain, rinse in cold water and drain again. Toss with 1 tsp (5 mL) of vegetable oil or sesame oil if you don't plan to use the noodles right away.

2. In a bowl, combine soy sauce and cornstarch and stir well into a smooth sauce. Add pork and toss to coat evenly. Set aside for 10 minutes.

3. In another bowl, combine chicken stock, sherry, salt and sugar and stir well. Set aside.

4. Heat a wok or a large deep skillet over high heat. Add oil and swirl to coat pan. Add garlic and ginger and toss well, until fragrant, about 15 seconds.

5. Add pork mixture, spreading into a single layer. Cook, undisturbed, until edges change color, about 15 seconds. Toss well and add carrots. Cook, tossing often, until carrots have begun to wilt and pork has changed color, about 1 minute more.

6. Add chicken stock mixture, pouring in around sides of pan and bring to a gentle boil, about 30 seconds.

7. Add noodles and spinach and toss well. Cook, tossing often, until spinach has wilted, noodles are hot, tender and evenly seasoned and pork is cooked through, 1 to 2 minutes. Add green onions and toss well. Transfer to a serving platter. Serve hot or warm.

Thai-Style Chile-Fired Pork with Noodles

Serves 2 to 4

This is my version of *nahm prik ong*, a robust specialty from Northern Thailand which combines ground pork, garlic and tomatoes in a chile-fired sauce. Traditionally enjoyed with sticky rice and crispy pork skins, it makes a wonderful sauce for tender Chinese-style egg noodles.

9 oz	fresh Chinese-style egg noodles	275 g
1 tbsp	Thai red curry paste	15 mL
3 tbsp	chicken stock	45 mL
2 tbsp	fish sauce	25 mL
2 tsp	brown sugar	10 mL
1 tsp	salt or to taste	5 mL
2 tbsp	vegetable oil	25 mL
1/3 cup	chopped onion	75 mL
1 tbsp	chopped garlic	15 mL
8 oz	ground pork	250 g
1 1/4 cups	coarsely chopped plum tomatoes	300 mL
1/4 cup	chopped fresh cilantro	50 mL
3 tbsp	chopped green onions	45 mL

1. In a large pot of boiling salted water, cook noodles until tender, 2 to 4 minutes. Drain, rinse in cold water and drain again. Toss with 1 tsp (5 mL) of vegetable oil or sesame oil if you don't plan to use the noodles right away.

2. In a small bowl, combine red curry paste and 1 tbsp (15 mL) water. Mash and stir to lightly mix and soften paste (no need to dissolve it or mix well). Set aside. In another small bowl, combine stock, fish sauce, sugar and salt and stir well. Set aside.

3. Heat a wok or a large deep skillet over medium heat. Add oil and swirl to coat pan. Add onion and garlic toss well, until fragrant, about 30 seconds. Add curry paste mixture and toss well. Cook, pressing and stirring to soften curry paste and help dissolve into a sauce, about 1 minute. Increase heat to medium-high.

4. Add pork and using a spatula or slotted spoon begin breaking up the meat into small chunks. Cook, tossing often, until pork is crumbly, evenly seasoned and no longer pink, 1 to 2 minutes.

5. Add chicken stock mixture, pouring in around sides of pan. Toss gently to mix well. Bring to a boil, tossing occasionally. Add tomatoes and toss well. Cook, tossing occasionally, until tomatoes are softened and everything comes together into a chunky, evenly seasoned sauce, 1 to 2 minutes more.

6. Add noodles to pan. Toss well, scooping and turning to season them evenly. Add cilantro and green onions and toss well. Transfer to a serving platter. Serve hot or warm.

Gingery Noodles with Pork in Spicy Bean Sauce

9 oz	fresh Chinese-style egg noodles (see Tip, page 283)	275 g
2 tbsp	Chinese-style hot bean paste (see Tips, right)	25 mL
2 tbsp	chicken stock	25 mL
1 tbsp	soy sauce	15 mL
1 tbsp	water	15 mL
2 tsp	brown sugar or granulated sugar	10 mL
2 tsp	Asian sesame oil	10 mL
2 tbsp	vegetable oil	25 mL
1 tbsp	chopped garlic	15 mL
1 cup	frozen shelled edamame beans	250 mL
3 tbsp	shredded fresh gingerroot (see Tips, right)	45 mL
8 oz	ground pork	250 g
3 tbsp	chopped green onions	45 mL
3 tbsp	chopped fresh cilantro	45 mL

1. In a large pot of boiling salted water, cook noodles until just tender, 2 to 4 minutes. Drain, rinse in cold water and drain again. Toss with 1 tsp (5 mL) of vegetable oil or sesame oil if you don't plan to use the noodles right away.

2. In a bowl, combine bean paste, chicken stock, soy sauce, water, brown sugar and sesame oil and stir well. Set aside.

3. Heat a wok or a large deep skillet over medium-high heat. Add oil and swirl to coat pan. Add garlic and toss well, until fragrant, 15 seconds. Add edamame beans and ginger and toss well. Cook, tossing often, for 15 seconds more.

4. Add pork and using a spatula or slotted spoon begin breaking up the meat into small chunks. Cook, tossing often, until pork is crumbly, evenly seasoned and no longer pink, 1 to 2 minutes.

5. Add noodles and toss well. Add bean sauce mixture, pouring in around sides of pan. Cook, tossing often, until pork is cooked through, noodles are evenly seasoned and edamame beans are hot, 1 to 2 minutes more. Add green onions and cilantro and toss well. Transfer to a serving platter. Serve hot or warm.

Serves 2 to 4

Fresh ginger provides the vibrant flavor in this hearty dish. Enjoy it Asian-style with chopsticks from a small bowl or use a fork and enjoy it like spaghetti with meat sauce.

TIPS

Chinese-style bean paste is available in small cans and big jars. Also called "bean sauce," this seasoning is made from preserved soybeans, which are seasoned and ground to a thick, rich purée with intensely salty flavor. The kind in jars is a thinner but still substantial sauce, chunky with whole or partially ground beans. Hot bean paste is also called Szechwan bean paste. In this recipe you could use regular bean paste and add 1 tsp (5 mL) chile-garlic sauce or hot pepper sauce to create the heat.

To shred fresh gingerroot, you will need a thick chunk. Peel and slice it crosswise against the grain into thin coins. Stack coins into little piles and cut them carefully into thin little strips.

Wide Rice Noodles with Pork and Zucchini

Serves 2 to 4

This recipe uses dried rice noodles cooked in a traditional way. The noodles are soaked in warm water for 15 minutes, until flexible and bright white. They are then cooked over medium-high heat until tender and deliciously seasoned.

TIP

Dried rice noodles come in 1-lb (500 g) packages, folded into a plump rectangular packet and wrapped in cellophane. I love the ones which are wide as fettuccine, but the slender, linguine-size ones work nicely in this recipe as well. Because they break easily, I usually soften about half the package of dried noodles and reserve the extra in the refrigerator for another dish within a day or two. Place the package of dried noodles in the sink before opening it, as dried rice noodles tend to scatter. Then put the remaining dried noodles into a resealable plastic bag and store it on your pantry shelf for up to 1 month.

4 oz	dried rice noodles, fettuccine-width (see Tip, left)	125 g
2 tbsp	soy sauce	25 mL
1 tsp	salt or to taste	5 mL
1 tsp	granulated sugar	5 mL
8 oz	zucchini (about 2 small or 1 medium)	250 g
2 tbsp	vegetable oil	25 mL
1 tbsp	chopped garlic	15 mL
4 oz	ground pork	125 g
1/3 cup	chicken stock	75 mL
3 tbsp	chopped green onions	45 mL
2 tsp	Asian sesame oil	10 mL

1. Place rice noodles in a bowl and cover with warm water. Set aside to soak for 15 minutes, until noodles are flexible and bright white. Drain well. Set aside.

2. In a small bowl, combine soy sauce, salt and sugar and stir well.

3. Trim zucchini and cut in half lengthwise. Cut crosswise into thin, bite-size slices.

4. Heat a wok or a large deep skillet over high heat. Add oil and swirl to coat pan. Add garlic and toss well, until fragrant, about 15 seconds.

5. Add ground pork and using a spatula, break up the meat into smaller chunks. Spread into a single layer. Cook, undisturbed, for 30 seconds. Toss well. Cook, tossing often, until no longer pink outside, about 1 minute more.

6. Add zucchini and toss well. Spread into a single layer. Reduce heat to medium-high and cook, undisturbed, for 1 minute.

7. Add soy sauce mixture, pouring in around edges of pan. Add rice noodles and toss well.

8. Add chicken stock, pouring in around sides of pan. Toss well. Cook, tossing occasionally, until noodles curl up and are tender and pork is cooked through, 2 to 3 minutes more. Add green onions and sesame oil and toss well. Transfer to a serving platter. Serve hot or warm.

Pad Thai (page 302)

Overleaf: Vietnamese-Style Bean Thread Noodles with Crab (page 311)

Rice Noodles
with Snow Peas and Ham

6 oz	dried rice noodles, linguine-width	175 g
1/3 cup	chicken stock	75 mL
2 tbsp	soy sauce	25 mL
1 tsp	salt or to taste	5 mL
1 tsp	granulated sugar	5 mL
2 tbsp	vegetable oil	25 mL
2 tbsp	chopped onion	25 mL
1 tbsp	chopped garlic	15 mL
1 1/4 cups	chopped ham (about 6 oz/175 g)	300 mL
1 1/2 cups	trimmed snow peas (see Tip, right)	375 mL
3 tbsp	chopped green onions	45 mL
2 tsp	Asian sesame oil	10 mL

Serves 2 to 4

This dish is an inviting mix of colors and textures. I love it with a big salad and tangy dressing, bringing together a contrast of flavors to make a memorable meal.

TIP
To trim snow peas, cut off and discard tip and cut stem end partway, pulling it down along the straight side of each snow pea to remove any strings.

1. Bring a large pot of water to a rolling boil over high heat. Add rice noodles and remove from heat. Stir gently to separate the noodles. Let stand for 5 to 7 minutes, stirring occasionally, until noodles are softened but still firm. Drain, rinse well in cold water. Drain and set aside.

2. In a bowl, combine chicken stock, soy sauce, salt and sugar and stir well. Set aside.

3. Heat a wok or a large deep skillet over high heat. Add oil and swirl to coat pan. Add onion and garlic and toss well, until fragrant, about 15 seconds.

4. Add ham, spreading into a single layer. Cook, undisturbed, for 15 seconds. Toss well and cook for 15 seconds more. Add snow peas and toss well. Cook, tossing often, until snow peas are bright green and beginning to wilt and ham is heated through, about 1 minute. Add noodles and cook, tossing often and pulling the noodles apart with tongs or spatulas to help them cook evenly, for 1 minute.

5. Add chicken stock mixture, pouring in around sides of pan. Cook, tossing often, turning and scooping noodles to heat and soften them, until noodles curl up and are tender, snow peas are tender-crisp and ham is hot, 1 to 2 minutes more. Add an additional 1 to 2 tbsp (15 to 25 mL) of water as needed to keep noodles from sticking or burning. Add green onions and sesame oil and toss well. Transfer to a serving platter. Serve hot or warm.

Overleaf: Thai-Style Roasted Chile Paste (page 336)

Candied Walnuts (page 341) and Toasted Sesame Seeds (page 342)

Yakisoba

This Japanese noodle-shop classic is uniquely delicious and very simple to make at home. Its distinctive flavor comes from a generous splash of Worcestershire sauce. If you like, serve your yakisoba with its traditional accompaniments, sliced red pickled ginger called *beni shoga* and fine shreds of the crisp seaweed sheets called *ao nori*.

8 oz	dried chukka soba noodles or dried Chinese-style egg noodles (see Tips, right)	250 g
3 tbsp	Worcestershire sauce	45 mL
2 tbsp	soy sauce	25 mL
4 tsp	granulated sugar	20 mL
2 tsp	Asian sesame oil	10 mL
1 tsp	dark soy sauce, optional	5 mL
2 tbsp	vegetable oil	25 mL
1 tbsp	chopped garlic	15 mL
1 tbsp	chopped fresh gingerroot	15 mL
1/3 cup	chopped onion	75 mL
6 oz	boneless pork (such as loin or tenderloin), thinly sliced	175 g
1 tsp	salt or to taste	5 mL
1/4 tsp	freshly ground pepper	1 mL
1 1/4 cups	shredded cabbage or napa cabbage	300 mL
3/4 cup	shredded carrots	175 mL
3/4 cup	thinly sliced mushrooms	175 mL
2 tbsp	water	25 mL
1/4 cup	chopped green onions	50 mL

1. In a large pot of boiling salted water, cook noodles until just tender, about 4 minutes. Drain, rinse in cold water and drain again. Toss with 1 tsp (5 mL) of vegetable oil or sesame oil if you don't plan to use the noodles right away.

2. In a bowl, combine Worcestershire sauce, soy sauce, sugar, sesame oil and dark soy sauce, if using, and stir well. Set aside.

3. In a wok or large deep skillet, heat oil over medium-high heat. Add garlic and ginger toss well, until fragrant, about 15 seconds. Add onion and toss well.

4. Add pork, spreading into a single layer. Cook, undisturbed, until edges change color, about 30 seconds. Toss well and sprinkle salt and pepper over pork. Toss well. Cook, tossing often, until pork is no longer pink, about 1 minute more.

5. Add cabbage and toss well until it begins to wilt, about 30 seconds. Add carrots and mushrooms and toss well. Add water, pouring in around sides of pan. Cook, tossing often, until vegetables are brightened in color and tender-crisp and pork is cooked through, 1 to 2 minutes.

6. Add noodles to pan and toss well. Add Worcestershire sauce mixture, pouring in around sides of pan. Cook, tossing often, to season the noodles evenly, about 1 minute. Add green onions and toss well. Transfer to a serving platter. Serve hot or warm.

Variation: Although pork and cabbage are the typical stars in this recipe, you could use chicken, beef or tofu and bok choy or spinach instead with tasty results.

TIPS

This dish is typically made with chukka soba, a curly wheat noodle sold in dried form in rectangular shapes which soften to a tender texture with about 4 minutes of cooking. I find it in my supermarkets in 5 oz (150 g) packages, not quite enough for this recipe. So I buy two and measure out about 8 oz (250 g).

In the name "yakisoba" the word "soba" refers generally to noodles, not to the particular kind of noodle known in Japan as "soba." Made from buckwheat, soba noodles are too tender in their texture to be a good choice for stir-fry cooking. "Yaki" in this case means "cooked."

Mee Goreng

Serves 2 to 4

More of a type of noodle dish than a tightly conceived recipe, mee goreng is typically egg noodles tossed with cabbage and dark soy sauce and topped with crisp-fried shallots or onions. Serve with the traditional accompaniments of sliced cucumber along with sliced tomatoes if they are in season or a big fruit salad.

9 oz	fresh Chinese-style egg noodles (see Tip, page 283)	275 g
1 tbsp	soy sauce	15 mL
1 tbsp	dark soy sauce	15 mL
1 tbsp	molasses or honey	15 mL
1 tbsp	chicken stock	15 mL
1 tsp	salt or to taste	5 mL
2 tbsp	vegetable oil	25 mL
2 tbsp	chopped shallots or onion	25 mL
1 tbsp	chopped garlic	15 mL
2 tsp	chopped fresh hot chile pepper, optional	10 mL
4 oz	skinless boneless chicken breasts, cut into 1-inch (2.5 cm) pieces	125 g
4 oz	medium shrimp, peeled, deveined and chopped crosswise into 3 pieces	125 g
1½ cups	shredded cabbage or napa cabbage	375 mL
¼ cup	chopped green onions	50 mL
¼ cup	Crisp-Fried Shallots, optional (see recipe, page 343)	50 mL

1. In a large pot of boiling salted water, cook noodles until tender, 2 to 4 minutes. Drain, rinse in cold water and drain again. Toss with 1 tsp (5 mL) of vegetable oil or sesame oil if you don't plan to use the noodles right away.

2. In a small bowl, combine soy sauce, dark soy sauce, molasses, chicken stock and salt and stir well. Set aside.

3. Heat a wok or a large deep skillet over medium-high heat. Add oil and swirl to coat pan. Add shallots, garlic and chile pepper, if using, and toss well, until fragrant, about 15 seconds.

4. Add chicken and shrimp and toss well. Cook, tossing occasionally, until chicken is firm and no longer pink, about 1 minute.

5. Add cabbage and toss well. Cook, tossing often, until cabbage is softened, shrimp are pink and both shrimp and chicken are cooked through, 1 to 2 minutes. Add noodles and toss well.

6. Add soy sauce mixture, pouring in around sides of pan. Toss well. Add green onions and cook, tossing often, until noodles are evenly seasoned. Transfer to a serving platter and sprinkle Crisp-Fried Shallots over noodles, if using. Serve hot or warm.

> **Variations:** Variations to this recipe abound. You could simplify a little by skipping the shrimp and increasing the amount of chicken.
>
> Add an egg or two, either scrambling it into the wok when the noodles are almost done, or making delicate pancakes and cutting them into ribbons, to be tossed into the noodles just before serving.
>
> For a vegetarian version, omit chicken stock, chicken and shrimp and add crisp-fried tofu and crisp-fried chunks of potato and add a generous dollop of tomato ketchup to the soy sauce mixture.

Thai-Style Rice Noodles with Beef and Spinach

Serves 2 to 4

I use dried rice noodles in my version of *pad si-yu*, one of my favorite noodle dishes. The fresh rice noodles used in Thailand can be difficult to find but dried ones make a delicious alternative. First choice would be the dried rice noodles which are similar in shape to fettuccine. You can also use the slender ones which are standard for pad Thai. *Prik nahm som*, which means chile-vinegar sauce, is a simple, tangy condiment Thai people love to mix in just before eating *pad si-yu*. It makes a perfect accent to this dish.

8 oz	dried rice noodles, fettuccine-width	250 g
3 tbsp	fish sauce	45 mL
2 tbsp	dark soy sauce or soy sauce	25 mL
1 tbsp	molasses or dark brown sugar	15 mL
½ tsp	salt or to taste	2 mL
¼ tsp	freshly ground pepper	1 mL
3 tbsp	vegetable oil, divided	45 mL
1 tbsp	chopped garlic	15 mL
8 oz	lean boneless beef, thinly sliced crosswise into 2-inch (5 cm) long strips (see Tip, right)	250 g
5 cups	loosely packed fresh spinach leaves	1.25 L
¼ cup	chicken stock or water	50 mL
2	eggs, lightly beaten	2
	Thai-Style Chile-Vinegar Sauce (see recipe, page 295)	

1. Bring a large pot of water to a rolling boil over high heat. Add rice noodles and remove from heat. Stir gently to separate the noodles. Let stand for 5 to 7 minutes, stirring occasionally, until softened but still firm. Drain, rinse well in cold water. Drain and set aside.

2. In a small bowl, combine fish sauce, dark soy sauce, molasses, salt and pepper and set aside. Set a bowl next to the stove to hold beef and spinach during cooking.

3. Heat a wok or a large deep skillet over high heat. Add 2 tbsp (25 mL) of the oil and swirl to coat pan. Add garlic and toss well, until fragrant, about 15 seconds.

4. Add beef, spreading into a single layer. Cook, undisturbed, until edges change color, about 30 seconds. Toss well. Cook, tossing often, until no longer pink, about 1 minute more.

5. Add spinach and cook, tossing often, until beginning to wilt and beef is cooked through, about 1 minute more. Transfer spinach and beef to the reserved bowl.

6. Add noodles to pan and toss well. Cook, tossing often and pulling the noodles apart with tongs or spatulas to help them cook evenly, for 1 minute. Add chicken stock, pouring in around sides of pan and toss well. Cook, tossing often, until noodles are tender, about 1 minute more.

7. Push noodles to side of pan. Add remaining 1 tbsp (15 mL) of oil. Pour in eggs and when they are almost set, toss to scramble and mix them with noodles. Return beef and spinach to pan and toss well.

8. Add fish sauce mixture, pouring in around sides of pan. Toss well. Cook, tossing occasionally, until noodles are tender and evenly seasoned, about 1 minute more. Transfer to a serving platter. Place Thai-Style Chile-Vinegar Sauce on the platter or next to it.

> **Variation:** You could use small broccoli florets or Chinese broccoli, in place of spinach. Allow a little extra cooking time for the broccoli florets, adding a splash of water to the pan to help them cook without overcooking the dish. Chinese broccoli, known as *gai lan* in Cantonese and *pahk kah-nah* in Thai, is a delicious dark green leafy vegetable with chubby stalks, large sturdy leaves and tiny white flowers. Use a combination of leaves cut into 2-inch (5 cm) pieces, and stalks peeled and sliced crosswise on the diagonal into thin pieces (about ⅛ inch/0.25 cm). Blanch briefly in boiling water, 1 to 2 minutes, and drain well before using here. You could also add it uncooked and allow extra cooking time, with splashes of water until it's tender.

TIP

To make it easier to cut thin slices, place the meat in the freezer for up to 1 hour before you plan to cut it. Partially frozen, it will be easier to slice into thin strips. If you use flank steak, cut it lengthwise into strips about 2 inches (5 cm) wide. This will make crosswise slices just the right dimension for slicing.

Thai-Style Chile-Vinegar Sauce

Makes ½ cup (125 mL)

½ cup	white vinegar	125 mL
2 tsp	granulated sugar	10 mL
2 tsp	finely chopped fresh hot chiles	10 mL

1. In a small bowl, combine vinegar and sugar and stir well.
2. Stir in chiles. Serve at room temperature.

Vietnamese-Style Rice Noodles with Pork and Shrimp

Serves 2 to 4

This is my version of the Vietnamese noodle dish, *hu tieu xao*.

6 oz	dried rice noodles, fettuccine or linguine-width	175 g
2 tbsp	fish sauce	25 mL
2 tbsp	soy sauce	25 mL
2 tbsp	water	25 mL
1 tsp	salt or to taste	5 mL
½ tsp	granulated sugar	2 mL
½ tsp	freshly ground pepper	2 mL
2 tbsp	vegetable oil	25 mL
1 tbsp	chopped garlic	15 mL
1 tbsp	chopped shallots or onion	15 mL
4 oz	boneless pork (such as loin or tenderloin), thinly sliced	125 g
12	medium shrimp, peeled and deveined	12
2½ cups	fresh spinach leaves	625 mL
1 cup	bean sprouts or finely shredded napa cabbage	250 mL
¼ cup	chopped green onions	50 mL

1. Bring a large pot of water to a rolling boil over high heat. Add rice noodles and remove from heat. Let stand for 5 to 7 minutes, stirring occasionally, until noodles are softened but still firm. Drain, rinse well in cold water. Drain and set aside.

2. In a small bowl, combine fish sauce, soy sauce, water, salt, sugar and pepper and stir well. Set aside.

3. In a wok or large deep skillet, heat oil over high heat. Add garlic and shallots and toss well, until fragrant, about 15 seconds.

4. Add pork, spreading into a single layer. Cook, undisturbed, until edges change color, about 30 seconds. Toss well. Add shrimp and toss well. Cook, tossing often, until shrimp are pink and firm and pork is cooked through, 1 to 2 minutes.

5. Add noodles and cook, tossing often and pulling noodles apart with tongs or spatulas to help them cook evenly, for 1 minute.

6. Add fish sauce mixture, pouring in around sides of pan. Cook, tossing often, turning and scooping noodles to heat and soften them, until noodles curl up and are tender and shrimp are cooked through, 1 to 2 minutes more. Add an additional 1 to 2 tbsp (15 to 25 mL) of water as needed to keep noodles from sticking or burning.

7. Push the noodles to one side and add spinach and bean sprouts to center of pan. Scoop noodles over them and cook, undisturbed, until bean sprouts are tender-crisp, about 15 seconds. Add green onions and toss well. Transfer to a serving platter. Serve hot or warm.

Variation: You could use chicken or ham in place of pork and add 2 tsp (10 mL) chopped fresh hot chiles with the garlic if you like a bit of heat.

Thai-Style Rice Noodles with Chicken

Serves 2 to 4

This quick Thai noodle dish, *kwaytiow kua gai*, is usually served on a bed of cool, crisp lettuce. You can serve it with a simple seasoning sauce of chopped fresh hot green chiles stirred into a small bowl of white vinegar.

TIP

For the traditional pickled cabbage used in this dish, you could use either *Tien-sien* pickled vegetable, which comes in tiny cans, or *tang chai*, which often comes in sealed plastic packages. You could also use chopped kimchi, for a tangy note with a bonus of chile heat.

8 oz	dried rice noodles, fettuccine-width	250 g
2 tbsp	fish sauce	25 mL
1 tbsp	soy sauce	15 mL
1 tsp	dark soy sauce, optional	5 mL
1 tsp	granulated sugar	5 mL
½ tsp	salt or to taste	2 mL
4 cups	shredded lettuce or mixed greens	1 L
2 tbsp	vegetable oil	25 mL
1 tbsp	chopped garlic	15 mL
1 tsp	finely chopped pickled cabbage, optional (see Tip, left)	5 mL
8 oz	skinless boneless chicken breasts or thighs, thinly sliced	250 g
2	eggs, beaten	2
¼ cup	chopped green onions	50 mL
3 tbsp	chopped fresh cilantro	45 mL

1. Bring a large pot of water to a rolling boil over high heat. Add noodles and remove from heat. Let stand for 5 to 7 minutes, stirring occasionally, until softened but still firm. Drain, rinse well in cold water. Drain and set aside.

2. In a small bowl, combine fish sauce, soy sauce, dark soy sauce, if using, sugar and salt and stir well. Set aside. Line a serving platter with lettuce leaves. Set aside.

3. In a wok or large deep skillet, heat oil over high heat. Add garlic and pickled cabbage, if using, and toss well, until fragrant, about 15 seconds.

4. Add chicken, spreading into a single layer. Cook, undisturbed, until edges change color, about 30 seconds. Toss well. Cook, tossing often, until no longer pink, about 1 minute. Push chicken to one side and add eggs, swirling to spread into a layer. Cook, undisturbed, until most of egg has set. Toss well, breaking into soft lumps while moist.

5. Add noodles and toss well. Cook, tossing often and pulling the noodles out into a single layer, for 1 minute.

6. Add fish sauce mixture, pouring in around sides of pan. Cook, tossing often, turning and scooping noodles to heat and soften, until tender and chicken is cooked through, 1 to 2 minutes more. Add 1 to 2 tbsp (15 to 25 mL) water as needed to keep noodles from sticking or burning. Add green onions and cilantro and toss well.

Rice Noodles with Fragrant Pork

8 oz	dried rice noodles, fettuccine-width	250 g
2 tbsp	soy sauce	25 mL
2 tbsp	chicken stock	25 mL
1 tbsp	dry sherry or Shaoxing rice wine	15 mL
1 tsp	salt or to taste	5 mL
1 tsp	granulated sugar	5 mL
¼ tsp	freshly ground pepper	1 mL
2 tbsp	vegetable oil	25 mL
2 tbsp	chopped shallots or onion	25 mL
1 tbsp	chopped garlic	15 mL
6 oz	ground pork	175 g
1½ cups	bean sprouts	375 mL
¾ cup	chopped green onions	175 mL

Serves 2 to 4

Add strips of sweet bell pepper to this dish if you want a little extra coolness, or dice up some fresh hot green chiles if you want to fire things up, adding either one after the pork is cooked. I've used dried rice noodles here, but if you can find fresh, soft rice noodles, follow the instructions in the Variation, below.

1. Bring a large pot of water to a rolling boil over high heat. Add rice noodles and remove from heat. Let stand for 5 to 7 minutes, stirring occasionally, until noodles are softened but still firm. Drain, rinse well in cold water. Drain and set aside.

2. In a bowl, combine soy sauce, stock, sherry, salt, sugar and pepper and stir well. Set aside.

3. Heat a wok or a large deep skillet over medium-high heat. Add oil and swirl to coat pan. Add shallots and garlic and toss well, until fragrant, about 15 seconds.

4. Add pork and using a spatula or slotted spoon begin breaking up the meat into small chunks. Cook, tossing and chopping, until pork is chopped down to very small chunks and is cooked through, 1 to 2 minutes. Add noodles and toss well.

5. Add soy sauce mixture, pouring in around sides of pan. Cook, tossing often, until noodles are hot, tender and evenly seasoned, 1 to 2 minutes. Add bean sprouts and green onions and toss well. Transfer to a serving platter. Serve hot or warm.

Variation: If you have freshly made soft rice noodles, cut them into fat ribbons about ¾ inches (2 cm) wide and toss to loosen them up. Omit cooking in Step 1 and add directly to the pan after the pork is done.

Rice Noodles with Beef and Bok Choy in Tangy Gravy

In this Thai comfort food classic, *kwaytiow laht nah*, beef and Chinese greens are cooked in a tangy gravy and served over rice noodles. Keep a spoon handy so you can savor all the delicious sauce.

TIP

Brown bean sauce is a salty condiment made from fermented soybeans. Thai cooks prefer a thin, whole-bean sauce called *dao jiow*, which is light brown in color. Any salty brown bean sauce, available in a jar, will work here and you can also omit it and still have a tasty dish.

8 oz	dried rice noodles, fettuccine-width	250 g
1 cup	chicken stock	250 mL
1 tbsp	fish sauce	15 mL
1 tbsp	soy sauce	15 mL
1 tbsp	white or cider vinegar	15 mL
1 tbsp	granulated sugar	15 mL
1 tbsp	brown bean sauce, optional (see Tip, left)	15 mL
1 tsp	dark soy sauce, optional	5 mL
3 tbsp	water	45 mL
1 tbsp	cornstarch	15 mL
3 tbsp	vegetable oil, divided	45 mL
2 tbsp	chopped garlic	25 mL
8 oz	lean boneless beef, thinly sliced crosswise into 2-inch (5 cm) long strips (see Tip, page 295)	250 g
2 cups	chopped bok choy or broccoli florets	500 mL

1. Bring a large pot of water to a rolling boil over high heat. Add rice noodles and remove from heat. Let stand for 5 to 7 minutes, stirring occasionally, until noodles are softened but still firm. Drain, rinse well in cold water. Drain and set aside.

2. In a bowl, combine chicken stock, fish sauce, soy sauce, vinegar, sugar, brown bean sauce and dark soy sauce, if using, and stir well. Set aside. In a small bowl, combine water and cornstarch and stir well into a smooth sauce. Set aside.

3. Heat a wok or large deep skillet over medium-high heat. Add 1 tbsp (15 mL) of the oil and swirl to coat pan. Add rice noodles and toss well. Cook, tossing often, turning and scooping noodles to heat and soften them, until noodles are curly and tender, about 2 minutes. Add an additional 1 to 2 tbsp (15 to 25 mL) of water as needed to keep noodles from sticking or burning. Transfer to a serving platter and set aside.

4. Increase heat to high. Add remaining 2 tbsp (25 mL) of oil, swirling to coat pan. Add garlic and toss well, until fragrant, about 15 seconds.

5. Add beef, spreading into a single layer. Cook, undisturbed, until edges change color, about 30 seconds. Toss well.

6. Add bok choy and toss well. Cook, tossing often, until very bright green and beginning to wilt and beef is no longer pink, about 1 minute.

7. Add chicken stock mixture, pouring in around sides of pan. Cook, tossing often, until beef is cooked through and broccoli is tender-crisp, about 1 minute. Stir cornstarch mixture and add to pan. Cook, tossing often, until sauce thickens to a smooth gravy, about 1 minute more. Carefully pour over the cooked rice noodles on the serving platter. Serve hot or warm.

> **Variations:** You could use *gai lan* or Chinese broccoli in place of bok choy (see Variation, page 295).
>
> Instead of beef, make this with pork, chicken or tofu, if you prefer.

Pad Thai

Serves 2 to 4

This popular dish is Thailand's take on the traditional Chinese stir-fry of rice noodles. Its salty, sweet, sour and chile-hot flavors give it the intensity and complexity typical of Thai dishes. You'll find it in night markets, corner cafés and elegant Thai restaurants, always tailored to that cook's vision of Thailand's signature noodle dish.

TIPS

Many supermarkets now carry dried rice noodles which are about the same width as linguine. This traditional choice for pad Thai is also available at Asian markets and from mail order (see Sources, page 346).

If using garlic chives, chop them into 1-inch (2.5 cm) lengths. If using green onions, chop the white portion of the green onions well, but leave the green tips in 1-inch (2.5 cm) lengths.

4 oz	dried rice noodles (see Tips, left)	125 g
¼ cup	chicken stock or water	50 mL
3 tbsp	fish sauce	45 mL
2 tbsp	soy sauce	25 mL
2 tbsp	granulated sugar	25 mL
1 tsp	hot pepper flakes	5 mL
3 tbsp	vegetable oil, divided	45 mL
1 tbsp	chopped garlic	15 mL
4 oz	boneless pork (such as loin or tenderloin) or skinless chicken breast or thighs, thinly sliced	125 g
8 to 10	medium shrimp, peeled and deveined	8 to 10
1	egg, beaten	1
½ cup	chopped garlic chives or green onions (see Tips, left)	125 mL
2 cups	bean sprouts, divided	500 mL
⅓ cup	chopped roasted salted peanuts	75 mL
3 tbsp	freshly squeezed lime juice	45 mL
4	lime wedges	4

1. Bring a large pot of water to a rolling boil over high heat. Add noodles and remove from heat. Let stand for 5 to 7 minutes, stirring occasionally, until noodles are softened but still firm. Drain, rinse well in cold water. Drain and set aside.

2. In a small bowl, combine chicken stock, fish sauce, soy sauce, sugar and hot pepper flakes and stir well. Set aside.

3. Heat a wok or a large deep skillet over medium heat. Add 2 tbsp (25 mL) of the oil and swirl to coat pan. Add garlic and toss well, until fragrant, about 15 seconds.

4. Add pork, spreading into a single layer. Cook, undisturbed, until edges change color, about 1 minute. Toss well. Add shrimp and toss well. Cook, tossing often, until shrimp are pink and firm and pork is cooked through, 1 to 2 minutes. Add noodles and cook, tossing often and pulling to separate noodles, for 1 minute.

5. Add chicken stock mixture, pouring in around sides of pan. Cook, tossing often, turning and scooping noodles to heat and soften them, until noodles curl up and are tender and shrimp are cooked through, 1 to 2 minutes more. Add an additional 1 to 2 tbsp (15 to 25 mL) of chicken stock or water as needed to keep noodles from sticking or burning.

6. Push the noodles to one side and add remaining 1 tbsp (15 mL) of oil. Add egg and swirl to expose to hot pan. Cook, undisturbed, until edges have begun to set, about 15 seconds. Cook, stirring often, until egg is softly scrambled but still very moist, about 1 minute.

7. Add garlic chives and 1 cup (250 mL) of the bean sprouts and cook, tossing often, until they have begun to wilt, about 1 minute more. Add peanuts and lime juice and toss well. Transfer to a serving platter. Place the remaining bean sprouts and lime wedges on one side. Serve hot or warm, mixing in the raw bean sprouts and squeezing a little lime juice over the noodles just before eating.

> **Variations:** For a more traditional version, add 2 tbsp (25 mL) tamarind liquid (see page 339) to the chicken stock mixture.
>
> Replace pork and shrimp with ½ cup (125 mL) small chunks of crisp-fried firm tofu, ⅓ cup (75 mL) dried shrimp and ¼ cup (50 mL) finely chopped *chai po*, pickled daikon radish, tossing them all together in the hot oil until heated through, right after the garlic is fragrant and just before adding the noodles. You could also add these ingredients in addition to the shrimp and pork or chicken.

Singapore Curry Noodles with Shiitakes and Shrimp

Serves 2 to 4

I love this classic noodle dish, which is often served in Chinese restaurants specializing in the dumplings, noodles and other special treats known as dim sum. Chinese dishes using curry powder are given the name "Singapore," since that cosmopolitan place is where the spice mixture found a place on the Chinese pantry shelf.

TIP

The very thin rice noodles traditionally used in this dish are often available in supermarkets as well as Asian grocery stores; cooked angel hair pasta would also work in this recipe.

6 oz	very thin dried rice noodles (see Tip, left)	175 g
2/3 cup	chicken stock or water	150 mL
2 tbsp	curry powder	25 mL
1 tsp	salt or to taste	5 mL
4 oz	shiitake mushrooms	125 g
3 tbsp	vegetable oil, divided	45 mL
1 tbsp	chopped garlic	15 mL
8 oz	medium shrimp, peeled and deveined	250 g
1 cup	chopped onion	250 mL
1 1/4 cups	thinly sliced green bell peppers	300 mL

1. Bring a large pot of water to a rolling boil over high heat. Add noodles and remove from heat. Let stand for 5 to 7 minutes, stirring occasionally, until noodles are softened but still firm. Drain, rinse well in cold water. Drain and set aside.

2. In a small bowl, combine chicken stock, curry powder and salt and stir well. Set aside.

3. Remove stems from shiitake mushrooms and slice each cap into long, slender strips. Set a bowl next to the stove to hold the shrimp and vegetables as they are cooked.

4. Heat a wok or a large deep skillet over high heat. Add 2 tbsp (25 mL) of the oil and swirl to coat pan. Add garlic and toss well, until fragrant, about 15 seconds.

5. Add shrimp, spreading into a single layer. Cook, undisturbed, until edges turn pink, about 1 minute. Toss well. Cook, tossing often, until shrimp are pink, firm and cooked through, 1 to 2 minutes more. Transfer to the reserved bowl and set aside.

6. Add onion, green peppers and mushrooms and toss well. Cook, tossing often, until mixture is fragrant and softened, about 1 minute. Transfer to the bowl along with the shrimp.

7. Add remaining 1 tbsp (15 mL) of oil to the wok. Add noodles and toss once. Add chicken stock mixture, pouring in around sides of pan. Toss well. Return shrimp and vegetables to pan and cook, tossing often, until noodles are tender and evenly seasoned, 1 to 2 minutes more. Transfer to the serving platter, arranging a few shrimp, green peppers and shiitake mushrooms on top of the noodles. Serve hot or warm.

Rice Noodles with Spicy Chicken and Basil

6 oz	dried rice noodles, linguine-width	175 g
2 tbsp	fish sauce	25 mL
1 tbsp	soy sauce	15 mL
1 tsp	dark soy sauce, optional	5 mL
1 tsp	granulated sugar	5 mL
1 tsp	salt or to taste	5 mL
2 tbsp	vegetable oil	25 mL
2 tbsp	chopped shallots or onion	25 mL
1 tbsp	chopped garlic	15 mL
2 tsp	finely chopped fresh hot green chiles	10 mL
4 oz	ground chicken	125 g
½ cup	halved cherry tomatoes	125 mL
⅓ cup	coarsely chopped fresh basil leaves	75 mL
2 tbsp	chopped green onions	25 mL

Serves 2 to 4

Chicken makes this noodle dish hearty while tomatoes and basil brighten its flavor. To capture their best flavor and aroma, chop the basil leaves just before you begin to cook this dish.

1. Bring a large pot of water to a rolling boil over high heat. Add noodles and remove from heat. Let stand for 5 to 7 minutes, stirring occasionally, until softened but still firm. Drain, rinse well in cold water. Drain and set aside.

2. In a small bowl, combine fish sauce, soy sauce, dark soy sauce, if using, sugar and salt and stir well. Set aside.

3. In a wok or large deep skillet, heat oil over high heat. Add shallots, garlic and chiles and toss well, until fragrant, about 15 seconds.

4. Add chicken and using a spatula or slotted spoon, begin breaking up the meat into small chunks. Cook, tossing often, continuing to break up meat, until crumbly and cooked through, 1 to 2 minutes. Add noodles and cook, tossing often, for 30 seconds.

5. Add fish sauce mixture, pouring in around sides of pan. Cook, tossing often, turning and scooping noodles to heat and soften, until tender and evenly seasoned, 1 to 2 minutes more. Add an additional 1 to 2 tbsp (15 to 25 mL) of water as needed to keep noodles from sticking or burning.

6. Add cherry tomatoes, basil and green onions. Cook, tossing gently to heat them a little, for 15 seconds more. Transfer to a serving platter. Serve hot or warm.

Variation: You could use ground pork or ground beef, or thinly sliced chicken breast in place of the ground chicken.

Rice Noodles with Lettuce and Fragrant Beef Gravy

Serves 2 to 4

I loved ordering this dish for lunch in a small café in Bangkok, where it is called *kwaytiow neua sahp*. Shredded romaine works nicely as the base for this satisfying dish, as does a combination of lettuces.

6 oz	dried rice noodles, fettuccine or linguine-width	175 g
¾ cup	chicken stock	175 mL
2 tbsp	soy sauce	25 mL
2 tbsp	fish sauce	25 mL
1 tsp	curry powder	5 mL
1 tsp	granulated sugar	5 mL
½ tsp	salt or to taste	2 mL
3 tbsp	water	45 mL
2 tsp	cornstarch or all-purpose flour	10 mL
4 cups	mixed salad greens	1 L
3 tbsp	vegetable oil, divided	45 mL
1 tbsp	coarsely chopped garlic	15 mL
12 oz	ground beef	375 g
½ cup	halved cherry tomatoes	125 mL
2 tbsp	chopped green onions	25 mL
¼ cup	chopped fresh cilantro	50 mL

1. Bring a large saucepan of water to a rolling boil. Add noodles and remove from heat. Let the noodles steep 5 to 7 minutes, stirring occasionally, until softened but still firm. Drain, rinse in cold water and drain again. Set aside.

2. In a bowl, combine chicken stock, soy sauce, fish sauce, curry powder, sugar and salt and stir well. Set aside. In a small bowl, combine water and cornstarch and stir well. Set aside.

3. Line a serving platter with lettuce leaves. Set aside.

4. Heat a wok or a large deep skillet over medium-high heat. Add 1 tbsp (15 mL) of the vegetable oil and swirl to coat pan. Add rice noodles and toss well. Cook, pulling them out into a single layer and tossing often, until noodles curl up and are tender, 1 to 2 minutes. Add 1 to 2 tbsp (15 to 25 mL) of water if needed to keep noodles from sticking. Transfer to the serving platter, piling noodles over lettuce. Set aside.

5. Add remaining 2 tbsp (25 mL) of oil to pan and swirl to coat well. Add garlic and toss well, until fragrant, about 15 seconds.

6. Add ground beef and using a spatula, break up the meat into smaller chunks. Spread into a single layer. Cook, undisturbed, for 30 seconds. Toss well. Cook, tossing often, until no longer pink, about 1 minute.

7. Add chicken stock mixture, pouring in around sides of pan. Toss gently as the sauce comes to a boil. Stir cornstarch mixture and add to pan. Cook, tossing often, until sauce thickens and beef is cooked through, about 1 minute more. Add cherry tomatoes and green onions and toss well. Pour meat sauce over warm noodles on the serving platter and sprinkle with cilantro. Serve hot or warm.

Thai-Style Bean Thread Noodles with Shrimp and Pork

Serves 2 to 4

This is my version of *pad woon sen*, Thailand's delicious take on stir-fried bean thread noodles. Their texture is silky soft and deliver flavor wonderfully.

TIP

Tongs make this dish easier to manage, since you can quickly grab, mix and separate the noodles as they cook. Metal tongs in a v-shape are ideal, but any kind you can handle easily is a plus. A spatula or a large spoon, slotted or otherwise, also work just fine.

4 oz	dried bean thread noodles (see Tip, left and right)	125 g
¼ cup	chicken stock or vegetable stock	50 mL
2 tbsp	fish sauce	25 mL
2 tsp	soy sauce	10 mL
1 tsp	granulated sugar	5 mL
½ tsp	salt or to taste	2 mL
½ tsp	freshly ground pepper	2 mL
2 tbsp	vegetable oil	25 mL
2 tbsp	chopped shallots	25 mL
1 tbsp	chopped garlic	15 mL
4 oz	ground pork	125 g
10	medium shrimp, peeled and deveined, each chopped into 4 pieces	10
¾ cup	thinly sliced mushrooms	175 mL
½ cup	chopped zucchini (½-inch/1 cm chunks)	125 mL
3 tbsp	chopped green onions	45 mL
2 tbsp	coarsely chopped fresh cilantro	25 mL

1. Place bean thread noodles in a bowl and add warm water to cover. Let stand for 10 minutes until they soften into flexible strands. Drain well and place on your cutting board. Shape them loosely into a long pile and cut crosswise into 3-inch (7.5 cm) lengths. Transfer to a bowl and set aside.

2. In a small bowl, combine chicken stock, fish sauce, soy sauce, sugar, salt and pepper and stir well. Set aside.

3. Heat a wok or a large deep skillet over medium-high heat. Add oil and swirl to coat pan. Add shallots and garlic and toss well, until fragrant, about 15 seconds.

4. Add pork and using a spatula or slotted spoon begin breaking up the meat into small chunks. Cook, tossing often, continuing to break up meat until crumbly, for 1 minute.

5. Add shrimp, mushrooms and zucchini and toss well. Cook, tossing often, until mushrooms and zucchini have softened, pork is no longer pink, shrimp are pink and firm and both are cooked through, 1 to 2 minutes.

6. Add chicken stock mixture, pouring in around sides of pan and toss well. Add noodles and cook, tossing often, until they have absorbed the sauce and are clear, curly, tender and evenly seasoned, 1 to 2 minutes. Add green onions and cilantro and toss well. Transfer to a serving platter. Serve hot or warm.

TIP

Enjoyed throughout Asia and widely available in the West, bean thread noodles are available only in dried form, most commonly formed into rounded rectangular skeins. Asian markets often carry sacks of 2-oz (60 g) skeins, as well as packages with one giant skein of around 8 oz (250 g). Many supermarkets carry them, in packages of 3.5 oz (100 g) or 7.5 oz (213 g). They may be labeled "*sai fun*" or "*harusame*" and are also called "glass noodles" and "cellophane noodles," because they become clear when cooked. They are made from mung beans and keep indefinitely on your pantry shelf.

Korean-Style Noodles with Sesame-Scented Beef

Serves 2 to 4

With its mix of delicate bean thread noodles and sesame-ginger beef, this Korean-style noodle dish is a year-round treat. My version of *chapchae* makes an appealing accompaniment to grilled salmon and a green salad tossed with avocado and cherry tomatoes.

4 oz	dried bean thread noodles (see Tips, pages 308 and 309)	125 g
6	dried shiitake mushrooms	6
2 tbsp	soy sauce	25 mL
¼ cup	chopped green onions, divided	50 mL
2 tsp	chopped garlic	10 mL
2 tsp	granulated sugar	10 mL
2 tsp	Asian sesame oil	10 mL
½ tsp	salt or to taste	2 mL
¼ tsp	freshly ground pepper	1 mL
4 oz	lean boneless beef, thinly sliced crosswise into 2-inch (5 cm) long strips (see Tip, page 295)	125 g
1 tbsp	sesame seeds	15 mL
3 tbsp	vegetable oil, divided	45 mL
1	egg, beaten	1
¾ cup	shredded cabbage	175 mL
¾ cup	shredded carrots	175 mL
¾ cup	bean sprouts	175 mL
1½ cups	loosely packed spinach leaves	375 mL
⅓ cup	chicken stock	75 mL

1. Place bean thread noodles in a bowl and add warm water to cover. In another bowl, place dried shiitake mushrooms and cover with warm water. Let each stand for 10 minutes until softened enough to be sliced into strips (see Step 5).

2. In a bowl, combine soy sauce, 1 tbsp (15 mL) of the green onions, garlic, sugar, sesame oil, salt and pepper and stir well. Add beef and stir to mix evenly with sauce. Set aside for 10 minutes.

3. Meanwhile, heat a wok or a large deep skillet over medium heat. Add sesame seeds and cook, stirring to toast them evenly and keep from burning, until light brown and fragrant, 3 to 5 minutes. Transfer to a plate and set aside to cool.

4. Add 1 tbsp (15 mL) of the oil to pan and swirl to coat. Add egg and swirl to spread into a thin pancake. Cook, undisturbed, until set but not dry and turn out onto a small plate to cool. Roll into a cylinder and slice it crosswise into thin ribbons. Set aside.

5. When the noodles are softened and flexible, drain them well. Place them on a cutting board and shape them into a long rectangle, parallel to the countertop. Chop the noodles crosswise into 3-inch (7.5 cm) lengths and fluff them with your fingers to loosen the strands before cooking. Set aside. Trim stems from soaked shiitakes and slice caps into long thin strips.

6. Heat a wok or a large deep skillet over medium-high heat. Add remaining 2 tbsp (25 mL) of oil and swirl to coat pan. Add beef mixture and spread into a single layer. Cook, undisturbed, for 15 seconds. Toss well. Cook, tossing often, until no longer pink, about 1 minute.

7. Add mushrooms, cabbage and carrots and toss well. Cook, tossing often, until vegetables are softened and beef is cooked through, 1 to 2 minutes. Add noodles, egg ribbons, bean sprouts and spinach leaves and toss well.

8. Add chicken stock, pouring in around sides of pan. Cook, tossing often, until noodles are clear and softened, and have absorbed most of the chicken stock, about 2 minutes. Transfer to a serving platter and sprinkle with remaining green onions and toasted sesame seeds. Serve hot or warm.

Vietnamese-Style Bean Thread Noodles with Crab

Delicate bean thread noodles make a fine stage on which to present sweet and savory chunks of crabmeat. Based on a classic Vietnamese dish called *mien xao cua*, this recipe makes an inviting tangle of peppery noodles studded with cilantro and fresh shiitake mushrooms. Dungeness crab is divine, with its rich flavor and gorgeous color, but any kind of fresh crabmeat works wonderfully and canned lump crabmeat makes a delicious dish.

TIP

In order to handle the noodles easily both in cooking and in eating, I cut the softened, drained bean thread noodles into short lengths before cooking them. I pile them onto the cutting board in something resembling a log, (a horizontal one, running parallel to the countertop) and cut through the mass of noodles crosswise at 3-inch (7.5 cm) lengths. You can leave them intact, or cut them into longer strands than mine.

4 oz	dried bean thread noodles (see Tips, pages 308 and 309)	125 g
¼ cup	chicken stock or vegetable stock	50 mL
¼ cup	water	50 mL
2 tbsp	fish sauce	25 mL
2 tsp	soy sauce	10 mL
¾ tsp	freshly ground pepper	4 mL
2 oz	fresh shiitake mushrooms	60 g
2 tbsp	vegetable oil	25 mL
2 tbsp	chopped shallots	25 mL
1 tbsp	chopped garlic	15 mL
8 oz	cooked lump crabmeat	250 g
2 tbsp	chopped green onions	25 mL
2 tbsp	coarsely chopped fresh cilantro	25 mL

1. Place bean thread noodles in a bowl and cover with warm water. Let stand for 10 minutes, until they soften into flexible strands. Drain well and place on cutting board. Shape noodles loosely into a long pile and cut crosswise into 3-inch (7.5 cm) lengths. Transfer to a bowl and set aside.

2. In a small bowl, combine chicken stock and water and stir well. Set aside. In another small bowl, combine fish sauce, soy sauce and pepper and stir well. Set aside.

3. Remove stems from shiitake mushrooms. Slice caps into thin strips, about ⅛ inch (0.25 cm) wide. Set aside.

4. Heat a wok or a large deep skillet over medium-high heat. Add oil and swirl to coat pan. Add shallots and garlic and toss well, until fragrant, about 15 seconds. Add mushrooms and cook, tossing often, until darkened in color, shiny and softened, about 30 seconds. Add noodles and cook, tossing often, for 30 seconds.

5. Add chicken stock mixture, pouring in around sides of pan. Cook, tossing occasionally, until noodles have absorbed the sauce and are clear, curly, tender and evenly seasoned, 2 to 3 minutes. There will be lots of liquid at first, but the noodles will absorb it as they cook.

6. Add fish sauce mixture and quickly toss well to season the noodles evenly. Add crabmeat and green onions and toss well, quickly mixing them into the tangle of noodles. Add cilantro and toss well. Transfer to a serving platter. Serve hot or warm.

Rice, Grains & Other Sides

Simply Jasmine

Serves 4

This naturally aromatic rice grows in Thailand's lush central plains. Its delicate, nutty aroma will perfume your kitchen.

- 2- to 3-quart (2 to 3 L) saucepan with tight-fitting lid

1 1/2 cups	jasmine rice	375 mL
2 cups	water	500 mL

1. Place rice in a saucepan and add water to cover by about 3 inches (7.5 cm). Stir and swirl with your fingers a few times. Carefully pour out most of the water.

2. Add 2 cups (500 mL) water to the pan and over medium heat bring to a gentle boil. Continue cooking until rice begins to look dry, about 5 minutes.

3. Stir well and then cover the pan with tight-fitting lid. Reduce heat to low and cook for 15 minutes more. Remove from heat and let stand, covered, for 10 minutes. Uncover and stir gently to fluff rice. Serve hot or warm.

Japanese-Style Rice

Serves 4 to 6

Many supermarkets carry short- or medium-grain rice, the types of rice favored in Japan and Korea. These plump-grained varieties of rice cook into moist, tender grains, easily scooped up with chopsticks from a rice bowl. One rule for this type of rice: The lid stays on until the rice is done — no peeking!

- 2- to 3-quart (2 to 3 L) saucepan with tight-fitting lid

2 1/2 cups	short- or medium-grain rice	625 mL
2 3/4 cups	water	675 mL

1. Place rice in a saucepan and add water to cover by about 3 inches (7.5 cm). Stir rice with your hand to rinse thoroughly. Carefully pour out most of the water. Repeat this process twice, until the rinsing water is fairly clear. Drain rice very well.

2. Add 2 3/4 cups (675 mL) water to the pan and cover it with tight-fitting lid. Place rice over high heat and bring to a rolling boil without removing the lid, about 5 minutes. (Pay attention to the bubbling sounds and tiny bursts of steam emerging from the pot as it comes to a full boil.)

3. Without removing the lid, reduce heat to low and let rice cook for 10 minutes more. Remove from heat and let stand, covered, for 10 minutes. Uncover and stir gently to fluff rice. Serve hot or warm.

Basmati Rice

- 2- to 3-quart (2 to 3 L) saucepan with tight-fitting lid

1 cup	basmati rice	250 mL
2 cups	water	500 mL
½ tsp	salt	2 mL

1. Place rice in a bowl and add cold water to cover by about 3 inches (7.5 cm). Stir rice with your hand to rinse thoroughly and then drain well.

2. In a saucepan over high heat, bring 2 cups (500 mL) water to a rolling boil. Add rice and salt and stir well. When the pot returns to a boil, cover with tight-fitting lid.

3. Reduce heat to low and cook, undisturbed, for 20 minutes. Remove from heat and let stand, covered, for 5 minutes. Uncover and stir gently to fluff rice. Serve hot or warm.

Serves 4

Fine, long grains of basmati rice make any stir-fried dish an elegant little feast. Grown in the foothills of the Himalayas, basmati rice is prized in kitchens throughout India and the Middle East. Look for it in Asian markets, health food stores, well-stocked supermarkets and via mail order (see Sources, page 346).

Parboiled Rice

- 2- to 3-quart (2 to 3 L) saucepan with tight-fitting lid

3⅓ cups	water	825 mL
1½ cups	parboiled rice (see Tip, right)	375 mL
2 tsp	butter or olive oil, optional	10 mL
1 tsp	salt	5 mL

1. In a saucepan over medium-high heat, bring water to a rolling boil. Add rice, butter, if using, and salt. Stir well.

2. Cover pan with tight-fitting lid. Reduce heat to medium-low and cook, undisturbed, for 20 minutes.

3. Remove from heat and let stand, covered, for 5 minutes. Uncover and stir gently to fluff rice. Serve hot or warm.

Serves 4 to 6

This form of long-grain rice is steam-cooked while still in the husk, increasing its nutritional value and allowing it to cook into firm, distinct grains.

TIP

Parboiled rice has an ivory color which distinguishes it from raw long-grain rice. A popular brand uses the term "Converted" to identify its parboiled rice. This type of rice will work interchangeably in this recipe.

Brown Rice

Serves 4

A nutty flavor, robust texture and wholesome benefits make brown rice worth the extra bit of cooking time it requires.

● **2- to 3-quart (2 to 3 L) saucepan with tight-fitting lid**

2¼ cups	water	550 mL
1 cup	long-grain brown rice	250 mL
2 tsp	butter or olive oil	10 mL
½ tsp	salt	2 mL

1. In a saucepan, combine water, brown rice, butter and salt and stir well. Place over medium-high heat and bring to a rolling boil.
2. Stir well. Reduce heat to maintain a gentle but visible simmer. Cover and cook, until rice is tender and cooked through, 30 to 40 minutes. Uncover and stir gently to fluff rice. Serve hot or warm.

White Rice

Serves 4

This recipe makes 4 cups (1 L) and is exactly the amount of cooked rice you will need for the recipes in the Fried Rice chapter.

TIP

Cooked rice should be refrigerated for no more than 2 days. You can also freeze for up to 1 month. To reheat for recipes other than Fried Rice, steam gently or heat in a microwave oven for 2 to 4 minutes, stopping every minute to stir well and encourage it to heat evenly.

● **2- to 3-quart (2 to 3 L) saucepan with tight-fitting lid**

1½ cups	long-grain white rice, such as jasmine	375 mL
2 cups	water	500 mL

1. Place rice in a saucepan and add water to cover by about 3 inches (7.5 cm). Stir and swirl with your fingers a few times, and then drain. Repeat this rinsing and draining two more times.
2. Add 2 cups (500 mL) water to the pan and place over medium heat. Stir well and then let it come to a boil, 7 to 10 minutes. Stir well and cook until the grains of rice look dry and the water level has dropped just below the surface of the rice, 3 to 5 minutes more.
3. Stir well and then cover the pan with a tight-fitting lid. Reduce heat to low and cook undisturbed until the rice is tender and cooked through, for 15 minutes more. Remove from heat, still covered, and set aside for 10 minutes. Remove the lid, stir gently to fluff up rice. Serve hot or warm.
4. For Fried Rice, bring cooked rice to room temperature first. Spread into a thin layer on a baking sheet. Let cool slightly (the steaming should have subsided), transfer to the refrigerator until cold to the touch.

Simple Sesame-Ginger Rice

4 cups	cooked rice, chilled (see Tip, right and page 316)	1 L
2 tbsp	vegetable oil	25 mL
1 tbsp	finely chopped fresh gingerroot	15 mL
1 tbsp	chopped garlic	15 mL
1/3 cup	chopped onion	75 mL
1 tsp	salt or to taste	5 mL
1/2 tsp	granulated sugar	2 mL
1/2 cup	very thinly sliced green onions	125 mL
2 tsp	Asian sesame oil	10 mL

1. Transfer cooked rice to a large bowl or turn it out onto a baking sheet. Using your hands or the back of a large spoon, gently break up clumps and work the rice into separate grains, so that it will heat up quickly and accept seasonings well.

2. Heat a wok or a large heavy skillet over high heat. Add vegetable oil and swirl to coat pan. Add ginger and garlic and toss well. Add onion and cook, tossing occasionally, until mixture is softened and fragrant, about 1 minute.

3. Add rice, gently breaking up any large clumps to help it cook evenly. Toss well and let cook, undisturbed, for 1 minute. Add salt and sugar and cook, tossing occasionally, until rice is tender and heated through, 2 to 3 minutes.

4. Add green onions and sesame oil and toss to mix well. Transfer to a serving plate. Serve hot or warm.

Serves 4

Since this rice dish uses cooked rice, which has been made in advance and chilled, it makes a good choice when you want a special accompaniment to stir-fried dishes without a lot of preparation time.

TIP

To store cooked rice, place in a shallow container and let cool slightly (the steaming should have subsided) and then refrigerate for no more than 2 days.

Indonesian-Style Yellow Rice Pilaf

This traditional rice dish, known in Indonesia as *nasi kuning*, provides a lovely and delicious centerpiece for a stir-fry meal. Its flavor and color are unique, but it is quite simple to make. If you don't have fresh lemongrass, add 1 tsp (5 mL) grated lime or lemon zest.

TIPS

To prepare lemongrass, trim the end to make a smooth base, and trim tops, leaving a 6-inch (15 cm) stalk. Quarter it lengthwise.

A 2-quart (2 L) or 3-quart (3 L) saucepan with a tight-fitting lid is perfect for cooking rice. The rice needs plenty of room since it triples in volume in the course of cooking. If your pan is too small, rice will probably boil over. The tight-fitting lid captures the steam, cooking the rice to tender perfection after its initial boiling stage.

- 2- to 3-quart (2 to 3 L) saucepan with tight-fitting lid

1 cup	long-grain parboiled white rice	250 mL
¾ cup	unsweetened coconut milk	175 mL
¾ cup	water or chicken stock	175 mL
3	slices fresh gingerroot	3
½ tsp	salt or to taste	2 mL
½ tsp	ground turmeric or curry powder	2 mL
1	stalk fresh lemongrass, trimmed and quartered, optional (see Tips, left)	1

1. Place rice in a saucepan and add water to cover by about 3 inches (7.5 cm). Stir rice with your hand to rinse thoroughly and then drain well.

2. Add coconut milk, water, ginger, salt and turmeric. Stir well. Add lemongrass pieces to pan. Bring rice mixture to a rolling boil over high heat, stirring well. Reduce heat to maintain a gentle boil and cook, covered, for 20 minutes. Remove from heat and let stand, covered, for 10 minutes.

3. Uncover and stir gently to fluff rice. Discard ginger and lemongrass. Serve hot or warm.

Sticky Rice

- Steamer or wok, fitted with bamboo steaming trays (see Tips, right)

| 2 cups | long-grain sticky rice | 500 mL |
| | Water for soaking and steaming rice | |

1. Place sticky rice in a bowl and add water to cover by about 2 inches (5 cm). Set aside to soak for 3 hours or for up to 12 hours.

2. Prepare a steaming vessel, such as a wok fitted with bamboo steaming trays, a traditional Thai or Laotian-style steaming basket and pot, or a vegetable-steaming device (see Tips, right). Fill wok or the base of your steamer with about 4 inches (10 cm) water and bring to a rolling boil over medium-high heat.

3. Meanwhile, prepare a steaming basket. If you are using Asian-style bamboo steaming trays, line the tray with cheesecloth, with a kitchen towel (not terrycloth) or with lettuce leaves, to prevent the rice grains from falling through the large openings in the trays. Drain the soaked rice well and then spread it out on the tray in an even layer.

4. When water comes to a boil, position the steaming basket over steaming water and place bamboo cover or a folded kitchen towel over rice. Reduce heat to maintain a lively flow of steam and cook, until rice softens to a pleasing chewy texture, 25 to 30 minutes. Test by scooping out a spoonful and rolling into a bite-size ball.

5. Turn rice out onto a baking sheet or a platter and quickly, using two dampened spoons spread it into an even layer. Allow rice to rest, releasing some steam, about 5 minutes. Then gather sticky rice into a large ball and place it on a small serving platter or in a sticky rice serving basket. Serve hot, warm or at room temperature.

Serves 4 to 6

This variety of long-grain rice grows in Laos and Northern Thailand, and is the everyday companion to family meals. It soaks in water for 3 hours to soften the grains, then it's steamed into plump, tender, chewy grains which stick together naturally. Sticky rice is easily rolled up into bite-size lumps, perfect for eating out of hand.

TIPS

You could use any kind of steaming device here as long as it suspends the soaked rice over steaming water during the cooking. If the steaming device has holes or perforations large enough for grains of rice to fall through, line it with cheesecloth, a kitchen towel or leaves of lettuce.

Look for long-grain sticky rice in Asian markets or via mail order (see Sources, page 346).

A traditional Thai or Laotian-style steaming basket and pot is available in Asian stores (see Sources, page 346).

Wild Rice

Serves 4

This gorgeous grain makes a delicious companion to stir-fried dishes. Technically not a rice but the seed of an aquatic grass, wild rice needs a longer cooking time than most varieties of rice, but I think it's worth the wait. My family loves it mixed with brown or white rice after cooking, as well as plain.

- 2- to 3-quart (2 to 3 L) saucepan with tight-fitting lid

4½ cups	water	1.125 L
1½ cups	wild rice	375 mL
1 tsp	salt	5 mL

1. In a saucepan over medium-high heat, combine water, wild rice and salt. Bring to a rolling boil and stir well.
2. Reduce heat to maintain a gentle boil, cover pan and cook, until rice is plump, cracked open and tender, about 45 minutes. Remove from heat and let stand, covered, for 10 minutes. Uncover and stir well. Serve hot or warm.

> **Variation:** You could add butter or olive oil to the rice after removing it from the stove. Or stir in finely chopped fresh herbs, such as cilantro or Italian parsley.

Fragrant Orzo with Tiny Peas

Serves 4

A serving of this tiny pasta looks like gigantic grains of rice and is most inviting on a plate.

1 cup	orzo pasta	250 mL
1 tbsp	vegetable oil	15 mL
2 tsp	chopped garlic	10 mL
½ tsp	salt or to taste	2 mL
¾ cup	frozen tiny peas (see Tip, page 232)	175 mL
2 tbsp	chopped green onions	25 mL

1. In a saucepan of boiling water, cook pasta until tender but firm, 7 to 9 minutes.
2. Meanwhile, heat a small skillet over medium-high heat. Add oil and swirl to coat pan. Add garlic and salt and cook, stirring once or twice, until garlic is fragrant, about 15 seconds. Add peas and cook, until peas are hot, about 2 minutes. Add green onions and toss well. Remove from heat and set aside.
3. When orzo is ready, drain well and return to saucepan. Add garlic and pea mixture and toss well. Serve hot or warm.

Couscous with Cilantro, Tomatoes and Peas

2¾ cups	water	675 mL
1¾ cups	quick-cooking couscous	425 mL
1 cup	frozen tiny peas	250 mL
1 tsp	salt or to taste	5 mL
2 tbsp	vegetable oil	25 mL
¾ cup	chopped onion	175 mL
1 tbsp	chopped garlic	15 mL
¾ cup	coarsely chopped plum (Roma) tomatoes (see Tip, right)	175 mL
¼ cup	chopped fresh cilantro	50 mL

1. In a saucepan over high heat, bring water to a rolling boil. Stir in couscous, peas and salt. Cover pan and remove from heat. Set aside for 5 minutes.

2. Meanwhile, heat oil in a skillet over medium-high heat. Add onion and garlic, and cook, stirring once, until garlic is fragrant and onions are softened, about 1 minute. Add tomatoes, stirring well, and cook for 1 minute. Remove from heat.

3. Uncover couscous and using a wooden spoon or a fork stir gently and fluff into a soft, grainy mixture. Add tomato mixture and stir well. Add cilantro, stirring well. Serve hot or warm.

Serves 4

A tiny form of pasta with roots in the Middle East, couscous cooks quickly and makes a satisfying companion to stir-fried dishes. In its quick-cooking form, couscous can be on your table in about 5 minutes time.

TIP

To prepare the tomatoes, cut off stem end, quarter tomatoes lengthwise and chop crosswise into small chunks, discarding any seeds or liquid left after chopping.

Bean Thread Noodles with Cilantro and Green Onions

Serves 4

This noodle with many names makes a wonderful accompaniment to almost any stir-fried dish. Also known as cellophane noodles, glass noodles, silver noodles and *sai fun*, they come in white, brittle little skeins. A little cooking time transforms them into clear, springy, chewy and curly noodles, which are easy to season and a pleasure to eat. You will need about 3½ cups (875 mL) of cooked noodles for this recipe.

TIP

Long-handled tongs made of lightweight metal are ideal for tossing noodles while they cook as well as while they are being seasoned.

3½ oz	bean thread noodles	100 g
1 tbsp	soy sauce	15 mL
1 tsp	Asian sesame oil	5 mL
1 tsp	granulated sugar	5 mL
1 tsp	salt or to taste	5 mL
2 tbsp	chopped fresh cilantro or mint	25 mL
2 tbsp	finely chopped green onion	25 mL

1. In a saucepan of boiling water, cook noodles for 2 minutes, stirring and pulling the noodles occasionally to separate and allow them to cook evenly. (Using metal tongs or two forks will make this process easier, see Tip, left.) Remove from heat and let stand about 3 minutes more, gently lifting, poking and pulling the noodles to separate them into strands.

2. When noodles are clear, soft, curly and chewy, drain well and rinse in cold water. Drain again. Transfer noodles to cutting board and arrange in a large rectangle. Cut through noodles crosswise in three places to shorten the strands to a more manageable length (or leave them whole if you like).

3. In a large bowl, combine soy sauce, sesame oil, sugar and salt and stir well. Add noodles and toss well to season evenly. Add cilantro and green onions and toss well. Serve at room temperature.

Noodles with Green Onions and Sesame Oil

8 oz	thin Asian noodles or pasta, such as spaghettini or angel hair pasta (see Tips, right)	250 g
1/3 cup	thinly sliced green onions	75 mL
2 tbsp	Asian sesame oil	25 mL
1/2 tsp	salt	2 mL

1. In a large pot of boiling salted water, cook noodles, stirring occasionally, until tender but firm, 6 to 8 minutes or according to package directions. Stir to separate noodles as they begin to soften. Drain well. Add cold water to cover the cooked noodles, and drain again.

2. Return cooked noodles to the pot. Add green onions, sesame oil and salt and toss well. Serve hot, warm or at room temperature.

Variation: For a heartier noodle dish, add thin strips of ham, shreds of roast chicken or cooked shrimp, tossing to mix them in well.

Serves 4

Serve these noodles instead of rice with any stir-fried dish. They can be made in advance and served at room temperature.

TIPS

If you are using fresh Asian-style egg noodles, they may cook more quickly than dry pasta. Begin checking them early so that they don't overcook.

If you've prepared these noodles in advance, cover and refrigerate for up to 1 day. Then allow the noodles to return to room temperature before serving, or warm them gently in the microwave or oven.

Egg Noodles with Shredded Cabbage, Parsley and Pepper

Serves 4

This simple, hearty dish nicely anchors colorful, bright-flavored dishes such as Seared Shrimp with Sweet Tiny Peas or Chicken with Sweet and Hot Peppers (see recipes, pages 123 and 31).

8 oz	egg noodles	250 g
2 tbsp	vegetable oil	25 mL
¾ cup	thinly sliced onion	175 mL
4 cups	finely shredded cabbage	1 L
1 tsp	salt or to taste	5 mL
½ tsp	freshly ground pepper	2 mL
¼ cup	chopped fresh Italian parsley or cilantro	50 mL

1. In a large pot of boiling salted water, cook egg noodles, until tender but firm, 7 to 9 minutes. Drain well and return to pot. Cover and set aside.

2. Heat a large, deep skillet over medium-high heat. Add oil and swirl to coat pan. Add onion and cook, tossing well, about 1 minute.

3. Add cabbage shreds and cook, tossing occasionally, until tender but not soft, 3 to 4 minutes. Add salt and pepper and toss well.

4. Add noodles and toss gently, turning and scooping to combine evenly with cabbage. Add 1 to 2 tbsp (15 to 25 mL) water if needed to soften noodles and mix well. Add parsley and toss well. Transfer to a serving plate. Serve hot or warm.

Cantonese-Style Crispy Noodle Pancake

8 oz	fresh thin Chinese-style egg noodles	250 g
5 to	vegetable oil, divided	75 to
6 tbsp		90 mL

1. In a large pot of boiling water, cook noodles until tender but firm, 1 to 2 minutes. (Noodles cook quickly so have a colander ready in the sink and drain them as soon as they are done.)

2. Rinse drained noodles well with cold water, then shake off as much water as possible. Transfer drained, cooked noodles to a tray or a shallow baking pan and spread into a thin layer. Let dry at room temperature for about 1 hour.

3. To cook the noodle pancake, heat a large skillet over medium-high heat. Add 3 tbsp (45 mL) of the oil and swirl to coat the pan well on the bottom and sides.

4. When oil is hot, add noodles, spreading into an even layer over surface of pan. Press down with spatula, and cook, until golden brown and crisp on the bottom, 6 to 8 minutes.

5. Carefully flip pancake over to cook other side. Add 2 tbsp (25 mL) of oil around sides of pan, and press pancake down with spatula. Cook, until golden and crispy, 4 to 6 minutes. Add remaining oil if needed to keep the noodle cake from sticking to pan.

6. Transfer to a serving plate. Serve hot or warm. Use as the base for a stir-fried dish or as a noodle dish to be divided at the table and enjoyed with other dishes (see Tip, right).

Variation: You could make four small pancakes to serve on individual plates. Use a small skillet and divide the noodles and oil into four portions, keeping the cooked pancakes warm on a platter in a 250°F (120°C) oven while you finish cooking the remaining noodles.

Serves 4

This classic stir-fry accompaniment is known as "two-sides brown," since it consists of cooked thin egg noodles pressed into a hot wok or skillet, quickly sautéed on each side, and then turned out onto a platter as a base for a hot stir-fried dish. Allow a little extra time for this dish, since the noodles need an hour to dry after they are boiled and before they are cooked into a crispy, delicious pancake.

TIP

Ideally, you would serve this noodle pancake hot with a just-cooked stir-fry ladled over top right before serving. If this is hard to manage, prepare for both dishes, making the pancake first. Transfer pancake to a serving platter and place in a 250°F (120°C) oven to keep warm while you quickly cook your stir-fried dish.

Dried Rice Noodles

Serves 4

Dried rice noodles are a pantry staple in my kitchen. They keep well and cook fast, and I love to use them instead of rice, as a companion to a stir-fried dish. You can use any size of dried rice noodles including linguine-size (the standard for pad Thai) or fettucine-size or very thin vermicelli-size.

TIP

Divide a 1-lb (500 g) package of dried rice noodles by cutting open the top and gently sliding the skein of noodles out onto your cutting board. Gently pull them apart into two portions. Some will break as you do this and there will be broken pieces in the package already; this is normal. Set aside half for this recipe and place the remaining 8 oz (250 g) in a resealable plastic bag.

8 oz	dried rice noodles (see Tip, left)	250 g
2 tbsp	vegetable oil	25 mL
3 tbsp	thinly sliced green onions	45 mL
2 tbsp	chopped garlic	25 mL
2 tsp	soy sauce	10 mL
1/2 tsp	salt	2 mL

1. In a saucepan of boiling water, place noodles, gently submerging completely in water. Immediately remove from heat. Set aside for 10 minutes, stir and pull the noodles occasionally to separate and allow them to cook evenly, until noodles are tender. (Using metal tongs or two forks will make this process easier.)

2. Meanwhile, heat a small skillet over medium-high heat. Add oil and swirl to coat pan. Add green onions and garlic and toss well. Cook, tossing often, until garlic is fragrant and onions are softened, about 2 minutes.

3. Drain noodles well and return to saucepan. Add green onion mixture (including oil), soy sauce and salt. Toss well to season noodles evenly. Serve hot or warm.

Variation: For a simple noodle side dish, rinse noodles well with cold water, drain well, and then toss with 2 tsp (10 mL) Asian sesame oil.

Soba Noodles with Green Onions and Sesame Oil

8 oz	soba noodles	250 g
2 tbsp	soy sauce	25 mL
1 tbsp	seasoned rice vinegar or other vinegar	15 mL
2 tsp	Asian sesame oil	10 mL
½ tsp	granulated sugar	2 mL
½ tsp	salt or to taste	2 mL
3 tbsp	thinly sliced green onions	45 mL

1. In a saucepan of boiling water, cook noodles until tender but firm, 7 to 9 minutes or according to package directions.
2. Meanwhile, in a large bowl, combine soy sauce, vinegar, sesame oil, sugar and salt and stir well.
3. When noodles are ready, drain well and transfer to bowl with soy sauce mixture. Add green onions and toss well to season noodles evenly. Serve warm or at room temperature.

Serves 4

Made from buckwheat flour, soba noodles have a nutty color and pleasing texture and taste. In Japan they are often served at room temperature with salty or tangy dressings. They are often sold in small cellophane covered boxes with a row of perfectly straight noodles gathered into skeins.

Quinoa

| 2 cups | water | 500 mL |
| 1 cup | quinoa, rinsed and drained | 250 mL |

1. In a saucepan over high heat, combine water and quinoa and bring to a rolling boil.
2. Stir well, cover pan, and reduce heat to maintain a gentle boil. Cook, until water has cooked away and grains have changed from white to ivory and developed a curly and nubby texture, about 15 minutes more. Serve hot or warm.

Serves 4

This ancient grain, pronounced "keen-wa," is exceptionally high in protein, cooks quickly, and has a soft, pleasing texture that goes nicely with stir-fried dishes. Look for it in health food stores and in many well-stocked supermarkets. Keep some on hand for a busy night.

Polenta

Serves 4

As an alternative to rice, polenta is simple to make, pleasing in its corn flavor and beautiful on your table. You can serve it hot as a soft, thick porridge, which sets up quickly, or pour it into a pan, let set and then cut into generous pieces. These can be pan-fried, grilled, baked or served as is, accompanying a hearty stir-fried dish or two.

TIP

Polenta sticks to the pan despite my most dedicated stirring during cooking and spatula use at serving time. To simplify cleanup, fill the empty pan with cold water and let it stand for about an hour. Then the remaining polenta will come off with ease.

3 cups	water	750 mL
1 tsp	salt or to taste	5 mL
1 cup	cornmeal	250 mL

1. In a saucepan over high heat, bring water to a rolling boil. Stir in salt.

2. Add cornmeal slowly in a thin stream, stirring constantly to avoid lumps. Continue to stir well as polenta returns to a rolling boil. Reduce heat to low and simmer, stirring often and scraping the bottom of the pan to discourage sticking, about 15 minutes.

3. When polenta is thick and tender and pulls away from sides of pan, remove from heat. Transfer to a bowl. Serve hot, warm or at room temperature. (Alternatively, pour and press polenta into a bowl, which you have first rinsed out with water, and turn out onto a serving plate in a handsome mound. You could also pour and press it into a square baking pan and cut into squares or other shapes once it has become firm and cool.)

Variation: For a softer, more delicate batch of polenta, use 4 cups (1 L) water instead of 3 cups (750 mL), and cook a little longer. The resulting polenta will be tender both before and after it sets up.

Spaghetti Squash

● **Preheat oven to 375°F (190°C)**

1	small spaghetti squash, about 1½ pounds (750 g)	1
2 tbsp	Asian sesame oil	25 mL
1 tsp	salt or to taste	5 mL
¼ cup	chopped fresh cilantro or parsley	50 mL

1. Cut spaghetti squash in half lengthwise and scoop out seeds. Place both pieces in a baking pan, cut side down. Add about ¾ cup (175 mL) water to pan around squash.

2. Bake squash in preheated oven, until tender and easily pierced with a fork, 30 to 45 minutes. Remove from oven and carefully turn each half cut side up to cool on a platter.

3. When squash is no longer steaming, scrape the flesh gently with a large fork, pulling the naturally shredded squash out of the two husks. Transfer squash strands to a bowl, and add sesame oil and salt. Toss well. Add cilantro and toss well. Transfer the tumble of seasoned squash strands to a serving bowl. Serve hot or warm.

Serves 4

This plump, yellow wintry squash naturally cooks into long, slender strands with a warm color and delicate flavor. Use as you would noodles, lightly seasoning it as a base for robustly flavored stir-fried dishes.

Mandarin Pancakes

**Makes
16 pancakes to
serve 4 to 6**

The traditional
companion to Peking
Duck and other
Northern-style Chinese
dishes, these warm,
soft flatbreads are
simple to make and
fun to eat. You can use
them as wraps for any
not-too-saucy stir-fry.
You'll need a rolling pin
to flatten them out.
Since these are at their
tender best when warm,
try to make them close
to serving time, or plan
to steam them briefly
just before you serve
them.

2 cups	all-purpose flour	500 mL
¾ cup	boiling water	175 mL
2 tbsp	Asian sesame oil	25 mL

1. Place flour in a bowl and add boiling water, quickly stirring to combine well.

2. When mixture is cool enough to handle, gather into a lump of dough and transfer to a lightly floured cutting board or counter.

3. Knead dough until very smooth and tender, about 10 minutes. Cover with a kitchen towel or a bowl and let rest for 15 to 20 minutes or for up to 1 hour.

4. Shape dough into a log about 12 inches (30 cm) long and then cut into 8 pieces. Cut each of these pieces in half and roll each half into a small smooth ball.

5. Flatten each ball into a plump little disk and then, using your fingers or a pastry brush, lightly oil the top of each disk with a little of the sesame oil. Press two disks together, oiled sides facing in, and continue until you have 8 double disks.

6. Using a rolling pin and working on a lightly floured surface, roll out each double disk into a thin pancake 5 to 6 inches (12.5 to 15 cm) in diameter. Do not separate layers. (They needn't be perfectly round.)

7. Cover pancakes that aren't being cooked with a cloth. Heat a heavy ungreased skillet over medium-low heat until hot. Place one pancake in skillet and let cook, until it puffs up and bubbles a little, about 1 minute. Turn and cook other side, until soft and tender but not brittle and drying out, about 45 seconds. (It may or may not get small brown spots, but don't wait for them, as they aren't needed.)

8. Remove pancake to a plate and look at the sides where the two disks are ready to separate from each other. Gently and carefully pull the two pancakes apart. Set them aside, oiled side up, while you finish cooking the remaining pancakes.

9. Serve pancakes warm or set them aside and let cool to room temperature for up to 2 to 3 hours. Store, covered, in the refrigerator for up to 3 days. If cooled, place in bamboo steamer trays suspended over boiling water and steam for about 10 minutes to soften and warm. Or place them in another steaming device and steam until soft and warm. Alternatively, warm pancakes in a large skillet over medium-low heat, turning often so they reheat gently without further cooking.

Extras

Chinese-Style Barbecued Pork

This luscious ingredient, known in Cantonese dialect as *char shiu*, is as versatile as cooked ham is in Western cuisine. Cooks serve it over rice with sliced cucumbers on the side. They also use it chopped or sliced in soups, buns, noodle dishes and fried rice. Plan ahead so that the meat has several hours to marinate before cooking.

TIPS

The classic version of this barbecued pork gets its red hue from food coloring. If desired, stir a drop or two of red food coloring into the marinade before you add the meat.

I sometimes use boneless country-style ribs in making barbecued pork. If sold in a large piece, slice them into individual ribs. If sold sliced into ribs, simply proceed with the recipe. Their size and shape are just right without further chopping and they cook up into a rich, tender version of *char shiu pork*.

● Roasting pan with wire rack

2 tbsp	soy sauce	25 mL
2 tbsp	dry sherry or Shaoxing rice wine	25 mL
2 tbsp	hoisin sauce	25 mL
2 tbsp	bean paste, optional (see Tip, page 287)	25 mL
2 tbsp	liquid honey	25 mL
2 tbsp	granulated sugar	25 mL
1 tsp	salt or to taste	5 mL
2 lbs	boneless pork shoulder blade (butt) or country-style ribs	1 kg
2 to 3 tbsp	honey for basting	25 to 45 mL
	Additional honey, for basting	

1. In a large bowl, combine soy sauce, sherry, hoisin sauce, bean paste, if using, 2 tbsp (25 mL) honey, sugar and salt and stir well into a smooth sauce.

2. Cut pork with the grain into long thick strips, about 1½ inches (4 cm) in diameter. Add soy sauce mixture and turn to coat it evenly with the marinade. Cover and refrigerate for 3 hours or overnight, turning occasionally to season the meat evenly.

3. Preheat oven to 350°F (180°C). Add ½ inch (1 cm) of water to roasting pan with wire rack. Place strips of marinated pork on rack, about 3 inches (7.5 cm) apart from each other so that they can brown and cook evenly. Cook, turning once, for 30 minutes.

4. Cook, turning once, for 20 minutes more. Remove meat from rack and place in a bowl. Increase heat to 425°F (220°C).

5. Drizzle 2 or 3 tbsp (25 to 45 mL) honey over meat and using tongs or a fork turn and coat with honey. Return meat to rack and cook, turning once more, until handsomely browned and beginning to char nicely around the edges, 10 to 15 minutes.

6. Transfer to a platter and let cool to room temperature. Cut on the diagonal into thick or thin slices and serve. Or cover and refrigerate until needed for up 2 to 3 days for use in recipes or for serving over rice.

Thai-Style Cucumber Salad

1 cup	white or apple cider vinegar	250 mL
1 cup	water	250 mL
1 cup	granulated sugar	250 mL
2 tsp	salt or to taste	10 mL
2 lbs	cucumbers	1 kg
½ cup	chopped shallots or purple onion	125 mL
¼ cup	chopped fresh cilantro	50 mL
3 tbsp	chopped roasted salted peanuts, optional	45 mL

1. In a saucepan, combine vinegar, water, sugar and salt and stir well. Bring to a gentle boil over medium heat, stirring often. Simmer until sugar is dissolved completely and thickened slightly into a thin syrup. Transfer dressing to a bowl and set aside to let cool to room temperature.

2. If using English cucumbers with delicate skin and tiny seeds, leave some or all of the peeling on for its beautiful color, but trim away the ends. Quarter lengthwise and then slice crosswise into little triangles about ¼-inch (0.5 cm) thick. Set aside. If using cucumbers with lots of large seeds, peel them completely and trim away the ends. Halve lengthwise and use a spoon to scoop out seedy centers, leaving hollow "boats" of cucumber. Slice each piece crosswise into ¼-inch (0.5 cm) pieces. Set aside.

3. Add cucumbers and shallots to cooled dressing and toss to coat. Cover and refrigerate until shortly before serving time.

4. Transfer cucumbers to a serving bowl or several small bowls using a slotted spoon. Add enough dressing to fill the bowl about three-quarters of the way. Sprinkle cilantro and peanuts, if using, over cucumbers.

5. To serve, stir well to mix in the peanuts and cilantro. The dressing can be mixed in with rice or noodles as well. Store remaining cucumbers, covered and refrigerated, for up to 2 days.

Variation: You could add fresh hot chiles or a dollop of hot pepper sauce to this little salad if you like. Thinly slice 2 serrano chiles or 1 jalapeño pepper into rounds and mix them in along with the shallots or onion. You could also use 1 tsp (5 mL) of finely chopped Thai chiles.

Makes about 4 cups (1 L)

This simple, refreshing dish appears alongside satay and other dishes throughout Southeast Asia. Known as *arjaht*, it is often provided as a cooling counterpoint to the richness of fried and grilled dishes. We love it not just as a relish or pickle, but also as a quick cool vegetable dish as part of a rice or noodle-centered meal.

TIPS

For simplicity, you can mix the cilantro and peanuts into the cucumber-dressing bowl shortly before serving, rather than arrange them on top, which is customary to preserve crunchiness of peanuts and aroma of cilantro. Both ways are delicious.

This recipe can be doubled or tripled with good results.

Indonesian-Style Pineapple and Cucumber Salad

Serves 4 to 6

Whether you use fresh pineapple or canned, this simple version of the pineapple-cucumber dishes enjoyed throughout Malaysia, Singapore and Indonesia makes a sparkling addition to a menu of rice and stir-fried dishes. This offers a refreshing counterpoint to spicy dishes, even with the fresh chiles, which bestow a bright heat on the salad. You can omit the chiles if you prefer a fruity note. It also works nicely as a vegetable side dish or a relish with most any stir-fry, rice or noodles and a simple soup.

TIP

If you use sturdy dark green cucumbers with big seeds, peel them completely and halve them lengthwise. Scoop out and discard the seeds and then chop the remaining "boats" into big bite-size chunks, about ½ inch (1 cm) in diameter.

Both the pineapple and cucumber should be chopped into bite-size chunks.

¼ cup	freshly squeezed lime or lemon juice	50 mL
2 tbsp	granulated sugar	25 mL
1 tbsp	dark brown sugar	15 mL
1 tsp	salt or to taste	5 mL
3 cups	chopped fresh pineapple or canned pineapple chunks (see Tips, left)	750 mL
2 cups	chopped English cucumber (see Tips, left)	500 mL
3 tbsp	chopped shallots or purple onion	45 mL
2 tbsp	chopped fresh cilantro	25 mL
1 tsp	finely chopped fresh hot green chiles, optional	5 mL

1. In a large bowl, combine lime juice, granulated sugar, brown sugar and salt and stir well into a smooth sauce.

2. Add pineapple, cucumber, shallots, cilantro and chiles, if using, and toss gently to mix everything well.

3. Cover and refrigerate for 30 minutes or for up to 2 hours. Serve chilled or at room temperature, as a salad or as a relish.

Variations: To add a traditional note, fortify the dressing with a spoonful of Southeast-Asian-style shrimp paste, such as Malaysian blachan or Indonesian trassi. Either of these could be toasted in a dry skillet over medium heat until hot and softened, 3 to 5 minutes, before being added to the dressing ingredients.

You could also add a big splash of tamarind liquid (see recipe, page 339) to the dressing and then sprinkle chopped peanuts over the dressed salad before serving.

Everyday Soup

3 cups	chicken stock or vegetable stock	750 mL
4	shiitake mushrooms or large button mushrooms	4
½ cup	shredded carrots	125 mL
4 oz	firm tofu, chopped into ½-inch (1 cm) chunks	125 g
1 cup	fresh baby spinach	250 mL
¼ cup	thinly sliced green onions	50 mL
2 tsp	Asian sesame oil	10 mL

1. In a saucepan, bring chicken stock to a boil over medium-high heat.
2. Meanwhile, remove stems from shiitake mushrooms and discard. Slice caps into thin strips. If using button mushrooms, slice them thinly.
3. When soup is boiling, add mushrooms and carrots and cook until carrots have brightened in color and are tender-crisp, about 2 minutes.
4. Add tofu, spinach and green onions and stir gently. Cook for 1 minute more.
5. Transfer to serving bowls and pour sesame oil over the top of the soup. Serve hot.

Variations: Add diced cooked chicken, shrimp or ham instead of tofu.

Beat an egg and then pour it slowly into the soup as it boils gently, to make egg-flower or egg-drop soup.

Add Crispy Garlic in Oil (see page 344) instead of Asian sesame oil at the end of cooking time.

Add shredded napa cabbage instead of spinach.

Add frozen shredded collard greens or turnip greens instead of spinach and carrot shreds and cook until they are tender, 2 to 3 minutes.

Add cooked salmon instead of tofu. Then add chopped fresh hot green chiles along with green onions and top the soup with a generous squeeze of lime juice and a handful of cilantro leaves just before serving.

Serves 4

Simple soups are standard on the weeknight menu in homes all over Asia. Unlike long-simmered hearty soups that anchor a lunch or suppertime meal in the West, these soups are part of a rice- or noodle-centered menu and are served with other dishes in one course. This recipe gives you a basic pattern for a "with-rice-and-stir-fry" soup, which you can vary according to what you enjoy and have on hand. We like this Asian-style, spooning the soup over our rice as well as eating it directly with a spoon.

TIP

Because this soup is simple and quick, you can make it just before serving time allowing only enough time to heat everything up. You could also prepare it ahead up to Step 4, adding tofu but reserving spinach, and then removing it from the heat. When you are ready to serve, heat it back up to a gentle boil, add spinach and green onions and then sesame oil. Serve hot.

Thai-Style Roasted Chile Paste

Makes about 1¼ cups (300 mL)

This signature Thai condiment provides extraordinary flavor and color to stir-fried dishes and soups. Known in Thai as *nahm prik pao*, it has the rustic color of dried red chiles. You can buy a commercial version in jars, often labeled "chili paste in soya bean oil." You can use the small, dried red chiles known as "chiles de arbol" and "chiles japones," or those sold in cellophane sacks at Asian markets. Traditionally, *nahm prik pao* started with chiles, shallots and garlic, which were roasted in or over the embers of a charcoal fire and then ground up using a heavy mortar and pestle. Here you brown them carefully in a dry skillet and then grind them to a fine paste using a blender or a food processor.

TIP

Roasted chile paste is very oily and the oil is part of the condiment. When measuring, stir well first to be sure that you get mostly chile paste but a good dollop of the oil as well.

Basic Roasted Chile Paste

½ cup	small dried red chiles	125 mL
½ cup	unpeeled shallots, halved lengthwise	125 mL
⅓ cup	unpeeled garlic cloves, halved lengthwise	75 mL
½ cup	vegetable oil, divided	125 mL

1. Heat a wok or large deep skillet over medium-low heat for 5 minutes. Add chiles, spreading into a single layer. Cook, stirring gently and shaking pan often, until they have darkened without burning and become fragrant and brittle, 3 to 5 minutes. Transfer to a plate and let cool.

2. Add shallots and garlic to pan and cook in the same way, turning them occasionally so that they soften, brown and char in spots without burning significantly, about 5 minutes. Transfer to a plate and let cool.

3. Once cool, break chiles open and shake out and discard most of the seeds, along with the stems. Chop into small pieces and transfer to a bowl.

4. Peel and trim shallots and garlic, discarding papery peels and root ends. Chop into small pieces and add to the bowl along with the chopped chiles.

5. In a blender or small food processor, combine ¼ cup (50 mL) of the vegetable oil with chiles, shallots and garlic. Grind to a smooth paste, stopping often to scrape down the sides and pulsing the machine to grind everything evenly and well. Scrape the mixture out into a bowl and set aside.

6. In a wok or skillet over medium heat, heat remaining vegetable oil for 1 minute. Test to check the oil is hot enough by adding a bit of the chile paste. When it sizzles at once, add all the paste to the oil. Cook, stirring often, until the paste becomes fragrant and deepens a little in color, about 5 minutes, reducing heat if necessary to reduce spattering. Let cool to room temperature. Transfer to a jar and store in the refrigerator for up to 3 weeks.

Seasoned Roasted Chile Paste

3 tbsp	palm sugar or brown sugar	45 mL
3 tbsp	tamarind liquid (see recipe, page 339)	45 mL
2 tbsp	pounded or very finely ground dried shrimp, optional	25 mL
1 tbsp	fish sauce	15 mL
1 tsp	salt or to taste	5 mL
1	recipe Thai-Style Roasted Chile Paste (see recipe, page 141)	1

**Makes about
1¼ cups (300 mL)**

Roasted chile paste can be used with or without this seasoning in soups and stir-fries. Commercial versions are almost always seasoned.

1. In a bowl, combine palm sugar, tamarind liquid, dried shrimp, if using, fish sauce and salt and stir well.
2. Add cooled Thai-Style Roasted Chile Paste to the bowl and stir very well to combine everything evenly. Transfer to a jar and store in the refrigerator for up to 3 weeks.

Variation: For a vegetarian version, omit dried shrimp and substitute 2 tsp (10 mL) soy sauce and ½ tsp (2 mL) salt for fish sauce.

Thai-Style Green Curry Paste

Makes about ¾ cup (175 mL)

You can buy very good curry pastes in supermarkets and in Asian markets. I use store-bought curry pastes as my weeknight standard, but when I have some time or a special occasion, I make my own curry paste and the results are delicious and well worth the effort and time.

TIP

Prepare fresh lemongrass at the last possible minute. Trim rough end to a smooth base just under the bulge of each stalk. Trim away grassy tops, leaving a base of about 3 inches (7.5 cm). Remove any very dry outer leaves and slice each stalk into very thin rounds. Mince and add to the bowl.

1 tbsp	whole coriander seeds	15 mL
1 tsp	whole cumin seeds	5 mL
6	whole black or white peppercorns	6
⅓ cup	finely chopped fresh hot green Thai chiles or serrano chiles (about 20 Thai chiles)	75 mL
⅓ cup	chopped shallots or onion	75 mL
¼ cup	chopped roots of fresh cilantro or stems and leaves	50 mL
3 tbsp	chopped garlic	45 mL
3 tbsp	finely chopped fresh lemongrass (see Tip, left)	45 mL
2 tbsp	coarsely chopped fresh or frozen galanga or gingerroot	25 mL
1 tsp	minced peel of wild makrut lime or regular lime zest	5 mL

1. In a dry wok or a small skillet over medium-high heat, toast coriander seeds, stirring and shaking the pan, until darkened a shade or two, about 2 minutes. Transfer to a plate. Add cumin seeds to the pan and toast the same way, about 1 minute. Transfer to the plate and add peppercorns.

2. Grind coriander, cumin and peppercorns in a spice grinder or with a mortar and pestle, until a fine powder. Transfer to a bowl.

3. Add chiles, shallots, cilantro roots, garlic, lemongrass, galanga and wild lime peel to the bowl and stir well.

4. Transfer mixture to a blender or small food processor in small batches if necessary. Grind or process to a smooth paste. Add water 2 tbsp (25 mL) at a time, using just enough to move the blades and grind everything well. The mixture will be more of a sauce if you needed to add water and more of a paste if you did not. Either texture is fine (it will cook the same way once added to a curry recipe). Transfer to a jar and refrigerate for up to 2 weeks. *Or freeze:* Divide it into ¼ cup (50 mL) portions and place in small bowls to freeze until hard. Unmold when frozen and combine frozen curry paste chunks in a tightly sealed freezer container, or in a small resealable bag enclosed within a larger resealable bag, both with air squeezed out of them before closing the bag. Use without thawing, adding frozen paste directly to the pan.

Tamarind Liquid

| ⅓ cup | soft processed tamarind pulp (see Tips, right) | 75 mL |
| 1 cup | warm water | 250 mL |

1. In a bowl, combine tamarind pulp and water and using your fingers break the pulp into small chunks and begin dissolving it in water. Set aside.

2. Soak for 20 minutes, working tamarind pulp 3 or 4 times, squeezing and mashing to combine with the water and separate seeds, husks and fibers from the fruit pulp.

3. Place a large, fine-meshed strainer over a bowl and pour entire contents of tamarind and water into strainer.

4. Using the back of a large spoon or a pestle, press and scrape the softened tamarind pulp against the mesh, separating out seeds, fibers and husks and pushing the luscious, light brown essence you have created through the mesh into the bowl. Lots of it will remain on the outside of the strainer, so stop now and then to scrape that rich portion off the strainer and into the bowl.

5. After you have worked the mixture well, discard remaining solids. Stir essence of tamarind well. Its texture should be that of applesauce, pea soup or a soft fruit purée. Thin it by stirring in a little water if need be. Transfer to a jar and cover and refrigerate for 3 to 5 days.

Variation: You can use fresh ripe tamarind pods, often available at Hispanic and Caribbean markets as well as Asian ones. Pull off and discard as much of the brittle peel first. Soak 3 to 5 pods in a bowl covered with warm water. Then proceed as directed in the recipe, mashing softened tamarind pulp through a strainer to extract its rich essence. Expect to discard a lot of seeds and strands when you start from whole pods.

Makes about 1 cup (250 mL)

The rich brown essence of tamarind fruit brings a complex flavor to the cooking of South and Southeast Asia. Its mix of sharp and sweet adds luscious depth to sauces and soups. Making it takes a little time and effort, but it yields a luscious reward.

TIPS

Look for tamarind pulp in Asian markets, sold in square blocks. Sometimes labeled "wet tamarind," it has been processed to remove a great deal of the seeds and strands. Once opened, the package should be enclosed within a resealable plastic bag and stored at room temperature. It keeps indefinitely.

You can buy prepared tamarind liquid in a plastic jar. Imported from Thailand, it makes a good and handy alternative to freshly made tamarind liquid. It should be refrigerated after opening. I also substitute Indian-style tamarind chutney in many recipes with good results.

Firm Tofu

Makes 8 oz
(250 g) very
firm tofu

Firm and even
extra-firm tofu are
available nowadays
in many supermarkets,
as well as in Asian
groceries and in health
food stores. You can
transform soft, delicate
tofu into a firm state by
pressing it to remove
much of its natural
water content. Firm
tofu works wonderfully
for stir-frying.

TIPS

Once pressed, the tofu
will be flat and oddly
shaped and denser and
firmer in texture than
purchased firm tofu.
It works wonderfully
in stir-fried dishes and
can be cut into the
size and shape you like.

You will lose about
half the weight of
your block of tofu by
pressing out much of
its water content, so
plan to buy and press
double the amount of
soft tofu you will need.

1 lb	soft tofu	500 g

1. Drain off excess liquid from tofu. Place block of drained tofu on a cutting board and cut into 4 pieces. Set out two dinner-size places and two kitchen towels. Fold one towel in half and place it on one plate. Cover it with the second towel, unfolded and centered on the plate.

2. Place tofu chunks on the open towel, about 1 inch (2.5 cm) apart. Fold in the towel to enclose them snugly but not tightly. Set the plate of towel-wrapped tofu chunks in the sink or on a large rimmed baking pan so that any liquid released won't make a mess.

3. Place second plate on top of tofu and then set a heavy object on top of plate to hold firmly in place and press down on tofu. A full teakettle, four full cans of food or a bag of sugar or flour would be good handy choices.

4. Leave your makeshift press to do its work for as little as 15 minutes and as long as 1 hour. Longer means firmer tofu. Remove weights and plate, unwrap towels and transfer firm tofu to a covered container or chop and use right away in cooking. Refrigerate, covered, for up to 2 days. It can be immersed in water or not, as you prefer.

Candied Walnuts

- Baking sheets

¾ cup	granulated sugar	175 mL
3 cups	walnut halves	750 mL
4 cups	vegetable oil	1 L
2 tsp	salt	10 mL

1. In a saucepan, bring 6 cups (1.5 L) water to a rolling boil.
2. Pour sugar into a large mixing bowl and have a wooden spoon or a rubber spatula handy for stirring nuts.
3. When water comes to a rolling boil, add walnuts and stir well. When water returns to a boil, cook walnuts for 1 minute. Drain nuts in a colander in the sink and quickly transfer them to mixing bowl. Gently but quickly stir walnuts to coat evenly with sugar. Continue tossing until nuts have cooled and absorbed as much sugar as possible.
4. Transfer sugared nuts to a baking sheet and scatter into a single layer. Set aside.
5. Heat vegetable oil in a wok or large deep skillet over medium heat until hot (about 350°F/180°C). Have a slotted spoon or a large spoon and a strainer handy, so you can quickly remove nuts when almost done.
6. Carefully add about half sugared walnuts to hot oil and stir gently to separate them as oil bubbles up and nuts begin to brown. Watch carefully and scoop nuts out as soon as their color approaches a handsome golden brown, about 1 minute (see Tips, right).
7. Transfer walnuts carefully to another baking sheet and spread out to cool completely. Repeat with remaining sugared nuts. When all walnuts are cooked, sprinkle with salt, toss together to coat evenly and scatter again to let cool. Store cooled nuts in an airtight container at room temperature or in glass jar for up to 5 days.

Makes 3 cups (750 mL)

These nuts require a little careful attention, but the ingredients and techniques involved are simple and the results are spectacular. Make more than you need for a given stir-fry recipe. These are a delight and you will most likely want to serve them as a snack, to share them as gifts and of course to nibble on while you cook.

TIPS

Remove nuts from hot oil before they are exactly the color you want, because they continue cooking for a short time once they are out of the oil. Keep a few raw walnuts handy on a small plate, to help you judge how much they have colored. Things happen fast here: better to take them out early than to let them burn; they will still be delicious.

In place of a baking sheet you can use a section of your counter top lined with waxed paper, parchment paper or foil.

Toasted Sesame Seeds

Makes 1 cup (250 mL)

Sesame seeds have a permanent place on the pantry shelf within the cuisines of East Asia. Japanese and Korean cooks use them extensively and they are also popular throughout China and in Vietnam. White sesame seeds are usually toasted before use and sometimes ground or chopped after toasting. Scatter the toasted seeds on salads, rice and noodle dishes.

TIPS

Seeds may pop as they heat up; a few may even pop up and out of the pan. Not too many, don't worry.

Keep a small dish of raw sesame seeds by the stove so that you can keep in mind the degree of browning that is taking place in the pan. The process is subtle and uneven, so I find it helpful to have the visual cue of how "browned" the seeds I am toasting have become.

This same technique is used to toast shredded or grated coconut and raw grains of rice in Thailand and for pine nuts in Western cooking.

1 cup	white sesame seeds	250 mL

1. Set a dinner plate by stove to hold toasted seeds as soon as they finish cooking.

2. In a wok or a small dry skillet over medium heat, toast sesame seeds, stirring often and shaking pan, until they just begin to change color to a warm wheat brown and release their nutty aroma, 4 to 6 minutes. They may cluster together as they heat and release some of their oil. Immediately remove pan from heat and turn out onto the reserved plate. Spread seeds out and let cool to room temperature. Seeds will continue browning and cooking a little even after they are removed from the heat and pan.

3. Transfer cooled toasted seeds to a jar and store at room temperature for 3 days or in the freezer for up to 1 month.

Crisp-Fried Shallots

| 1 lb | small shallots | 500 g |
| 3 cups | vegetable oil | 750 mL |

1. Cut shallots in half lengthwise. Remove papery peel and outer layers, while leaving root end intact.

2. Place half a shallot cut side down and slice thinly crosswise. Continue slicing all the shallots. Fluff and sift through shallots to separate. (You should have about 2 cups/500 mL.)

3. Place a baking sheet or platter lined with paper towels by the stove. Have handy a metal strainer or two slotted spoons with which to quickly remove cooked shallots from the oil.

4. Heat oil in a wok or a large deep skillet over medium heat. When a bit of shallot dropped into oil sizzles at once, add about one-third of the shallots and let fry, turning gently to brown evenly, about 1 minute.

5. Before shallots are completely brown, scoop out and scatter over paper towels. They will continue to cook for a little while after being removed from the pan. Continue with remaining shallots layering between paper towels.

6. Let cool completely and then transfer to a jar. Store at room temperature for up to 3 days.

> **Variation:** You can used small yellow onions in this way. Halve onions lengthwise and slice crosswise into large, half-circle pieces. Cut each of these sections in half lengthwise, so that you have small pieces.

Makes about ¾ cup (175 mL)

These delectable golden brown bits of shallot add texture, color and a tasty depth of flavor to an array of dishes enjoyed throughout Southeast Asia. They are a particularly popular finishing touch to fried rice and noodle dishes in Indonesia.

Crispy Garlic in Oil

**Makes about
½ cup (125 mL)**

Thai people enjoy this simple condiment on soups. It is wonderful tossed with noodles, spooned over rice or grilled food, or tossed with a simple stir-fried dish for a marvelous burst of nutty rich flavor. Keep the oil and garlic together and use both, or scoop out the garlic bits, or use the oil alone for cooking or as a seasoning.

TIP

The garlic should be chopped but not minced here. You want pleasing very small chunks, which take on a handsome color and yield a minimalist crunch. Minced garlic would burn in the hot oil rather than brown in a pleasant way.

| ½ cup | vegetable oil | 125 mL |
| ⅓ cup | chopped garlic (see Tip, left) | 75 mL |

1. In a wok or a skillet over low heat, warm oil for 2 to 3 minutes.
2. When a bit of garlic dropped into oil sizzles at once, add all the garlic and stir well to break up any clusters and help cook evenly.
3. Cook, gently stirring occasionally, until about half the garlic is a handsome, wheaty golden brown, about 2 minutes. (Don't worry about the uneven coloring. The garlic will continue to cook and brown after being removed from the heat.)
4. Remove pan from stove and set aside. Let pan of garlic and oil cool to room temperature.
5. Transfer cooled garlic and its oil to a jar and cover. Store, refrigerated, for 2 days.

Library and Archives Canada Cataloguing in Publication

McDermott, Nancie
300 best stir-fry recipes / Nancie McDermott.

ISBN-13: 978-0-7788-0157-3
ISBN-10: 0-7788-0157-8

1. Stir frying. I. Title. II. Title: Three hundred best stir-fry recipes.

TX689.5.M33 2007   641.7'74   C2006-905907-1

A Bibliography for Further Reading and Cooking

Alford, Jeffrey and Naomi Duguid. *Hot, Sour, Salty, Sweet: A Culinary Journey Through Southeast Asia*. New York: Artisan, 2000.

Cost, Bruce. *Asian Ingredients*. New York: Quill, 2000.

Joachim, David. *The Food Substitutions Bible*. Toronto: Robert Rose, Inc., 2005.

Kuo, Irene. *The Key to Chinese Cooking*. New York: Alfred A. Knopf, 1977.

Lin, Florence. *Florence Lin's Chinese Regional Cookbook*. New York: Hawthorn Books, 1975.

Nguyen, Andrea Quynhgiao. *Into the Vietnamese Kitchen: Treasured Foodways, Modern Flavors*. Berkeley: Ten Speed Press, 2006.

Oseland, James. *The Cradle of Flavor: Home Cooking from the Spice Islands of Indonesia, Singapore and Malaysia*. New York: W.W. Norton, 2006.

Solomon, Charmaine. *Encyclopedia of Asian Food*. Boston: Periplus Editions, 1996.

Tropp, Barbara. *The Modern Art of Chinese Cooking: Techniques and Recipes*. New York: Hearst Books, 1982.

Yee, Rhoda. *Chinese Village Cookbook: A Practical Guide to Cantonese Country Cooking*. San Francisco: Yerba Buena Press, 1975.

Young, Grace and Alan Richardson. *The Breath of a Wok: Unlocking the Spirit of Chinese Wok Cooking through Recipes and Lore*. New York: Simon and Schuster, 2004.

Yueh, Jean. *The Great Tastes of Chinese Cooking: Contemporary Methods and Menus*. New York: Times Books, 1979.

Sources

Here are an array of sources for ingredients, equipment, and herb and vegetable seeds with which to enhance your stir-fry cooking. Many offer catalogs as well as websites and a number have recipes as well. Those without a designation of "cookware" or "plants and seeds" carry kitchen tools and cookware as well as ingredients for stir-fry cooking.

ImportFood.com
P.O. Box 2054
Issaquah, WA 98027
Tel: (888) 618-8424 or (425) 687-1708
Fax: (425) 687-8413
www.importfood.com

Kalustyan's
123 Lexington Avenue
New York, NY 10016
Tel: (800) 352-3451 or (212) 685-3451
Fax: (212) 683-8458
www.kalustyans.com

**Kitazawa Seed Company
(plants and seeds)**
P.O. Box 13220
Oakland, CA 94661
Tel: (510) 595-1188
Fax: (510) 595-1860
www.kitazawaseed.com

Melissa's/World Variety Produce
P.O. Box 21127
Los Angeles, CA 90021
Tel: (800) 588-0151
www.melissas.com

Ming Wo (cookware)
23 East Pender Street
Vancouver, B.C. V6A 1S9
Canada
Tel: (877) 864-6496 or (604) 683-7268
Fax: (604) 683-3848
www.mingwo.com

Oriental Pantry
423 Great Road (2A)
Acton, MA 01720
Tel: (978) 264-4576
Fax: (781) 275-4506
www.orientalpantry.com

Penzey's Spices
Multiple locations
Tel: (800) 741-7787 or (262) 785-7676
Fax: (262) 785-7678
www.penzeys.com

Richters Herbs (plants and seeds)
357 Highway 47
Goodwood, ON L0C IA0
Canada
Tel: (905) 640-6677
Fax: (905) 640-6641
www.richters.com

Sur La Table
Tel: (800) 243-0852
www.surlatable.com

TempleofThai.com
14525 SW Millikan Way
RCM #10102
Beaverton, OR 97005
Tel: (877) 811-8773
Fax: (877) 811-8773
www.templeofthai.com

The Wok Shop (cookware)
718 Grant Avenue
San Francisco, CA 94108
Tel: (888) 780-7171 or (415) 989-3797
www.wokshop.com

Index